ScottForesman Science

Discover the Wonder

Series Consulting Author

David Heil
Associate Director,
Oregon Museum of Science & Industry
Portland, Oregon

Consulting Authors

Maureen Allen
Science Resource Teacher/Specialist
Irvine Unified School District
Irvine, California

Dr. Timothy Cooney
Professor of Earth Science & Science Education
Earth Science Department
University of Northern Iowa
Cedar Falls, Iowa

Angie Matamoros
Lead Science Supervisor
Broward County Schools
Ft. Lauderdale, Florida

Dr. Manuel Perry
Manager, Educational Programs
Lawrence Livermore National Laboratory
Livermore, California

Dr. Irwin Slesnick
Professor of Biology
Biology Department
Western Washington University
Bellingham, Washington

 ScottForesman

A Division of HarperCollins*Publishers*

Editorial Offices: Glenview, Illinois
Regional Offices: Sunnyvale, California • Tucker, Georgia
Glenview, Illinois • Oakland, New Jersey • Dallas, Texas

Content Consultants

Dr. Linda Berne
University of North Carolina
Charlotte, North Carolina

Dr. Kurt Brorson
Laboratory of Cellular and Molecular
Immunology
National Institutes of Health
Bethesda, Maryland

Dr. Bonnie Buratti
Jet Propulsion Laboratory
California Institute of Technology
Pasadena, California

Dr. Michael Garcia
Department of Geology and Geophysics
University of Hawaii
Honolulu, Hawaii

Dr. Norman Gelfand
Fermi National Accelerator Laboratory
Accelerator Division
Batavia, Illinois

Dr. Roger Pielke
Department of Atmospheric Science
Colorado State University
Fort Collins, Colorado

Dr. Harrison H. Schmitt
Former Astronaut (Apollo 17) and
United States Senator
Geologist and Science and Technology
Consultant
Albuquerque, New Mexico

Dr. Richard Shippee
Department of Biology
Vincennes University
Vincennes, Indiana

Dr. David Stronck
Department of Teacher Education
California State University at Hayward
Hayward, California

Dr. Merita Thompson
Department of Health Education
Eastern Kentucky University
Richmond, Kentucky

Dr. Antonio Garcia Trejo
Arizona Department of Environmental
Quality
Chandler, Arizona

Dr. Lisa Wagner
Department of Biology
Georgia Southern University
Statesboro, Georgia

Multicultural Consultants

Dr. Thomas Crosby
Department of Biology
Morgan State University
Baltimore, Maryland

Dr. Frank Dukepoo
Department of Biology
Northern Arizona University
Flagstaff, Arizona

Dr. Amram Gamliel (Ben-Teman)
Educational Consultant/Professional
Writer
Newton Center, Massachusetts

Dr. Hilda Hernandez
Department of Education
California State University at Chico
Chico, California

Dr. Luis A. Martinez-Perez
College of Education
Florida International University
Miami, Florida

Safety Consultant

Dr. Jack A. Gerlovich
Science Education Safety
Consultant/Author
Waukee, Iowa

Reading Consultant

Dr. Robert A. Pavlik
Professor of Reading/Language Arts
Reading/Language Arts Department
Cardinal Stritch College
Milwaukee, Wisconsin

Activity Consultant

Mary Jo Diem
Science/Educational Consultant
Croton-on-Hudson, New York

Acknowledgments

Photographs Unless otherwise acknowledged, all photographs are the property of ScottForesman. Page abbreviations are as follows: (T)top, (C)center, (B)bottom, (L)left, (R)right, (INS)inset.
Cover Design Sheldon Cotler + Associates
Cover Background: F. Stuart Westmorland/ALLSTOCK, INC. Inset: Norbert Wu/ ALLSTOCK, INC. Magnifying Glass: Richard Chesnut
Page v(T) Chemical Design/SPL/Photo Researchers **v(BR)** From CORPUSCLES by Marcell Bessis, ©1974, Springer-Verlag, Berlin, Heidelberg, New York
vii(BL) Culver Pictures **viii(T)** L. Tobey Sanford **ix(R)** William Meyers/Third Coast Stock
x(B) Greg Vaughn/Tom Stack & Associates **xi(B)** Wes Thompson/The Stock Market
xiii(BL) Erika Craddock/Tony Stone Worldwide **xiv(T)** David M. Dennis/Tom Stack & Associates

Illustrations Unless otherwise acknowledged, all computer graphics by Ligature, Inc.
Page ix Randy Verougstraete **xi** Wild Onion Studio **xii** Teri McDermott **xiv** Carl Kock

Acknowledgments continue on page 47.

About the Cover

The amusing creature on the cover is a clownfish. It was photographed in its salt-water habitat in the Pacific Ocean. The underwater background photograph was taken near the island of Truk in the Pacific Ocean.

Reviewers

Take a Closer Look

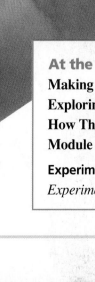

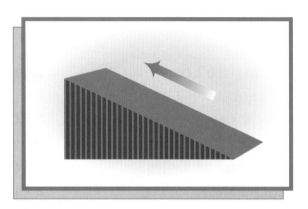

CHAPTER

3 Pedal Power

Fun in Motion

CHAPTER 3 Playing by the Rules

Running on Sunlight

3 Using Sunshine

Electricity

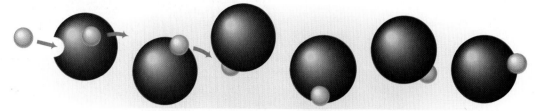

CHAPTER 3 Signals in the Air

Living Off the Land

CHAPTER 3 Gardening Plants

Take a Closer Look

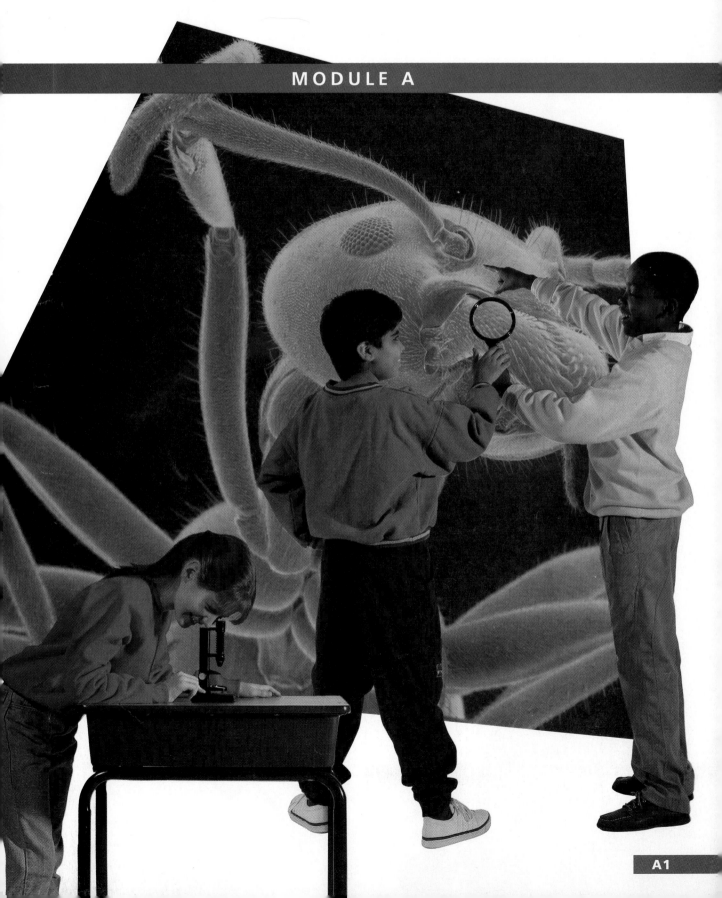

Take a Closer Look

Are we all made out of the same stuff? It depends on how closely you look! Along with everything else on the earth, people are made of tiny particles called atoms. In this module, you'll take a closer look at matter on the earth. You'll see the crystals in rocks, the compounds in matter, and the cells in your body, and find that all are made of atoms.

CHAPTER 1 Exploring the Unseen

How close can you get? By using lenses and microscopes, people can begin to solve the mystery of what's inside.

CHAPTER 2 Structure of Mattter

How small is small? Atoms are small, but electrons, protons, and neutrons are even smaller. Quarks may be the smallest of all.

CHAPTER
3 Organized Organisms

We're all in this together!

The human body contains many types of cells, yet all work together to keep us alive.

In this module

1

Exploring the Unseen

Now I know why they call it sandstone.

Wear cover goggles for this activity.

Discover Activity

What's a rock made of?

Examine a piece of granite using a hand lens. Then rub two pieces of granite together while holding them over a piece of paper. Use a hand lens to examine the pieces that fall onto the paper. Use a toothpick to sort the material by color. Repeat this process with two pieces of sandstone.

For Discussion

1. What rock is made of the greatest variety of pieces?

2. How many kinds of particles are in each rock?

1.1 *Let's Get Small*

▶ **What is the smallest object you can see?**

You may think that you've seen just about everything. Looking at your classroom, your home, and the rest of your world may not hold many surprises for you. However, with a little imagination and the tools of science, you can see new worlds full of creatures you may not even know exist.

What if you could make yourself smaller just by wishing it so? Think small for a minute—very small. Even smaller. A pebble now towers over you like a boulder. A blade of grass looks like a giant redwood tree. An ant the size of a truck rushes past you. Things are very different when you're small!

Scale

Of course, you can't make yourself that small in order to take a closer look at things. You're used to seeing objects in detail that are about your size, or scale. Sure, some things that you can see are a lot bigger than you are—like a giant skyscraper. You also might occasionally see something very small, such as the pieces of rock you viewed in the Discover Activity. However, it may surprise you to learn that your eyes can't see everything there is to be seen.

The earth, for example, is on a very different scale than you—it is far too big for you to see in its entirety. Until 30 years ago, when spaceflight began, no one had ever seen the earth from space. This changed when astronauts first orbited high above the surface of the earth, and saw how the earth looked from space.

▼ *Much of the world around you is on a different scale.*

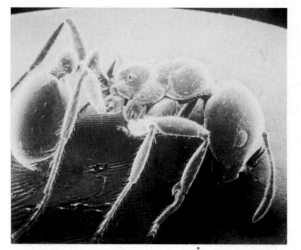

10x

25x

▲ *The red number followed by an X above the pictures tells how many times larger than life size the ant looks. Look for these magnifications by many of the pictures in this module.*

▼ *This magnification tells you the girl is shown just half as big as the girl really is.*

0.5x

Another world exists where the scale is so small that your eyes alone cannot possibly see all that there is to see. Thousands of different organisms can live in a single drop of pond water. Yet if you looked at a drop of water containing all of these organisms, you'd be lucky if you saw a few specks. Your eyes simply cannot see things that small.

Magnification

Because you can't change the size of your body, you must magnify, or enlarge, very small objects to a size that your eyes can see. To change the scale of very small objects, different instruments are used. The hand lens is one tool for making small things appear larger. The microscope is another tool for making tiny objects look huge. These instruments can help you see incredible details on small objects enlarged to fantastic sizes.

If you want to see tiny details on an ant like the ant above, you must put it under a high-powered microscope. Magnifying the ant to these scales makes the ant look larger than a professional football player!

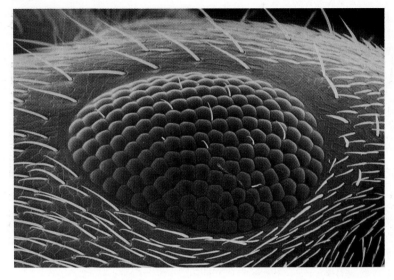

One type of microscope—a scanning electron microscope—uses electrons to make things look many thousands of times bigger. Even a magnification of 10,000 would produce an ant over 50 meters long! It would be hard to look at an ant that big, so it's shown below compared to human scale.

To magnify the ant so that it appears to be the size of an average fifth-grade student, you would need to enlarge it about 250 times. Magnified 350 times, you can see that the ant's eyes are made of hundreds of tiny lenses. Equipped with a microscope, you can take a closer look at unseen worlds. You might be surprised—things are not always what they seem to be!

▼ *Find how much this ant was magnified to put the girl and the ant on the same scale.*

60x

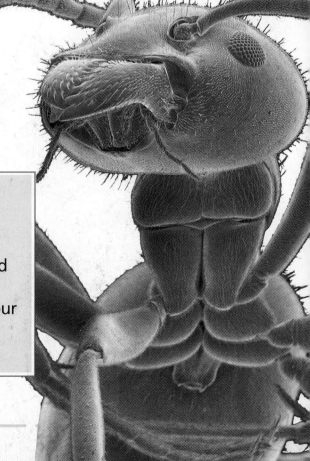

Checkpoint

1. Name some other animals that might need to be studied at a different scale due to their small size.
2. Name two tools that are commonly used to magnify the images of small objects.
3. Take Action! Imagine you've changed your size to very large or very small. Write a journal entry about the experience.

Activity

Scaling Up and Down

You can make a small drawing of yourself, and then magnify it to make your picture look big. Try this activity to find out how.

Picture A

Picture B

Picture C

Gather These Materials

graph paper   measuring tape
hand lens

Follow This Procedure

Part A

1 Make a chart like the one on the next page. Record your observations in your chart.

2 Use a measuring tape to measure the parts of your body listed on the chart. Record your measurements on your chart. (Picture A)

3 Now make a drawing that is much smaller than your actual body. Decide on the scale of your drawing. For example, 1 cm on your graph paper might represent 10 cm of body length. Use a scale that will allow you to draw your whole body on your paper. Write your scale on your chart.

4 Fill in the second column of the chart to show how long each body measurement will be in your scale drawing. Use your scale drawing measurements to make a scale drawing of yourself. (Picture B)

Part B

5 Place a hand lens on top of your scale drawing. Move your head so that your eyes are about 30 cm above the hand lens.

6 Count the number of graph paper lines you see through the hand lens.

7 Without moving your drawing or your head, move the hand lens closer to your eyes. Stop when your picture looks as large as possible but is still in focus. Then count the number of lines you can see on the graph paper. (Picture C)

Predict: *How many times does your hand lens magnify an image?*

8 Find out the magnifying power of your lens. Divide the number of lines you counted when the hand lens was against the drawing by the number of lines you counted in the enlarged image.

Record Your Results

Scale: _____ cm = 10 cm		
	Actual size	Size in scale
Head		
Arm		
Leg		
Hand		

State Your Conclusions

1. How many times smaller was your height in your scale drawing compared to your actual body height?

2. What is the magnifying power of your hand lens?

Let's Experiment

Now that you've learned about scale drawings and magnifying power, how would you make a scale drawing of an object larger than its actual size?

1.2 Minerals and Crystals

▶ **What are rocks made of?**

Take a closer look at many of the living and nonliving things around you—ants, plants, and even rocks. Rocks might seem to be quite simple at first glance. But a closer look reveals that rocks are not at all simple. For instance, rocks are made of different little pieces. These pieces can form arrangements so beautiful they're worn as jewelry.

Miniature Minerals

The little pieces that make up rocks such as the granite and sandstone used in the Discover Activity are called minerals. A **mineral** (min′ər əl) is nonliving solid matter from the earth. In a piece of granite, such as the one pictured below, you can see the various minerals as different flecks of color. The lighter specks are bits of the mineral quartz, and the darker ones are feldspar and other minerals. These are but a few different minerals. Over 2500 different kinds of minerals exist on the earth.

▼ *Breaking apart rocks reveals the different minerals within them.*

With all of these different minerals, how can you tell one from another? One characteristic that differs among minerals is the way they break apart. Some minerals cleave—or break apart—along smooth surfaces. Galena breaks into cubes and mica splits into thin sheets. Other minerals are said to fracture because they break unevenly. Quartz fractures, or shatters, like glass. The way that a mineral breaks apart depends on the arrangement of the particles inside it.

You can also understand the structure of minerals by taking a closer look at the crystal shapes of minerals. A **crystal** (kris′ tl) is a structure that shows the regular arrangement and order of the particles within a mineral. You'll learn more about particles that minerals are made of in the next chapter.

Crystals have fascinated people for centuries. The word *crystal* comes from the Greek word for "icy cold." For a long time people thought crystals were ice, frozen so hard they would never thaw.

Crystals often form in hollow spaces between rocks or even inside of them. Because of this, many crystals take the shape of the hollow area in the rock where they grow. Rocks with crystals lining their insides are called geodes. You can see the ordered structure of crystals in the picture.

All minerals, no matter how different they look, share certain properties. These are properties that can either be seen or tested, such as color, luster, hardness, and cleavage or fracture. The deeper you look into this world of miniature minerals, the more neatness and order you find.

▼ *Quartz crystals*

Properties of Minerals

Gemstones are minerals, and they have mineral properties such as color, luster, hardness, and cleavage or fracture.

Color The color of crystals depends on what substances form them. Adding different chemicals can produce the greens, blues, reds, and yellows in gems and other crystals. Notice the range of color in the gems pictured—all are forms of the mineral corundum. Corundum is a deep red when it contains chromium. This forms a gemstone known as a ruby. Iron and titanium produce blue. Other chemicals produce other colors in corundum.

Luster The amount of shine, or luster, on the surface of a crystal varies. Sapphires and other gemstones can be polished to a high luster, so they're often used in jewelry.

Color

Luster

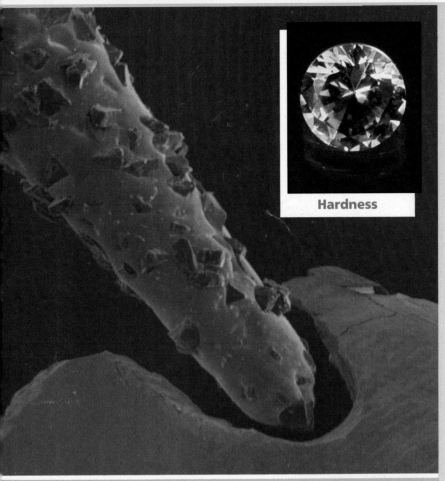

Hardness

Cleavage

Hardness The hardness of a crystal depends on the strength of the forces holding its particles together. Many crystals possess great hardness. Diamond is the hardest mineral of all. Diamonds are often cut to make jewelry, but uncut diamonds are useful, too. Pieces of diamond are in many tools that cut and drill. Many saw blades contain diamond dust. The microscopic view of your dentist's drill allows you to see the small bits of diamond that drill into teeth.

Corundum is second to diamond in hardness. Jewelry made of rubies and sapphires doesn't break or chip easily. Corundum is also used in tools that require a hard cutting material.

Cleavage Some diamonds show cleavage, but like this large "uncut" diamond, most don't break along flat surfaces. The polished diamond was skillfully cut with a very sharp knife—a technique that results in a beautiful gem or a pile of chips.

Common Crystals

Imagine this: early on a winter's morning you're awakened by the rumble of the snow plow and the salt truck as they pass your apartment. You rush to the window and look out—snow blankets the ground! You get dressed, put on your watch, and sit down to breakfast, sprinkling a bit of salt on your eggs. As you listen to your portable radio, the phone suddenly rings—a friend is calling to say she'll meet you on the way to school. This all seems simple, but it wouldn't be possible without crystals. The world around you is chock full of crystals, as long as you don't think of crystals only as rocks or gems.

Every day you're depending on common crystals all around you. They all share the properties seen in gemstones: color, hardness, luster, and cleavage or fracture. Although some crystals are colorless, dull, and jagged, they're very precious to you.

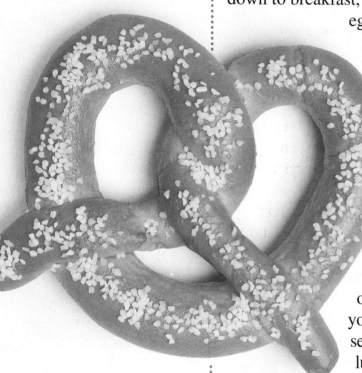

▲ Crystals of salt have many different uses.

Salt is one of these colorless, dull, useful crystals. The mineral salt can be gathered either from mines deep in the ground or by evaporating ocean water. Salt is such a necessity to life that in ancient times it was traded in equal amounts with gold. The Romans used salt as a form of payment called salarium or "salt money." The word *salary* comes from this Roman word.

When you think of salt, you probably think of the crystals used as a seasoning. But salt also is used for many other purposes. Salt is used to help melt ice on roads in the winter, to preserve foods such as fish, and to make soap, glass, and many other products.

▲ Sugar crystals form by evaporating water from sugar syrup.

Another crystal that's used every day is sugar. Unlike salt, sugar is not a mineral, because it comes from living things. Sugar is refined from plants such as sugar cane and sugar beets, and is used mostly as a sweetener in foods. But like salt, sugar crystals dissolve in water—and in your mouth!

Take away another common crystal—quartz sand—and concrete buildings would collapse and sidewalks would disappear. Concrete is a mixture, and sand is one of the main ingredients. Quartz sand is also melted to make glass. Without crystals of the mineral quartz, you might not be able to listen to your friends on the phone. When you put the phone against your ear, a piece of quartz reproduces the sound of your friend's voice on the other end of the line.

Crystals may be common, but crystals are far from ordinary. To look more closely at crystals, simply take a look around you!

➤ A quartz crystal inside the watch keeps the watch running.

Scratch Test

The Mohs scale was developed in 1822 by German mineralogist Frederich Mohs. It lists ten minerals in order of increasing hardness—from the softest, talc, to the hardest, diamond.

Hardness	Mineral
1	Talc
2	Gypsum
3	Calcite
4	Fluorite
5	Apatite
6	Feldspar
7	Quartz
8	Topaz
9	Corundum
10	Diamond

Scientists measure a mineral's hardness using a "scratch test." Harder minerals will scratch softer ones. For example, galena can scratch gypsum but it can't scratch calcite. Gypsum has a hardness of 2, and calcite has a hardness of 3. So galena has a hardness between 2 and 3.

What Did You Find Out?
1. *Mineral A scratches feldspar but doesn't scratch quartz. About what hardness is this mineral?*
2. *Iron has a hardness of 4.5. What minerals on the scale can iron scratch?*

Crystal Shape

Certain items around you can help you understand how crystals are put together. For instance, think about the shape of a checkerboard—the entire board is square, but many black and red squares make up this square board. One of the walls of your school building might be a large rectangle, built out of many smaller rectangular bricks. The entire school may be a large rectangular prism, the same shape as a much smaller brick. So small shapes put together can make a big shape—the same shape, just a bigger size.

These patterns of shapes are very orderly. Crystals possess this same kind of order and organization. As you know, crystals can be large or small, some as tiny as a grain of salt. A closer look at salt reveals that each grain is a tiny cube. Notice the cube shapes of these grains of salt shown under increasing magnification. But what if you break apart a grain of salt and make it smaller—what shape will the pieces be? Lots of smaller cubes, the same as the original grain of salt.

▼ *The closer you look, the more organized the structure of salt appears to be.*

30x

In addition to cubes, many other crystal shapes exist. Also, different samples of one mineral might not all have exactly the same crystal shape.

However, many minerals appear most often in one particular crystal shape. If you can identify that shape, you stand a good chance of identifying the mineral. For example, galena usually appears as shiny metallic cubes. Both quartz and ice often form six-sided crystals. Although sugar isn't a mineral, it forms crystals shaped like flat, thin books.

Although different substances have different crystal shapes, the crystals of each substance are the same shape, whatever their size. Large chunks of salt are cubic crystals, as are tiny salt grains.

You can see that crystals have organized structures. Remember, the reason for the order and neatness within crystals is the arrangement of the particles within them. But what are these particles and how are they put together? To find out you need to look inside crystals using an instrument that can see inside even the tiniest grain of sand.

Into The Field

How are salt crystals and sugar crystals alike yet different?

Use a hand lens to observe crystals of salt and crystals of sugar. Make a sketch and write a description of what you see.

325x

Checkpoint

1. What are rocks composed of? What is the structure of their parts?
2. What is the hardest mineral known? What tools is it used in?
3. List three crystals that you encounter every day. Explain how they are used.
4. If you break apart sugar crystals into smaller shapes, what shapes will they be?
5. Take Action! Fold a piece of paper four times, then unfold it. Count the smaller rectangles and compare them to crystals.

Activity

How Do Your Crystals Grow?

Crystals form and seem to "grow" in areas between or inside of rocks. In this activity, you will grow crystals of your own.

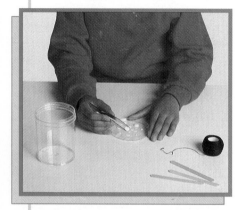

Picture A

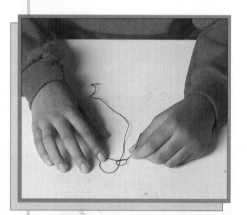

Picture B

Picture C

Gather These Materials

cover goggles

saturated alum solution

saucer

hand lens

seed crystal

piece of string

cooled alum solution

plastic jar

craft stick

piece of paper

Follow This Procedure

Part A

1 Make a chart like the one on the next page. Record your observations in your chart.

2 Put on your cover goggles.

3 Pour a small amount of warm, saturated alum solution into a saucer. Place the saucer in a warm, sunny place or near a heater where it will not be disturbed.

Predict: What will happen as the liquid evaporates?

4 Observe the saucer the next day. Use a hand lens to examine what has happened.

Part B

5 Put on your cover goggles again. Pick the most even-growing crystal you have grown in the saucer. It should be about 3 to 6 mm across. This will be your seed crystal. (Picture A)

6 Use the string to make a loop that you will tie around the seed crystal. (Picture B)

7 Pour cooled alum solution into the plastic jar. Be careful not to pour in any crystals.

8 Tie the loose end of the string to a craft stick. Place the stick on the top of the jar. The crystal should be in the solution without touching the sides or bottom. (Picture C)

9 Keep the jar in an undisturbed area. Place the piece of paper on top of the jar. Observe frequently.

State Your Conclusions

1. What did your crystal look like? Describe its appearance.
2. How did the crystal grow?
3. What do you think would happen if particles of dust or other impurities got into the jar?

Record Your Results

	Observations
Saucer	
Crystal: Day 1	
Crystal: Day 2	

Let's Experiment

When you made your seed crystals, you had to wait for the solution to evaporate in order for the crystals to form. How does the rate of evaporation affect the size of crystals? Design an experiment and use what you know about scientific methods to find out.

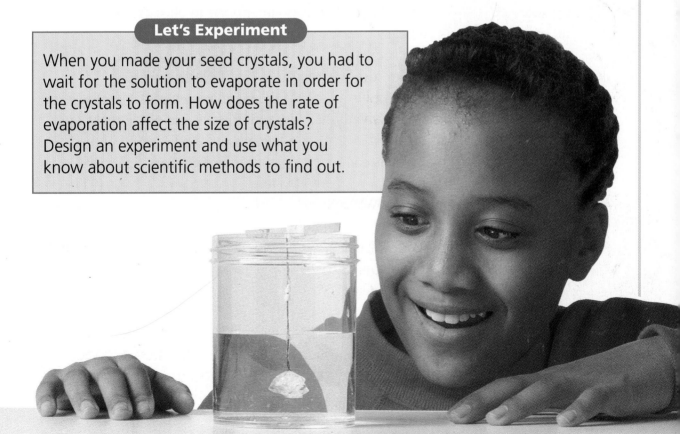

Classifying by Physical Properties

Classifying is a way to group objects or ideas according to a system. Classifying is a good way to see what different items or subjects have in common. Arranging items such as books according to a system also makes them easier to find and use.

Thinking It Through

Suppose you are planning a display of the following crystalline substances: kitchen salt, rock salt, sugar, sand, sulfur, quartz, a model of a snowflake, a model of an ice cube.

There are several ways you can classify these crystals. Here are some to think about.

By size: You could decide to put the model of the snowflake with other small items such as sugar, because real snowflakes are small. Their crystals can be seen only when magnified.

By temperature at which it formed: The salts probably formed at around room temperature. The snow and ice formed at very low temperatures. The other materials formed at high temperatures.

Living and nonliving: Only one item is from a living thing; sugar is from a plant.
Edible and nonedible: The sugar, salt, and ice cube are edible—able to be eaten, unlike the other items.
By whether or not they dissolve easily in water at room temperature: How could you find out for sure which items belong in the "easily dissolved" group? You could mix each item in a cup of room-temperature water.

There are many ways to arrange the same group of items. Can you think of any other ways to classify, or group, the crystals?

Your Turn

Make up your own rock classification system. Place some of the rocks and other substances discussed in the chapter into your classification system.

Chapter Review

Thinking Back

1. How does the microscope aid scientists in their study of the world?
2. How are rocks, **minerals**, and **crystals** related?
3. Name one characteristic that differs among minerals. Give an example.
4. What four properties do gemstones share with all other crystals?

5. Name three kinds of crystals and describe how they are used.
6. Describe what you would see if you crushed a grain of salt and observed the pieces through a microscope.
7. Name two facts about the shapes of all crystals.

Connecting Ideas

1. Copy the concept map. Use the terms at the right to complete the map about rocks and minerals to show their structure.

salt   crystals

minerals   rocks

mica

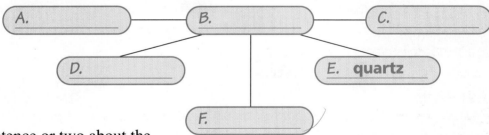

2. Write a sentence or two about the ideas shown in the concept map.

Gathering Evidence

1. In the Activity on page 8, how many times smaller was your scale drawing than your actual body?
2. In the Activity on page 18, what information did you use to predict what would happen when the alum solution evaporated?

Doing Science!

1. *Design an activity* to show that all crystals of a particular substance have the same shape.
2. *Develop a skit* that describes how life would be different if organisms were as large as they appear when magnified by an electron microscope.

2

Structure of Matter

*Hey!
Is this some kind
of magic trick?*

Wear cover goggles
for this activity.

Discover Activity

Is matter made of particles?

Use a dropper to place two drops of perfume in a large balloon. Be careful not to get any perfume on the neck or the outside of the balloon. Blow up the balloon and tie it in a knot. Smell the outside of the balloon. Then wave the balloon in the air for two minutes. Smell the balloon again.

For Discussion

1. When did you first smell the perfume?

2. How did the perfume get outside the balloon?

2.1 *Inner Structure*

▶ *What are the particles inside a crystal?*

Looking into crystals shouldn't be difficult—some quartz crystals are bigger than you are, such as the quartz in the picture. Yet no matter if the crystals are big or small, you know that their particles are arranged in an ordered pattern. But the particles that give crystals their shape are far too small to be seen by your eyes alone. How then can these particles be studied?

Atoms

The particles within crystals are **atoms**—the basic units of all matter. The way that atoms are arranged in crystals determines the shape of the crystal. For example, the atoms in a salt crystal connect in a structure shaped like a cube. When many of the atoms in salt join together, they form a small cube the size of a grain of salt. Many more atoms connect to make even larger cubes of salt.

Other substances are made of different arrangements of atoms. Quartz crystals are formed of atoms, but the atoms in quartz connect in a six-sided shape.

Instruments can help you see the arrangement of atoms inside crystals. The same X rays that show bones within your body and that the dentist uses to examine your teeth can be sent through crystals. Just like doctors and dentists, scientists use X-ray images to learn about inner structure.

▼ *A crystal of quartz can be as small as a grain of sand or as large as you!*

X-Ray Diffraction

X-ray diffraction helps scientists study the structure of crystals.

Crystals—like all matter—are composed of atoms. In each type of crystal, atoms are arranged in a different, orderly way. For example, salt crystals are always made of atoms of sodium and chlorine. The particles are arranged in a cubic pattern like this model. No other crystal has these kinds of particles arranged in exactly this way.

Scientists use X rays to study the structure of crystals. A machine like the one shown beams X rays through a crystal. As X rays pass through the crystal, many rays are diffracted—or bent—by the atoms inside the crystal. The diffracted X rays then strike a piece of film, forming an image of the crystal's diffraction pattern.

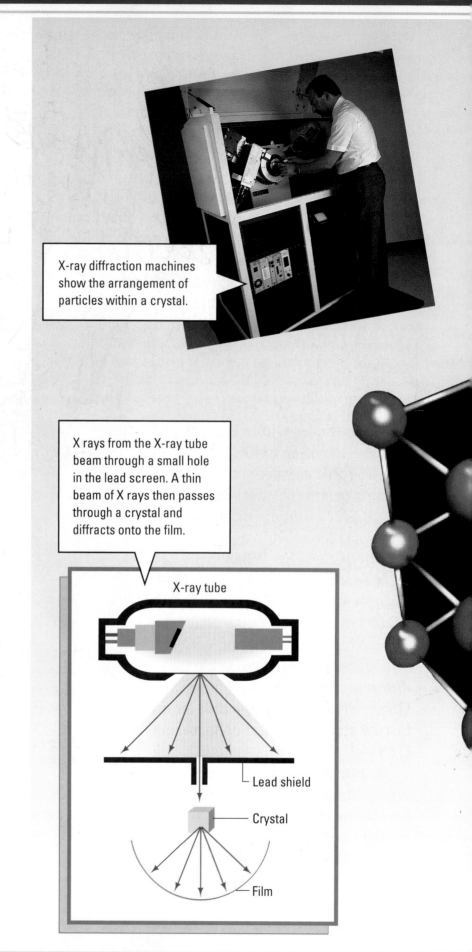

X-ray diffraction machines show the arrangement of particles within a crystal.

X rays from the X-ray tube beam through a small hole in the lead screen. A thin beam of X rays then passes through a crystal and diffracts onto the film.

X-ray tube

Lead shield

Crystal

Film

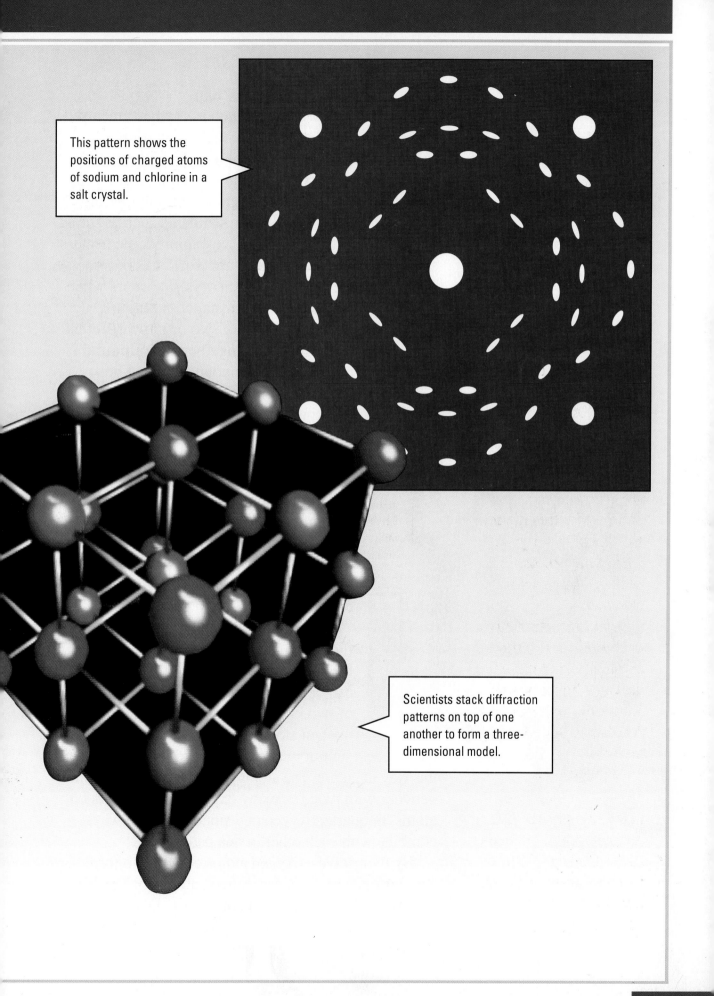

This pattern shows the positions of charged atoms of sodium and chlorine in a salt crystal.

Scientists stack diffraction patterns on top of one another to form a three-dimensional model.

Comparing Compounds

You know that matter—such as the perfume used in the Discover Activity—is made of particles called atoms. You've been taking a closer and closer look at how matter is put together, going from rock to mineral to atom. You've zoomed in on tiny bits of matter using X rays and instruments such as the microscope. The deeper you've explored, the neater and more orderly that miniature world has become. The same order that's found in crystals occurs when atoms of other substances combine.

When atoms of two or more different substances join together, a **compound** is produced. A compound forms when different kinds of atoms combine. Looking closely at compounds reveals that their atoms are also organized in various patterns and arrangements.

Different compounds are made of different combinations of atoms. Later in this chapter, you'll learn about various types of atoms—over 100 different kinds! The structures of these different atoms determine how they combine into different compounds.

You know that sand is small pieces of rocks and minerals, including quartz— the same type of crystals of quartz that can be as big as you are. Quartz is made of two kinds of atoms: silicon atoms and oxygen atoms. The diagram represents the smallest unit of quartz, but the atoms don't appear this way in nature. The atoms form a three-dimensional network with twice as many oxygen atoms as silicon atoms. In quartz, oxygen and silicon atoms always combine with each other in this pattern.

By themselves, oxygen atoms combine to form an odorless, colorless gas. Silicon atoms make a hard, grey solid. But together, silicon atoms and oxygen atoms form a colorless, solid mineral called quartz!

▼ Silicon and oxygen atoms combine to form the quartz that is found in sand.

Si

O

O

Although carbon dioxide is a waste product that you exhale, carbon dioxide in the air is used by plants to make sugars.

The compound carbon dioxide is not a crystal—it's a colorless gas that's mixed with other gases you exhale. Carbon dioxide is also made of two different kinds of atoms: carbon atoms and oxygen atoms. Two oxygen atoms are attached to each carbon atom—one on each side. Carbon dioxide is always arranged in this way.

One compound that you can't live without is water. The atoms in water are arranged in a pattern that looks like a "mouse head." Water contains one oxygen atom for every two hydrogen atoms.

Compare the three compounds—quartz, carbon dioxide, and water. Each contains oxygen atoms combined with one other kind of atom. At room temperature, sand is a solid, carbon dioxide is a gas, and water is a liquid. The kinds of atoms and the links between them determine whether the compound is a solid, a liquid, or a gas at room temperature.

Hydrogen and oxygen atoms form the compound water, which can be found as a solid, a liquid, or a gas.

So atoms combine in certain ways to form different substances called compounds. But how do atoms arrange and rearrange themselves? Can you put atoms together in a compound and take them apart? Yes, and you can even predict what will happen!

Reaction Patterns

Compounds are always being made from atoms in the world around you. Mixing baking soda and vinegar produces bubbles of carbon dioxide gas. The atoms in baking soda and vinegar are rearranged to make carbon dioxide. This process is a **chemical reaction** (rē ak′ shən)—a process that produces one or more substances that are different from the original substances.

A compound often looks different from the substances whose atoms combine to make it. Notice the clear liquid in the flask. This liquid contains white, solid potassium iodide dissolved, or mixed, in water. The clear liquid in the dropper is white, solid lead nitrate dissolved in water. When the liquids mix, a yellow solid—lead iodide—forms!

Chemical reactions occur in many different ways. One way is that two different kinds of atoms combine to form a compound, as shown in the diagram. This happens when hydrogen atoms and oxygen atoms combine to make water.

▲ Lead nitrate and potassium iodide combine to form lead iodide.

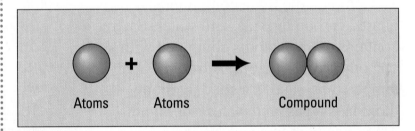

A second type of reaction occurs when a compound breaks down into different types of atoms. Notice the compound in the diagram below breaks down into two kinds of atoms. This occurs when the compound water breaks apart, and hydrogen and oxygen atoms are released.

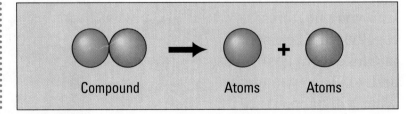

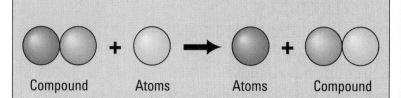

Compound + Atoms → Atoms + Compound

In a third type of reaction, one kind of atom replaces another kind of atom in a compound. When the compound iron oxide combines with carbon, the iron oxide separates into iron and oxygen atoms. Oxygen and carbon atoms combine, leaving iron atoms by themselves.

The reaction below involves compounds dissolved in water. The diagram shows their atoms switch places, and new compounds form. This process formed the yellow lead iodide in the picture. You know potassium nitrate formed too, but you can't see it because it's dissolved in the water.

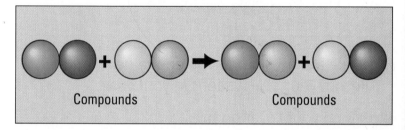

Compounds → Compounds

Reactions don't happen by chance. You can predict how certain substances will react. If you know how to organize atoms, you can cause quite a reaction!

Checkpoint

1. How are the particles within salt crystals and quartz crystals arranged?
2. How do X rays reveal the structure of atoms within crystals?
3. Compare quartz, water, and carbon dioxide. How are they similar and different?
4. What are four kinds of chemical reactions that can occur?
5. **Take Action!** Bite into an apple and let it sit five minutes. What reaction appears?

A Very Clear Reaction

Heating sand with other compounds produces the chemical reaction needed to make common window glass. Glass is one of the few substances that does not form a crystal structure when it cools. Instead, its atoms remain in a state similar to those of a very thick liquid.

The graph below shows the major ingredients in window glass. The "Other" category includes sodium and calcium.

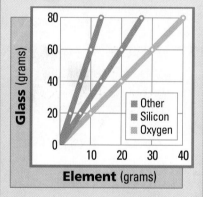

What Did You Find Out?
1. *In 60 grams of glass, how much silicon is used?*
2. *If 20 grams of silicon are available, how much oxygen and sodium and calcium would be needed to make the greatest amount of glass from all of this silicon?*
3. *Which ingredient would you need the most of to make 60 grams of glass?*

Activity

Observing a Chemical Change

What is an example of a chemical reaction where the atoms of two different compounds trade places? Try this activity to find out.

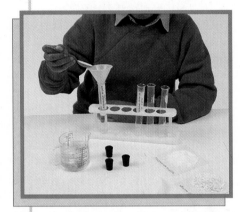

Picture A

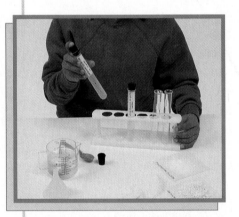

Picture B

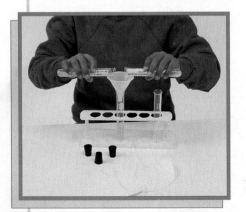

Picture C

Gather These Materials

cover goggles
4 test tubes with
   stoppers
funnel
spoon

magnesium sulfate
calcium chloride
filter paper
water
test tube holder

Follow This Procedure

1 Make a chart like the one on the next page. Record your observations in your chart.

2 Put on your cover goggles.

3 Half fill one test tube with water.

4 Using the funnel, add 1 level spoonful of magnesium sulfate to the test tube. (Picture A) Put the stopper in and shake until the solid dissolves.

5 Fill a second test tube halfway with water, then add 1 level spoonful of calcium chloride. Put the stopper in and shake until the solid dissolves. (Picture B)

> **Predict: *What would happen if you combined the contents of the 2 test tubes?***

6 Pour the contents of the 2 test tubes together into a third test tube. (Picture C) Observe for 5 minutes. Record your observations.

7 Fold a round piece of filter paper into a cone shape. Place the filter cone into the funnel. Place the funnel into a fourth test tube.

8 Slowly pour the combined mixture into the funnel.

9 Record the results.

State Your Conclusions

---

1. What happened when you mixed together the contents of the first and second test tubes?

2. How can you tell that a chemical reaction took place?

Record Your Results

Compound	Observations
Magnesium sulfate	
Calcium chloride	
New compound	

Let's Experiment

How is the amount of the new substance that forms affected by the amount of magnesium sulfate and the amount of calcium chloride used? Use your knowledge of scientific methods to find out.

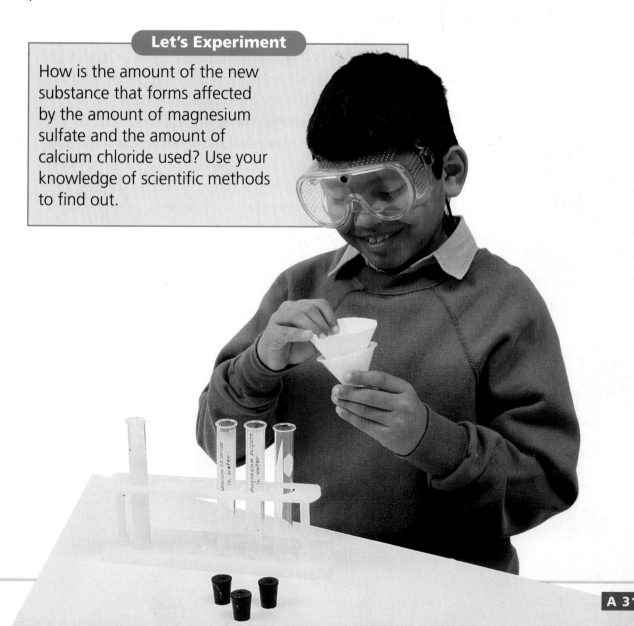

2.2 Model Changes

▶ What do atoms look like?

Many chemical reactions are easy to see. Baking soda and vinegar combine quickly, producing many bubbles of carbon dioxide. Some reactions are much slower. Rust forms so slowly that you hardly notice it. In any reaction, you can't see the compounds breaking apart or the atoms combining. Atoms are much too small to see with your eyes alone.

People have long wondered exactly what atoms look like. Because atoms are so small, models have been built to represent atoms. A model is a picture or a structure that helps explain how something looks or works. Models of atoms have changed over time. But models aren't just guesses about what atoms look like—they're based on scientific information gathered through experiments. An experiment can produce information that adds to a model or changes it completely.

Certain instruments magnify atoms so they can be seen. Even powerful microscopes produce only hazy images of atoms, like those shown below. Pictures of atoms taken through microscopes don't show much detail—atoms look like little round balls. But experiments and models have produced a clearer picture of atoms. And experiments have helped show that atoms are made of even smaller parts.

▼ Models of atoms help us understand what actual atoms may look like. Observing atoms through scanning tunneling electron microscopes gives us information too. The yellow "balls" are carbon atoms in graphite.

Model Atoms

Over 2000 years ago, the Greek philosopher Democritus suggested that everything was made of atoms, and that atoms could not be divided. But Democritus and the Greeks didn't prove their ideas or models with experiments. And although the Greek idea lasted for many centuries, it changed as more information was gathered.

In the early 1800s, the British scientist John Dalton took the Greek model further. He agreed with the Greek idea that everything is made of atoms shaped like solid, round balls. He also thought that different substances were made of different atoms. But Dalton's atom model was still quite simple.

The model next changed in 1897 due to the experiments of J. J. Thomson, another British scientist. He made electricity pass through a tube, and noticed that a green glow formed at the end of the tube. Thomson found that when he held a magnet next to this glow, the glow was attracted to the magnet. He realized that the glow must be made of very small charged particles. Thomson called each of these negatively charged particles an **electron** (i lek′ tron). The atom model that Thomson proposed had electrons inside of solid atoms—like raisins in bread. Scientists don't use Thomson's atom model today, but his discoveries paved the way for later atom models.

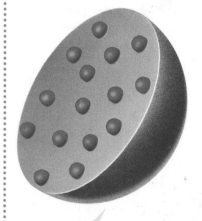

Thomson's model
J. J. Thomson believed that electrons were found inside solid atoms.

Dalton's model
John Dalton's model of the atom was similar to that of the ancient Greeks.

If atoms contained particles such as electrons, were there also other pieces? And if so, how were the other pieces arranged in the atom? Another scientist named Ernest Rutherford—also working in England in the early 1900s—set up an experiment to find out. Rutherford beamed atom-sized particles at a piece of gold foil. If the gold atoms were solid, he knew that the particles would bounce back off of them. But most of the particles passed right through the foil! Rutherford then knew that the atoms in the foil were mostly empty space. He used this evidence to construct a new atom model.

What about the few particles that bounced back—what were they bouncing off of? Rutherford believed each atom contained a **nucleus** (nü′ klē əs)—the central part of the atom. He thought that the nucleus was made of a positively charged particle called a **proton** (prō′ ton). And in his model, Rutherford placed electrons around the protons in the nucleus. Between them was empty space.

This model of the atom was changed a bit by the Danish scientist Niels Bohr. In 1913, Bohr proposed that electrons traveled in certain orbits around the nucleus of an atom. Each layer contained only a certain number of electrons. And Bohr thought electrons often jumped from one layer to another. But even this model eventually changed.

Rutherford's model
Rutherford's model looks like a tiny solar system, with protons in the nucleus surrounded by electrons.

Bohr's model
Bohr's model of the atom shows electrons orbiting at different levels around the atom's nucleus.

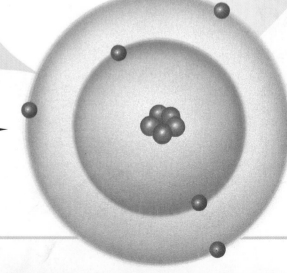

In 1932, another British scientist, James Chadwick, proved that another particle was contained in the atom's nucleus. This particle is the **neutron** (nü′ tron)—a particle with no charge. The model of the atom changed again, with the nucleus containing protons and neutrons orbited by electrons in different layers.

Today another model, the electron cloud model, is used. Scientists aren't certain how electrons move as they orbit the nucleus. That's because the behavior of electrons is more complicated than simply orbiting the nucleus and jumping from one layer to another. In this model, you can see the darker area in the center where the nucleus is. But you can't see the different layers of electrons. In fact, you can't say exactly where electrons will be in any atom.

So not only do atoms combine into orderly compounds and react in predictable ways, atoms also have an orderly arrangement of parts. It has taken the experiments of many scientists to arrive at the model of the atom in use today. Perhaps the model will change in the future as the result of another discovery. It's amazing to think that so much is known of something that couldn't even be seen until quite recently.

Electron cloud model
Electrons are less likely to be found in the fuzzy parts of the "cloud" than in the darker parts nearer the nucleus.

Particle Accelerators

Tools other than microscopes can be used to study atoms. In fact, some of these tools are machines so large that they're wider and longer than entire towns. The machines are particle accelerators, and with them scientists can look much more closely at atoms. It's possible even to find parts of atoms smaller than protons, neutrons, or electrons.

Although some particle accelerators are long and straight, most accelerators are built as large rings under the ground. They shoot protons and electrons around and around in circles at high speeds. Then the electrons and protons collide and some break apart. When these subatomic particles break apart, you can study what the parts inside of them do.

Recent experiments proved that protons and neutrons are made of smaller parts called quarks. Using larger rings, scientists spin electrons and protons around with greater energy and smash them apart into smaller particles.

▼ Particles travel through accelerators at almost the speed of light.

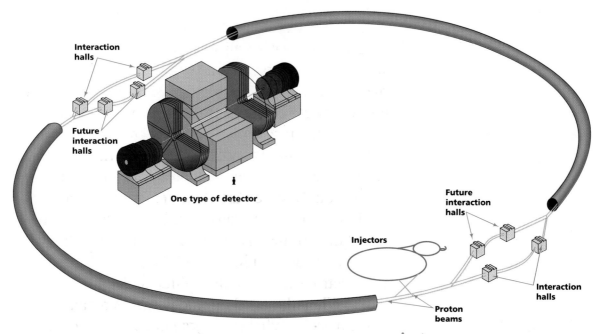

Interaction halls

Future interaction halls

One type of detector

Future interaction halls

Injectors

Interaction halls

Proton beams

The Superconducting Super Collider, or SSC, under construction in Texas will be about 85 kilometers across, and will be located under the town of Waxahachie. With the SSC, scientists hope to find the basic particle which makes up everything—quarks and all other particles of matter. Scientists may also be able to construct a model that explains how the basic forces in the universe may have at one time acted together.

This giant machine should greatly increase knowledge about things very small. In the beginning, it seemed that atoms could not be divided—now the number of parts seems endless!

▲ *Huge machines called particle accelerators are used to study the smallest bits of matter.*

Checkpoint

1. How did the Bohr model change the model of the atom proposed by Rutherford?
2. What particles, smaller even than protons, electrons, and neutrons, have scientists discovered using particle accelerators?
3. Take Action! Pretend you are a scientist who discovers a part of the atom. Write a journal entry about your experiment.

2.3 Setting the Table

> **How are atoms different from one another?**

All atoms contain the same parts—protons, electrons, and neutrons. The difference between atoms is the number of parts they contain. And because of this difference, certain atoms form solid metals and others compose invisible gases.

Elements

An **element** (el′ ə mənt) is any substance made of only one kind of atom. The mercury inside a thermometer is an element. So is the iron in an iron frying pan. An atom is the smallest part of these and other elements.

In 1869, a Russian scientist named Mendeleev (Men′ dl ā′ ef) organized the different elements known at the time. He made a list in which he arranged all of the elements that he knew about, starting with hydrogen. He noticed that certain elements in his list had similar properties. So Mendeleev constructed a table with rows and columns that organized the elements according to their properties. This chart—called the **periodic table**—is an orderly arrangement of the different elements.

Mendeleev left blank spaces where he thought an element should fit, even though he didn't know if that element existed. His predictions turned out to be accurate when these elements—gallium, scandium, and germanium—were later discovered.

▼ Mendeleev left blank spaces on his periodic table, predicting the existence of three elements that were not yet discovered.

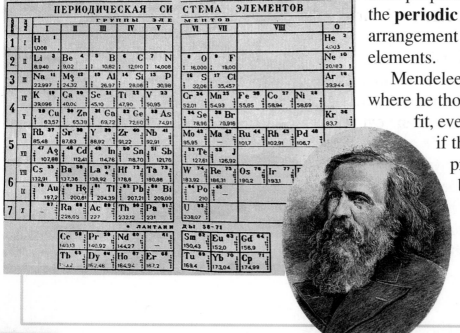

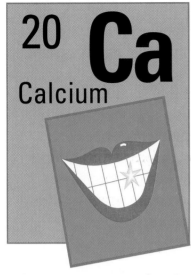
20 Ca
Calcium

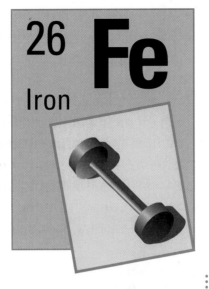
26 Fe
Iron

74 W
Tungsten

Element Symbols

When addressing letters to friends, you probably use abbreviations to indicate the states where they live. All of the elements also have abbreviations, or symbols, to represent their names.

Symbols have one, two, or even three letters. Some symbols are easy to remember and understand. Other symbols might seem odd because they represent words in other languages.

Elements are used in many ways, a few of which are shown in the pictures above. Calcium—symbol Ca—is an important element found in many foods you eat. Calcium helps your bones and teeth grow. It also helps your blood clot and your muscles contract. The symbol for calcium is simply made up of the first two letters of its name.

But the symbol for iron doesn't match its name. That's because its symbol—Fe—comes from the ancient Latin word *ferrum*, meaning iron. Iron was one of the first metals used by ancient civilizations to make tools.

Tungsten has an unlikely symbol—W. This symbol comes from the German word *wolfram,* another name for tungsten. And the word tungsten comes from a Swedish phrase meaning "heavy stone." Learning symbols of elements is like learning several languages at once!

▲ *Different elements have different uses.*

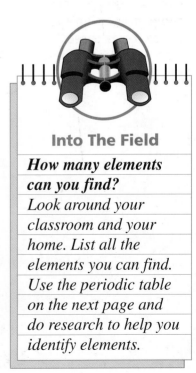

Into The Field

How many elements can you find?
Look around your classroom and your home. List all the elements you can find. Use the periodic table on the next page and do research to help you identify elements.

The periodic table is arranged in rows and columns based on the structure and properties of different atoms.

Periodic Table

You can use the periodic table to learn more about the elements. You can read the table two different ways. One way is to read across, from left to right. Notice that starting with hydrogen, the numbers for each element get larger. These atomic numbers tell you how many protons are in each atom of each element. As atomic numbers increase through the table, atoms of the elements become more massive. For example, an atom of lead has 82 protons, 82 electrons, and an average of 125 neutrons!

1	**2**	**3**	**4**	**5**	**6**	**7**	**8**	**9**
1 **H** Hydrogen								
3 **Li** Lithium	4 **Be** Beryllium							
11 **Na** Sodium	12 **Mg** Magnesium							
19 **K** Potassium	20 **Ca** Calcium	21 **Sc** Scandium	22 **Ti** Titanium	23 **V** Vanadium	24 **Cr** Chromium	25 **Mn** Manganese	26 **Fe** Iron	27 **Co** Cobalt
37 **Rb** Rubidium	38 **Sr** Strontium	39 **Y** Yttrium	40 **Zr** Zirconium	41 **Nb** Niobium	42 **Mo** Molybdenum	43 **Tc** Technetium	44 **Ru** Ruthenium	45 **Rh** Rhodium
55 **Cs** Cesium	56 **Ba** Barium	71 **Lu** Lutetium	72 **Hf** Hafnium	73 **Ta** Tantalum	74 **W** Tungsten	75 **Re** Rhenium	76 **Os** Osmium	77 **Ir** Iridium
87 **Fr** Francium	88 **Ra** Radium	103 **Lr** Lawrencium	104 **Unq** Unnilquadium	105 **Unp** Unnilpentium	106 **Unh** Unnilhexium	107 **Uns** Unnilseptium	108 **Uno** Unniloctium	109 **Une** Unnilennium

57 **La** Lanthanum	58 **Ce** Cerium	59 **Pr** Praseodymium	60 **Nd** Neodymium	61 **Pm** Promethium	62 **Sm** Samarium	63 **Eu** Europium
89 **Ac** Actinium	90 **Th** Thorium	91 **Pa** Profactinium	92 **U** Uranium	93 **Np** Neptunium	94 **Pu** Plutonium	95 **Am** Americium

A second way to read the table is from top to bottom. Every column is a family of elements with similar properties. Elements in families resemble each other and react in similar ways. For example, lithium, sodium, and potassium—all in the first column—react strongly with water. When placed in water they explode, releasing large amounts of heat.

The periodic table is also divided into metals and nonmetals. Metals can be polished, and both heat and electricity pass easily through them. Nonmetals have opposite properties. Also, elements on opposite sides of the table easily react with each other to form compounds.

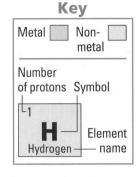

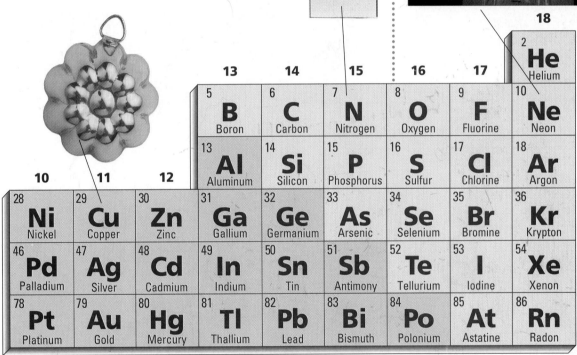

			13	14	15	16	17	18
								2 **He** Helium
			5 **B** Boron	6 **C** Carbon	7 **N** Nitrogen	8 **O** Oxygen	9 **F** Fluorine	10 **Ne** Neon
			13 **Al** Aluminum	14 **Si** Silicon	15 **P** Phosphorus	16 **S** Sulfur	17 **Cl** Chlorine	18 **Ar** Argon
10	11	12						
28 **Ni** Nickel	29 **Cu** Copper	30 **Zn** Zinc	31 **Ga** Gallium	32 **Ge** Germanium	33 **As** Arsenic	34 **Se** Selenium	35 **Br** Bromine	36 **Kr** Krypton
46 **Pd** Palladium	47 **Ag** Silver	48 **Cd** Cadmium	49 **In** Indium	50 **Sn** Tin	51 **Sb** Antimony	52 **Te** Tellurium	53 **I** Iodine	54 **Xe** Xenon
78 **Pt** Platinum	79 **Au** Gold	80 **Hg** Mercury	81 **Tl** Thallium	82 **Pb** Lead	83 **Bi** Bismuth	84 **Po** Polonium	85 **At** Astatine	86 **Rn** Radon

64 **Gd** Gadolinium	65 **Tb** Terbium	66 **Dy** Dysprosium	67 **Ho** Holmium	68 **Er** Erbium	69 **Tm** Thulium	70 **Yb** Ytterbium
96 **Cm** Curium	97 **Bk** Berkelium	98 **Cf** Californium	99 **Es** Einsteinium	100 **Fm** Fermium	101 **Md** Mendelevium	102 **No** Nobelium

Over time, ideas about the elements have changed greatly. The ancient Greeks thought that everything was made of some combination of earth, air, fire, and water. They thought that these substances were the four basic elements. Again, the Greeks didn't do any experiments to try to prove their ideas.

Later, people called alchemists did many experiments with elements. They tried to change one element into another. For example, they tried to make gold by changing the properties of copper and lead. Although they couldn't change one kind of element into another, alchemists made many discoveries as they heated, melted, evaporated, and combined materials. In doing so, they discovered the existence of phosphorus, and perhaps zinc, arsenic, bismuth, and antimony.

▼ *The periodic table is a tool that can help you answer questions about atoms and elements.*

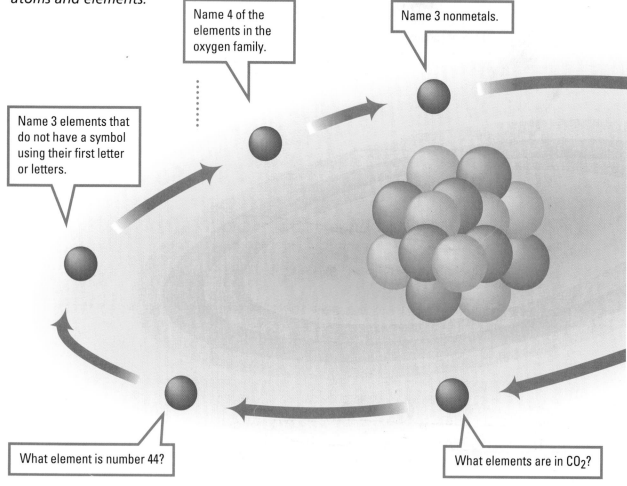

Name 4 of the elements in the oxygen family.

Name 3 nonmetals.

Name 3 elements that do not have a symbol using their first letter or letters.

What element is number 44?

What elements are in CO_2?

More recently, scientists working with particle accelerators and in other laboratories have been able to change the atoms of elements. The process in nuclear reactors causes a nuclear reaction, changing the nucleus of an atom of uranium to a nucleus of plutonium. And scientists in laboratories can now do what alchemists tried for hundreds of years to accomplish—change lead atoms into atoms of gold. But too few gold atoms are made for this process to be valuable.

Scientists sometimes discover new elements and add them to the periodic table. New elements are made in the laboratory, but their atoms quickly decay and break apart. Perhaps someday you'll help make an element to be added to the periodic table!

Find an element in the lithium family that combines with an element in the fluorine family.

Checkpoint

1. How did Mendeleev arrange the different elements in a table?
2. Why do some elements have symbols that are unlike their names?
3. You know that lithium, sodium, and potassium are very reactive. What other elements share this property?
4. **Take Action!** Make flashcards with symbols of elements on one side and their names on the other. Learn these symbols by quizzing yourself and your friends.

Making a Model of an Atom

Scientists use models of the atom to describe how atoms are put together. In this activity, make a model of your own.

Picture A

Picture B

Picture C

Gather These Materials

periodic table of the elements

3 different pieces of colored modeling clay

craft sticks

plastic knife

metric ruler

Follow This Procedure

1 Make a chart like the one on the next page. Record your observations in your chart.

2 Choose an element from the periodic table of the elements. Find the atomic number in the box next to the name of the element you chose. This number represents the number of protons and electrons that this atom contains. In your model, also use this number to represent the number of neutrons in the atom.

3 Place 3 different colors of modeling clay on your desk. Choose one color of clay for protons and slice off a piece using a plastic knife. (Picture A)

4 Separate that slice of clay into smaller pieces. Roll each piece into a ball about 1 cm in diameter. Make the same number of protons as the atomic number of the element you chose.

5 Use another color of clay for neutrons. Make them the same size and form the same number of clay balls as you did for protons.

6 With the third color of clay, make smaller clay balls to represent electrons. Make the same number as you did for the protons and neutrons. (Picture B)

Predict: How many particles are contained in the nucleus of your model atom?

7 Press the protons and neutrons together gently to form the nucleus of your model atom. Insert one of the craft sticks all the way through the nucleus. Place an electron on each end. These represent the 2 electrons closest to the nucleus.

8 Gently insert other craft sticks into but not through the nucleus. Place one electron on the end of each stick. Do this until you use all your electrons. These represent the electrons farther away from the nucleus. (Picture C)

9 Write the name of the element on the data table. Then draw a diagram of your model.

State Your Conclusions

1. How is your model of the atom different from the true structure of an atom?
2. How could you change your model of the atom to make it more realistic?

Let's Experiment

The mass number of an atom is the total number of the protons and neutrons it possesses. Carbon-14 is a form of carbon with 2 extra neutrons. Find carbon on the periodic table of the elements and construct a model of an atom of carbon-14.

Record Your Results

Model of element
Name of element:

Making Time Lines

A time line is a good way to organize and study a series of events. It lets you see when each event occurred in relation to other events.

Thinking It Through

The time line on this page was made from the notes shown to the right. These are the steps you would take to make the time line.

1. Gather the information you need to make the time line. In this case, the information is in the form of notes such as those you might take while reading.

2. Draw a vertical or a horizontal line. The earliest year will be at the bottom of the vertical line or to the left on the horizontal line.

3. Find the earliest and latest events you plan to use. Mark the earliest and latest times on the time line.

4. Decide on a reasonable time interval. One that is too large will crowd all your information together. One that is too small will not allow space for all your information. Mark off the intervals.

5. Place your data at the appropriate points on the time line. Draw a line from the time line to each piece of data.

6. Give your time line a title.

Notes

1977:*Voyager I* and *II* launched. They were spacecraft without crews, designed to explore the Solar System.

1957:*Sputnik I,* the first satellite, was launched by the Soviet Union.

1969:*Apollo 11,* astronauts landed on the moon for the first time.

1966:First satellite docked with a fuel-carrying rocket in space.

1973:*Skylab,* an orbiting laboratory, was launched into space.

Your Turn

Use events from the chapter, starting with Dalton. Make a time line to show the history of the model of the atom.

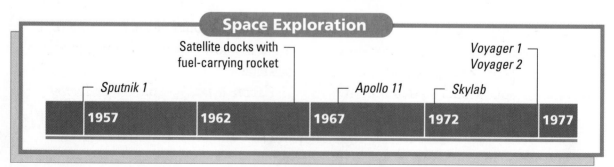

Space Exploration

Satellite docks with fuel-carrying rocket

Sputnik 1

Apollo 11

Skylab

Voyager 1
Voyager 2

| 1957 | 1962 | 1967 | 1972 | 1977 |

Chapter Review

Thinking Back

1. What determines the shape of a crystal?
2. Explain the process in which X-ray diffraction is used to determine the structure of crystals.
3. Compare **atoms** and **compounds.**
4. What is a **chemical reaction**?
5. Explain the reaction that occurs when iron oxide combines with carbon.
6. What makes up the **nucleus** of an atom?
7. What is the difference between **electrons** and **protons**?
8. How are atoms and **elements** related?
9. How does a **neutron** differ from the other particles that make up an atom?
10. What are the two ways you could read the **periodic table**? What information would you find using each method?

Connecting Ideas

1. Copy the concept map. Use the terms at the right to complete the map about compounds and atoms to show how they are structured.

atoms   **compounds**
neutrons   **protons**

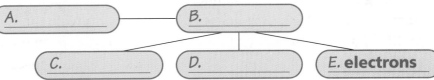

2. Write a sentence or two about the ideas shown in the concept map.

Gathering Evidence

1. In the Activity on page 30, how did you know a chemical reaction occurred?
2. In the Activity on page 44, how could you change your model so that it more accurately shows an atom's structure?

Doing Science!

1. **Design a model** of the structure of an atom to show a group of younger students.
2. **Create a skit** in which Mendeleev explains his periodic table to a group of scientists.

Organized Organisms

Alright, look at this! Oh yuk, look what's in this one!

How do the parts of a microscope work?

Compare your microscope to the one below. Identify as many parts as you can. Place a prepared slide on the microscope stage. Bring the low-powered objective to within 3 millimeters of the slide. Then adjust the slide, objective, and light level to give you a clear image of the slide.

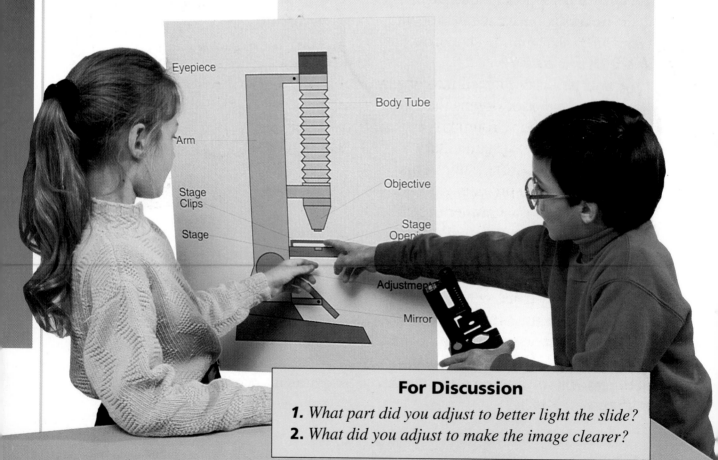

Eyepiece

Body Tube

Arm

Stage Clips

Objective

Stage

Stage Openi...

Adjustmen...

Mirror

For Discussion

1. *What part did you adjust to better light the slide?*
2. *What did you adjust to make the image clearer?*

3.1 *An Inside Look*

▶ *What kind of a picture is this?*

Doctors can't use their eyes to see everything inside people's bodies. However, they have instruments to help them. To design these instruments, scientists use their knowledge of the order and structure of nature. One example of advanced technology is the MRI—magnetic resonance imaging—machine. It uses atoms to produce images like the one shown. Because scientists understand how atoms are arranged and how to use them, doctors can learn more about the human body.

Organ Systems

What would you find if you looked inside a human body? Remember that the closer you looked at crystals, the more order you found. This order is true of the human body.

Your body is organized into **organ systems**—groups of organs that work together to do a job. Your skin, hair, and nails make up the integumentary (in teg′ yə men′tə rē) system. This system covers and protects your body.

Your bones form another organ system—the skeletal system. This system holds you up and protects you. Muscles attached to bones help you to move. All of your muscles are another organ system: the muscular system.

The circulatory system carries blood through your heart, lungs, and all around your body—every twenty seconds. All your organ systems are working at the same time. You're more organized than you might have thought!

▼ *The inside of the human body is visible when viewed with an MRI machine.*

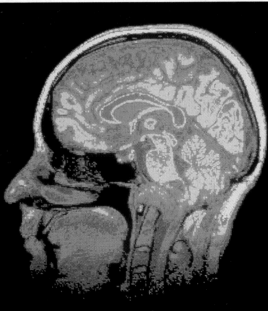

Organized Labor

To discover more about the structure of crystals, you made their scale larger and larger so you could take a closer look at them. What would you discover if you looked more closely at organ systems? First you would see **organs**—groups of tissues that work together to do a certain job. The pictures on this page show two organs of the circulatory system—the heart and the blood vessels.

Next, you would see that different types of **tissues** form the organs in each organ system. Tissues are groups of cells of the same kind that do the same job. In the circulatory system, for instance, the heart and blood vessels are made of different tissues. Blood, which is also a tissue, differs from the tissues of the vessels and heart.

Next, you might look at different types of tissues under a microscope. You would discover that the tissues are made of cells. A **cell** is the smallest living part of the body. However, cells do not look alike. The cells in muscle tissue look long and stringy. The cells in bone tissue form circular patterns. A drop of blood reveals disk-shaped red blood cells and round white blood cells.

▲ *Your heart is one organ in your circulatory system.*

3300X

➤ *Tissues, like those lining the blood vessel below, are made of cells. You can also see cells of blood, which is a tissue.*

From *Tissues and Organs: A Text-Atlas of Scanning Electron Microscopy* by R.G. Kessel and Randy H. Kardon, p.37. ©1979 W. H. Freeman and Company.

Your body is made of many kinds of cells—each of which has its own set of tasks. Imagine that your class wants to prepare a meal. The class decides to divide tasks to get the work done. Some students shop, others cook, and others clean up. By dividing the jobs, your class serves a delicious meal easily.

Your body is also made of many different parts working together. Every day, you breathe, digest food, sleep, smell, touch, move, and learn. Down to the tiniest cell, each part of your body works so your whole body can do these things. For instance, each organ does a job in an organ system. In turn, each type of tissue does its job as part of a certain organ. And finally, groups of cells do certain tasks as part of different tissues.

Each organ system performs many functions at one time. Your body is made up of many organ systems, so it can perform many different tasks at once. Your body works hard to get you through a busy day!

▼ *The smallest living parts of your body are cells.*
50,000X

Checkpoint

1. Name two organ systems and tell what role they play in the body.
2. What is the smallest living part of the tissue lining a blood vessel?
3. Take Action! Make a collage of photographs of people, labeling the organ systems being used in each picture.

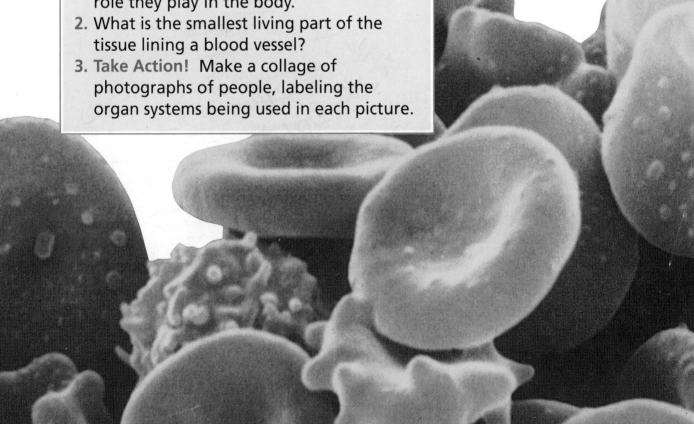

Activity

Onions Are Made Of Cells Too

You can see the cells that form the skin of an onion and the lining of a pork casing. Try this activity to find out how.

Picture A

Gather These Materials

cover goggles
piece of onion
tweezers
2 microscope slides and
   cover slips

dropper and water
microscope
pork casing
plastic knife
iodine solution

Follow This Procedure

1 Make a chart like the one on the next page. Record your observations in your chart.

2 Put on your cover goggles.

3 Bend a small piece of onion until it breaks in two. Look for a layer of onion skin holding together the thin layers. (Picture A) Use tweezers to remove the skin.

4 Spread the onion skin on a microscope slide using the tweezers.

Picture B

5 Add a couple of drops of water from a dropper to the slide. Use the dropper to add enough water to cover the skin.

6 Place a cover slip over the onion skin. (Picture B)

7 Place the slide on the microscope stage. View the onion under low power. Draw what you see.

8 View under high power. Focus on one cell and draw what you see.

Picture C

9 Place 2 drops of water in the middle of the second microscope slide.

10 Firmly scrape the inside of a pork casing with a plastic knife. Gently tap the knife edge into the water on the slide. (Picture C)

11 Add a coverslip. Observe under high and low power. Draw what you see under each magnification.

Predict: *How would your view of both kinds of cells improve with staining?*

12 Remove the cover slips and add several drops of iodine solution to each of your slides.

Onion cells	
Low power	High power

Pork casing cells	
Low power	High power

State Your Conclusions

1. Both the onion and the pork casing are made of cells. What cell parts are the same? What cell parts are different?

2. What other living things could you examine that would resemble the onion cells? What other living things could you examine that would resemble the pork casing cells?

Let's Experiment

All living things are made of cells. Use the same procedure to observe cells of algae and parts of plants such as the thin "skin" of leaves. Make drawings and compare the various cells.

Into The Field

What is the smallest object that you can find and pick up?
Use a hand lens to examine your classroom. Find the smallest object that you can see and try to pick it up. Lay the object on paper to examine it.

➤ Leeuwenhoek took notes and made drawings of the tiny organisms he saw.

3.2 *Looking at Cells*

▶ **What's in a cell?**

The Dutch scientist Anton van Leeuwenhoek (lā′vən húk), who lived during the 1600s, was not trained in science. He sold silk, wool, and cotton for a living. He became interested in magnification after using lenses to inspect his cloth. In his spare time, he ground lenses and used them to make small, powerful microscopes.

One day, Leeuwenhoek filled a dish with cloudy water from a lake near his town. Then he looked at a drop of the water through his microscope. He was surprised at what he saw—a zoo of tiny, living organisms wriggled in the drop of water!

Animalcules

Leeuwenhoek called the organisms he discovered "animalcules." His discovery changed the way scientists thought about living things. Before Leeuwenhoek saw living things in a drop of water, people didn't know about single-celled organisms. In fact, nobody knew that life existed on such a small scale.

Using his microscopes, Leeuwenhoek looked at everything from the hairs of his wig to the eyes of certain insects. Like scientists today, he kept a record of his observations. His simple instruments and records, as shown in the picture, began to focus attention on these little-known microscopic organisms.

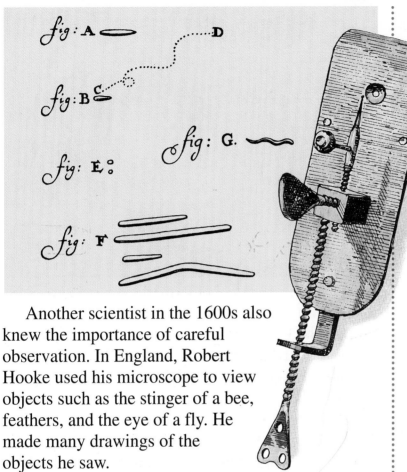

Leeuwenhoek kept careful notes and made drawings of the "animalcules" that he observed through his microscope.

Another scientist in the 1600s also knew the importance of careful observation. In England, Robert Hooke used his microscope to view objects such as the stinger of a bee, feathers, and the eye of a fly. He made many drawings of the objects he saw.

When Hooke looked at a thin slice of cork, he saw a pattern similar to a honeycomb. He called each box in the pattern a *cell* because it resembled the small rooms that monks live in. He suggested that cork cells formed part of a larger organism.

Using scientific instruments, Leeuwenhoek and Hooke glimpsed a new world. Leeuwenhoek saw single-celled organisms. Hooke saw small parts of larger organisms. Technology helped them better understand nature.

Since then, many more microorganisms have been observed. Improved technology—microscopes and other instruments—have helped scientists learn more and more about living things and their structures. By looking at the structures of tiny cells, scientists have discovered order in nature, even on a very small scale!

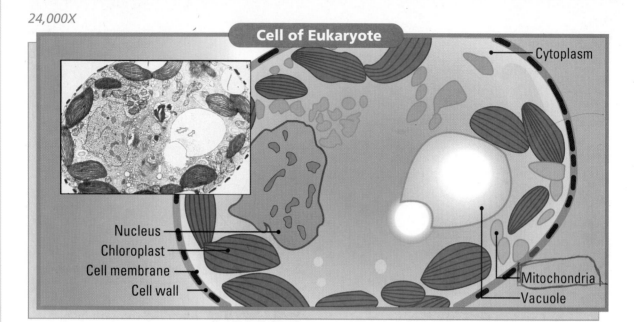

24,000X

Cell of Eukaryote

- Cytoplasm
- Nucleus
- Chloroplast
- Cell membrane
- Cell wall
- Mitochondria
- Vacuole

▲ Cells of eukaryotes are very organized—all of the structures you see here have different jobs.

Viewing Cells

Because of advanced microscopes, scientists know about many tiny organisms that have only one cell. Other organisms are made of many cells—your body contains many trillions of cells.

Scientists divide cells into two groups based on their structure. One cell group includes bacteria, a type of organism that's single-celled. But you can't see their inner structure using a light microscope. You'll learn more about them in the next section.

Scientists classify the second group as eukaryotes (yü′kar′ē ōts). All other single-celled and many-celled organisms fall in this group. A **eukaryote** is made of cells that contain many different structures surrounded by thin coverings called membranes.

Imagine changing the scale of a cell from a eukaryote such as a plant. You make it bigger until you're holding it in the palm of your hand. What would you see? You'd probably first notice the rectangular shape of the cell, although cells are different shapes.

Looking inside the cell, you would see a round shape. This is the cell's **nucleus** (nü′klē əs)—the cell part that controls activities of other cell parts. The nucleus is covered by the nuclear membrane.

The part of the cell surrounding the nucleus is a jellylike fluid called **cytoplasm** (sī′tə plaz′əm). Notice the tiny structures within the cytoplasm in the diagram. Most of these structures are surrounded by membranes too. These structures, called organelles, or "tiny organs," do the work of the cell.

For instance, chloroplasts are organelles in plant cells that trap sunlight to make sugars that provide energy for the plant. Other organelles such as vacuoles and mitochondria (mī′tə kon′drē ə) have different jobs. These cell parts carry out many jobs at the same time, helping keep the cell alive. Different parts doing different jobs also allow cells to specialize and form tissues.

Now imagine that you make the eukaryotic cell in your hand smaller again. Then you place it under a light microscope like the one you used in the Discover Activity. You see the nucleus, the cytoplasm, and many other organelles clearly.

However, if you looked at eukaryotic cells under a compound light microscope—like the one shown—you wouldn't see much detail involving the structures inside the cell. Only by using powerful electron microscopes can you see inside an organelle such as a chloroplast. And at this smaller scale, there's a whole new level of structure.

➤ *Cells in eukaryotes can be seen using a compound light microscope.*

INVESTIGATE

By a Hair's Width

How can you estimate a cell's size? Let's investigate.

What To Do
A. Take a hair from your head and place it on a slide.
B. Cover the hair with a moss leaf.
C. Add a drop of water and a cover slip.

Hair strand — Cover slip
Moss leaf
Water
Glass slide

D. Examine the slide using the low power of a microscope. Locate the hair and the moss cells.
E. How many moss cells in a row cover the width of your hair strand?
F. Draw what you see in a chart like the one below.

Record Your Results

Cells and Hair

What Did You Find Out?
1. *Hair is about 0.1 millimeter in width. How wide is a moss cell?*
2. *If 10 algal cells cover a hair, how wide are they?*

Scanning the Cell

Understanding electrons—nonliving matter—has added to knowledge about living things.

Using beams of electrons instead of light, scientists use electron microscopes to view cells in detail. Scientists can magnify objects hundreds or thousands of times with electron microscopes. Images seen in electron microscopes are also very clear. Compare the chloroplasts below— seen through a light microscope—with the electron microscope images of chloroplasts on the next page. You can see that electron microscopes are useful instruments for viewing the inside of cells.

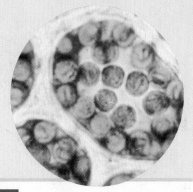

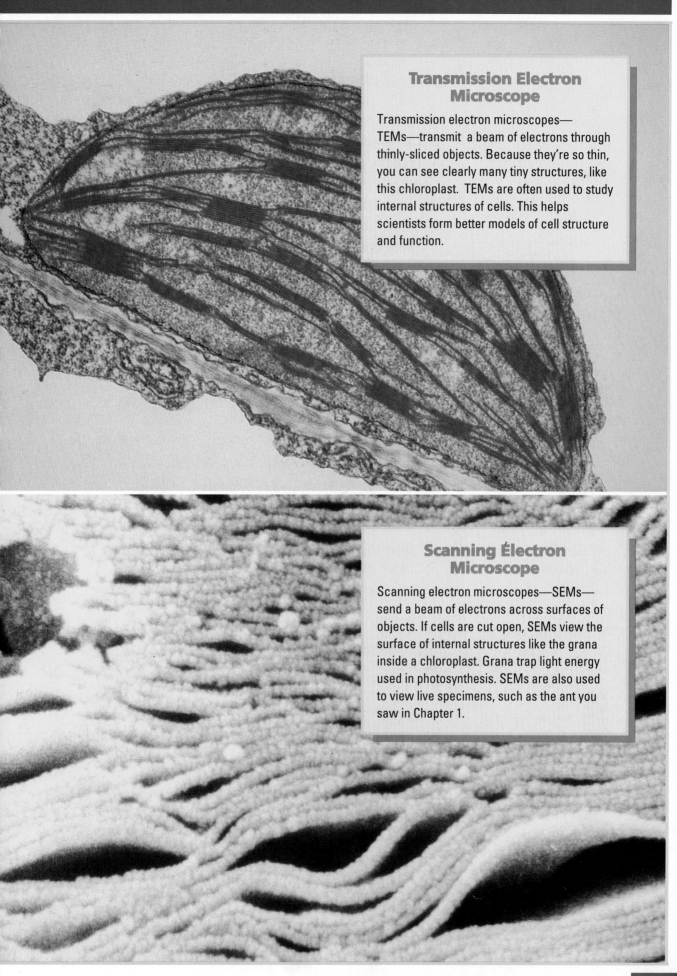

Transmission Electron Microscope

Transmission electron microscopes—TEMs—transmit a beam of electrons through thinly-sliced objects. Because they're so thin, you can see clearly many tiny structures, like this chloroplast. TEMs are often used to study internal structures of cells. This helps scientists form better models of cell structure and function.

Scanning Electron Microscope

Scanning electron microscopes—SEMs—send a beam of electrons across surfaces of objects. If cells are cut open, SEMs view the surface of internal structures like the grana inside a chloroplast. Grana trap light energy used in photosynthesis. SEMs are also used to view live specimens, such as the ant you saw in Chapter 1.

Prokaryotes

How can scientists see inside bacteria? Imagine a giant fly over a kilometer long. That's how big an electron microscope can magnify objects. Electron microscopes show details very clearly. For example, you can even see individual atoms of an element. No wonder this technology finally allowed scientists to examine the smallest of cells—bacteria.

You know bacteria as "germs," but bacteria both help and harm people. When you wash your hands before meals, you try to wash off bacteria that might make you ill. Helpful bacteria can turn apple cider to vinegar, and form yogurt from milk.

Scientists classify bacteria separately from eukaryotes. A **prokaryote** (prō kar′ē ōt) such as a bacterium is made of cells without a membrane separating organelles from the cytoplasm.

Under an electron microscope, prokaryotic cells look different from eukaryotic cells. You learned that cells of eukaryotes have many organelles. Try to find these structures in the picture of the bacterium. The material from the nucleus of a bacterium isn't inside a membrane. Without membranes forming organelles, prokaryotic cells have fewer internal structures than eukaryotic cells.

▼ *Cells from prokaryotes are not as organized as cells from eukaryotes.*

41,600X

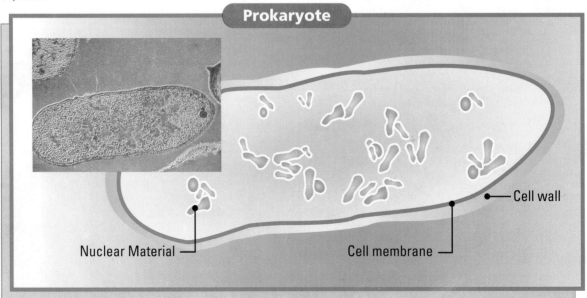

Prokaryote

Nuclear Material

Cell membrane

Cell wall

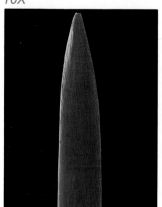

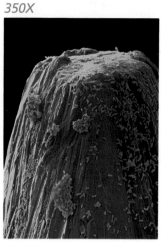

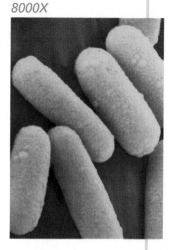

▲ *The tip of this pin is covered by many bacteria.*

Because prokaryotes don't have organelles covered by membranes, they aren't as organized as the cells of eukaryotes. They can't do as many tasks at one time as the cells of eukaryotes can. Because they can't carry out many tasks at once, prokaryotes aren't as specialized as eukaryotes.

Prokaryotes are surrounded by a cell membrane and a cell wall. The cell membrane holds the contents of the cell. Outside this membrane, the rigid, nonliving cell wall supports the cell.

Eukaryotes have these structures too. The cells of animals—such as those from your body—are surrounded by cell membranes only. However, the cells of plants and fungi are surrounded by both cell membranes and cell walls.

Checkpoint

1. Name one similarity and one difference between Leeuwenhoek's and Hooke's observations.
2. List two organelles in eukaryotic cells.
3. What kind of electron microscope shows images of the outer surfaces of objects?
4. In what way is the inside of a bacterium different from a eukaryotic cell?
5. **Take Action!** Write a "Help Wanted" advertisement describing a number of jobs that a cell and its parts can do.

Activity

Building a Model of a Cell

How can you build a simple model of a cell? Try this activity to find out.

Picture A

Gather These Materials

cover goggles

large plastic jar with lid

iodine solution

water

plastic mixing bowl

package of unflavored gelatin

plastic spoon

cornstarch

perfume

self-sealing sandwich bag

marble

Follow This Procedure

1. Make a chart like the one on the next page. Record your observations in your chart.

2. Put your cover goggles on.

3. Fill the large plastic jar about half full of water. Carefully add enough iodine solution to make the water a dark orange color. (Picture A) *CAUTION: Do not spill any of the iodine solution on your skin or clothing.*

4. Put the lid on the jar and set it aside.

5. In the mixing bowl, prepare the unflavored gelatin according to the package directions. Add 1 spoonful of cornstarch and 5 drops of perfume to the gelatin mixture in the bowl. (Picture B)

6. Fill the self-sealing bag about three-fourths full of the gelatin mixture. The gelatin will represent the cell cytoplasm.

Picture B

Picture C

7 Put the marble into the bag and seal tightly. The marble will represent the cell nucleus. The bag will represent the cell membrane.

8 Open the plastic jar and gently put the bag into the iodine solution. Replace the lid. (Picture C)

Predict: **What will happen in the jar after 30 minutes? after 24 hours? after 48 hours?**

9 Record your observations of the jar after 30 minutes, after 24 hours, and after 48 hours on your chart. You may open the jar and the bag to make observations.

Time	Observations
After 30 mins.	
After 24 hrs.	
After 48 hrs.	

State Your Conclusions

1. What happened to the mixture in the bag? How do you know?

2. When iodine comes in contact with a starch, like cornstarch, it turns the solution a bluish-black color. Based on your observations, what happened to the contents of the bag and the solution in the jar?

3. How is your model like a cell?

Let's Experiment

How could you make models of prokaryotic cells and eukaryotic cells to show some simple similarities and differences between the 2 kinds of cells?

3.3 Specialized Cells

> **Why are cells different?**

When you look around your classroom you probably see objects such as desks and books. However, you've learned that many things exist that you cannot see. For example, you can't see the atoms that make up your desk. Although you can see your classmates, you can't see the cells of their bodies. But imagine for a moment that you *could* see the cells that make up one of your friends—a eukaryote. You would notice cells of different shapes and sizes doing different kinds of work. You'd also notice how cells work together so your friend's body can do different things.

Axon

Cell body

Dendrite

▲ *Nerve impulses travel from the dendrites, through the cell body, and along the axon.*

Cells with a Difference

If you had to describe the cell at the top of this page, you might say that it looks like a bug. The cell at the bottom of the page may look like a blob of jelly to you. Both of these cells are in your body. They look different because they do different jobs.

The first picture is a nerve cell. You have billions of nerve cells. They make up the tissues of your brain, your spinal cord, and your nerves.

▼ *Extensions of the white blood cell, called pseudopodia, engulf harmful bacteria so the cell can digest them.*

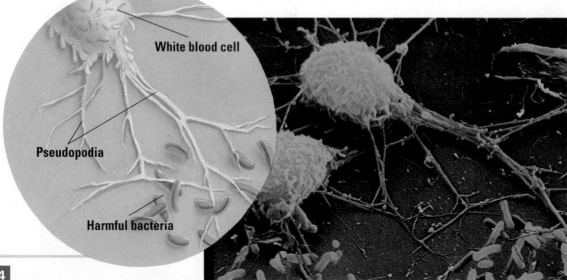

White blood cell

Pseudopodia

Harmful bacteria

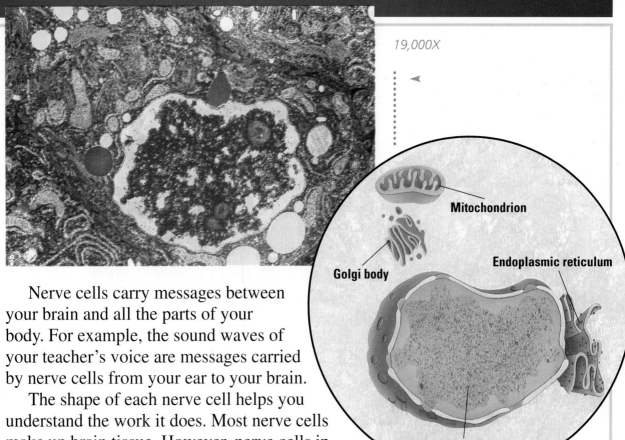

Mitochondrion

Golgi body

Endoplasmic reticulum

Nucleus

Nerve cells carry messages between your brain and all the parts of your body. For example, the sound waves of your teacher's voice are messages carried by nerve cells from your ear to your brain.

The shape of each nerve cell helps you understand the work it does. Most nerve cells make up brain tissue. However, nerve cells in other parts of your body can be a full meter long! Their structure is very long, which helps carry messages the length of the body.

The other cell you saw is a white blood cell called a macrophage (mak′rō fāj). White blood cells protect the body from disease. For instance, if disease-causing bacteria enter your body, white blood cells attack them. Macrophage cells travel through the body, gobbling up bacteria. A macrophage changes shape, surrounds bacteria, and digests them.

Find the epithelial (ep′ə thē′lē əl) cell shown on this page. Epithelial cells form some of the tissues and organs that cover the inside and the outside of your body, such as your skin and the lining of your mouth. Notice how the epithelial cell looks different from the other two cells you observed. The various structures inside this cell enable it to carry out many processes. Some structures keep the cell in working order. Other structures help the cell carry out its role in the body. There seem to be cells and cell structures for every job!

▲ Epithelial cells contain many structures that help the cells do several tasks at one time. For example, mitochondria release energy while the endoplasmic reticulum transports materials to the Golgi bodies for sorting and packaging.

Cells at Work

Red blood cells are different from all other cells in your body.

Red blood cells are specialized cells—certain properties enable them to do many jobs in your body. For example, red blood cells carry oxygen to your cells and take away wastes. Their disk shape allows them to move through very small veins and arteries. And red blood cells contain hemoglobin—a compound that helps transport both oxygen and carbon dioxide.

Red blood cells are part of your body's circulatory system. They're also part of your respiratory system, because they carry oxygen and carbon dioxide to and from the lungs.

A drop of blood like this one contains about 250 million red blood cells. Your body holds about 12 trillion red blood cells!

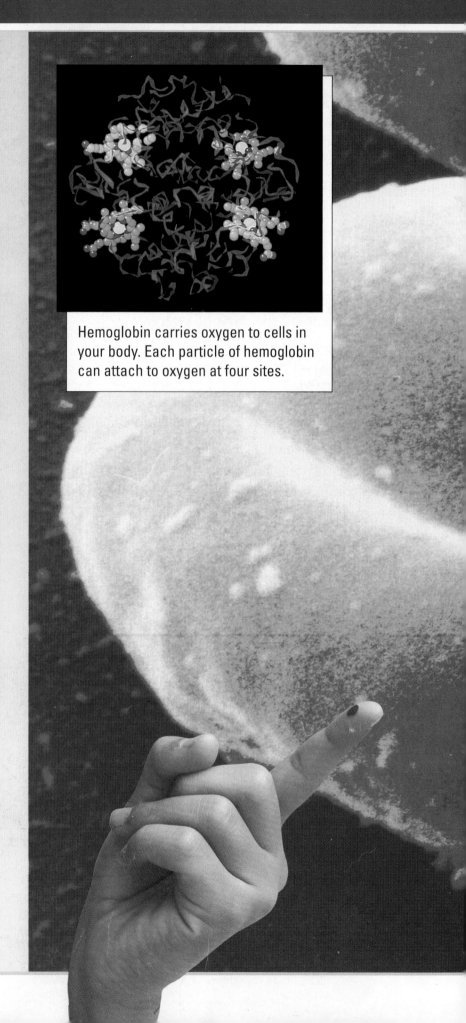

Hemoglobin carries oxygen to cells in your body. Each particle of hemoglobin can attach to oxygen at four sites.

The shape of red blood cells helps them pass through blood vessels. Some vessels are so tiny, blood cells must line up to squeeze through.

During its formation, a red blood cell "spits out" its nucleus. Without a nucleus, the cell takes the shape of a flat disk with a depression in the middle.

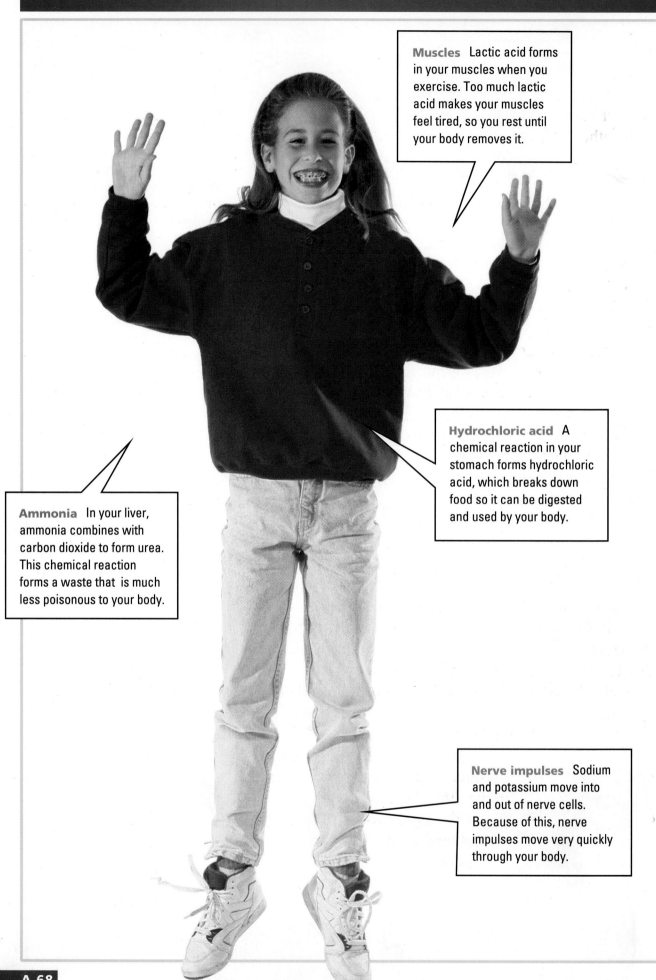

Body Chemistry

When you're perfectly still, does your body do any work besides breathing? Absolutely! The cells in your body are always hard at work. Many of the useful activities they perform involve chemical reactions. In fact, you can think of your body as a chemical factory.

Remember that when atoms are rearranged, new substances result—for example, vinegar and baking soda combine to form carbon dioxide. Chemical reactions also take place inside your body, and without them you couldn't exist. Many of the chemical reactions inside you help your body use energy that keeps you warm and on the go. For instance, each time you eat, chemical reactions break down food into substances that your body can use. One reaction begins when charged atoms in your stomach combine to form hydrochloric acid. This very strong acid would burn your skin, but in your stomach it helps to break down protein in meats and other foods. A chemical reaction in the small intestine breaks protein down further.

In the nervous system, chemical reactions help messages travel along nerve cells. These chemical reactions involve potassium and sodium. The elements potassium and sodium move into and out of the nerve cells, causing nerve impulses to move forward through the body.

Ammonia, a poisonous waste product of the body, changes form in the liver. There ammonia combines with another waste: carbon dioxide. The two substances combine to form urea, a compound that is much less poisonous.

◄ Hydrochloric acid, carbon dioxide, and ammonia are just a few of the compounds in your body.

Organic system

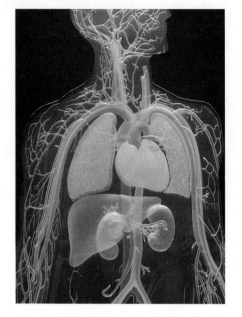

Organ system

▲ *Your body is made of many organ systems working together.*

The Natural Order

In this module, you learned about the smallest parts of living and nonliving things. You know that elements are substances made of one kind of atom. You also know that atoms combine to make new substances called compounds. In addition, you learned about chemical reactions, which rearrange atoms to make compounds.

What do atoms have to do with you? Think about it for a moment—if everything you can see, touch, and smell is made of atoms, what are you made of? You're also made of atoms! The same atoms that make up the earth and all the objects on it also form you.

How do you get from the scale of your body down to the scale of atoms? You know that your body consists of many different organ systems, such as your circulatory system. And each organ in each organ system consists of different tissues. For example, an organ in your circulatory system—your heart—is composed of tissues. These tissues are made of different cells. Going from organ systems down to the level of cells is familiar enough.

Cell

Compound

Atom

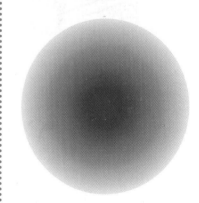

What if you broke a cell apart again and again, until you got to its smallest parts? You'd find chemicals—compounds that are combinations of elements such as carbon, hydrogen, oxygen, nitrogen, sulfur, and phosphorus. Finally, you'd see that compounds are made of individual atoms. Living things, like you, are an incredible organization of atoms. Atoms really are the building blocks of everything!

Checkpoint

1. How does the structure of a nerve cell help it do a specific job?
2. How does the shape of red blood cells help them move through your body?
3. Describe one of the chemical reactions in your body and the job that it helps to do.
4. What are some elements that make different compounds in the human body?
5. **Take Action!** Write a fun poem about the different jobs that cells, compounds, and atoms do in your body.

Organizing Information

Imagine a grocery store where the food is put on the shelves in the order in which it is received. Apples are next to milk, and butter is across the store with the soap. It would take you a lot of time to find what you wanted. This is why food stores organize products into categories such as canned goods and fresh fruits.

Scientists organize information for much the same reason—to make it easier to use and understand. Here are some ways to organize information:

- Classify
- Make graphs
- Make models
- Make time lines

Thinking It Through

When organizing objects or data, it's important to choose a useful way to organize. Suppose you wanted to organize everything you own on some shelves. Which way of organizing would you choose? Classifying seems the best choice here, because it is a way to group objects or ideas according to a system. You might decide to group

items into similar categories. You could put puzzles on the first shelf, books on the second, and miniature figures on the third.

Now suppose you wanted to make a record of your coin collection by age of the coins. You might choose to use a time line here, because a time line is a way to order objects or events by time.

In each case, the method of organization is appropriate to what is being organized. The toys would be easier to locate on the shelves, and the coins' ages would be easier to locate and compare to each other.

Your Turn

1. Organize the objects in your desk. Describe what you did. Which method did you choose?

2. Choose a subject to organize in the form of a time line. You might choose the main events of your own life or the events that occur in a book. Make a time line of these events.

Chapter Review

Thinking Back

1. Why are your blood vessels, heart, and blood considered an **organ system**?
2. How are **tissues** and **organs** related?
3. How are tissues and **cells** related?
4. Describe the structure of a **eukaryote cell**.
5. How is the **nucleus** of a cell important?
6. Explain the relationship between **cytoplasm** and organelles in a eukaryote cell.
7. What are two materials transported by red blood cells in your body?
8. Compare the internal structures of **prokaryote** and eukaryote cells.
9. How do the structures of white and red blood cells help them do their jobs?
10. What type of electron microscope sends a beam of electrons through a very thinly sliced specimen?
11. Describe a chemical reaction that occurs in the nervous system.

Connecting Ideas

1. Copy the concept map. Use the terms at the right to complete the map about body systems to show how your body is organized.

organs   **organ systems**
          tissues

(A. **cells**)—(B. _____)—(C. _____)—(D. _____)

2. Write a sentence or two about the ideas shown in the concept map.

Gathering Evidence

1. In the Activity on page 52, how could you tell the difference between cells from plants and cells from animals?
2. In the Activity on page 62, what information did you use to describe the differences between a model of a prokaryotic cell and a eukaryotic cell?

Doing Science!

1. *Create a skit* in which Robert Hooke describes his observations of a slice of cork to a group of scientists.
2. *Design an activity* that classifies an unknown cell as either a eukaryote cell or a prokaryote cell.

Plastic or Not?

Plastic is made of carbon, hydrogen, oxygen, nitrogen, and other elements that are combined under heat and pressure. Because of its structure, plastic does not rot or corrode. It also should not be burned in waste incinerators, because burning plastic releases chemicals that can cause disease.

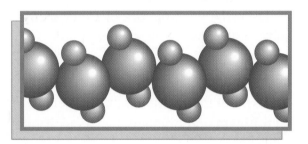

Needs and Goals

Landfills in the United States are filling up with all kinds of trash—plastic, paper, metal, and other materials. And much of this trash doesn't break down easily. Even paper that has been in landfills for decades may not break apart. Reducing the amount of trash placed in landfills is an issue that continues to concern many people.

> By recycling plastic, you can keep from adding to overcrowded landfills.

Gathering Information

One alternative to throwing away items you use every day is to reuse or recycle them. Items made of plastic and other materials don't have to end up in landfills. For example, using disposable plastic dishes and bags over again means they won't end up in the garbage.

And by recycling plastic material when you're done using it, you can keep from adding to overcrowded landfills. Buying items that can be used over again is often a wise choice.

Possible Alternatives

Your decision about what kinds of materials to use may depend on the situation. For instance, paper cups and plates can be used to serve cold foods, but they don't insulate well. Holding paper cups or plates with hot foods in them may hurt your hands. China dishes can replace paper or plastic dishes, but no one wants to carry 25 china plates to a picnic.

Evaluating Alternatives

Copy the table. Make extra rows to add other disposable items you or your family use.

Making the Best Choice

Fill in the third column of the table. Remember, the situation may make a difference in your decision about what to use. Sometimes plastic is the best material. For example, bake sales and picnics are not great places to use metal utensils—some are bound to get lost and they might be unsafe. And if you have ever used a paper bag on a rainy day, you know what can happen!

Plastic or Paper

Item	Use	Alternative
Plates	Family picnic	
Plates	School lunches	
Utensils	Home	
Bags	Shopping	
Cups	Hot drinks	
Cups	Cold drinks	

Now You Do It

1. When did you decide to use paper? When might you replace plastic with another material? When did you decide to use plastic? Explain your choices.
2. What plastic kitchen items do you have that you could use over again?
3. *On Your Own* In a supermarket, look for items packaged in plastic, and similar items packaged in paper, cardboard, or glass. Make a list of the items that have two kinds of packaging. List items that you can find packaged only in plastic.
4. *Critical Thinking* Some companies now use recycled plastic for packaging. But only a small percentage of plastic is recycled in the United States. Pretend you run a company. Develop a plan to get people to recycle plastic items.

What Can You Learn From a Swab?

Reine Makiya

Occupation: Medical technologist
Hobbies: Sewing, watching sports
Attitude: "We're all working for the good of the patient."

Remember the last time you went to the doctor because you had a sore throat? Most likely, the doctor stuck a long, cotton-tipped stick, called a swab, down your throat and you gagged. That was the last time you saw the swab. What happened next?

Reine Makiya might have received the swab. She's a medical technologist. It's her job to oversee running tests that the doctors in her clinic have ordered. The first thing Reine would have done with your swab was to wipe it on gel in a petri dish. The gel contains food that allows cells to grow. If any bacterial cells were on the swab, they would have formed groups of cells. Then Reine would have studied these cells to find out if they were the type of bacteria that causes sore throats. If they were, she would have done one more test to check her results. Then your doctor could order the right kind of medicine to help you get well.

How do you know which type of tests to run?

"Almost every disease leaves clues that show up in the blood or other body fluids. And when someone is sick, the doctor usually has some idea of what's causing the problem. You could think of this idea as a hypothesis. Think of the lab tests as the experiment. The lab tests can prove or disprove the hypothesis. Sometimes results come back that the doctor did not expect. That's when we might suggest another kind of lab test."

How do you know what other tests to suggest?

"We learn a lot in school about the kinds of lab results from different types of diseases. It's like detective work. You have the pieces of a puzzle and you try to put them together to find the cause of the problem."

Microscope: Tool for Exploration

How might you explore a world that is too small to be seen with just your eyes? One way is by using a microscope. The compound light microscope uses lenses to make objects look larger than they really are.

6 Objective lenses are mounted on a revolving nosepiece attached to the bottom of the main tube; lenses in the eyepiece enlarge the image.

1 A compound light microscope is used to examine transparent or thinly cut specimens mounted on slides.

2 The coarse adjustment knob raises and lowers the tube; the fine adjustment knob makes tiny movements to focus the objective lens.

5 Under the stage is the diaphragm, which adjusts the amount of light.

4 A mirror beneath the stage reflects light up through the opening and through the slide.

3 Clips hold the slide firmly over the opening in the stage.

Find Out On Your Own

Observe a specimen under a microscope and discover what happens when you carefully switch from one objective lens to the next. Draw pictures of the results.

Module Review

Making Connections

Scale and Structure

1. Compare the number of oxygen and hydrogen atoms in a sample of water.
2. How has the microscope helped scientists learn more about the structure of living and nonliving things?
3. How does the structure of living things compare with the structure of objects such as rocks and icebergs?

Modeling

4. How are models helpful to scientists?

5. Compare Dalton's model of the atom with that of Bohr and the current electron cloud model.

Systems and Interactions

6. What two elements are produced in the chemical reaction that occurs when the compound water is separated?
7. Describe the levels of organization that are found in living things, beginning with organ systems and ending with cells.

Using What I Learned

Communicating

1. Draw a diagram that shows the structure of a neon atom.

Observing

2. Look at the diagram of the atom below. Use the periodic table to determine which element it represents.

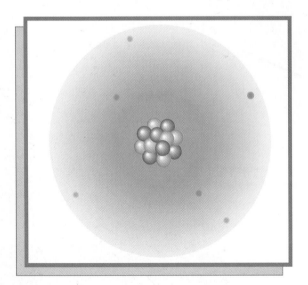

Comparing

3. Compare an element and a compound.
4. How are all types of chemical reactions alike?
5. What kinds of tools enable scientists to explore the inner structure of matter? How do they vary with the amount of detail that the scientist wants?

Relating

6. How are a mineral and a cell alike?

Applying

7. Explain how you could identify an unknown mineral specimen.
8. Two elements lie in the same vertical column of the periodic table. What does this indicate about the elements?

Categorizing

9. What characteristics could you use to classify a cell as either eukaryotic or prokaryotic?

Applying What I Learned

Performance Task

Use toothpicks and balls of different colored modeling clay to show the structure of the compound water.

Drawing

Make a drawing to show the structure of a typical plant cell.

Science Theater

Create a skit that shows how the model of the atom changed over time. Be sure to include the work of Dalton, Thomson, Rutherford, Bohr, and Chadwick.

Exhibitions

Design a bulletin board that shows how crystals are found in common items and that they have widespread uses.

What If

What if technology had not used the knowledge of science to produce tools that enable scientists to magnify objects? How might the inability to see microscopic organisms have changed the study of disease and medicine? Describe how this might change your daily life.

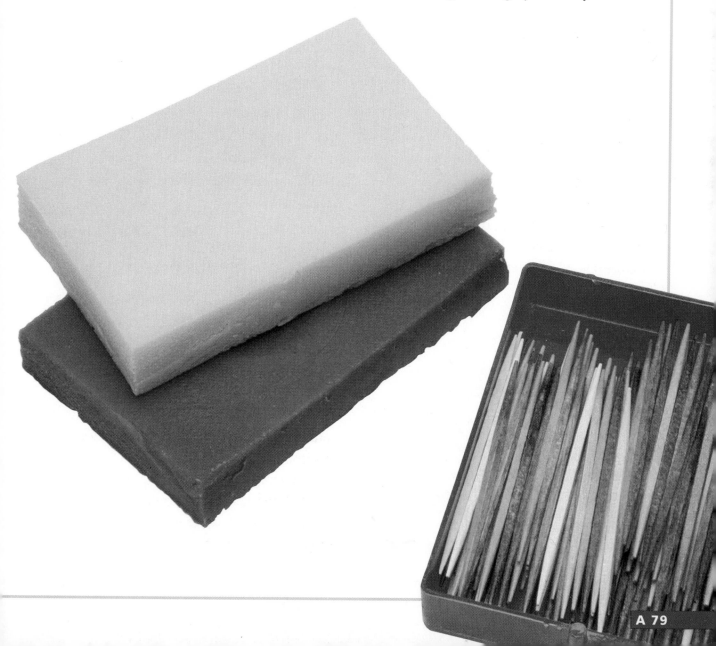

Pedaling Uphill

Pedaling Uphill

Down with up! For thousands of years, people have waged an uphill struggle against the forces of gravity and friction. It's hard work, but now we have machines of all kinds to help us along the way. In this module, you'll explore different types of machines, find out how they work, and discover that the use of simple machines to perform great feats is nothing new!

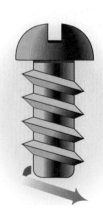

CHAPTER

1 Work and Play

When does work stop and play begin? Even the simplest machines can turn hard work into child's play.

CHAPTER

2 Everyday Machines

It's complex! It's a compound machine! Some machines may seem complicated, but they're really just a group of simple machines working together.

CHAPTER

3 Pedal Power

Use your head when you pedal with your feet. Different bikes are suited to different needs, yet all require care in upkeep and use.

Work and Play

I hope this is a strong
rubber band!

Wear cover goggles
for this activity.

Discover Activity

How can you move a brick

Tie one end of a string around a brick, and tie the
other end of the string to a rubber band. Pull on the
rubber band until the brick slides across the floor.
How much does the rubber band stretch? Now what
can you do to make the brick easier to move? Find
at least one other way.

For Discussion

1. What is the purpose of the rubber band?
2. What is the easiest way to pull the brick?

1.1 *Get Moving*

Why is it so hard to ride a bike uphill?

You and your friends in the science club have planned this bike trip for weeks. The weather's great—sunny and warm. But it's getting late and you're getting tired. The wind is at your back, and seems to push you along. You're thankful for this "help," because it's at the end of a long day.

Suddenly a steep hill looms before you. "Oh no, not again," you think. Your bike begins to slow down. You have to pedal harder and harder. You might even stand up on the pedals so you can push still harder. Why do you have to pedal so much harder to move your bike uphill than along a level road?

Force—a Push or Pull

Even on level ground, a bike doesn't move by itself. Like any other object, a bicycle starts to move only when something pushes or pulls on it. A push or a pull on something is called a **force**.

When you ride a bike, you apply force with your legs to keep the bike moving forward. On level ground, most of your effort goes into pushing the bike forward. But when you come to a hill, you also have to work against gravity—a force that pulls down on you and the bike. So when you ride up the hill you not only have to push the bike forward, you also have to push it and yourself up against the force of gravity. That's why pedaling uphill is such hard work.

▲ *When you ride uphill you are doing work against gravity.*

Into The Field

How does friction change when a surface is wet?

Test a ground surface, such as a concrete sidewalk, for friction when it's wet and when it's dry. Record the test results.

Work—Moving Things Around

Do you think of riding a bike as "work?" What about taking out the garbage or pushing against a rock that won't budge? In science, **work** is done when a force moves an object through a distance that is in the direction of the force. When you are moving objects, such as a bike or the garbage, you are doing work. In the scientific sense, you haven't done work on the rock if you haven't made it move!

The amount of work done depends on how much force is used to move an object and how far the object moves. For example, the amount of work the boy in the picture does depends on the number of his friends he pushes on the sled at one time and how far he pushes the sled.

Friction—a Force Between Surfaces

Would the sled glide over a bare sidewalk like it does over snow or ice? It couldn't. Friction would stop the sled in a hurry! **Friction** is a force that resists the motion of one surface past another surface, as shown in the picture. This force creates a resistance on moving objects, such as the sled, and causes them to stop.

What can you do to reduce friction when you're moving heavy trash barrels? It's easier to use a wagon with wheels to move the barrels than it is to drag the barrels. Wheels or rollers help cut friction between moving, touching surfaces. Using pencils as rollers in the Discover Activity probably made it easier to move the brick.

▼ *Work is done when a force moves an object through a distance. The distance must be in the direction of the force.*

◄ *Friction prevents the tires from slipping and moves the bike forward.*

You also can use a thick liquid like oil or grease to reduce friction. Oil and grease are lubricants— substances that reduce friction. But watch out for grease spots on the kitchen floor! Grease forms a smooth layer between the bottoms of your feet and the floor. This layer makes it easy for your feet to slip on the floor and fly out from under you.

Ball bearings, which are shown in the picture, are small balls that help cut down on friction inside machines by keeping metal surfaces from rubbing against each other. A bicycle has ball bearings where the wheels are joined to the frame.

But wait! Friction isn't always bad news. You couldn't ride a bike at all if it weren't for friction between your tires and the ground. The opposing force of friction prevents the tires from slipping and moves the bike forward.

▲ *Ball bearings cut down on friction between moving parts.*

Checkpoint

1. Why is it so hard to ride a bike up hill?
2. Is studying for a test "work?" Explain.
3. Name three things used to reduce friction.
4. **Take Action!** Rub your hands together. Wet your hands, then rub them together again. Which way is easier? Explain.

1.2 *Simple Machines*

▶ *How do tools make work easier?*

Imagine you want to build a ramp for a skateboard. What would you need? Wood? Nails?

"I'll need tools," you respond, "I can't build a skateboard ramp without tools!"

Saws, hammers, and nails aren't really complicated, but they make work much easier.

Using Inclined Planes

Tools with only one or two parts are known as **simple machines**. You'll look at several kinds of simple machines—the inclined plane, screw, wedge, lever, pulley, and wheel and axle.

Why do tools make it easier to do a job? It's what happens to the force you apply to the tool that counts. A simple machine can make your force stronger, change its direction, or change its speed.

"What kind of simple machine do I need to lift heavy boards?" You need an inclined plane for this job. An inclined plane, shown here, is a flat surface with one end higher than the other. When you walk up a ramp, you are using an inclined plane to get yourself to a higher place! The girl in the picture is using a ramp to lift herself up to the door of a building. It's easier to push, pull, or carry something up a ramp than it is to lift it up to a higher place. The job is even easier if the ramp has a gentle slope rather than a steep one.

▼ *The ramp, an inclined plane, makes it easier for people to lift things.*

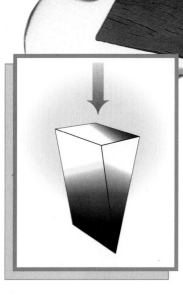

"What simple machine can I use to split wood?" You can use a wedge, which has inclined planes as its sloping sides. Nails, axe blades, needles, and knife blades like the one in the picture are wedges. A wedge changes the direction of the force you apply. What happens, for example, when you cut a tough chunk of meat into pieces? The knife blade changes the downward force of each cut to a sideways force that splits the meat.

You can find wedges in some unusual places. The bow, or front, of a boat is a wedge that allows the boat to move through the water more easily. Also, some burrowing animals, such as moles and earthworms, have wedge-shaped body parts that help them push through the soil.

"I need something to fasten two pieces of wood together. What can I use?" For this, use a screw, which is an inclined plane wrapped around a center post. Screws work by increasing the force you apply and by changing its direction. As you turn the screw around, it moves downward and the force you applied to turn the screw increases!

Screws and bolts are used to fasten things together. Propellers are screws that turn water or air, helping boats and airplanes move. Screws also are used in machines for lifting heavy objects such as houses or cars. Read on to find out what else you can do with simple machines.

▲ *A knife is a wedge because it has inclined planes as its sloping sides.*

▲ *The bottle top has an inclined plane wrapped around it, so it is an example of a screw.*

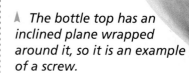

Levers in the Park

A *lever* makes it easier to lift things.

A lever is a simple machine used to lift things. You do work when you use a lever to lift something.

Many, but not all, levers look like a metal bar or a board. By pushing down on one end of a bar, you can lift something resting on the other end.

A lever can increase your force many times over, and it can change the direction of the force too.

The force you put into a lever (or any other simple machine) is called the applied force. The object that you lift with a lever is called the load. Finally, the balance point of a lever is called the fulcrum.

Can you find four levers in the park picture? Hint: These levers might not look like boards or bars!

Crowbar, a Lever

A crowbar is a lever. You can push down on one end of a crowbar with the applied force to lift a big rock, or the load, at the other end. The fulcrum is the balance point of a lever. On a crowbar, the fulcrum separates the applied force from the load. But the fulcrum isn't between the applied force and the load for all levers.

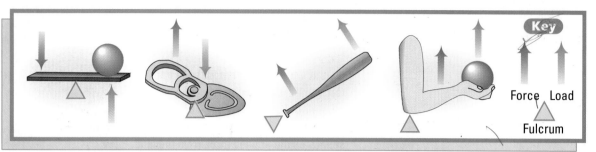

Force   Load

Fulcrum

▲ Each lever has an applied force, a load, and a fulcrum. Use the Key to find these parts.

Using Levers

How many levers did you find in the park picture? You're right if you spotted the seesaw, the tab opener on the can, and the baseball bat. But did you guess that the pitcher's arm is a lever too? It is.

Suppose you're on one end of the seesaw and a friend is on the other. The fulcrum is in the middle. When your end of the seesaw is in the air, your weight provides the "applied force" that lifts the "load"—your friend's weight. You go down and your friend goes up. As you start up again, your weight serves as the load. The applied force and load switch sides as the seesaw goes up and down. Compare the seesaw drawing with the other drawings.

Do you have to learn about applied force and loads before you can use levers? Of course not! You open a can of juice automatically. You use your arm as a lever when you swing a bat, hammer a nail, or even lift a forkful of food to your mouth!

Hold on. You're not finished with levers yet. The pulley is a simple machine that looks like a wheel with a rope around it. You might not have guessed it, but a pulley is a type of lever.

▲ The pulley at the top of the flagpole changes the direction of the force.

Notice the pulley on the flagpole. You apply force when you pull down on the rope and the "load" is the flag. In this machine, the fulcrum is at the pulley itself. Notice that the pulley changes the direction of the force. Pulling down on something usually is easier than lifting it up. Think how awkward it would be to climb a flagpole just to raise the flag!

Look at the wheel and axle diagram and then get ready for a surprise. It's another lever! This simple machine contains a wheel attached to a rod, called the axle. In many cases, the wheel part of the machine is actually a handle or a crank that turns in a circle, as you can see in the diagram. When you turn the axle, the wheel turns. When you turn the wheel, the axle turns.

The crank, or wheel, is the part of the lever where you huff and puff and apply a force. The axle is the part of the lever where the work gets done—the load.

The boy on the unicycle applies force on the cranks and pedals, which make up the "wheel" part of the machine. The "axle" is the rod through the center of the unicycle. As he turns the pedals around one time, the axle also makes one turn. The unicycle wheel goes around once each time the axle turns. Would you like to take a ride on a unicycle?

Checkpoint

1. What is a simple machine?
2. What is the fulcrum of a lever?
3. How does a flag pulley change your force?
4. Take Action! Make a drawing with arrows to show moving wagon wheels and the axles between the wheels. Are they simple machines? Explain.

▲ The unicycle has a wheel and axle machine.

Activity

Pulling on Pulleys

How can pulleys make jobs easier? Try this activity and see.

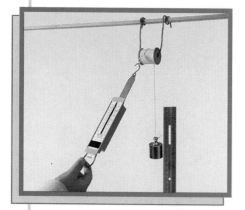

Picture A

Picture B

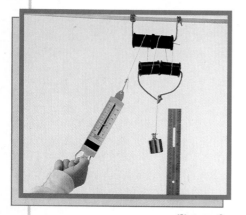

Picture C

Follow This Procedure

1 Make a chart like the one on the next page. Record your observations in your chart.

2 Make a single fixed pulley by running wire through a spool. Hook the wire ends over a meter stick, and hang the meter stick between two desks. Stick the ruler in clay to stand it up.

3 Run a piece of twine over the spool. Tie a 200-gram mass to one end of the twine and the spring scale to the other end. (Picture A)

4 Pull down on the spring scale to raise the mass 10 centimeters. Note the force needed to raise the mass—the applied force. It's shown on the spring scale. Record the applied force in your chart.

5 Make a single movable pulley using a spool and string. Attach the mass to the spool. Tie one end of some string to the meter stick. Attach a spring scale to the other end of this string. (Picture B) Practice balancing the spool on the string as shown.

6 Pull up on the spring scale to raise the mass 10 centimeters. Record the applied force in your chart.

7 Make a combination pulley using four spools. Tie one end of a string around one of the spools. Make two wire hooks for your pulley. Attach one hook to the meter stick. Attach the mass to the other hook. Tie a spring scale to the free end of the string. (Picture C)

Predict: *Is the combination pulley the best one to use for lifting the mass?*

8 Pull on the spring scale to raise the mass 10 centimeters. Record the applied force in your chart.

State Your Conclusions

1. Compare the applied forces for the three pulleys.
2. Do you think more or less force would be needed to lift the mass if you used a combination pulley with even more spools?

Let's Experiment

Through what distance does the string move with each pulley? Repeat the procedure without the spring scale. Use what you know about scientific methods to find out.

Record Your Results

Pulley type	Applied force
Single fixed pulley	
Single movable pulley	
Combination pulley	

1.3 *The Pyramids*

> ### *How much can you do with simple machines?*

Think of some tools you commonly use—knives, forks, hammers, maybe a wrench or a screwdriver. While building the pyramids with simple machines such as these might seem impossible, it wasn't. Let's find out how the Egyptians did it.

A Look into the Past

More than 4000 years ago, in 2500 BC, builders in Egypt had few of the machines that builders have today. They had no cranes, trucks, and electric drills. They didn't even have metal nails, screws, or wheels. Even without these things, the Egyptians managed to build huge stone statues and pyramids, like the ones in the picture. How the master builders of ancient Egypt constructed the pyramids is one of the great mysteries of all time.

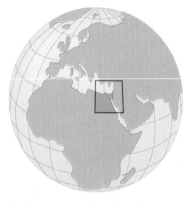

▲ *Egypt is in North Africa.*

▼ *The pyramids at Giza*

The Egyptians built the pyramids as monuments to their pharaohs, or kings. A pyramid is a tomb with a burial room hidden underneath its huge rectangular base. The four triangular sides of the structure represent the rays of the sun. The triangles meet at a point on top.

People exploring the tombs have found many pictures showing scenes of life in ancient Egypt. No pictures show how the pyramids were built, but some pictures do give scientists a few clues. In some of the pictures, workers are using stone or wooden tools, such as the adze on the right. In other pictures, Egyptians are measuring blocks with rope and wood, and workers are building ramps of mud. Carved pictures in the stone walls of some burial chambers show barges carrying heavy objects down the Nile River.

Scientists have found other evidence that these pictures tell a true story. They found some of the simple tools of wood, rock, and copper, along with the remains of dirt ramps and mud walls near some unfinished pyramids. Using these and other clues, scientists and historians have tried to recreate the past and explain how the pyramids were built. Let's go through the building of a pyramid—from beginning to end.

▲ *A worker using an adze*

Measuring and smoothing a cut stone

Working with the Stones

A pyramid contains an enormous amount of stone. For many pyramids, workers cut large stones from granite cliffs. To find out how hard it is to cut granite, try breaking a piece of granite yourself.

Skilled stone cutters started by cutting notches in solid rock. They used drills, such as the one in the picture, to pierce the stone. Also, they used wooden mallets to hammer chisels against the stone. Chisels act as wedges, changing downward forces from the hammer into sideways forces powerful enough to chip hard rock.

When the notches were large enough, stone cutters hammered in wedge-shaped pieces of wood and poured water over the wedges. Water caused the wedges to swell, splitting the stone from the cliff.

The picture shows quarry workers carefully measuring the cut stone. Workers smoothed out the stones by scraping off rock with chisels. Then they used sand, pieces of very hard rock, ropes, and wooden mallets soaked in water to polish the blocks. The blocks had to fit snugly when they were put into place.

Once the blocks were shaped, they had to be lifted and moved to the building site. For lifting, Egyptians used logs as levers, ropes, a few kinds of pulleys without wheels, and lots of muscle power.

An Egyptian drill

What's a pulley without a wheel? For the flagpole pulley, you pull *down* on a rope to lift the flag *up*. The Egyptians threw the rope over a wooden beam instead of a pulley. The beam was firmly fixed to two upright posts in the ground. One end of the rope was tied to a stone. Workers could pull down on the free end of the rope to lift the stone. The rope squeaked and got very hot as it slid along the beam. The Egyptians oiled the rope to help reduce this friction.

Thousands of workers were needed to pull huge stone blocks from nearby quarries to the site of the pyramid. For this job, they used timber rollers or sledges or both. A sledge looks like a big wagon that has runners instead of wheels. The stone movers pulled the sledges with ropes over paths paved with mud and brick. The people in the drawing are using ropes and log levers to get the stone block off the sledge. Many stones came from quarries far up the Nile River. Quarry workers stowed these stones on large flat-bottomed barges and floated them down the river to the work site.

▼ *Using levers to lift a block*

Ramps got higher as the pyramids got higher.

Building Up Layers

Many people at the work site moved the blocks into place for the bottom layer of the pyramid. At the same time, others built walls and ramps with mud, stones, and brick. Egyptian workers used the ramps as inclined planes to lift the stones. Then they moved the stones along the walls.

At first, the ramps and walls were as high as the foundation. During the building of the pyramid, workers added more and more layers to the walls and ramps. The diagrams show that ramps became higher and longer with each pyramid layer.

The laborers in the picture have put rollers under a huge block to get it up the ramp. Many people are needed to pull the ropes. As the block goes forward, it moves off its back rollers. People behind the block are moving these rollers from behind to in front of the block.

One person is pouring water and oil on the ramp in front of the block. Water and oil cut down on friction between the rollers and the ramp.

Moving a block up a ramp

When the block gets to the top of the ramp, it is level with the top of the foundation layer. Laborers can move the stone along the top of a wall and into place in the second layer of the pyramid.

In time, the pyramid looked like a giant's staircase. Each step was as tall as one layer of stone blocks. Workers added stones to the top layer where they were needed for an even surface. Also, they polished the stones with sand and chisels.

Then ramp workers started lowering the ramps and walls, one layer at a time and smoothing the stones as they went. The finished pyramid was visible proof of the genius of the Egyptian builders in their use of simple machines.

Checkpoint

1. What is the shape of a pyramid?
2. How did wedges help in cutting stones ?
3. What drawback do rollers have?
4. **Take Action!** Build a lever using two pencils. Show where the applied force, load, and fulcrum are on the lever.

An Easier Way

Do inclined planes make it easier to lift things? Let's investigate and find out.

A. Use a string or rubber bands to fasten a spring scale to a stone. Use the spring scale to lift the stone to a height of 10 centimeters.
B. Read the force you used on the spring scale and record it in a chart like the one shown here.
C. Make an inclined plane—or ramp—by propping a board on books so that one end of the board is raised 10 centimeters above the desk or floor. The height of the ramp is 10 centimeters.
D. Read the spring scale again as you pull the stone up the inclined plane.

Record Your Results

	Applied Force
Stone lifted	
Stone moved up ramp	

What Did You Find Out?
1. *Compare the applied force for the two trials.*
2. *How will the applied force change if the height of the ramp doesn't change, but you use a longer board? a shorter board?*

Activity

Lifting Weights

A lever can help you lift weights, if you know how to use it. Try this activity to find out how.

Picture A

Picture B

Picture C

Gather These Materials

cardboard rectangle,
  10 cm by 15 cm
masking tape
meter stick

2 paper cups
modeling clay
marbles

Follow This Procedure

1. Make a chart like the one on the next page. Record your observations in your chart.

2. Draw two lines across your cardboard rectangle to divide it into three sections, each 5 centimeters by 10 centimeters. Fold the cardboard along these lines.

3. Tape the long edges together to make a triangular tube. This tube is your fulcrum. (Picture A)

4. Tape one cup at each end of a meter stick. Put a ball of modeling clay that's 2 centimeters in diameter in one of the cups. Place the fulcrum 20 centimeters from the end with the empty cup.

5. Drop marbles into the empty cup, one at a time until the lever balances. Record the number of marbles in your chart. (Picture B)

6. Take the marbles out of the cup and move the fulcrum so that it's 40 centimeters from the end of the meter stick with the empty cup.

Predict: *Will you have to add more marbles or fewer marbles to balance the lever now?*

7 Repeat step 5 with the fulcrum at 40, 60, and 80 centimeters. (Picture C)

State Your Conclusions

1. Where was the fulcrum when you needed the fewest marbles to balance the lever? the most marbles?

2. If you want to use a lever to lift a heavy weight, where would you place the fulcrum to make the job easiest?

Let's Experiment

What would happen if you left the fulcrum in one position but moved the marbles closer or farther away from the fulcrum? Use what you know about scientific methods to find out.

Record Your Results

Distance of fulcrum from empty cup	Number of marbles to balance lever
20 cm	
40 cm	
60 cm	
80 cm	

Making a Line Graph

When doing activities in science, you need to decide the best way to show your results. Graphs are a good way to show how two kinds of measurements are related. For example, bar graphs are helpful for making comparisons while line graphs show how one quantity changes with another.

Thinking It Through

Follow these steps to see how the line graph shown was constructed.

1. Use graph paper, if you have it. If not, make your own grid—a pattern of evenly spaced horizontal lines and vertical lines. Horizontal lines are left to right, and vertical lines are up and down.

2. Draw each axis, or base line, of the graph. The horizontal axis runs across the bottom of the graph. The vertical axis goes up the left side of the graph.

3. Label each axis to indicate what it shows. In this graph, the horizontal axis shows the mass of the object. The vertical axis shows the distance the object moved.

4. Choose the scale of the graph. To do this you should think about the highest and lowest values you have to graph. Number each axis so that the complete set of points and lines cover most of the graph.

5. Plot your data as points on the grid. In the graph shown here, a 20 g object moves 30 cm. To plot that point, first find the 30 cm mark on the vertical axis. Then follow the line from the 30 cm mark to the right until you are directly above the 20 g mark on the horizontal axis, and mark this point.

6. Plot the rest of the points: 40 g for 25 cm; 60 g for 15 cm; and 80 g for 5 cm. Connect the points by drawing straight lines from point to point.

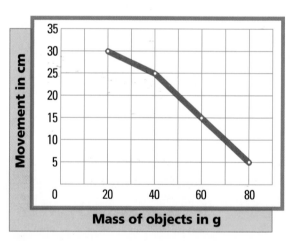

Mass of objects in g

Your Turn

Make your own graph showing how distance (vertical axis) changes over time (horizontal axis). Use these measurements: 20 km for 2 hours; 40 km for 4 hours; 80 km for 8 hours.

Chapter Review

Thinking Back

1. How can **friction** help a bicycle move forward?
2. Name three ways a **simple machine** can change an applied force.
3. What are the applied force, load, and fulcrum of a lever?

4. How are **work** and **force** related?
5. Explain how three kinds of simple machines were used by the Egyptians in building the pyramids.
6. What effect does a wedge have on the force applied to it?

Connecting Ideas

1. Copy the concept map. Use the terms at the right to complete the map about work and simple machines.

simple machines strength
speed direction
force

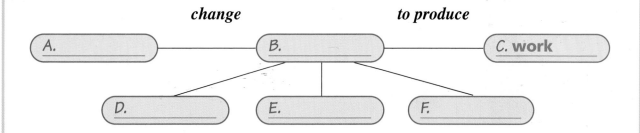

2. Write a sentence or two that summarizes the ideas shown in the concept map.

Gathering Evidence

1. In the Activity on page 14, what did you learn about combining pulleys?
2. In the Activity on page 22, what did you learn about the position of the fulcrum?

Doing Science!

1. *Design an activity* to show that a rough surface creates more friction than a smooth surface.
2. *Design a tool* that makes it easier to remove a book from inside your desk.

CHAPTER 2

Everyday Machines

It works . . . but what do I do if I catch one?

Discover Activity

Can you build a mousetrap?

Imagine that you have a pesky mouse in your house. You want to catch it, but you don't want to hurt it. Look around your classroom for some things that you might use to make a gentle mousetrap. Then build it!

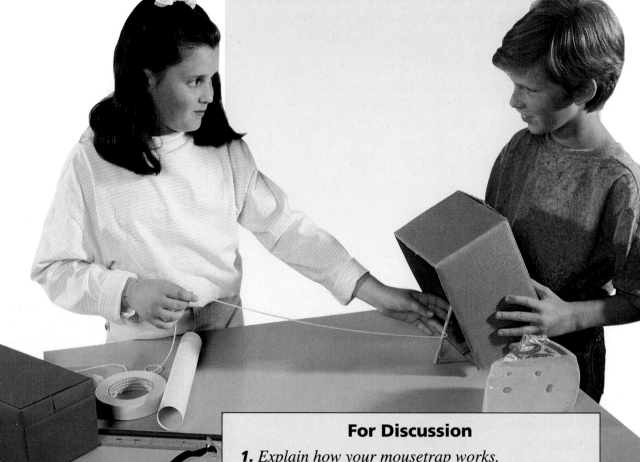

For Discussion

1. Explain how your mousetrap works.
2. Which simple machines does your trap use?

2·1 *Compound Machines*

How is a pair of scissors a machine?

Maria found the red letters that she needed for her poster on a cardboard box. When she tore some letters off the box, a few of them ripped. When she used a knife to cut them out, the *B's* and *P's* were sloppy. Then Maria got some scissors and started over again. The letters she cut this time were perfect. Maria smiled as she studied the scissors.

Putting Machines Together

Take a look at the scissors and find the simple machines. If you spotted levers and wedges, you're on the right track. Scissors are made of two levers that work together. You put force on the handles and work is done at the blades. The levers share a fulcrum at the place where the levers are joined. The scissors' blades are two sharp wedges.

What's going on in the scissors when you cut a piece of paper? When you move the handles, the levers change the small applied force on the handles into a large force on the blades. If you move the handles together, the blades close with a downward force. The wedges of the blades turn this downward force into a sideways force that splits the paper apart.

Scissors and most of the other tools you use every day are made up of several simple machines. A combination of two or more simple machines is called a **compound machine**. The mousetrap you made in the Discover Activity is a compound machine. Like simple machines, compound machines change the force you put into them.

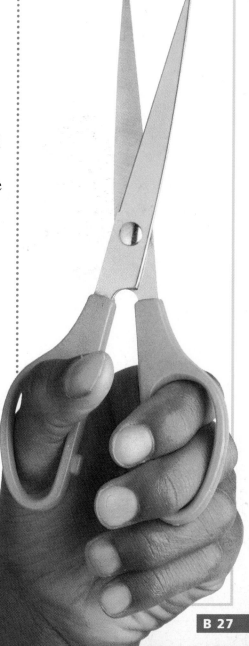

▼ *Most tools and machines you use every day are made up of simple machines.*

Hand brakes are levers with the fulcrum joining the two parts of each brake.

Screws hold many parts of the bicycle together.

SX-1000

The **cranks, pedals,** and **sprockets** make up two wheels and axles.

The Bicycle—A Compound Machine

What has a seat, two pedals, two wheels, and is a compound machine? You guessed it—a bicycle! Take a look at the picture. It shows some of the simple machines in a bicycle.

The two toothed wheels on the bike are called sprockets. The bicycle chain runs around the two sprockets and connects them. Links of the chain fit over the teeth on the sprockets.

The big sprocket and the cranks and pedals are one wheel and axle. The pedals and cranks are the "wheel" and the big sprocket is the "axle." When the pedals turn, the big sprocket turns too.

The little sprocket and the rear wheel itself are a second wheel and axle. The little sprocket is the "wheel" and the rear wheel is the "axle." When the little sprocket turns, the rear wheel turns too.

Okay. The big question is: How do these parts work together to move a bike? The answer is: The force applied by your legs travels through two wheels and axles—from the pedals to the back wheel—and it makes the wheels turn. The distance the bike moves is greater than the distance through which your pedal turned.

Can you follow the force as it travels? The force travels from the pedals to the big sprocket and through the bicycle chain to the little sprocket and the rear wheel. The spinning of the rear wheel causes the front wheel also to turn. Phew! Did you follow the force all the way?

Into The Field

How many simple machines are on your playground?

Find as many simple machines as you can on a playground. Describe each, tell how it works, and draw it.

Checkpoint

1. Describe the two simple machines on a shovel.
2. How is the bicycle an example of a compound machine?
3. **Take Action!** Take apart a pencil sharpener. Identify the simple machines that make up this compound machine.

Activity

Putting Sprockets Together

On machines other than bicycles, sprockets are called gears. How do gears work together? Try this activity and see.

Picture A

Gather These Materials

2 big plastic lids
2 small plastic lids
2 long corrugated
  cardboard strips
2 short corrugated
  cardboard strips

glue
scissors
protractor
marker or grease pencil
2 push-pins
shoe-box lid

Follow This Procedure

1 Make a chart like the one on the next page. Record your observations in your chart.

2 Make four sprockets, or gears, from the four plastic lids. To make each sprocket, glue a cardboard strip around the edge of a lid. The long strips are for the big lids and the short ones are for the small lids.

3 Use a protractor and a marker to find and mark the center of each lid. Draw an arrow from the center to the edge. (Picture A)

4 Use push-pins to mount the two largest sprockets on the lid of a shoe-box. Make sure the edges of the sprockets are locked together. Make a mark on the shoe-box lid just above each sprocket. Label the left gear the *input gear*.

5 Line up the arrows on the gears with the marks on the shoe-box lid. (Picture B)

Picture B

Picture C

6 Turn the input gear around once. You might need to push down on the flat part of the gear as it turns. Find out how many turns the second gear makes and whether the second gear turns in the same direction as the input gear does. Record your data in your chart.

Record Your Results

Gear combination	Number of turns for second gear	Direction of second gear compared to input gear (same, opposite)
Large input gear/ large second gear		
Large input gear/ small second gear		
Small input gear/ small second gear		

Predict: **What will happen if you replace the second gear with one that is smaller?**

7 Replace the second gear with a smaller gear. Now the input gear is bigger than the second gear. Repeat steps 5 and 6. (Picture C)

8 Now replace the input gear with the other small gear. This time, both gears are small. Repeat steps 5 and 6 again.

State Your Conclusions

1. How do you know the small gear moves faster than the big gear?

2. Where is the applied force on your model? Explain.

Let's Experiment

How do a big, a medium, and a small gear (in that order) work together? Describe the speeds and directions of the second and third gears compared to the first one. Use what you know about scientific methods to find out.

2.2 Gearing Up

> ### How can a dog do all this work?

▼ As gears turn, they change the speed and the direction of the force the dog supplies.

Would you like somebody to find the right outfit for you, brush your teeth, and comb your hair when you get ready for school in the morning? The machine in the picture can do all these things. It makes getting ready for school faster and easier.

But you can't get this machine unless you have a dog, because the dog provides the force needed to keep the machine parts moving. Also, machines like this one are hard to find at most stores!

Big and Little Gears

Gears are toothed wheels that developed from the wheel and the lever. Gears are an important part of this machine and many others.

One gear by itself doesn't do much work. But if you put two or more gears together, they can change the speed, direction, and strength of the force put into the machine.

When two gears of the same size work together, they turn at the same speed. If the two gears are different sizes, the smaller gear turns faster than the larger one does. The bigger the difference in gear size, the bigger the difference in their speeds.

Bicycle gears are called sprockets. What do the sprockets have to do with the speed of a bicycle? Let's see what happens in a one-speed bike. When the pedals turn around once, the big sprocket also turns once. Because of the bicycle chain, one turn of the big sprocket turns the little sprocket.

But the little sprocket on this bike makes two turns, because it's spinning faster than the big sprocket. The other part of this wheel and axle—the rear wheel—also makes two turns. What do you have so far? Well, for one turn of the pedals, the rear wheel turns twice.

But wait! The distance around the rear wheel is much greater than the distance marked by one turn of the pedals. So, in the time needed to pedal around once, the bike moves the distance covered by two turns of the rear wheel. Because of the sprockets, the bike goes far and fast with little pedaling effort! Gears really do make work easier.

Taking a Spin

Gears come in many sizes and shapes. They are used to change the direction and the speed of the applied force. Here's how.

Gears work in pairs. When one gear turns, it causes the second gear to rotate in the opposite direction. Thus, the direction of the applied force changes.

Gear A has twenty teeth. Gear B has half as many or ten teeth. If you apply force to, or turn, Gear A once, Gear B will rotate twice. Gear B will spin twice as fast as Gear A. Thus the speed of the gear doubles.

What Did You Find Out?
1. *If one gear has 50 teeth and the other gear has 10, how many times will the second gear rotate for each revolution of the first gear?*
2. *How could you use gears to triple the speed of the applied force?*

The Tower Crane

The tower crane is a complex machine.

As you walk down a city street, you see a tower crane perched atop a tall building. Today's workers use complex machines like the tower crane to build skyscrapers.

A complex machine is one that is made up of many compound machines and usually is powered by electricity or fuel. Complex machines, like compound machines, can be broken down into the simple machines you have studied.

Pulleys

Pulleys are used to lift building materials.

Wheel and Axle

Wheel and axles are used to wind the pulley cable.

Lever

The arms of the tower crane are a lever.

Ancient Levers

In 1500 BC, an Egyptian farmer in the fields lifted water from the Nile with the help of a shaduf. The shaduf is a lever with a counterweight on it. The counterweight is something that's put on a lever to balance the load. For the shaduf, the load is the basket of water.

Modern Machines

The ancient Egyptians used "muscle power" to add force to the simple machines they used. Today, people use all sorts of machines—from crowbars or ramps to complex machines such as the ones shown here. The force put into most complex machines comes from the energy in electricity or fuel.

People have found bigger and stronger forces to run machines, but they haven't found ways to get rid of friction. What's worse, the faster the machine runs and the more parts it has, the faster friction can wear down the parts. So, friction is as much of a problem today as it was in ancient Egypt.

How is friction a problem? Friction means a loss of useful work. The energy that is put into a machine is changed to work. Because of friction, however, some of the energy used to run the machine changes into useless heat, which goes off into the air. This change means that a machine doesn't do as much work as it should.

Also, friction makes machines overheat, break down, and wear out quickly. To avoid the effects of friction, a machine should be kept in good working condition. Oiling and greasing a machine regularly cuts down on friction between metal parts that rub together and makes the machine last longer.

Complex machines do a lot of work in a very short time, and that's good. But they do something else that's not good. Using energy such as electricity and fuel has created the problem of pollution. For example, people burn fuel to move assembly lines in factories, to power cars, and to make electricity. But when the fuel burns, it produces smoke and gases that can be harmful to the environment.

⋏ The force that runs the motorcycle comes from the energy released from burning fuel.

Scientists are trying to find fuels that create less pollution. They are looking for cheaper ways to use the energy in water, wind, and the sun's rays. They also are designing more efficient machines—ones that run quickly using very little energy, such as the car shown here.

What will the machines of the future be like? For one thing, "robots" will probably become more important in industry. Watch a science fiction movie! You might get a clue about what's ahead.

Even today, engineers are building unusual robots, like the one below. Other robots are designed to perform tasks thought to be too dangerous, boring, or unpleasant for humans. Today in Japan, automobile manufacturing is almost completely automated. In many plants, only robots are working on the assembly lines! Who knows? In a few years, you might be able to get a robot to do dishes for you and clean your room!

▲ *Designed for maximum efficiency*

Checkpoint

1. How do gears change the applied force?
2. What is a complex machine?
3. How can friction be reduced?
4. **Take Action!** Calculate how far you actually pedal to travel one kilometer. Use these figures: the distance around one turn of the pedals is 50 centimeters, and around the back wheel is 200 centimeters.

▼ *Robots are complex machines that can perform a variety of tasks.*

Activity

Falling Water Runs A Machine

Some machines run on water power. Try this activity to see how falling water can run a machine.

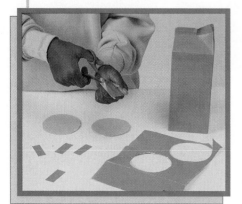

Picture A

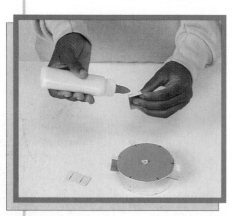

Picture B

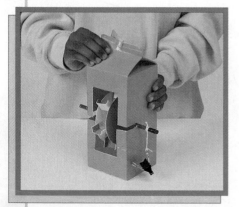

Picture C

Gather These Materials

2 milk cartons
pencil
compass
ruler

scissors
stapler or glue
tape and string
small object

Follow This Procedure

1 Make a chart like the one on the next page. Record your observations in your chart.

2 Cut open one carton along its corner seam. Lay it out flat. From this, you will get 2 circles (wheels) and 6 rectangles (paddles) to make a paddle wheel. (Picture A)

3 First, trace two circles, each with a radius of 4 centimeters. Cut them out. Poke a pencil hole in the center of each circle. Draw six marks around the outside of each circle. To correctly space the marks, imagine you are marking a clock at 2:00, 4:00, 6:00, 8:00, 10:00, and 12:00.

4 Next, trace and cut out six rectangles, each 2 centimeters by 4 centimeters. Draw a line— 1 centimeter from the end—along the short sides of each paddle. Fold up along these lines to make tabs.

5 Line up the tabs with the six marks on the wheels. Staple or glue the tabs to the wheels with the tabs facing up. (Picture B)

6 Stick a pencil through the holes in the centers of the wheels. Tape the pencil to the wheels so the pencil won't spin unless the wheel does.

7 Now you're ready to fit the water wheel into the second carton. Use Picture C to help you finish the model. Start by cutting a 4 centimeter by 12 centimeter hole in one side of the second carton.

8 Cut two slots for the pencil on the sides of the carton, as shown in Picture C. Make each slot halfway up the side and about 3 centimeters long. Stick the pencil through the slots so that the wheel is inside the carton and the paddles stick out of the hole. Tie a string to one end of the pencil and tie a small object to the other end of the string.

> **Predict: *Will your water wheel be able to lift the object tied to the pencil?***

9 Put your model under running water from a faucet so water hits the paddles and turns the wheel. Record your findings in your chart.

Record Your Results

Water flow	Objects raised? (yes or no)
Fast	
Slow	

State Your Conclusions

1. What kind of simple machine did you make?
2. On your model, find the applied force, the load, and the axle.

Let's Experiment

Can you get your water wheel to lift heavier objects? Use what you know about scientific methods to find out.

Predicting Which Tool To Use

When you make a prediction, you guess that something's going to happen based on your experience or knowledge. You might predict it will rain when you see gray clouds. You base this prediction on what has happened on other cloudy days.

Thinking It Through

You can use what you know about simple machines to predict what kind of object to use as a tool for a particular job. For example, suppose you need to open a big paint can. The lid's too tight for you to pry it open with your fingers, and you don't have a paint can opener. What can you use as a substitute for a paint can opener?

You might think through a list of questions like these.

1. Which simple machine could I use to do this job? The simple machines I learned about are the lever, pulley, wheel and axle, inclined plane, wedge, and screw. I'm not sure which one to use on the lid.

2. Do I need to drag, carry, or lift an object? In this case, I need to lift the lid to get the can open.

3. Which simple machines are good for lifting? All the simple machines can be used to lift something, but I want a tool I can use to pry open a metal lid. So, I probably would want to use a lever of some kind.

4. What kind of lever would be best for prying open a lid? I need something fairly small, hard as a metal, and shaped like a bar. A crowbar is the right shape and it's metal, but it's too big. A penny is metal, but it's not the right shape.

5. Would a spoon or a screwdriver work? Both are metal and about the right shape and size. But the metal in the spoon isn't strong enough. It'll bend and the spoon will break. So I'll try a screwdriver instead.

Your Turn

You're riding on a seesaw with a person who is bigger than you. To balance the seesaw, which person should sit closer to the middle, or fulcrum? Use what you learned in the lever activity to make a prediction.

Chapter Review

Thinking Back

1. Why is a pair of scissors called a **compound machine**?
2. What kind of simple machine is made up of the pedals and cranks and the big sprocket of a bicycle?
3. Why is the distance a bicycle moves greater than the distance a rider pedals?

4. What effect do gears have on a force put into a machine?
5. What is a **gear**?
6. What is a complex machine?
7. What effect does friction have on the amount of useful work done by a machine?

Connecting Ideas

1. Copy the concept map. Use the terms to the right to complete the map about machines.

compound machine
complex machine

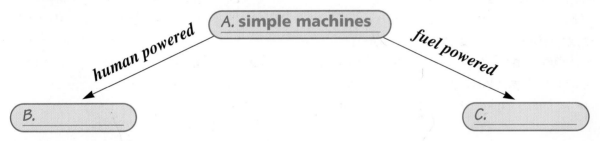

2. Write a sentence or two that summarizes the ideas shown in the concept map.

Gathering Evidence

1. In the Activity on page 30, how did you know the number of turns for the second gear depended on the input gear?
2. In the Activity on page 38, how did you know that work was done?

Doing Science!

1. **Design a machine** that would make it easier for you to do a job, such as cleaning your room.
2. **Draw a picture** showing how energy passes through a bicycle and makes it move forward.

CHAPTER 3

Pedal Power

Look how fast it's spinning!

Discover Activity

How do ball bearings work?

Try to spin a large juice can while it's standing on its end. Then think of a way to use marbles and a plastic lid to make this task easier. Use these materials to make ball bearings.

For Discussion

1. How do the marbles help move the can?

2. How is the number of marbles important?

3.1 Old and New Bikes

How have bicycles changed over the years?

Nobody knows for sure when the first bicycle was invented, but the one in the picture was built in the late 1700s. It had wooden wheels and they called it a "hobbyhorse."

Hobbyhorses didn't have pedals, so people rode them by pushing their feet along the ground. With no sprockets, you had to huff and puff just to move a hobbyhorse. And with no brakes, people had to drag their feet on the ground to stop. Even though these "bicycles" were just for fun, only strong, daring people rode hobbyhorses!

While you still might ride your bicycle just for fun, they have also become an important form of transportation throughout the world. An estimated 3 million bicycles are in Beijing, China alone! But the Chinese don't ride all of these bikes just to get from one place to another. Look at the street cleaner. The Chinese have modified bikes to do jobs that, here in the United States, usually take machines that use fuel. How did the bicycle move from the simple hobbyhorse to such a specialized tool? People used machines to develop new technologies.

⋏ *Modern bicycles have come a long way from this primitive hobbyhorse.*

◄ *Bicycles have become specialized for many tasks.*

Bicycling Through History

Inventors combined simple machines to create today's bicycle.

The bicycle has been around for only about 200 years. But it is made up of simple machines that are quite ancient. For example, wheeled vehicles existed by about 3000 B.C. in Mesopotamia and India. The chain-drive was first invented in China during the 10th century, even though it was not used on bicycles until 1869.

The idea of a wheeled vehicle with gears took many years to develop. The forerunner of the bicycle consisted of just two wheels connected by a bar.

Steering, brakes, gears, pedals, and rubber tires were added over the years. Each addition made the bicycle safer, faster, and more comfortable.

1850-60. Ernest Michaux of France built bikes with crank pedals and large front wheels. This increased speed but made it difficult for the rider to balance.

1791 French inventor M. De Sivrac built a two-wheeled vehicle that worked like a scooter. It moved when its rider pushed against the ground.

1839 Kirkpatrick MacMillan of Scotland built a wooden bike that had pedals for its front wheel. Connecting levers turned the back wheel.

1790 | 1840

A modern dirt bike

1884 John Starley of Great Britain began making a "safety bike". His bike had a diamond-shaped frame for strength. It was driven by its rear wheel, which was connected to the pedals by a chain and sprocket.

1888 Scotsman John Dunlop began manufacturing inflatable rubber tires in 1888. This added comfort greatly increased the popularity of bicycling.

1940s By this time, bike racers in Europe were using bikes with gears that gave them five speeds. Today many bikes have ten speeds or even more.

1990s Bikes today have frames made of aluminum and other light materials. Soon you might be riding a bike like this one.

| 1890 | 1940 | 1990 |

➤ *Compare the treads on the two tires. The tire with smaller treads makes this racing bicycle easier to ride on smooth surfaces.*

▼ *Touring bikes are good for long trips.*

Bike Design

Would you like to have a dirt bike like the one you just saw on the timeline? If so, you're not alone. Many children choose to ride bikes with small frames and wheels like that one. These bicycles have high handlebars that let you sit upright. In this position, you have good visibility and control over the front wheel.

The "balloon" tires of small bikes are soft and fat with deep grooves. They have a tough rubber inner tube that holds air and a tougher outer tube that touches the pavement. Bicycles with thick "squashable" tires are good for riding on dirt roads, rough surfaces, and all-around use. Small wheels will not take you as far when you pedal, but they do help you make fast turns.

What kind of bike would you want to ride on a long bicycle trip? Racing bicycles or touring bicycles like the one this woman is riding have full-sized frames, high seats, thin tires, and big wheels. They are designed for fast riding and long trips. The tires on a big-wheeled bike are thin and hard. They're great for long, fast rides on smooth roads. Because the wheels are big, every push of the pedal takes you a long distance.

Many racing bicycles have dropped handlebars that make the rider lean forward. Leaning forward "streamlines" the body, cutting down on friction between the rider and the air. Straight handlebars, on the other hand, are good for everyday riding. They allow you to sit upright, so you can see well and better control the bicycle.

Tires, Treads, and Friction

If riders have to stop in a hurry, then it's "Hooray for friction!" The tires on a bicycle provide you with the friction you have to have for turning the wheel and for stopping. This friction is produced where the rolling tires touch the road.

Bicycle tires must be able to grip the road in both wet and dry weather. But friction is lost if a thin layer of water gets between the tire and the pavement. So, most tires have special grooves and ridges—called treads—that help keep a layer of water from forming.

How can treads do this? On wet days, water squeezes up into the grooves as the tire rolls along, and the tire is still able to touch the road. The deeper the tread, the better the tire grips the road. If you ride a bike where there's a lot of rain and mud, you need tires with deep treads.

Checkpoint

1. Which three basic parts of today's bikes were missing from early models?
2. What kind of bicycles are best for long trips on the open road?
3. What kind of tires are best for fast stops on wet pavement?
4. **Take Action!** Map out an area where you frequently ride a bike. Which kind of bicycle would be best for your route?

A Canned Bicycle

How could you estimate the mass of a bicycle? Let's investigate to find out.

What To Do
A. Use a balance to find the mass of an aluminum can. Record the mass in a table like the one below.

	Aluminum	Steel
Mass of one can		
Number of cans	577	229
Estimated mass of bike		

B. An all-aluminum bicycle has about as much aluminum as 577 cans. Use this fact to find the estimated mass of an aluminum bicycle. Record the estimated mass.
C. Now find the mass of a steel or tin can. Record the mass.
D. An all-steel bicycle has about as much steel as 229 steel cans. Find the estimated mass of a steel bicycle.

What Did You Find Out?
1. *Which bicycle is lighter?*
2. *Which bike would you have expected to be lighter?*
3. *Would you rather ride a steel or an aluminum bike for long distances? Explain.*

Getting a Bicycle in Gear

What can three metal lids and some rubber bands tell you about bicycle gears? Try this activity and see.

Picture A

Gather These Materials

cover goggles shoe-box lid
large metal lid metric ruler
medium-sized metal lid 2 pushpins
small metal lid small hammer
compass rubber bands
grease pencil scissors
 wooden block

Follow This Procedure

1 Make a chart like the one on the next page. Record your observations in your chart.

2 Use a compass to find the center of each lid. Then mark this point with a grease pencil on the underside of the lid.

3 Draw an arrow from the center to the edge of each lid.

Picture B

4 Put on cover goggles before you do this step. Set each lid on the wooden block, and hammer a pushpin into the center of each lid. (Picture A)

5 Use the pushpins to fasten the large and small lids, top down, on the shoe-box lid so that they are about 15 centimeters apart.

6 Write labels for the gears on the shoe box. Label the large lid the *pedal gear* and the small lid the *rear-wheel gear*.

Picture C

7 Cut several rubber bands and tie them together so that they form one large rubber band that will encircle both gears. Make sure that the large rubber band will fit around the two gears, stretching only slightly. (Picture B)

Record Your Results

Size of rear-wheel gear	Number of turns for rear-wheel gear	Direction of rear-wheel compared to pedal gear
Small gear		
Medium-sized gear		

8 Turn the pedal gear one complete turn. Note the direction and the number of times the rear-wheel gear turns. Record this information. (Picture C)

Predict: *What will happen if you replace the small lid with the medium-sized lid?*

9 Repeat step 8, replacing the small lid with the medium-sized lid.

State Your Conclusions

1. How does the pedal gear work to turn the rear-wheel gear?

2. How is this similar to the way a bicycle works?

Let's Experiment

How would the motion of the gears change if you twisted the rubber band once and placed it around the two gears? Use what you know about scientific methods to find out.

LESSON

3.2 *Safe Wheels*

▶ *How can I tell if my bike is safe to ride?*

It was late on a cold, rainy afternoon. Juan was riding home from a friend's house when suddenly, BANG! His bike tire had a blowout. As Juan walked the bicycle home, he thought, "Did this have to happen right now? Why did I have to get a flat tire when it's cold and rainy? What rotten luck."

Was it bad luck or was it carelessness that caused the flat tire? It's hard to say. Often, though, flat tires and many other problems can be avoided by taking good care of a bicycle. What do you have to do to keep your bicycle running well?

Keep It Running

Why is it important to keep a bicycle—or any machine you use—in good shape? Common sense tells you that one reason for maintaining a machine is because it's safer to use a machine that runs well than one that is ready to break down. If Juan had been riding in heavy car traffic, the effects of the blowout might have been much more serious. Juan could have been involved in a traffic accident.

If you ask Mr. Lee, a bicycle mechanic, how to take care of a bike, chances are he will start talking about tires. He'll tell you to make sure you have the "right amount" of air in the tires. This means using a tire gauge to check the tires once every two weeks.

Usually, you will have to inflate, or put air into, the tires, because air slowly seeps out of rubber tires. It leaks out because rubber is porous, which means it has openings that are big enough to let air pass through.

▶ *Bicycle maintenance is easy and important.*

The right amount of air varies with the tire. For example, the bike mechanic says a dirt bike tire might hold about up to three kilograms per square centimeter of air, but a racing bike tire holds about seven kilograms per square centimeter of air. You can see how much air the tire holds written on the side of the tire.

Why all the fuss about tires? Underinflated tires—those with not enough air—make you do more work. Part of the force you put into the pedals is wasted just getting "squishy" tires to roll. Not only that, hitting bumps with underinflated tires damages the wheels and causes flat tires.

On the other hand, overinflated tires—those with too much air—have drawbacks too. For one thing, it's hard to control a bike when you are riding on overinflated tires. Also, rubber tires can pop just like balloons do. Only you call the popping of a rubber tire a blowout!

When you inflate a tire, you are pushing air molecules into the inner tube. Once inside the tube, the molecules are squeezed closer together, so they press on the walls of the inner tube. Since rubber is elastic, it stretches and the tire gets bigger. If the rubber has stretched as far as it can, and you keep adding more air molecules, watch out! It's a blowout.

Bike experts also think checking the bicycle chain and the brakes is important. They'll tell you to clean and lubricate, or oil, the chain about once a month. When the chain turns around the sprockets, metal rubs against metal. Oiling the chain reduces friction, which makes the chain work better and last longer. Bicycle shops sell a special spray that cleans and oils the chain at the same time.

▼ *Inspect your bicycle regularly.*

▲ *This bike rider is signaling left turn, right turn, and stop.*

➤ *Bicycle helmets help save lives.*

As for the all-important brakes, make sure the brakes grip the wheel rims and not the tires. If the brakes rub against the tires, they won't work properly and they'll wear down the tire. Because you need friction to stop the bike, keep the rubber blocks of the brakes clean and free from grease. Use a glass cleaner to wipe off the rubber blocks, and, while you're at it, wipe the metal wheel rims too.

Finally, the bike mechanic will tell you to bring the bike in once a year for a "checkup," even if it seems to be working all right. If, at any time, something isn't right—loose or broken spokes, bent sprocket teeth, weak brakes—then head for the repair shop in a hurry!

Getting There in One Piece

When a little child starts riding a tricycle, someone is there to make sure the child rides where it's safe. By the time children are old enough to ride two-wheel bicycles, however, they're old enough to ride in the streets. When you jump on a bicycle and zoom down the street, make sure you follow bicycle safety rules.

Speaking of safety, what are you wearing today? Is it important? It is if you will be riding a bike. In fact, what you wear can save your life! A helmet like this one makes you more visible, and it protects your head if you fall or are knocked off the bike. *Always* wear a helmet when you ride.

Both you and the bike need to be visible. Bright, light-colored clothes make it easier for drivers to see you, especially at night. Make sure the bicycle has good reflectors and bright lights too. Attaching a bright orange flag on a tall stick to your bike helps others see you better too.

Follow the same road rules motorists use, and remember the first rule of the road: Stay to the right! That means ride with traffic, not against it. Learn the hand signals shown here and use them when you turn corners or change lanes. The hand signals alert the people in the cars or on the bicycles around you to which direction you're going. You might find out other important safety tips from your community safety council.

Over 40,000 car–bicycle accidents alone occur each year. That's one group you don't want to join! Play it safe by practicing good bicycle safety habits.

Into The Field

How can people ride their bikes safely?
Watch people riding their bikes. Identify and record any unsafe practices you see. Explain why they're unsafe.

Checkpoint

1. Why is it important to keep a bicycle in good repair?
2. What are three hand signals bicycle riders should use?
3. **Take Action!** Organize a *Bicycle Safety Check* with an adult and the other bicycle riders in your school or neighborhood.

Activity

Slip-Sliding Away

Bicycle riders need to pay attention to riding surfaces. Try this activity to learn more about surfaces and friction.

Picture A

Picture B

Picture C

Gather These Materials

big rectangular cake pan
  or cookie sheet
small block of wood
waxed paper

masking tape
water
cup with a spout
sand

Follow This Procedure

1 Make a chart like the one on the next page. Record your observations in your chart. Keep in mind as you go that you are to compare the surfaces for slipperiness.

2 Slide a block of wood across the bottom of the pan. (Picture A) Record whether or not the block slides easily across the metal surface by writing yes or no in the chart.

3 Cover the bottom of the pan with a sheet of waxed paper. Tape down the waxed paper so that the surface is smooth and the edges of the paper stay down.

4 Repeat step 2, sliding the block of wood across the waxed paper (Picture B) and record your observation.

5 Pour a thin layer of water into the pan. Make sure the water is no deeper than 0.5 centimeter.

6 Repeat step 2, sliding the block of wood through the water (Picture C) and record your observation.

Record Your Results

Surface	Does block slide easily? (yes or no)	Rank slipperiness (1, 2, 3, or 4)
Smooth metal		
Waxed paper		
Water layer on smooth metal		
Wet sand		

Predict: *Do you think the block of wood will slide easily across a layer of packed sand?*

7 Pour a layer of sand in the pan. Use enough sand to soak up the water in the cake pan, and pack the wet sand down.

8 Repeat step 2, and record your observation.

9 To compare the surfaces, write a 1, 2, 3, or 4 in each box of the righthand column of the chart. The number *1* is for most slippery; the number *4* is for least slippery.

State Your Conclusions

1. Which surface was most slippery? least slippery?
2. If a bicycle is skidding, what kind of surface is safest? most dangerous?

Let's Experiment

How would the block slide if you put several rubber bands around it? Use what you know about scientific methods to find out.

Organizing Your Data

When you do an activity or solve a problem, you need to show your information, or data, in a form that is clear and easy to read. You need to organize your data.

There are many good ways to organize data, including bar graphs, tables, line graphs, maps, and models. Let's look at two different kinds of "organizers"—bar graphs and tables.

Thinking It Through

Suppose you're going to buy a bike. You see three bikes that cost about what you want to spend. All three have different features. You want to compare the costs and the features of the bikes. Begin by organizing the information.

How is a bar graph useful? A bar graph lets you compare the costs at one glance. It's a simple, clear way to show part of your information. A bar graph is especially useful if you need to compare the costs of many bikes.

How is a table useful? Take a look at the information in the table at the right. You can't take in all the information at a glance. You have to read each item listed, but the information that's important to you is there. The table lets you compare both costs and features at

one time. For your purposes, using the table is better than using the bar graph.

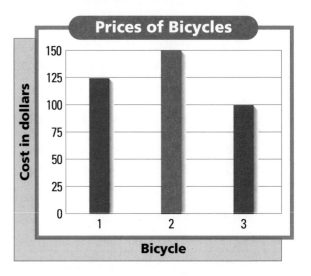

Bike	Cost	Features
1	$125	5-speed, favorite color
2	$150	10-speed, racing bike
3	$100	3-speed, off-road bike

Your Turn

Pretend you're going shopping for a bike. You can't decide whether to get a dirt bike or a racing bike. To help you decide which bike to buy, organize the information found in this chapter. Design a table to show this information.

Chapter Review

Thinking Back

1. Name three things added to bikes over the years to make them safer.
2. Describe two ways in which a dirt bike is good for use on dirt roads and rough surfaces.
3. What's one reason why racing bicycles have dropped handlebars?
4. How are tire treads a safety feature?
5. How often should you check the amount of air in a bicycle's tires?
6. How can underinflated tires cause a bicycle rider to do extra work?
7. Explain how overinflating a tire can cause a blowout.

Connecting Ideas

1. Copy the concept map. Use the terms at the right to complete the map describing bicycle care and safety.

tire pump   no reflectors
oil   overinflated tires

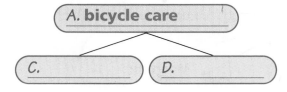

A. bicycle care
C.
D.

B. bicycle hazards
E.
F.

2. Write a sentence or two that summarizes the ideas shown in the concept map.

Gathering Evidence

1. In the Activity on page 48, how did you know that the direction in which the rear-wheel gear turns depends upon the way the rubber band connects the gears?
2. In the Activity on page 54, how did you know that less friction is created when the block runs on a smooth surface than on a rough surface?

Doing Science!

1. *Make a poster* showing the design for a new bicycle. Describe the features that make the bike different from those used today.
2. *Write a skit* that could be presented to a group of first- or second-graders demonstrating the importance of bicycle safety rules.

The Bicycle of Your Dreams

I t might seem like a dream come true. You've been promised a new bicycle for your birthday. Now it's time to choose which one you will buy.

Go into any bike shop. You'll see many different kinds of bikes: mountain bikes, road bikes, and hybrid bikes—which are bikes of different sizes and with different kinds of features. How can you decide which of these bicycles is best for you?

The ideal bicycle is lightweight, sturdy, and economical.

Needs and Goals

To choose a bicycle, think about these factors:

- Type: Is the bicycle right for the kind of riding you do?
- Size: Is the bicycle the right height for you?
- Features: What sort of brakes do you prefer? Are additional comfort features, such as a special seat, or safety features, such as reflectors, important to you?

Road Bike

Mountain Bike

Hybrid Bike

Gathering Information

To decide on a type of bicycle, think carefully about how and where you will ride it. Make a checklist of ways you plan to use your bike, as shown on the chart. Then you can rate how often you might use the bicycle in this way.

A bike that doesn't fit you isn't safe to ride. Be sure that your knees bend slightly when you push all the way down on the pedals.

Make sure the seat is comfortable and that it's easy to reach the handlebars.

Bicycle Comparison

Type of bicycle and activities	Frequency of Use		
	Often	Sometimes	Never
Road Bicycles			
Riding on a smooth, paved surface			
Covering long distances (20-30 km)			
Participating in bicycle races			
Lifting bicycle up flight of stairs with ease			
Mountain Bicycle			
Riding on dirt roads, beaches, park trails			
Riding up and down steep hills			
Hybrid bicycle			
Riding on rough and smooth surfaces			
Riding on hills and flat surfaces			
Lifting bicycle up flight of stairs with ease			
Riding on dirt or other unpaved surfaces			

Possible Alternatives

Road bikes are best for riding on smooth, paved roads and covering long distances. Mountain bikes are better suited for riding on dirt roads and up and down steep hills. Hybrid bikes are best for people who ride in a variety of conditions.

Evaluating Alternatives

Copy the table and fill it in to show your riding habits. Then think about which additional features you might want. Consider comfort, safety, and the additional cost of the feature.

Making the Best Choice

Use the table to decide what type of bike would be ideal for you. Then consider the prices of different bikes before deciding which one to buy.

Now You Do It

1. How do the bicycles in the diagram compare in terms of tires and handlebars?

2. Which of the three types of bicycles do you think would be best for you? Why?

3. *On Your Own* Finding the ideal bike for the right price isn't always possible. Visit some bike stores and gather information on the prices of different bikes. Which of these bikes would you choose, given its price?

4. *Critical Thinking* How is riding a bicycle better for the environment than driving a car? What are some ways that state and local governments could encourage the use of bicycles as a form of transportation?

Searching for Clues

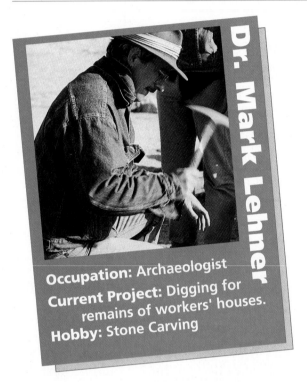

Dr. Mark Lehner

Occupation: Archaeologist
Current Project: Digging for remains of workers' houses.
Hobby: Stone Carving

Imagine walking along a dry stream bed. At your feet are large bones, white with age. Your grandfather tells you that these are bones from buffalo that lived hundreds of years ago. Why did the buffalo come here? What people lived here? What was it like in the past?

Mark Lehner first started asking questions like these on his grandfather's farm. Today, Dr. Lehner asks the same types of questions. He's an archaeologist who studies the people who built the great pyramids of Egypt.

Who built the pyramids?

"Men were drafted into service to work on the pyramids. They lived in large camps not far from the work site. After about a year or so, they would go back to their families and farms. You could compare it to a military system, the way they were drafted and organized."

What have you learned about the builders of the pyramids?

"When a group of workers hauled a stone up to the pyramid, they wrote their group name in red paint on the stone. It's like graffiti that's lasted for 5000 years! The workers were advertising that they had moved that big, heavy stone into place."

Can you learn other details from the tomb paintings?

"Many paintings have been discovered, and they show people catching fish, herding cattle, and dancing. But they don't show anyone building pyramids."

Where did the stones come from?

"The large blocks of limestone came from nearby quarries. Granite and other special stones used inside the tombs were brought up the Nile."

What's the best part of your job?

"The best part is discovering things from 5000 years ago and salvaging them for future generations."

Jackscrew: Lifting a Heavy Load

It seems incredible, yet a very simple, small tool called a jackscrew can lift a 27.2 metric ton house. The strength of a lever and a screw working together makes this unlikely feat possible.

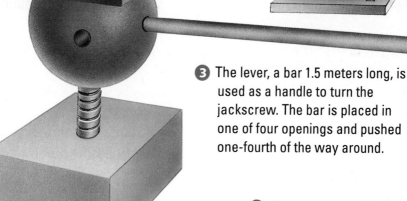

1 Because the threads on the screw part of a jackscrew are close together, the lifting force of the screw is very powerful.

2 The screw is set on a steel platform. Neither the screw nor the platform move.

3 The lever, a bar 1.5 meters long, is used as a handle to turn the jackscrew. The bar is placed in one of four openings and pushed one-fourth of the way around.

4 Then the bar is removed from that opening, put into the next opening, and pushed another one-fourth turn. This process is repeated for each opening. As the bar turns, the house is lifted.

Find Out On Your Own

On a Saturday or a Sunday, record in a journal how many times you use a lever or a screw. Make a note of how these machines were helpful.

Module Review

Making Connections

Energy

1. In order to do work, a machine needs a source of energy. What provides the energy to run a bike?
2. What provided the energy for the machines used to build the pyramids?
3. How is a compound machine different from a complex machine?
4. Name at least three kinds of energy used to run today's machines.

Systems and Interactions

5. Can a compound machine work properly if one of the simple machines it contains breaks down? Explain.
6. How do tire treads help the bike rider?

7. What kinds of machines make up a complex machine?
8. Describe what a pulley without wheels looks like and how it works.

Scale and Structure

9. Today's bike goes fast without a big front wheel, such as the one on the 1800s model. What parts help modern bikes go fast?
10. Two ramps leading to a building are the same height—2 meters. But Ramp A is 4 meters long and Ramp B is 3 meters long. If you needed to push a cart full of books into the building, which ramp would you use? Explain your answer.

Using What I Learned

Comparing

1. Compare a crowbar to a seesaw.

Ordering

2. Order the following tools from simplest to most complicated: electric can opener, crowbar, pencil sharpener.

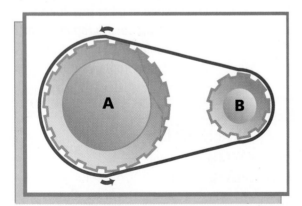

Categorizing

3. Name two things you could use to describe how much work a machine does.

Relating

4. Why is it easier to walk down, rather than up, a flight of stairs?

Observing

5. Study the diagram. Compare the speeds and directions of the two gears.

Communicating

6. Explain how ball bearings help cut down on friction.

Applying What I Learned

Performance Task

Use a meter stick and a chalkboard eraser to make a lever. The eraser can act as the fulcrum. Use your lever to lift 3 small books. Place the fulcrum so that the lever can lift the weight as easily as possible. Wear cover goggles while testing your lever and be careful not to break the meter stick. Draw a picture of your lever.

Action Project

Complex machines use a great deal of electricity. Make a list of complex machines used in your home. Tell which ones could be replaced with simpler machines in order to conserve energy.

Drawing

Make a drawing of a bicycle that is best-suited for use on wet, rough, roads.

Science Theater

Write a skit that shows some simple machines the Egyptians used to build the pyramids.

Exhibitions

Make a poster or bulletin board promoting good bicycle safety habits.

What If

Your town plans to create a bicycle path between your home and school. Write a letter to your local planning board describing the route you want the path to take. List reasons why you selected this particular route.

Fun in Motion

Fun in Motion

Zoom! The ball hurtles toward you. Pow! You kick it with your foot. Whoosh! As the ball flies through the air, you sprint around the bases. Kickball is just one of many sports that involves motion— the ball's motion, your motion, and the motion of the other players. Thanks to the laws of motion, you can play the game and make your body move.

CHAPTER
2 Get Moving

You're just a bundle of bones, muscles, and nerves. But what a bundle! Your body's muscular, skeletal, and nervous systems work together to get you moving.

CHAPTER
1 Kickball in Motion

When you kick a ball, does the ball kick back? Balls aren't people, but both balls and people move and both obey three basic laws of motion.

CHAPTER 3 Playing by the Rules

Can you play kickball on the moon? It's possible—but you might have to change the rules. Motion on the moon is far different than motion on the earth.

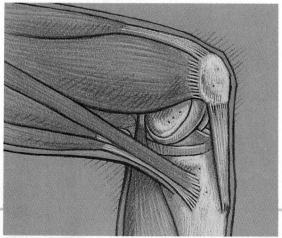

Kickball in Motion

Let's race!

Why do some things slide more easily than others?

Select a variety of small objects like a button, coin, stone, and a rubber eraser. Line these objects up at one edge of a board. Examine each object carefully. Predict the order in which objects will move as you slowly lift up the edge of the board. Then test your prediction. Try this with another set of objects.

For Discussion

1. Which objects slide easily and which don't?

2. Why do certain objects slide easily ?

1.1 *Play Ball!*

▶ *What kind of movement takes place in a game of kickball?*

Playground games include many different kinds of motion that involve a ball or a human body. For example, a lot is going on in this kickball game. Your team—the Accelerators—takes the field. The first kicker for the other team—the Forces—steps up to home plate. The pitcher reaches back. Then she rolls the ball forward as hard as she can.

The kicker stands at home plate. He kicks the ball toward the third baseman. The kicker takes off for first. The third baseman throws to first, but the kicker beats the throw. Safe! The second kicker takes a running start. She kicks the ball to the outfield fence, and both runners cross home plate.

What did the Forces just do? Sure, they scored two runs. But they also used the three laws of motion. Perhaps you don't understand that right now. But come back to this kickball game at the end of the chapter to test your knowledge. Because if you understand the laws of motion, you might have the winning edge.

▼ *Many kinds of motion are involved in a game of kickball.*

Inertia

Have you ever run down a steep hill? When you got to the bottom you might have tried to stop quickly. But your legs kept taking you forward until you shuffled to a stop.

Think back to your own games of kickball. Maybe you've kicked the ball to the outfield once or twice. Do you remember what happened then? The ball kept rolling—while the outfielders chased it. Maybe the ball didn't stop until it hit the schoolyard fence.

These two situations show inertia (in ėr′ shə). **Inertia** is the tendency of an object to stay either in constant motion or at rest. That is, moving objects tend to keep moving in the same direction at the same speed. Objects that are not moving tend to stay still. The only thing that can change the situation is an outside force. A force applied to a moving object—like a kickball—can send it off in a different direction and at a different speed. A force such as friction slows down a moving object. Or a force applied to a motionless object can start it moving. For example, a kickball sitting in the grass needs a force—such as the force provided by your foot— to move it.

Think about running down a steep hill. Inertia is the reason you can't stop right away when you run down a steep hill. It's why you sometimes go past home plate when you slide. Your body and other objects have inertia. Inertia is also why a kickball keeps rolling once your kick gets it started.

▼ *A moving kickball exhibits inertia.*

Inertia controls your motion off the field too. For example, you might be riding in a car when the driver suddenly slams on the brakes. What happens to your body? You keep moving forward, even though the car has stopped—but your seat belt and harness stop you from hitting the dashboard. In this case, something stops the car carrying you forward. But because your body is traveling at the same speed as the car, inertia keeps your body going at that speed until the seat belt and harness stop you.

Inertia can be used to do amazing things, too. Inertia is the reason the *Voyager 2* space probe is taking a fantastic journey through space. NASA sent *Voyager 2* into space in 1977 to take pictures of the solar system's outer planets. In 1989, *Voyager 2* reached Neptune, its last encounter in the solar system. Then it sped toward the edge of the solar system at about 100,000 kilometers per hour.

Voyager 2 does not have big rocket engines to boost it along. It does not need them because it's already moving very fast and will coast for years because of its inertia. In fact, *Voyager 2* should speed through the vacuum of space for millions of years without stopping—as long as no outside force changes its motion.

Starting and Stopping

Let's return to the kickball game. The pitcher rolls the ball toward home plate, but the pitch is wide. The kicker lets it pass. But the ball gets away from the catcher and rolls off the field. The ball bounces off the curb, then starts down a long hill. Soon it's completely out of sight.

No one can tell just where the ball will end up. But it will stop rolling somewhere. That's because the forces of gravity and friction can act to stop the motion of moving objects.

Suppose the kickball rolls down the hill and across a level field. What will happen? It will roll more and more slowly until it comes to a stop.

How do gravity and friction change the motion of the kickball? Gravity is the force that interacts with all objects on the earth. Gravitational force from the earth pulls on the kickball, and an equal amount of gravitational force from the kickball pulls on the earth. Which object will move more easily—the kickball or the earth? The kickball moves because it's much less massive than the earth is. Even if you kick the ball into the air, the force of gravity will bring it back to the ground. It will end up rolling on the ground before coming to a complete stop.

The rolling is where friction comes in. You saw in the Discover Activity that friction resists the motion of one surface against another. As the ball rolls along, the ball and the dirt rub against each other, producing friction. Friction pushes backward on the moving kickball, until it comes to a stop.

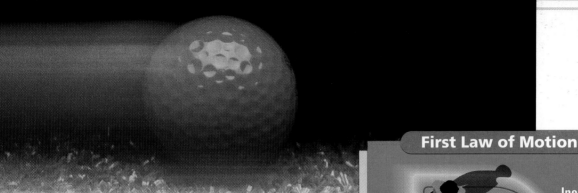

First Law of Motion

Look around you at all the objects that move—your body, cars, bikes, and baseballs. Believe it or not, you have already learned the idea behind what scientists call the First Law of Motion.

The First Law of Motion states that objects that are at rest tend to stay at rest unless acted upon by some outside force. Remember, a kickball won't move unless you kick it. The First Law of Motion also states that objects in motion will continue in motion with the same speed and direction until some outside force acts on them. For instance, the force from an outside source such as your foot can change the motion of a kickball. And the more force from your foot, the more change!

First Law of Motion

Inertia of ball at rest

Inertia of ball in motion

Friction slows ball

Gravity pulls ball down

▲ *In miniature golf, the ball moves in accordance with the First Law of Motion.*

Checkpoint

1. What are two different ways that an object can show inertia?
2. What two forces combine to stop objects in motion?
3. Why could you call the First Law of Motion the Law of Inertia?
4. Take Action! Roll a ball down a ramp across a carpet and then across a tile floor. Compare the distances rolled and explain any difference.

How Can You Lose a Marble Race?

In this activity, you'll build a maze for marbles so they'll go as slowly as possible. Use friction and gravity to keep your marble going in "slow motion."

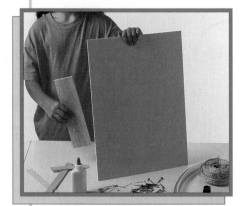

Picture A

Picture B

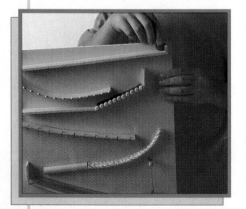

Picture C

Gather These Materials

cover goggles
tape
scrap wood
wood strips
white glue
marble

obstacles such as
  cardboard tubes,
  blocks of wood, nails,
  or rubber bands
stopwatch

Follow This Procedure

1. Make a chart like the one on the next page. Record your observations in your chart.

2. Put on your cover goggles.

3. Prop up a large piece of scrap wood using wood strips. You will build a marble maze on the wood. (Picture A)

4. Use white glue to attach several wood strips to begin your maze. Before you attach each one, experiment with a marble to make sure the wood is in a good position to be a marble run. (Picture B)

5. Add obstacles for your marble to go over or through. Try cardboard tubes, blocks of wood, nails, rubber bands, and any other things you can think of.

Predict: *Would a marble go faster down a steep angle or a slight angle?*

6 Let your marble go through the maze a few times. Use the stopwatch to see how long it takes. Decide what you can change to slow down the marble. Record your results. (Picture C)

7 When you have completed your maze, let your marble go down the track at the same time as your neighbor's. The marble with the slowest time wins. Record your results.

	Time
Trial 1	
Trial 2	
Trial 3	

State Your Conclusions

1. Where did friction slow down the marble the most?
2. Where did the marble speed up the most? Why?

Let's Experiment

Now that you have made a slow track, what would you have to do to increase the speed of the marble through the maze? Use what you know about scientific methods to plan and build another maze that's designed for speed.

LESSON

1.2 We Want a Hit!

▶ **What affects the distance a ball is kicked?**

It is not hard to kick a kickball. Its mass is less than a kilogram. But what about kicking a 500 kilogram kickball? That would be a different story. You'd need a lot more force than your foot could supply to get *that* ball moving through the air.

The law of motion at work here involves the relationship between force and mass. The greater the mass, the more force you need to get the mass to move. This is why you can't kick a home run with a 500 kilogram kickball. It's also why you—a fifth grader—don't use an adult bowling ball. Its mass is too great for you to move easily!

▼ *Moving a 500 kilogram kickball takes a lot of force!*

Mass and Force

The force needed to move an object depends on its mass and how fast you want to move it. You've already learned that a force is a push or pull. These pushes and pulls can move objects. The wind can apply a force. A swinging hockey stick, a hand hitting a volleyball, or a foot kicking a kickball can also apply a force.

▼ *Increasing the mass of javelins affects how far they're thrown.*

Mass is the amount of matter or material in a substance. You need more force to move an object with a large mass than you do to give the same motion to an object with less mass. That's why you need far more force to give a 500 kilogram kickball the same motion as you would a baseball.

What happens once you get an object moving? The mass of the object affects the way it moves. For instance, imagine the same amount of force acting on two bowling balls. One bowling ball has more mass than the other. The same amount of force will move the bowling ball with less mass faster than it will move the bowling ball with greater mass.

The people who make the rules for the sport of javelin throwing used the relationship of force and mass to increase safety. Athletes train and eat better today than in the past. So they're bigger and stronger—that's why they often set new records.

With stronger athletes throwing them, javelins were going farther and farther. The sharp javelins were putting nearby spectators in danger. So the people who manage the sport decided to make javelins more massive. If the athletes threw with the same force, how did more massive javelins solve the problem?

This girl's foot changes the velocity of the ball.

Excel with Acceleration

A force acts on an object. For example, a foot kicks a kickball. Or a lacrosse player uses his stick to hurl the ball at the opponent's goal. Then the object moves off at a certain speed and in a certain direction. **Speed** measures how quickly an object moves over a certain distance. **Velocity** (və los′ ə tē) measures the speed and the direction that an object travels. A change in speed causes a change in velocity. Changing direction without changing speed also changes velocity.

Back at the kickball game, you kick the ball. The ball travels toward third base at 20 meters per second. That is its velocity. Suppose the ball hits a rock in the field. It keeps the same speed, but it bounces toward second base. How has its velocity changed? Suppose you kick the kickball again toward third base. It doesn't change direction. But friction slows the ball from 20 to 10 meters per second. How has its velocity changed this time?

As you know, the velocity of moving things can change. Suppose the kickball is lying in the grass. You have two chances to give it a kick. The first time, you just give it a gentle tap. The second time, you kick with all your might.

The velocity of the kickball changed slowly the first time. It went from 0 to perhaps 5 meters per second. The velocity really shot up fast the second time. It went from 0 to maybe 20 meters per second in the same amount of time. The ball's velocity changed more the second time you kicked it than the first time. **Acceleration** (ak sel′ ə rā′ shən) measures the rate of change in velocity.

Acceleration occurs when you first kick a kickball and it speeds up. Acceleration also happens when an object slows down—remember, the speed is changing. Another way acceleration occurs is when an object changes direction. When a kickball flies through the air and curves toward the ground, it accelerates as it changes direction.

When you want to accelerate an object, greater force over the same amount of time means greater acceleration. For example, a running start increases the force of your kick because your foot is moving faster. That means greater acceleration and distance for the kickball. It also might mean a home run.

▼ *Getting a running start changes the amount of force that your foot provides.*

Speeding Through Time

People have used machines to help them travel faster and faster.

Long ago, people traveled under their own power. After people learned to tame and ride animals, riding horses was the fastest form of land transportation. The fastest travel on water was using ships with oars and sails.

Transportation changed little until the early 1800s, when steam power began to drive ships and trains. In the mid 1900s, steam engines in trains were replaced by engines that burned fuel directly and provided more force.

During this century, fuel-powered engines have moved trains, ships, cars, and planes at greater and greater speeds. Today, jet and rocket power can accelerate humans to speeds faster than sound.

1807 Steam Power
Robert Fulton's steamboat, the *Clermont*, moved at a speed of about 8 kph on its first voyage in 1807.

1829 Steam Power
In 1829, the *Rocket*, a steam-driven locomotive, set a new human land speed record. The *Rocket* reached about 58 kph carrying a load.

1800

1850

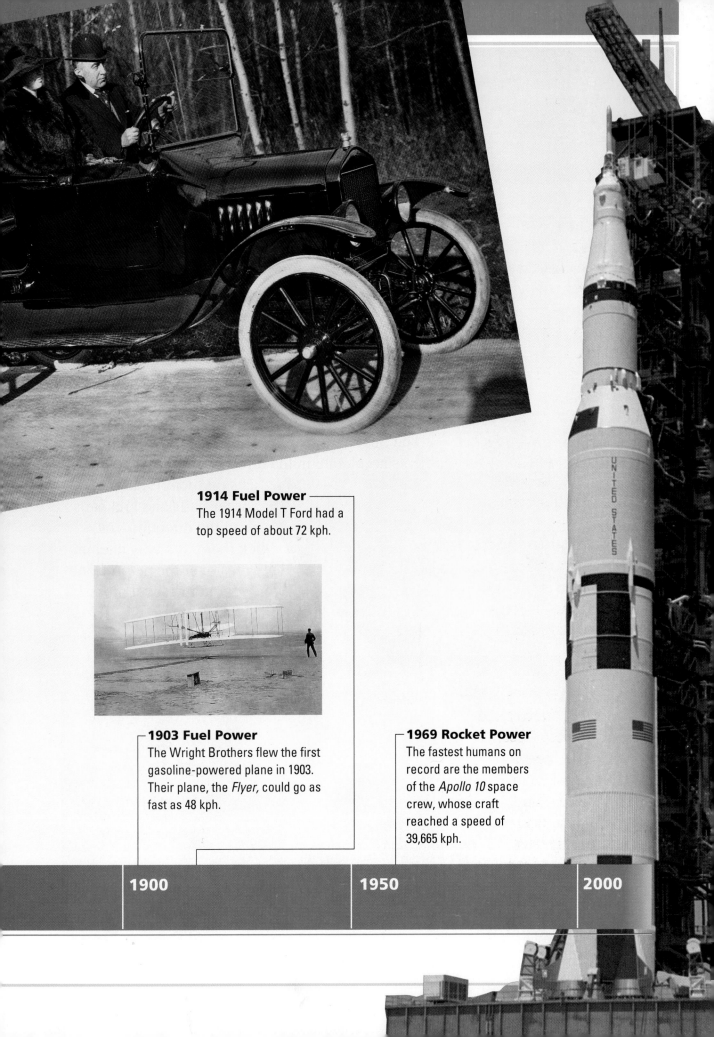

1914 Fuel Power
The 1914 Model T Ford had a top speed of about 72 kph.

1903 Fuel Power
The Wright Brothers flew the first gasoline-powered plane in 1903. Their plane, the *Flyer,* could go as fast as 48 kph.

1969 Rocket Power
The fastest humans on record are the members of the *Apollo 10* space crew, whose craft reached a speed of 39,665 kph.

1900

1950

2000

Second Law of Motion

You just read all about the Second Law of Motion. The Second Law of Motion explains that forces can change the motion of objects. The Second Law of Motion also explains how an object's motion changes when a force acts on it. The law can be written as this equation.

$$F = M \times A$$

The equation shows the relationship among force, mass, and acceleration. *F* is the force applied to the object. *M* is the mass of the object. *A* is the object's acceleration. This equation tells you that the force you need to move a mass equals that mass multiplied by the acceleration you want. The greater the mass acted upon by a given force, the smaller its acceleration.

The Second Law of Motion also explains that objects accelerate in the direction of the force that acts on them. That's why soccer balls and kickballs go in the direction you kick them. It's why a tennis ball goes over the net in front of you after your racket moves forward and hits it.

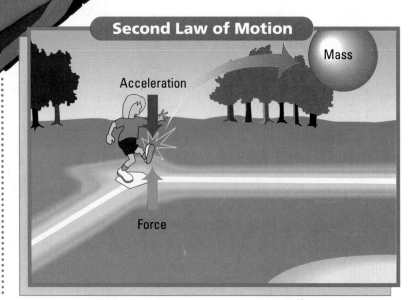

Second Law of Motion

Mass

Acceleration

Force

➤ *Your foot provides the force to accelerate the mass of a kickball.*

The Second Law of Motion also states that a change in the mass of an object means a change in the amount of force you need to give it the same acceleration. For example, accelerating a 750 kilogram car 20 meters per second per second requires a certain amount of force. Exactly twice as much force is needed to accelerate a 1500 kilogram car the same amount. You have to apply more force as the mass you are trying to move increases.

The Second Law of Motion also says that when the acceleration of an object changes, the amount of force acting on it must also be changing. A kickball doesn't speed up or slow down all by itself—forces move it or slow it down. And these same forces speed up and slow down the action in many other sports as well.

Checkpoint

1. What are two things that determine how big a force you need to apply in order to move something?
2. How is speed different from velocity?
3. Compare how long it would take to travel the 8000 kilometers from San Francisco to Tokyo on the *Clermont,* the *Flyer,* and with the *Apollo 10* space crew.
4. How much more force is needed to give the same acceleration to a 1500 kilogram car as to a 500 kilogram car?
5. **Take Action!** Diagram the force, mass, and acceleration involved in several sports. Vary one factor and show the results.

Forcing the Issue

How does force change as you ride your bike? You know that the force needed to move an object, F, is equal to the mass of the object, M, multiplied by the rate of acceleration, A.

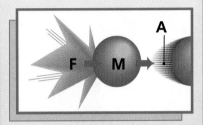

You can see that when the mass of an object stays the same, the greater the force, the greater the acceleration. If force doubles and mass stays the same, the rate of acceleration also doubles.

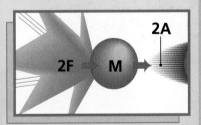

What Did You Find Out?
1. *If an object's mass stays the same, what happens to the force if the acceleration triples?*
2. *The same force is acting on both a small mass and a larger mass. Compare their accelerations.*

Activity

Look Out Below!

What happens to the speed of objects when they travel down a ramp? Try this activity to find out.

Picture A

Picture B

Picture C

Gather These Materials

piece of wood
3 thick books
meter stick
masking tape

ball
watch with second hand
  or stopwatch

Follow This Procedure

1. Make a chart like the one on the next page. Record your observations in your chart.

2. Prop a piece of wood against a thick book to make a ramp. (Picture A)

3. Use a meter stick to measure 300 centimeters from the top of the ramp to a spot on the floor in line with the ramp. Place a piece of masking tape there. (Picture B)

4. Release a ball at the top of the ramp and let it roll down.

5. Use a stopwatch to time how many seconds the ball takes to reach the tape. Release the ball and measure the time twice more. Record your times. (Picture C)

6. Add another book of the same thickness to make your ramp higher. Repeat steps 4 and 5.

Predict: *How long do you think it will take the ball to roll the distance with two books?*

Record Your Results

	Times for each trial (in seconds)			Average time (in seconds)	Average speed (centimeters per second)
Trial 1 (one book)					
Trial 2 (two books)					
Trial 3 (three books)					

7 Add a third book to the ramp and repeat steps 4 and 5.

8 Calculate the average time of the ball in each trial. To calculate the average speed, divide 300 centimeters by the average time in seconds. Record the average speed in your chart.

State Your Conclusions

1. How did the average speed of the ball change as the number of books increased?

2. What were two forces acting on the ball as it rolled down the ramp?

3. How did friction affect the speed of the ball?

Let's Experiment

Now you have seen what happens to the speed of a ball as you increase the angle of a ramp. What happens if you change the amount of friction acting on the ball? Use what you know about scientific methods to find out. Try covering the ramp with a thick towel, and doing the activity in a room with carpeting.

1.3 *Obeying the Law*

> ### *How else are forces used in games?*

Lots of forces are at work in a kickball game. You already know about some of them. Certain forces move a ball and some forces stop the ball's motion. These are the same forces that stop your body's movement.

Other forces are also at work at the ballgame. They help you run the bases and throw the ball. These same forces work in other sports and games, too. They're important in swimming, in boating, and in riding a bike. They help archers propel arrows and gymnasts to tumble.

Action and Reaction

Forces work in pairs. An action force pushes in one direction, and a reaction force pushes equally in the opposite direction. The two forces act on different objects. You can see this clearly in the pictures on this page. The child pushes backward against the raft. This is the action force. The raft pushes back against the child equally. The reaction force pushes the child forward and the raft backward—in opposite directions.

▼ *Pushing on the side of this raft causes the raft to push back.*

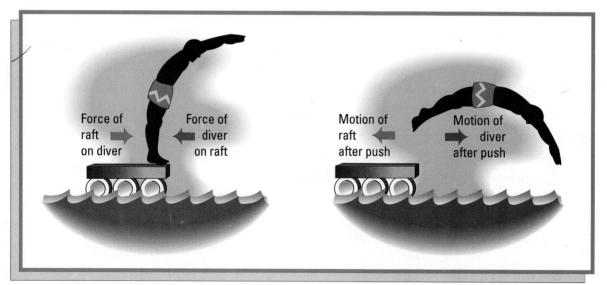

Force of raft on diver

Force of diver on raft

Motion of raft after push

Motion of diver after push

This girl experiences a reaction force when she throws a javelin.

You're ready to run. You dig your toe into the ground and push off. You might not know it but the ground is pushing back against you. Each time you apply force to another object or person, it applies an equal force back.

So when you push down on the ground, the ground pushes up equally. The force you exert has very little effect on the ground. The earth is too massive for you to accelerate. But the push the earth gives you gets you going.

Forces push a car along the road. A car sits on tires, and they press against the ground. When the tires turn, they push against the earth. Again, the earth pushes back equally. The car moves because it's less massive than the earth. The action force is the car's tires pushing against the ground. The reaction force is the earth pushing back.

Sometimes a person can really feel action and reaction forces. For example, when this girl throws a javelin forward, a reaction force jolts her back against her wheelchair.

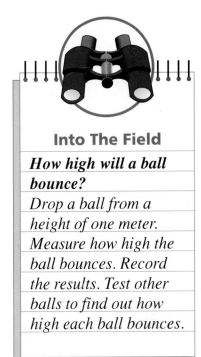

Into The Field

How high will a ball bounce?
Drop a ball from a height of one meter. Measure how high the ball bounces. Record the results. Test other balls to find out how high each ball bounces.

Third Law of Motion

Ground pushes forward

Foot pushes backward

▲ *Pushing in one direction causes an equal push in the opposite direction.*

Third Law of Motion

By understanding pairs of forces, you can understand the Third Law of Motion. The Third Law of Motion states that for every action there is an equal and opposite reaction.

The Third Law of Motion affects your everyday life. A boy on a skateboard pushes back with his toe to accelerate. The push of the ground sends him and his skateboard forward in the opposite direction.

A swimmer paddles through the water. Her arms push down through the water from front to back. The water pushes back against the swimmer's arms and hands and sends her forward. When the swimmer reaches the end of the pool, she pushes off and keeps swimming in the opposite direction. The action force of her push causes a reaction force to occur and helps move her along. A sprinter pushes down and back on the starting blocks before a race. The blocks push back and help her spring forward to a good start.

Scientists learned to use this principle to get into space. A rocket engine pushes hot gases out from under it. The reaction force pushes the rocket in the opposite direction—up into the air.

Newton's Laws

The laws of motion were devised by an English scientist named Isaac Newton more than 300 years ago. At that time, most scientists agreed with many of the ideas of the ancient Greeks, who thought that all matter was naturally at rest. Forces had to push constantly to keep anything moving. So a rolling ball would stop rolling when the force moving the ball stopped acting. Newton's calculations proved that many of the ancient Greek ideas about motion were wrong.

Newton's three laws can explain almost anything about the way objects move. Now that you know more about the three laws of motion, ask yourself these questions. Should you slide into a base to stop yourself quickly or go in standing up? Think back to the First Law of Motion. Will a running start give your foot greater velocity and more force as you kick the ball? The Second Law helps you there. Will you get more reaction force when you kick a fast pitch or a slow pitch? Look to the Third Law for clues. As you can see, Newton's Laws of Motion really do give you a competitive edge!

▲ In his book, the Principia, Isaac Newton proposed the three laws of motion.

Checkpoint

1. Explain the relationship between action forces and reaction forces.
2. What is Newton's Third Law of Motion?
3. How is the ancient Greek idea of force and motion different from Newton's First Law of Motion?
4. **Take Action!** Cut out pictures and make a collage showing examples of action and reaction forces.

Analyzing Bar Graphs

When you read a bar graph, it often shows measurements that have been made at different points in time. The graph helps you to see changes over time—whether they are large changes or small ones.

Thinking It Through

The bar graph shows the Olympic records for the men's long jump since 1912. Use these questions to help you analyze the information in the graph.

How often were measurements made?
Although the Olympics are held every four years, this graph shows only the record long jumps. The measurements shown on the graph are only for years when the record was broken.

What does the graph show between two record-setting years?
The graph shows nothing between two record years. But you know that the record must have been the last record before that time that was measured. For example, the record in 1950 must still have been 8.07 meters.

What trends, events, or ideas of interest do you notice about the records?
Some records lasted a short time. Others lasted a long time. Some made large increases in the record. Others did not.

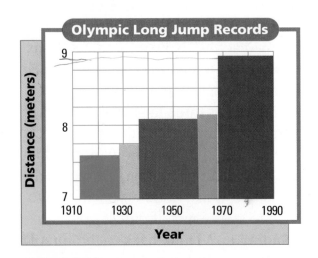

Olympic Long Jump Records

1912	Albert Gutterson, USA	7.60 m
1928	Edward B. Hamm, USA	7.74 m
1936	Jesse Owens, USA	8.07 m
1960	Ralph Boston, USA	8.12 m
1968	Bob Beamon, USA	8.90 m

Your Turn

Use the bar graph and the chart to answer these questions.
1. What was the record in 1920?
2. What was the record in 1980?
3. Whose record lasted the longest?
4. Whose record do you think is the most remarkable? Why?
5. Construct a bar graph that shows the records in another Olympic event. Look for trends and interesting facts.

Chapter Review

Thinking Back

1. How does a boulder rolling down a mountain show **inertia** once it reaches the bottom and continues rolling?
2. Compare the effects of gravity and friction on a moving object.
3. Describe the relationship between mass, force, and motion.
4. A pitcher throws a ball 150 km per hour. Explain how this is an example of **speed.**
5. What are two ways that the **velocity** of a moving object can change?
6. What kinds of changes have led to faster and faster means of transportation?
7. Explain the relationship between the force, mass, and **acceleration** of a moving object.
8. A skier pushes backward with her poles, causing her to move forward in the opposite direction. Explain which law of motion this illustrates.
9. Explain the view of force and motion accepted by most scientists at the time of Isaac Newton.

Connecting Ideas

1. Copy the concept map. Use the terms at right to complete the map about motion.

force   friction
mass   speed

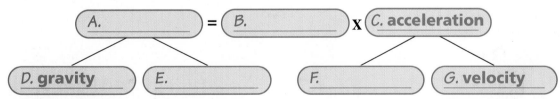

2. Write a sentence or two about the ideas shown in the concept map.

Gathering Evidence

1. In the Activity on page 10, what information did you use to predict that the marble would move faster?
2. In the Activity on page 20, how did you conclude gravity acted on the ball?

Doing Science!

1. **Demonstrate** the Second Law of Motion to an audience.
2. **Develop a skit** that shows for every action there is an equal and opposite reaction.

Get Moving

Way to go... that's your best kick yet!

How does practice help your aim?

Make an "X" on the gym wall with two pieces of tape. Place a kickball on the floor at least 5 meters from the wall. Try to kick the kickball so that it will hit the X. Measure the distance between where your ball hits and the center of the X. Kick the ball two more times, each time trying to hit the X.

For Discussion

1. How did practice help to improve your aim?
2. How close were you able to come to the X?

2.1 Pump 'Em Up

How does my body move things?

The right moves can win any game. A sharp swing of a bat drives a baseball into the bleachers. A leap and a push send a basketball sailing through a hoop. A hard slide gets a runner safely to second base just before the kickball is thrown in. Newton's three laws of motion describe the way objects move. But it's a team of systems in your body—your muscles, bones, and nerves—that keep you in the action.

This team of body systems produces the movement that keeps you in the game. They keep your heart and lungs pumping and protect them from harm. They help to produce the force that makes lacrosse balls fly, jump ropes turn, and hockey pucks slide.

Your body contains more than 600 muscles, about 206 bones, and a nerve network about 72 kilometers long. The muscles in the arms of this bodybuilder work together with all of her other body systems. Your muscles also use teamwork to help move you along.

◄ This bodybuilder trains regularly to keep her body systems healthy.

Muscles At Work

Your muscular system is made up of all the muscles in your body. Your muscles get their job done by working in opposing pairs—like the action and reaction forces you learned about in the last chapter. When a pair of muscles goes to work, one muscle contracts or shortens. The contracting muscle pulls on the bone attached to it, so the bone moves. At the same time, the other muscle in the pair relaxes or lengthens.

The muscles in the arm shown here are a good example of an opposing pair. Find the biceps in the front of the upper arm and the triceps in the back of the upper arm. They work together to raise and lower the forearm.

Muscles can only pull—not push. You might want to raise your forearm to catch a ball as it zooms toward you in a game of stoopball, as pictured here. A message from your brain tells the biceps to contract. It shortens, pulling the bone in your forearm up toward the ball. At the same time, another message tells the triceps to relax. To lower your forearm, the opposite muscle takes over. A signal tells the biceps to relax. Then the triceps contracts and pulls your forearm down.

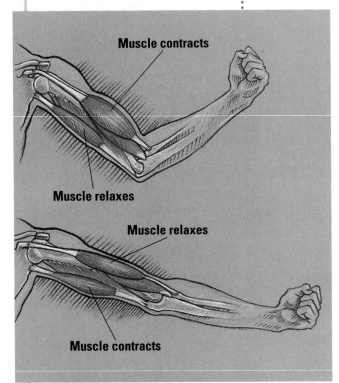

Muscle contracts

Muscle relaxes

Muscle relaxes

Muscle contracts

▲ *Muscles contract to move bones.*

➤ *Stoopball requires quick arm movement.*

Your muscles are always contracting and relaxing. They do it when you walk, run, talk, smile, or write. They contract and relax even when you don't know it's happening. You might think you're sitting perfectly still. But many muscles are working inside of you. Your heart beats. Muscles move air in and out of your lungs. In your stomach, muscles contract and relax to help digest your food. Your muscles are *always* hard at work.

Involuntary Muscles

Even when you're asleep, your body uses a set of muscles called involuntary muscles. An **involuntary muscle** (in vol′ ən ter′ē) works without you having to think about it. Some of these muscles help you to breathe. Involuntary muscles also control the beating of your heart, as well as helping you to blink and to digest food.

You can control certain involuntary muscles by thinking about them. You can breathe either fast or slow. This boy can wink one eye if he thinks about it. But you don't need to think about the actions of most of your involuntary muscles. They work even while you sleep, day in and day out.

You can't control most of your involuntary muscles. For example, "goose bumps" form when you're cold because tiny involuntary muscles in your skin contract. The hairs on your skin then stand up, causing the air near your skin to slow down and hold heat better. This action is probably more helpful to other animals with thicker fur than yours! The muscles of your heart also work involuntarily. The chart shows how many times your heart beats—without you thinking about it—over different periods of time.

Time	Number of Beats
1 minute	70
1 hour	4200
1 day	100,800
1 year	36,792,000

▲ *The muscles of your heart continue to work throughout the day and night.*

▼ *Some involuntary muscles can be controlled.*

Make Your Move

Skiers need coordination to twist and turn their way down a mountain. They put most of their body's muscles into action as they glide along. Of course, many involuntary muscles are working to keep them alive. But most of this skier's moves—and yours—are the work of voluntary muscles.

A **voluntary muscle** (vol′ ən ter′ē) is a muscle that a person can control with thought. These muscles move your legs, arms, fingers, toes, and other bones of your skeleton. They're at work when you laugh, read, chew, sing, or play a video game.

▼ *Tendons in your knee attach muscles to bones.*

Muscle

Tendon

Bone

Voluntary muscles come in many shapes and sizes. The smallest muscle in your body moves the bones of your middle ear, and is shorter than the thickness of a dime. Your body's longest muscle stretches all the way from your hip to your knee and moves your legs.

No matter how big they are or which bone they move, all voluntary muscles have the same structure. Voluntary muscles are made of bundles of overlapping fibers. Each fiber is thinner than one of your hairs. Each fiber is so tough, though, that it can move over 1000 times its own weight!

In order to move your body, muscles must be attached to your bones. **Tendons** (ten′dəns) like the ones in this skier's knee connect your muscles to your bones. Muscles pull on the ropelike tendons, and tendons then pull on the bones of your skeleton to make you move.

You don't always use the same number of muscle fibers to swing a baseball bat. Are you swinging for the fences, or do you just want to tap the ball slowly toward the pitcher? Your brain figures out how many muscle fibers are needed to do the job. For a strong swing, many of the fibers in your triceps pull together. For a weaker swing, fewer muscle fibers pull.

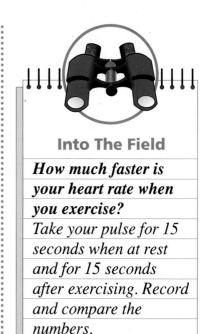

Into The Field

How much faster is your heart rate when you exercise?
Take your pulse for 15 seconds when at rest and for 15 seconds after exercising. Record and compare the numbers.

Checkpoint

1. How do pairs of muscles work together to make parts of your body move?
2. List three of the functions in your body controlled by involuntary muscles.
3. Would you use a greater number of muscle fibers jumping rope slowly or quickly?
4. Take Action! Prepare a slide of muscle tissue using thinly sliced meat. Sketch the fibers in the muscle tissue when viewed under a microscope.

Activity

Work In Pairs

Your muscles work in pairs. See pairs of muscles in action when you make a model of your foot.

Picture A

Picture B

Picture C

Gather These Materials

two shapes made of
  heavy paper
scissors

brass fastener
2 pieces of string
tape

Follow This Procedure

1 Make a chart like the one on the next page. Record your observations in your chart.

2 Your teacher will give you two shapes made of heavy paper. These shapes represent your lower leg and your foot. Cut out the shapes. Then poke a hole in the paper, and carefully cut out the holes. *CAUTION: Be careful when using pointed objects.* (Picture A)

3 Place shape B on top of shape A as shown.

4 Attach the two pieces with a brass fastener at letter X. What does your paper model look like? (Picture B)

5 Put a piece of string through each hole. Then tape down the one end of each piece of string as shown.

6 Pull the string that is closest to the "heel" of the "foot." How does the foot move? Record your observations. (Picture C)

7 Now pull the string closest to the "toe."

	Direction that foot moves	Length of string near heel	Length of opposite string
String near toe pulled			
String near heel pulled			

Predict: *What will happen to the foot now?*

8 Feel the muscle in the calf of your own leg. What happens to your calf muscle when you stand on your toes? What happens to your calf muscle when you stand back on your heels?

State Your Conclusions

1. What does the metal fastener represent in your model?

2. What do the strings represent? Do they act alone or together to move the foot?

3. When one string was getting longer, what was happening to the other? How does this observation apply to what happens to pairs of muscles?

Let's Experiment

Now that you've made a model of the muscles in the leg that move the foot, try making a model of the arm. Make another model by cutting out two similar pieces of heavy paper. What happens when these two muscles shorten or lengthen? Use what you know about scientific methods to find out how muscles work in your upper arm.

2.2 *You're Really Put Together*

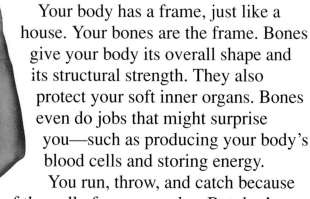

▶ *What role do bones play in movement?*

▼ *Bones protect your body while allowing great range of movement.*

Your body has a frame, just like a house. Your bones are the frame. Bones give your body its overall shape and its structural strength. They also protect your soft inner organs. Bones even do jobs that might surprise you—such as producing your body's blood cells and storing energy.

You run, throw, and catch because of the pull of your muscles. But don't forget—these muscles pull on your bones. You couldn't move a finger or an arm or a leg without your bones.

Skeletal System

If the boy here could take a look under his own skin, he would see a system of bones from his head to his toes. But why can't your skeleton be just one piece? Because it would make your body stiff and very hard to move. Having many bones in your body keeps you flexible, making many kinds of movement possible.

Your 206 bones come in different shapes and sizes. For example, your skull is actually over 20 flat bones joined together. These bones form a "helmet" that protects your brain. Ring-shaped vertebrae—33 in all—form your backbone, allowing you to bend, twist, lift, and push. The femur is a long, thick bone in your upper leg. All of the bones in your body work together as one unit. They give your body structure, protection, and flexibility.

Your skeletal system doesn't only include bones. The brown sections of this skeleton show **cartilage** (kär′ tl ij)—a flexible, bonelike substance. Notice where cartilage connects your ribs to your breastbone. This cartilage in your chest makes your rib cage flexible so it can expand as you breathe. Cartilage helps give shape to other parts of your body. Whether or not your ears are large or small or your nose is flat or pointed depends on the shape of the cartilage that forms these features.

Actually, the shapes of all your bones were determined by cartilage. A cartilage skeleton developed in your body before you were born. Bone then slowly took the place of cartilage, beginning at about two months and continuing after birth. Even then, your legs contained so much cartilage that you probably couldn't walk during your first year. Your bones continue to develop for years. For instance, the bones forming your skull grew together so slowly that a "soft spot" existed on the top of your head until you were about two years old.

A **joint** is a place where bones come together. Some bones are connected tightly at joints and do not move. The bones of your skull are this way. But most joints do allow movement.

Most of the parts of your body that move do so because of joints. For example, joints at your knee, wrist, and elbow allow you to move in different ways. Your body has five different kinds of joints—four kinds of joints that move and one that does not. The many movements that your bones and joints make possible keep you going strong.

▼ *Joints are located throughout the body's skeleton.*

Move It!

How does your body move?

What's your favorite sport? Are you the star of your neighborhood basketball games or terrific at tennis? Or is flipping a flying disk in the park with your dog just fine with you?

How can you perform all of the movements that different sports and activities demand? You know that your bones provide the framework and that your muscles do the work. Your joints—the places in your body where bones meet—are the connections that allow for movement. Different types of joints in the body allow for different types of movement. Whatever sport you like, it's your joints that help you move.

Take a look at how your body moves when you participate in different sports. What joints are called into action?

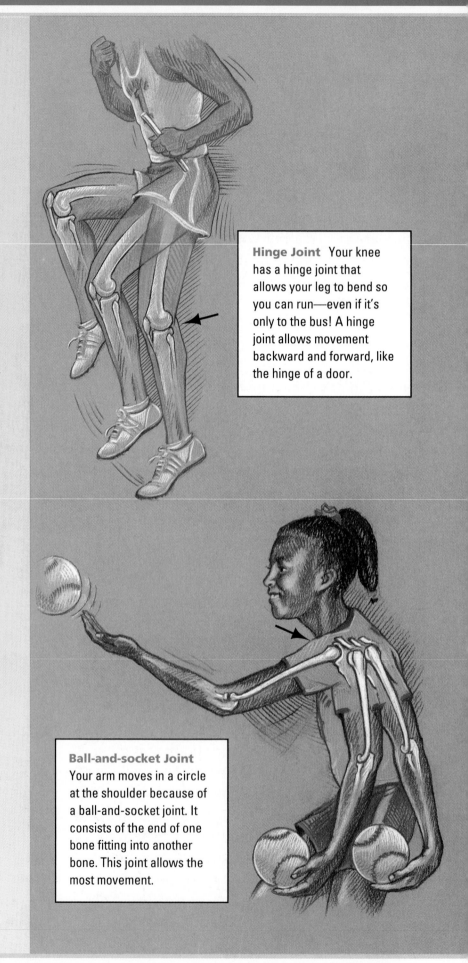

Hinge Joint Your knee has a hinge joint that allows your leg to bend so you can run—even if it's only to the bus! A hinge joint allows movement backward and forward, like the hinge of a door.

Ball-and-socket Joint Your arm moves in a circle at the shoulder because of a ball-and-socket joint. It consists of the end of one bone fitting into another bone. This joint allows the most movement.

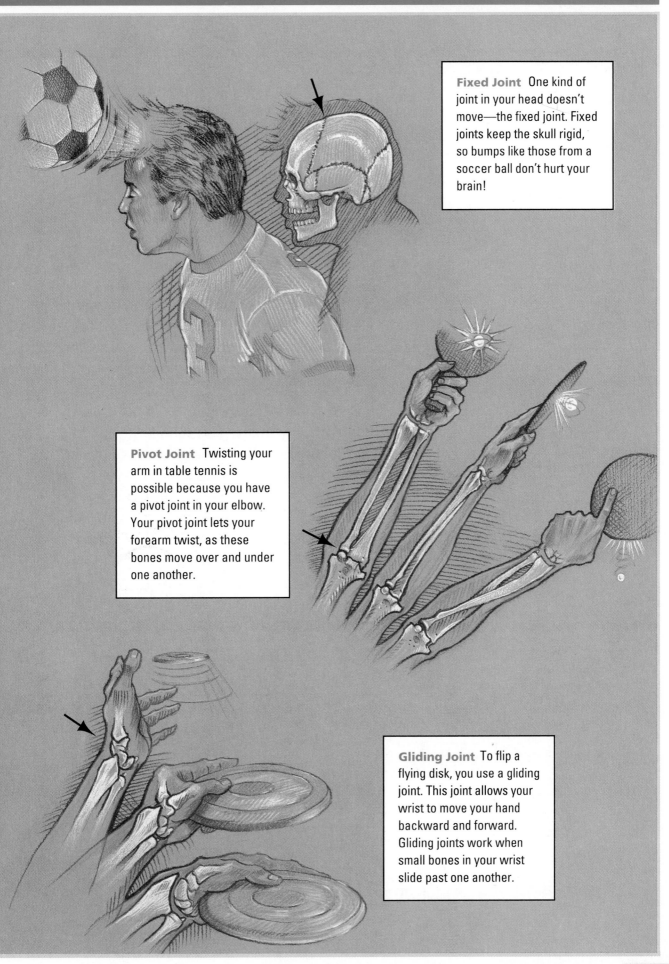

Fixed Joint One kind of joint in your head doesn't move—the fixed joint. Fixed joints keep the skull rigid, so bumps like those from a soccer ball don't hurt your brain!

Pivot Joint Twisting your arm in table tennis is possible because you have a pivot joint in your elbow. Your pivot joint lets your forearm twist, as these bones move over and under one another.

Gliding Joint To flip a flying disk, you use a gliding joint. This joint allows your wrist to move your hand backward and forward. Gliding joints work when small bones in your wrist slide past one another.

Inside Bones

How do your bones withstand the stress and strain of so much movement? Although bones might look solid from the outside, they're not. Bones not only give your body support and protection, they're also light enough to make your body easy to move.

If you cut open a human bone, it would look like the picture below. Notice the different layers of bone. The hard outer layer is made of living cells. Minerals such as calcium and phosphorus surround the cells, giving the bones their strength. Bones inside your body are covered by a thin membrane of soft tissue that protects the hard outer layer. This membrane also helps heal damaged bone tissue.

If your bones were completely solid, they would be heavy and hard to move. Underneath the hard outer layer of bone is the spongy layer—a layer of bone filled with tiny holes. The spongy layer of bone is hard, but it's called spongy because of its open structure. The holes in the spongy layer help make your bones lighter and easier to move.

Bone centers contain a hollow cavity. You can see such a cavity if you crack open the bone of a chicken leg. The cavity in human bones contains a special tissue called bone marrow. Blood vessels run through the marrow, carrying food and oxygen to bone cells and taking away waste.

▼ *The structure of bones helps them perform several functions.*

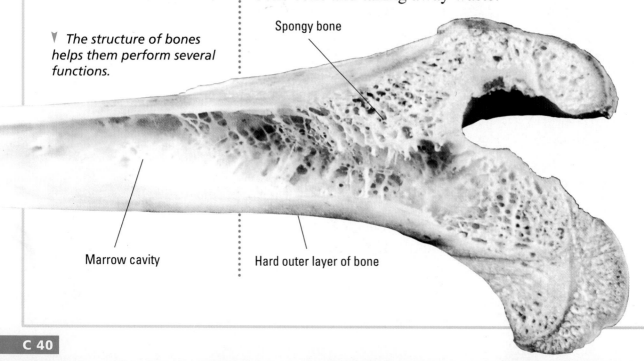

Spongy bone

Marrow cavity

Hard outer layer of bone

Your bones contain two types of marrow. Red marrow produces your blood cells. Yellow marrow is made of cells of fatty tissue that can be converted to energy when the body runs low on fuel.

Athletes such as the girl in the picture often jump as high and as far as they can. Why don't her bones break when she lands? Because her bones—and yours—are made to take just such a pounding.

Joints absorb much of the pounding when you jump, run, or fall. Again, cartilage aids your bones by helping to absorb shocks when bone pushes hard against bone. Find the cartilage in the diagram. Cartilage also reduces friction, letting bones slip against one another easily.

Ligaments (lig′ ə mənts) are tough strips of tissue that hold bones together at joints. Several ligaments hold together the bones in the knee. The ligaments allow joints to bend and turn, but they keep the joints from bending too far in the wrong direction.

Bones, ligaments, and cartilage make a great team. Strong but light. Tough but flexible. You're really put together!

Bone

Cartilage

Ligaments

▲ *Jumping and landing are cushioned by cartilage.*

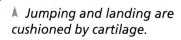

Checkpoint

1. What parts of your body are shaped by cartilage?
2. What kind of joint is important to a baseball pitcher? Why?
3. How are the holes in the spongy layer of bones important to your movement?
4. **Take Action!** Inspect the bones and joint of a chicken wing. Make a diagram of the ligaments and the structure of this joint.

Activity

How Fast Can You Respond?

Did anyone ever tell you that you have quick reflexes? Work in pairs in this activity to see how long it takes you to catch a falling meter stick.

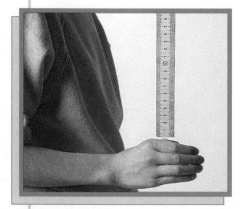

Picture A

Picture B

Picture C

Gather These Materials

meter stick

Follow This Procedure

1 Make a chart like the one on the next page. Record your observations in your chart.

2 Have your partner hold a meter stick vertically with the 0 centimeter mark at the bottom. Place your hand around the bottom of the meter stick without touching it. (Picture A)

3 Look at the meter stick—not at your partner. Your partner will get ready to drop the meter stick.

4 When your partner drops the meter stick, catch it as quickly as you can. Read the number of centimeters that the meter stick fell from above your hand. (Picture B)

5 Repeat step 4 two more times. Record your observations.

Predict: Do you think that your reaction time will improve each time?

6 Add together the distances and divide the total by 3 to get the average distance. Record your calculations.

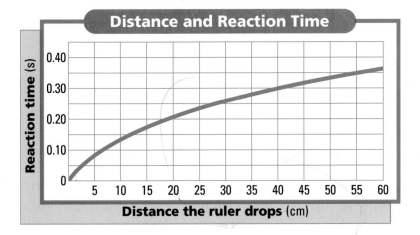

Distance and Reaction Time

Reaction time (s)

0.40
0.30
0.20
0.10
0

Distance the ruler drops (cm)

5 10 15 20 25 30 35 40 45 50 55 60

Record Your Results

	Reaction Distance
Trial 1	
Trial 2	
Trial 3	
Average distance	
Reaction time— see graph	

7 Look at the graph above. Find your average distance along the bottom of the graph. Then find that point along the curve. Trace a line with your finger over to the left side of the graph to find the reaction time in seconds.

8 Find out the reaction times of your classmates. Make a bar graph to show the number of students with each reaction time. (Picture C)

State Your Conclusions

1. What was your reaction time? What did your body have to do to react to the dropping meter stick? What force was at work pulling the meter stick downward?
2. Why do you think a graph was used to estimate reaction time and not a stopwatch?

Let's Experiment

Try this activity at some other time during the day. Is your average reaction time always the same? What factors might increase or decrease your reaction time? Use what you know about scientific methods to find out.

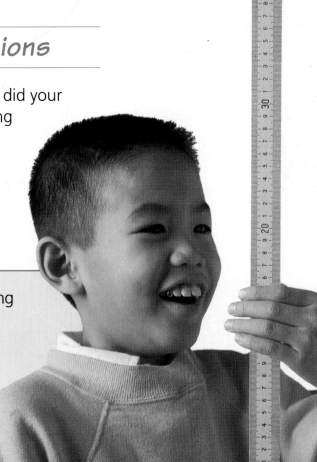

2.3 *It Takes Nerve*

▶ **What controls the movement of your body?**

Most movement starts with a decision: for example, "I want to jump rope." That's where your nervous system comes in. Your muscles move your bones to turn the jump rope. But first, your nervous system has to tell your arms, wrists, hands, and legs to move.

Nervous Energy

Your nervous system is made up of your brain, spinal cord, and nerves. It's the control system of your body. The central nervous system consists of the brain and the spinal cord. Your brain is in charge of those 72 kilometers of nerves that branch out from your brain and spinal cord. The nerves go to muscles in every part of your body—including those muscles needed to jump rope. Nerves are the pathways for messages between your brain and your muscles. These signals—called nerve impulses—are flashing around your body all the time at high speeds. Your body might seem to be on automatic, but lots of communication is going on.

Not all your moves are voluntary. A part of your nervous system called the autonomic nervous system controls involuntary processes such as breathing and digestion. Involuntary messages come from the lower-back part of the brain and move around the body without you having to think about them. These messages keep your body stable.

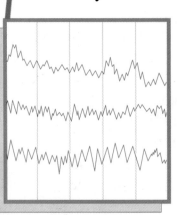

▼ *Nerve impulses are transmitted normally in a healthy nervous system, as indicated by the pattern shown.*

▲ *Hours of practice can improve your reaction rate.*

Waiting For A Reaction

You're playing volleyball. The score is close. You dive for the ball and make a save. This all takes place in about a second, but you *decided* to move your body. Your brain sent out a command that traveled through your nerves to your muscles. Then your muscles went into action.

One kind of movement doesn't require any thinking. It's a **reflex**—a movement that happens automatically. For example, when you exercise, your body uses too much oxygen. A reflex replaces this lost oxygen so your body returns to normal.

When you use too much oxygen, carbon dioxide builds up in your blood. The carbon dioxide enters nerve cells in your brain and causes messages to be sent to the muscles in your chest. These messages tell your chest and diaphragm muscles to work harder and faster. You breathe heavily, pull more oxygen into your lungs, and "catch your breath" after a while. All of this occurs without you having to think about it. It's why you can't hold your breath forever—a reflex tells your muscles to breathe!

Reflexes keep you safe. But quick voluntary reactions are handy too—especially in sports. Some sports and games improve reaction time more than others. Don't expect to improve your reaction rate playing board games. But sports like baseball, hockey, and volleyball need quickness. This volleyball player's movements may look like reflexes, but her reaction is due to practice.

Penny Practice

Can you catch a penny that you flip off of your elbow and improve with practice? Let's investigate.

What To Do
A. Bend your arm so that your hand rests on your shoulder. Make sure your arm is flat.
B. Place a penny on your elbow.
C. Quickly swing your elbow down and try to catch the penny in your hand.
D. Try to catch the penny ten different times. Record how many times you catch and miss the penny in a data table such as the one shown below.
E. Do three more trials of 10 attempts. Record how many times you catch and miss the penny in each trial.

Record Your Data

Trial	Misses	Catches
1		
2		
3		
4		

What Did You Find Out?
1. *Check your results. Did your actions improve with practice over several trials?*
2. *In this investigation, did you use voluntary muscles or involuntary muscles to flip the penny? Explain your answer.*

Teamwork and concentration help these girls to perform at their best.

Practice Makes Perfect

Many sports and games need quick reaction times. Jumping double dutch is one such sport. Through long hours of practice, teams develop routines that dazzle spectators. You might not start out a champ, but practice can make you a winner.

Why does practice make perfect? Remember that your nerves are specialized cells with long branches. These nerve cells carry impulses that pass messages from one part of your body to another. But the nerve cells don't touch one another. They're separated by tiny gaps called synapses. Chemicals move nerve impulses across the synapses.

Whenever you jump rope or kick a kickball as in the Discover Activity, you move the same way—and use the same nerve cells and synapses to carry messages to your muscles. Practice makes messages move across the synapses faster. So you spring into action more quickly with practice.

Some sports and games improve reaction time more than others. Sports such as soccer, four square, and footbag need speedy reactions. So lots of play makes you get better and better. Practice might not make perfect, but it can get you pretty close.

Destructive Drugs

Some decisions don't mean much. Should you have an apple or an orange for a snack? What difference does it make? However, some decisions can change your life.

Remember that practice and study can make you better at things—volleyball, multiplication tables, or playing the guitar. So a decision to practice is a good choice. But take a look at the decisions the two people below are thinking about. Are they making the right choice?

Maria wants to try out for the baseball team. She knows that she will be the only girl on the field, and the boys have been teasing her. She plays well, but she's very nervous and she wishes that she could feel more confident. Then Maria gets an idea. Why not try drinking some wine or beer to make her feel more in control?

Robert has a test tomorrow, but he has not read the book. He decides to stay up very late to study. Robert wonders whether he can get some pills to keep him awake.

Decisions involving drugs affect both physical and mental health. Drugs cause the nervous system to lose its ability to control both voluntary and involuntary processes. Jumping rope, taking a test, or even breathing can be a problem.

Maria and Robert are each making decisions about drugs. In both instances drugs seem like the easy answer to a problem. But answers that seem easy now could turn into trouble later. Drugs only fool your muscles and your nerves into feeling like a problem has gotten better. The feelings that drugs give do not last very long, but the damage they do to the body can last a lifetime.

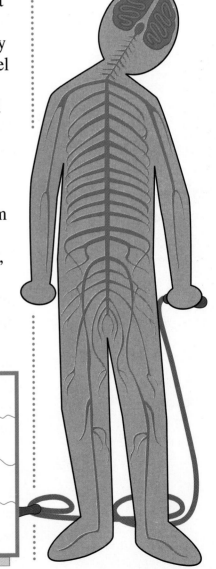

▼ Drug use affects the nervous system, as shown by the smaller peaks in this pattern of nerve impulses.

➤ *Playing the Northern Cheyenne wheel game requires concentration.*

▼ *You are a winner without drugs.*

Certain drugs are taken for health reasons. But some people take drugs just to change the way their nervous systems work. People who use drugs for this purpose are abusing drugs. Some abused drugs are prescription drugs, which are supposed to treat illnesses. Other abused drugs have no legal use.

Scientists put many drugs—both legal and illegal—into two groups: depressants and stimulants. Depressants—alcohol and other drugs such as tranquilizers—slow down the nervous system. That's why they seem to give a calming feeling. However, they slow down messages going from the brain or spinal cord to the muscles. Nerve impulses do not move through a drug user's body as fast as they should and the user's reaction rate drops. A drug user cannot react to situations that call for quick action. A person using depressants cannot concentrate either—not even enough to play simple games like these children.

Nerves also control involuntary processes. Depressants slow down the heart and lungs. Large amounts or doses can stop a user's body from working at all.

Stimulants such as cocaine, crack, and amphetamines have the opposite effect—they speed up the way the body works. Stimulants are dangerous because they strain the heart. At first, users are on a high. They talk a lot and feel full of energy. Then the rebound effect sets in. They crash from the high and become very tired and depressed. They want more of the drug.

All stimulants and depressants are addictive. The body gets used to the drug and develops a tolerance for it. Soon people who start taking drugs must take more and more to get the same feeling. The user's body now needs, or "depends on," the drug. Users feel sick if they don't get the drug. Addicted people find it hard to stop taking the drug—even if they want to.

Now think about Maria's and Robert's choices. It's clear that drugs are not the answer. Maria decides to talk about her problem with an adult that she trusts. Robert decides to study a little more, then get some sleep and continue reading in the morning. In what other ways would you suggest they solve their problems without drugs?

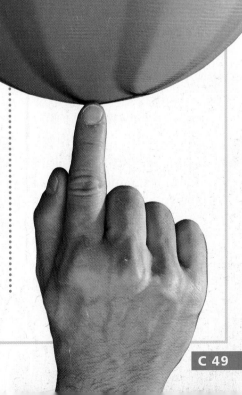

▼ *A decision not to use drugs is a smart one.*

Checkpoint

1. What organ controls your nervous system?
2. What reflex movement does your body exhibit when your hand touches something very hot?
3. How does doing something over and over improve your reaction time?
4. List some of the body's reactions to depressants and stimulants.
5. Take Action! Make a poster that tells of the dangers of drug use.

Analyzing Structure and Function

The parts of your body are adapted to do different jobs. For example, the structure of most joints allows certain types of movement. Their structures allow them to perform certain functions. Your teeth are another example of structure and function in your body. You have four kinds of teeth.

- Incisors: eight teeth in the front of the mouth—four on top, four on the bottom—with sharp, flattened edges.
- Canines: four large, sharp pointed teeth—two on top, two on the bottom—next to your incisors.
- Bicuspids or premolars: four teeth—two on top, two on the bottom—next to your canines. They have two parts, or cusps, and broad, irregular surfaces.
- Molars: the large teeth at the back of the jaw, with broad, irregular surfaces.

Thinking It Through

Why do you have so many types of teeth? Your teeth allow you to eat all kinds of foods. Each type of tooth has a certain function. Some of your teeth have similar functions to the teeth in each of the following kinds of animals.

1. Meat eaters like cats and dogs have long, sharp, canine teeth. Their teeth are used to kill prey and to tear flesh.

2. Rodents have large incisors that come together in a scissors action that can slice through food. The food then slides to the back of the mouth where it's ground up by broad molars.

3. Horses and many other plant eaters have large, flat molars for chewing and grinding tough grasses.

How do the structures of each animal's teeth aid in their functions? The structure allows the animal to eat the sort of food that the animal needs to survive.

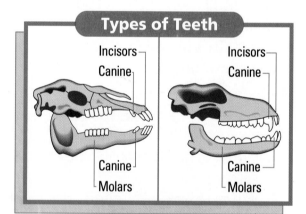

Types of Teeth

Incisors
Canine
Canine
Molars

Incisors
Canine
Canine
Molars

Your Turn

Think about how the animals above use each type of tooth. Use what you know about the structures and functions of their teeth to decide which pictured animal is a meat eater, and which eats grasses.

Chapter Review

Thinking Back

1. How might muscular pairs be compared to forces?
2. Compare **voluntary muscles** and **involuntary muscles.**
3. Why is **cartilage** considered part of the skeletal system?
4. Identify a place in your body where the bones cannot move. What causes this lack of motion?
5. How does the spongy inner layer of your bones aid in your movement?
6. How do bones, **tendons, joints, ligaments,** and muscles work together?
7. Explain how your nervous and muscular systems work together to help you regain your breath after exercising.
8. How does a **reflex** differ from a voluntary movement?

Connecting Ideas

1. Copy the concept map. Use the terms at the right to complete the map about body systems to show how you move.

bones   joints
ligaments   muscles

A. tendons — *connect* — B.

to

C. — *hold* — D. — *together at* — E.

2. Write a sentence or two about the ideas shown in the concept map.

Gathering Evidence

1. In the Activity on page 34, how did you predict the action of the foot when you pulled the string closest to the "toe"?
2. In the Activity on page 42, how did you predict improvement in your reaction time?

Doing Science!

1. *Develop a skit* that you could present to a group of first grade students which shows how muscles work in pairs.
2. *Design an experiment* to compare the reaction times of people of different ages.

Playing by the Rules

Discover Activity

How can you make a piece of paper fall more slowly?

Drop a 15 x 15-centimeter sheet of paper from above your head. How long does it take to touch the floor? Now change this paper so that it falls more slowly when dropped from the same height. You can cut, bend, or fold the paper, but you must use the entire sheet.

For Discussion

1. *What design keeps the paper afloat longest?*

2. *How can you make the paper fall very fast?*

3.1 *Rules of the Game*

When you're moving, why do you stop?

Wouldn't it be great if one leap could send you flying over a 6-meter fence? How would you like to throw a ball that would travel for kilometers? Imagine riding your bike all through town—and never having to pedal at all.

Sure, it would be nice. But Newton's Laws of Motion won't let you move like this. Balls, bikes, and all the parts of your body move according to certain rules. And you can't play unless you follow the rules of the game.

Types of Friction

It's going to be close—the throw is coming in fast. So you flop down to slide the last few feet. Your foot touches a corner of the base as you skid to a stop. Why didn't you slide all the way across the field? Friction brought you to a halt.

◄ *Friction brings this runner quickly to a stop.*

Two kinds of friction are sliding friction and rolling friction. Pushing a box can help explain how they work. Suppose you put the box on a concrete floor. Then you put a friend inside and push. Unless you have a lot of strength, not much happens. You're working against sliding friction. Sliding friction results when two solid surfaces slide across one another. Friction depends on the weight of the object doing the sliding and the surface it slides on. A heavier friend is harder to push than a light one— greater weight means more friction. And it's harder to push a box over a rough floor than a smooth one.

How could you make the box easier to push? You might add wheels. That would replace sliding friction with rolling friction. Rolling friction occurs when a round object rolls over a surface. Rolling friction opposes motion less than sliding friction. That's why you can push a car, which weighs far more than your friend in the box.

A substance on the surface where two objects meet can change the amount of friction. Notice that as the blades of the ice skates press into the ice, the pressure melts a thin layer of ice. So the skates glide on a thin layer of water. This reduces friction.

▼ *Olympic speed skater Bonnie Blair's skate blade glides along the ice on a thin layer of water.*

Friction

Pressure

Skate glides on water └Blade melts ice

In the Discover Activity, you saw that friction with the air opposes the motion of some objects, such as a piece of paper. A kickball slows down when traveling through the air because the ball pushes against particles in the air and the air particles push back. This type of friction is called **air resistance** (ri zis′təns)—the opposition to movement caused by air particles.

Engineers streamline objects to reduce air resistance. Streamlining is the rounding of the surfaces of objects—getting rid of parts that stick out, catch the air, and slow an object down. Air slips more easily over streamlined surfaces. That's why planes, race cars, and this bouncing ball are all rounded—to reduce air resistance.

Sport racers use streamlined equipment, too. The helmets of bike racers are streamlined. So are the wraparound poles some skiers use. People who race on bikes and skis streamline their bodies, too. They pull their arms and legs close in, tucking their heads down between their shoulders.

Force of Gravity

When you drop a ball, it falls toward the earth because the earth is pulling on it with a gravitational force. But the ball also is pulling on the earth with an equal gravitational force. Why does the same size force cause a ball to move but not the earth? Consider the masses of the earth and ball. The earth doesn't move toward the ball because the earth is so massive. However, the less massive ball does move. It accelerates toward the earth.

Earth's gravity determines your weight. An object's weight is the amount of force that gravity exerts on its mass.

◄ *The round shape of a ball allows it to move easily through the air.*

What do you think would happen to your weight if you went to a world with a different size and mass than the earth's? Your weight would change because the pull of gravity would be different. For example, the pull of gravity between you and the moon isn't nearly as strong as between you and the earth, because the moon is smaller and less massive. So you would weigh only one-sixth of your earth weight on the moon. Remember that your mass—the amount of matter that you contain—doesn't vary from place to place. But your weight changes as gravity changes.

Suppose you went to a place such as the huge planet Jupiter. What would happen to your weight there? You would weigh more on Jupiter than you do on Earth, because Jupiter is far bigger and more massive than Earth is. The attraction between you and Jupiter would cause you to weigh over twice as much.

The gravitational attraction between the earth and objects on the earth's surface is strong. Gravity keeps objects near the earth's surface, although they can go up into the air. That's why the different balls you see here go up and then fall back to the ground.

▼ *Because of gravity, all three balls have the same acceleration.*

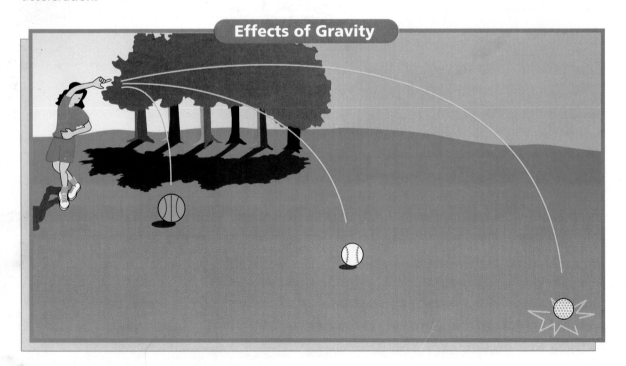

Effects of Gravity

Of course, some objects do escape the earth's gravitational attraction. Rockets that go into space and break free from the earth's pull must reach a velocity of 40,000 kilometers per hour. Any rocket that does not reach that velocity will fall back to the earth.

What would happen if gravitational attraction on the earth's surface was reduced? Balls would zoom into the air. Maybe they would never return. Perhaps you could leap over tall buildings. Many things that you never thought possible might occur. The rules of motion would not change, but the effects might!

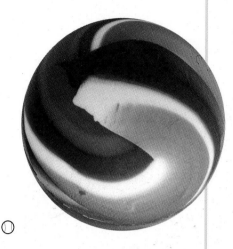

No Gravity

◄ If there were no gravity on the earth, a moving ball would keep on going!

Checkpoint

1. What kind of friction does a ball meet when it is thrown?
2. How would your weight change on the surface of Mars, a planet with less than half of the surface gravity of Earth?
3. Take Action! Design several paper airplanes. Experiment to see which will stay in the air for the longest amount of time.

Activity

Pull Out
The Stops

Cars are designed to reduce air resistance. Do this activity to see why cars are streamlined.

Picture A

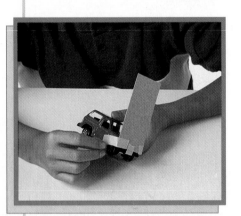

Picture B

Picture C

Gather These Materials

scissors	masking tape
shoe box lid	piece of cardboard
ruler	shoe box
model car	meter stick

Follow This Procedure

1 Make a chart like the one on the next page. Record your observations in your chart.

2 Use the scissors to carefully cut two slots opposite one another near one end of the shoe box lid. The slots will hold the ruler to act as a "starting gate" for your race car. Place your slots so a car fits in back of the starting gate. (Picture A)

3 Use the scissors to carefully cut one edge off the other end of the shoe box lid.

4 Place a piece of cardboard in front of your car. Tape it with masking tape. The cardboard can be as high as the car is long. (Picture B)

Predict: *What will happen to the air resistance when you add the cardboard?*

5 Turn the shoe box upside down. Place the shoe box lid against it to form a ramp. Put the ruler through the slots and place the model car behind it. (Picture C)

6 Make sure that the area in front of the ramp is clear. Then quickly remove the ruler and watch your car roll down the ramp. Mark how far it travels with a piece of masking tape.

7 Fold the cardboard back down onto the car roof. Repeat steps 5 and 6.

Predict: *How far will the car travel after you adjust the cardboard?*

8 Use a meter stick to compare the distance traveled each time.

Distance traveled	
with cardboard	
without cardboard	

State Your Conclusions

1. How did the cardboard affect the distance traveled by the car?

2. Make a side-view sketch of the front end of a car that you like. How does car design cut down the amount of air resistance?

3. Some race cars have no brakes. Instead they stop with a big parachute that inflates at the end of the race. How would that stop the car?

Let's Experiment

Now that you have discovered how air resistance affects distance, use what you know about scientific methods to find out how air resistance affects speed. Repeat the experiment using a stopwatch. Record the amount of time it takes for your car to travel to a point marked on the floor. Calculate the average speed for each trial.

3.2 *Moving Through Space*

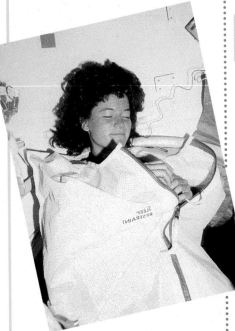

How is motion different in space?

It's breakfast time. The menu is nothing special: chunks of dry cereal and orange juice. You start with the cereal. You don't need a bowl—the little chunks float in front of you. You pluck the chunks of cereal out of the air one by one and pop them into your mouth.

You're ready to wash down your cereal with juice. You stick your straw into a big orange ball of juice that floats in front of you. The ball gets smaller as you drink, until it disappears.

Breakfast was never like this on the earth, because gravity always holds people and objects in place. But go into orbit around the earth like these astronauts, and your spacecraft would become a weightless environment. You would not see or feel many of the effects of gravity.

➤ *Away from the earth, astronauts enjoy a weightless environment.*

▲ *Liquids such as water move differently in space.*

Weightlessness

In space, it's hard to tell up from down because everything just floats. The reason is weightlessness. **Weightlessness** is a condition in which there is no pull of gravity—or the pull is so small that its effects aren't noticeable. Gravity holds things down to the earth's surface. As you move away from the earth, gravity's pull gets weaker. Objects in deep space become almost weightless, so they float.

The space shuttle astronauts experience weightlessness for a different reason, as you will see. They learn that objects do not act the same way as they do on the earth. Things that weigh a lot on the earth are suddenly easy to move. It's a snap for you to do a triple flip in the air as you cross a room.

NASA is learning more about the effects of weightlessness on people. A trip to the moon is short, only taking about three days. But trips to other planets will take much longer. Mars astronauts may have to make a nine-month journey. Shuttle trips and stays in orbiting space stations tell doctors how weightlessness affects the body.

These space journeys proved that weightlessness does things to the body. Muscles get weaker since they do so little work. The body also stretches a little because weight doesn't squeeze it down.

People are suited to living with weight. In deep space, people will have to survive with very little gravity and weight.

Planetary Pull

Weight and mass differ. Weight measures the pull of gravity between objects. Mass is the amount of matter in an object.

You're used to measuring your weight in pounds. But scientists measure weight in newtons. One newton is a little less than a quarter pound. The chart shows the pull of gravity on other planets in the solar system.

Your weight on Jupiter differs from that on Earth because Jupiter's pull of gravity is greater than that of Earth. So your weight on Jupiter is 2.54 times your weight on Earth.

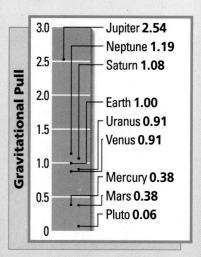

Gravitational Pull	
3.0	Jupiter **2.54**
	Neptune **1.19**
2.5	Saturn **1.08**
2.0	
	Earth **1.00**
1.5	Uranus **0.91**
	Venus **0.91**
1.0	
	Mercury **0.38**
0.5	Mars **0.38**
	Pluto **0.06**
0	

What Did You Find Out?
1. *How would the mass of your body change if you traveled to Neptune?*
2. *How would the weight of your body change if you traveled to Pluto?*
3. *Calculate your weight on the surface of Mars.*

Going Into Orbit

A **satellite** (sat′l īt) is an object that revolves around another object. For example, the moon is a natural satellite of the earth. Hundreds of artificial satellites, or those made by people, also orbit above the earth each day. They record the weather, relay phone calls, and track pollution. Some are just a few hundred kilometers up, while others are more than 35,000 kilometers above the earth.

To keep a satellite in space, it has to move forward at thousands of kilometers per hour. But if it moves too fast, it could shoot off into space. If it moves too slowly, the earth's gravitational attraction will pull it down toward the ground. It also has to be up high enough above the earth's surface. If a satellite is less than 300 kilometers above the earth, air resistance will slow the satellite allowing gravity to drag it through the atmosphere toward the earth.

Satellites must travel a certain speed at a certain distance from the earth to maintain orbit.

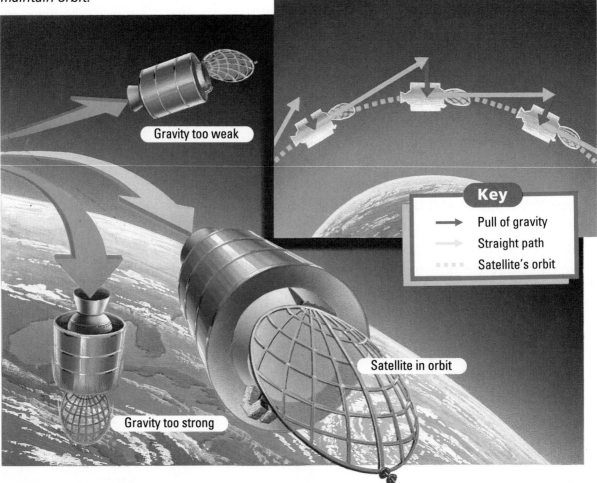

Gravity too weak

Gravity too strong

Satellite in orbit

Key

→ Pull of gravity
→ Straight path
▪▪▪▪ Satellite's orbit

Space engineers plan a satellite's orbit carefully. A satellite's **orbit** is the path it follows as it circles the earth. Satellites must travel forward fast enough to overcome the earth's downward pull. But the diagram shows that the earth's pull still acts on them. Satellites drop a certain distance toward the earth for every kilometer they travel. But the curved earth drops away under satellites the same distance. So the satellites are always falling around the earth. But they never hit the ground—they always stay above the earth in orbit.

The "free fall" of a satellite produces the weightlessness shuttle astronauts experience. This is different than the cause of weightlessness in deep space. In deep space, very little gravity pulls on objects. No nearby planet causes any gravitational attraction.

The shuttle does not go into deep space. It orbits about 320 kilometers above the earth. That is not far enough to decrease the pull of the the earth's gravity much. Astronauts and objects aboard the shuttle are always falling toward the earth with the shuttle. In the shuttle, people and objects don't press down on the bottom of the spacecraft at all, making them seem weightless.

Some satellites are released into orbit from the space shuttle. Astronauts can even intercept and repair orbiting satellites. Someday you may feel weightlessness as you work aboard the shuttle!

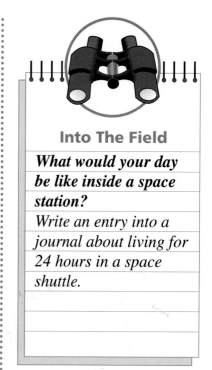

Into The Field

What would your day be like inside a space station?

Write an entry into a journal about living for 24 hours in a space shuttle.

Checkpoint

1. Why are objects weightless in space?
2. How is the weightlessness experienced in the space shuttle different from the weightlessness in deep space?
3. Take Action! Attach a paper clip to a piece of string and twirl it so that it wraps around your finger. How is this like a satellite traveling too slow?

Activity

Balloon Blast Off

Action forces and reaction forces can make a balloon move. Try this activity to see how a balloon can move like a rocket.

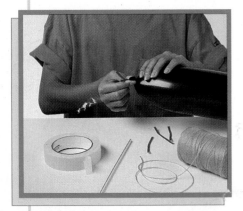

Picture A

Picture B

Picture C

Gather These Materials

cover goggles
long, narrow balloon
twist tie
masking tape

drinking straw
10 meters of string
2 chairs

Follow This Procedure

1 Make a chart like the one on the next page. Record your observations in your chart.

2 Put on your cover goggles.

3 Blow up a long, narrow balloon. Carefully use a twist tie to keep it closed. (Picture A)

4 Use masking tape to attach a drinking straw along the length of the balloon. (Picture B)

5 Thread the free end of the string through the straw attached to the balloon. (Picture C) Measure and cut 10 meters of the string.

6 Tie the free ends of the string to the backs of the two chairs. Separate the two chairs as much as possible.

Predict: *How far will the balloon travel between the two chairs?*

7 At one end of the string, untwist the twist tie, hold the mouth of the balloon closed, and then let the balloon go.

State Your Conclusions

1. How far did your balloon rocket go?

2. On a piece of paper, draw an arrow to show air escaping from your balloon rocket. Draw another arrow to show the direction that the balloon moves. How are these two directions related?

3. What are some of the factors that stopped your balloon from going farther?

Diagram of balloon rocket motion

Let's Experiment

Now that you have seen how to power a balloon rocket, what can you do to make your balloon travel faster or farther? Use what you know about scientific methods to find out. Experiment with the location of the chairs and the shape and size of your balloon.

3.3 *Space Games*

▶ *Does anybody live out in space?*

Humans have made short trips into space. Astronauts visited the earth's nearest neighbor, the moon. They did not find any living things there, but they did find that movement on the moon is very different than movement on the earth. Although the laws of motion still apply, having fun on the moon is a whole new ballgame.

All-Star In Space

Astronauts like to explore space, and they have fun while doing so. One Apollo astronaut packed a golf club with his gear when he went on a mission to the moon. He bounded around the moon's surface collecting samples for a while. Then he set up his golf ball and gave it a good whack. The ball sailed farther and higher than any earth golf ball ever had. Playing on the moon is full of surprises like that.

You're familiar with the effects of gravity here on the earth—when you throw a ball up in the air, it comes back down to the ground. But what would happen if you went to a place like the moon? Gravitational attraction on the moon isn't as strong as gravity on the earth because of the moon's smaller mass. Your weight is less on the moon, and the weight of other objects—such as a kickball—is less too. So the rules of games on the moon might be very different—and a whole lot more fun!

▼ *Movement on the moon is different than movement on the earth.*

Imagine running and jumping on the moon. With each step you would bound up into the air. If you tried to jump, you could jump about six times as high as you could on the earth. How high can you leap to shoot a basketball—less than a meter? You could leap perhaps two meters on the moon. That would make slam dunking a basketball easier—even for the shortest person on the team.

Hitting and throwing would also be easier on the moon. Think back to that astronaut and his golf ball. You could throw a ball or a flying disk great distances. Every football player would be able to pass like a professional quarterback. Each hitter in baseball could slam the ball over the fence like an all-star slugger.

Gymnasts would do great tumbles and flips. Weightlifters could lift weights that would be impossible here on the earth.

Of course, problems might arise if everyone hit the baseball out of the park. Because of less gravitational force and no friction from air resistance, you might need to have a much bigger ballfield on the moon than on the earth.

Space Kids

Would you like to jump on the space shuttle for a trip to the moon?

You can't do that just yet, but you can prepare for the trip at U.S. Space Camp® in Huntsville, Alabama. Children your age go through a one-week training camp using the same equipment astronauts use to train for space travel.

First, campers get used to the feeling of floating in a swimming pool. There they might build a frame structure to help them get used to the effects of weightlessness. Also, campers use space-age rocking chairs to give them the sensation of being turned this way and that in a spacecraft. Sometimes you don't know which end is up!

The trip is worth the discomfort, though, when campers get to hop on the moon-walk trainer. Their own space mission may be only one small step away!

Model Rockets
All of the trainees at Space Camp build and fire a simple rocket when they first arrive. This teaches them some of the basic principles of rocket flight. Model rocketry is a popular hobby with campers and other children across the country.

5DF Chair
The 5DF chair's name stands for "five degrees of freedom of movement." It moves up and down, side to side, sideways, around like a top, and over and over.

SPACE SHUTTLE

Mission Control

Campers take part in a simulated space mission. Students divide into two teams. While one team acts as the flight crew, the other group takes the job of Mission Control. Mission Control is in charge of making sure all of the systems are in order.

Moon-walk Trainer

Campers feel the same lack of gravity the astronauts felt when they stepped onto the surface of the moon. At only one-sixth their normal weight, they feel almost as though they're flying!

Space Playground

Chances are you will not be living in space anytime soon. But someday people might live in space settlements. They might be on the moon or on Mars. Whole families would live there, including children like yourself. And those children would want to play many of the games played now on the earth. In what ways would playground games be different on the moon, where gravity isn't as strong as on the earth?

Imagine a game of space kickball on the moon. What would be different about the rules? Perhaps the bases would be a greater distance apart, because the ball would travel so much farther on the moon. Remember that the moon is much colder and has no atmosphere, so if children were playing outdoors they would need to play in spacesuits. Maybe they would wear small jet packs on the backs of their suits. They would turn on the jets to move around the playground.

Imagine the start of a kickball game. The ball might sail high into the air when kicked. If the fielders had a hard time keeping up with the kickball they might fire up their jet packs and zoom around the field to catch it. The kicker would also fire her jet pack as soon as the ball was kicked and fly up the line toward first base. The fielders might have to tag out the runners with the ball because throwing the ball the right distance to a base might be hard to do. So games of kickball might have higher scores and lots more action. That would make the kickball and the other games you play at lunch and recess a lot more interesting!

I'M KICKING IT ALL THE WAY TO EARTH!

Double dutch jump rope would be different on the moon, too. Since people can jump higher on the moon than on the earth, the jump rope would have to be much longer, to make bigger loops. Jumpers might wear jet packs to help them do tricky maneuvers.

These moves are possible on bodies in space with less gravity than on the earth. But what about planets with more gravity? Jupiter is such a planet. It's not likely that people will ever live on Jupiter. Imagine how games would change in a place like Jupiter. Would it be as fun as floating on the moon?

Think back to the space kickball game. The kickball on Jupiter would be heavier than on Earth. It would be harder to kick as far as you can kick it on Earth. Kicking a fly ball would be difficult—forget about long home runs. The force of gravity would hold most balls on the planet's surface. Because of gravity, throwing the ball in the air would be hard. People might roll the ball from base to base.

Different amounts of gravitational force change how you have fun. With a few rule changes, games on the moon might be more fun than they are on the earth. How might you want to change the rules of your favorite sport? Think of all the new ways you might play soccer, volleyball, and stoopball—making up the rules would really be fun!

Checkpoint

1. Why would slam dunking a basketball be easier on the moon?
2. What are two ways that campers at Space Camp get used to the feeling of weightlessness?
3. What would be the effect of more gravity on a sport such as running?
4. **Take Action!** Design a new game to be played in a place with either stronger or weaker gravity.

Analyzing Diagrams

Suppose you're a swimming coach. One of the members of your team asks for your advice in increasing his swimming speed. You know that you can apply scientific principles to help him swim faster. You decide to analyze how he swims and compare it to how faster swimmers swim. One way to analyze data is to interpret diagrams.

Thinking It Through

You know that one way to increase speed is to reduce friction on the body. Swimmers can swim faster if they have a more streamlined body shape, like that of a dolphin or a fast car. Streamlining also reduces drag—the disturbance of air or water caused by motion that slows the body down. Of course, swimmers can't do much to change the shape of their bodies. But they can change the position of their bodies in the water. We can't "see" friction or drag. The best way to study these effects is in a diagram.

Study the two diagrams at the top of the next column. Notice the friction and drag caused by the body of each swimmer. You think that by changing the position of his body, your swimmer can reduce the effects of forward resistance, skin friction, and drag.

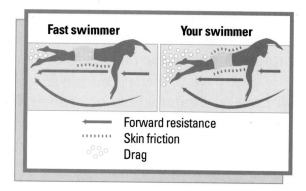

What advice would you give your swimmer? Notice that if he keeps his head down and his legs up, he reduces forward resistance, skin friction, and drag. His body is then in a more streamlined position. He is able to move through the water more quickly.

Your Turn

Look at the picture below. Tell which swimmer's position best reduces the problems of forward resistance, skin friction, and drag. Explain why.

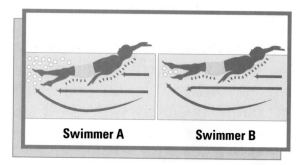

Swimmer A   Swimmer B

Chapter Review

Thinking Back

1. Which would be easier to push along a concrete sidewalk—a wheelbarrow filled with bricks or a cardboard box with an equal number of bricks? Explain why.
2. How can **air resistance** be reduced?
3. Explain how **weightlessness** can affect an astronaut's body.
4. Describe the relationship between a **satellite** and an **orbit.**

5. What determines your weight?
6. What would happen to a satellite that was traveling too close to the earth?
7. Would a football kickoff travel a greater distance on the moon or the earth?
8. How does Space Camp model the training of astronauts?
9. Why would it be more difficult to play a game of baseball on Jupiter?

Connecting Ideas

1. Copy the concept map. Use the terms at the right to complete the map about forces that affect movement.

air resistance   **rolling**
motion   **sliding**

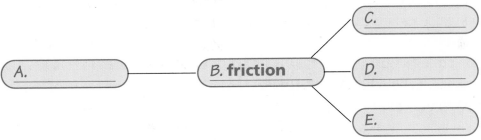

2. Write a sentence or two about the ideas shown in the concept map.

Gathering Evidence

1. In the Activity on page 58, how did you predict how the cardboard would affect the car?
2. In the Activity on page 64, what led you to conclude that air escaping from the balloon exerted a force?

Doing Science!

1. **Design an invention** to add to your bicycle that uses air resistance to stop the machine instead of hand brakes.
2. **Develop a skit** that shows a basketball game on Jupiter.

Run, Don't Walk

Learning to turn a problem into a strength is an important part of growing up. Just ask twelve-year-old Sarah East of Anadarko, Oklahoma. Sarah was born with only one complete leg. This disability might have held a lot of kids back. But Sarah has found a way to help other people who have lost a leg. She does this by testing leg prostheses (pros thē′ sēz), or artificial body parts, for John Sabolich, a researcher in Oklahoma City.

Sarah's left leg stops above the knee. Sabolich fitted her with her first prosthesis when she was a baby. Learning to use two legs early in her life helped Sarah become more active and confident.

Not too long ago, no prosthesis existed that could help people without knees run normally. It was too difficult to make an artificial knee joint and foot that worked like natural ones. Sarah helped Sabolich find a way to fix that. As Sarah's friend

"I want people to know that someone with an artificial leg can do the same things everyone else can do."

Sabolich explains, "When Sarah was 3 or 4 years old, she told me that she wanted to run. I said she wouldn't be able to do that. She replied, 'I could, if you would make something so I could.' "

Testing Technology

Sabolich went to work on a better prosthesis. Sarah tested his ideas and reported to him about how well each leg worked. At last he came up with what is now called the *Oklahoma City running leg.* This is a lightweight leg made of plastics and other space-age materials. The flexible socket fits comfortably against what remains of the person's own leg. Using this leg, Sarah became the first person without a knee to run like other kids.

Sarah continues to test prostheses for Sabolich. One new prosthesis she is testing has a *Sense of Feel.* Wires and a transmitter send signals from the foot of the prosthesis to the wearer's skin.

These signals let the wearer "feel" the ground. The wearer gets a better sense of where the foot is in relation to the ground. This feeling also helps the wearer balance better while walking. If the Sense of Feel technique works out, it will also be used in artificial hands. Someday, inventors may even come up with prostheses that can "feel" both heat and cold!

This year, Sarah played her first season of basketball on a team in Anadarko's basketball league. As she says, "I want people to know that someone with an artificial leg can do the same things everyone else can do."

On Your Own

1. How does Sarah help John Sabolich build better prostheses?
2. How does the Sense of Feel help a person such as Sarah?
3. What are some ways that the Sense of Feel might be used in the future?
4. Pretend you are a researcher who designs prostheses. List some of the features that you might try to include in your designs for improved prostheses. Make a drawing of your design, labeling each feature.

The Wellness Center

Caroline San Juan

Occupation: Director of wellness center
Hobbies: Jogging, teaching aerobics, playing piano, reading, learning Spanish

When Caroline was growing up, she wished her grandparents could've been healthier than they were. That wish spurred her on to her future career. "Wouldn't it be so much better," she thought, "to keep people from getting sick, rather than trying to make them well again?" Then she found out about exercise physiology, which helps people keep their bodies in shape so that they stay fit and well. Today Caroline San Juan is the director of a wellness center.

What's a wellness center?

"It's several things in one. People come here to exercise together, to learn about a good diet, and to get help stopping habits that are not healthy."

Which habits should people stop?

"One of the habits that's especially bad is smoking. When your grandparents were children, people didn't know how bad smoking was. Now everyone knows it's bad, but habits can be hard to break."

Are there good habits too?

"People can get in the habit of exercising and eating foods that are good for them. You just have to eat the foods your body needs. And you don't have to be an athlete, or even be good at sports. But you do need exercise—playing outside, riding a bike—anything that keeps you active."

What happens if you don't eat right and exercise?

"You just won't feel as well as you could. A child who lies around watching TV is likely to grow into an adult who lies around in front of the TV. And then that adult may no longer be able to do much else. That adult is also more likely to have a heart attack or to have diabetes.

"Think about it—it's not fun to be sick. And you have a choice—you can do your best and be your best."

Autopilot: Using Inertia

Imagine an aircraft flying without a pilot! When an aircraft flies on autopilot, the aircraft keeps moving in the same direction at the same altitude—and inertia is responsible for this action.

4 Simple accelerometers detect and measure movement, sending signals to the controls of the aircraft to correct its course.

5 Three different accelerometers detect changes in motion in all directions—side to side, up and down, and changes in forward acceleration.

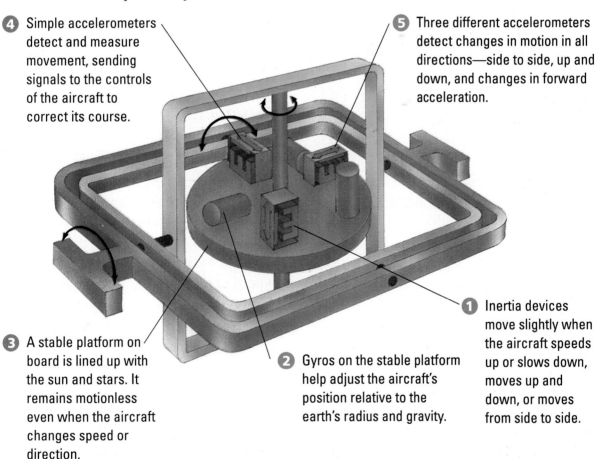

1 Inertia devices move slightly when the aircraft speeds up or slows down, moves up and down, or moves from side to side.

3 A stable platform on board is lined up with the sun and stars. It remains motionless even when the aircraft changes speed or direction.

2 Gyros on the stable platform help adjust the aircraft's position relative to the earth's radius and gravity.

Find Out On Your Own

Use encyclopedias or do other research to find out about the flight-path control system used to guide the space shuttle into orbit and to bring it back to the earth after a mission in space.

Module Review

Making Connections

Systems and Interactions

1. Explain how gravity and air resistance could be helpful to an aircraft coming in for a landing.
2. Use the Third Law of Motion to explain why a ball thrown in a downward direction bounces back in an upward direction.

Scale and Structure

3. Describe how the structure of your bones helps your skeletal system do its job.
4. Suppose the structure of a muscle was rigid and inflexible. What effect would this have on the ability of the muscular system to do its jobs?

Using What I Learned

Comparing

1. Explain why you could throw a football a greater distance on the moon than on the earth.
2. Explain why you can move the muscles in your toes but not the muscles in your stomach.

Applying

3. How is the action of muscles similar to forces in the Third Law of Motion?
4. Use the Second Law of Motion to explain what is occurring in the diagram.

Ordering

5. Suppose you were able to visit Jupiter, Mercury, and Venus. Would your weight be the same on these planets as it is on Earth? Order the planets from the planet where your weight would be the greatest to the planet where your weight would be the least. Include Earth in your list.

Relating

6. Describe the relationship that exists between the nervous, muscular, and skeletal systems.

Categorizing

7. What characteristics could you use to classify a muscle as either voluntary or involuntary?

Communicating

8. Diagram the relationship between a satellite and its orbit around the earth.
9. Act out the motions of a kickball game. Identify the three laws of motion whenever they control the motions you display.

Applying What I Learned

Performance Task

Use a book, ruler, model car, roll of pennies, and tape to show the relationship between mass, the force of gravity, and acceleration.

Drawing

Suppose you drop a bowling ball and a basketball from a second-story window. Make a drawing to show what will happen when the balls strike the sidewalk below.

Science Theater

Prepare a skit that pantomimes several activities that require a quick reaction rate. Perform the skit for your classmates. Have them guess what activities are being portrayed and tell why quick reaction rates are important.

Exhibitions

Make a poster or bulletin board illustrating each of the laws of motion. Include pictures that show everyday actions. Label them to show which law of motion is shown by each action.

What If

What if an acquaintance encouraged you to take a depressant such as alcohol? List reasons why you should decline the offer and write possible responses.

Running on Sunlight

Running on Sunlight

The sun never sets on the world of solar energy. All across the earth, producers store the sun's energy and convert it into forms that consumers can use. Now people are trying to harness the sun as well. In this module, you'll follow solar energy as it lights fires, powers machines, and feeds the earth.

CHAPTER

1 Energize!

Do you have the potential to be kinetic? Every time you move, you convert potential energy into kinetic energy. Welcome to the club.

CHAPTER

2 Solar Energy

The sun is the wave of the future! Waves of energy from the sun may soon provide the earth with all the electricity it needs.

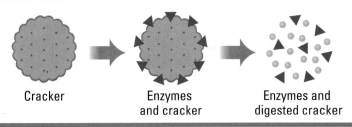

Cracker

Enzymes and cracker

Enzymes and digested cracker

3 Using Sunshine

You know that you can't eat sunshine. But without sunshine, you wouldn't have anything to eat!

Energize!

Cool!
I didn't touch the water!
It moved all by itself.

How much water can sunlight move in a day?

Half fill a tall bowl with water. Put a stone in a short cup. Place the cup in the center of the bowl. The top of the cup must be lower than the top of the bowl. Cover the bowl with plastic wrap and place a stone in the center of the cover directly over the cup. Move the bowl to a warm sunny place. Observe what happens for one day.

For Discussion

1. *What happens to the water in the bowl?*

2. *Devise a way to make more water move into the cup in the same amount of time.*

1.1 *Work and Energy*

What is energy?

"It's so hot I could fry an egg on the sidewalk!"
John mutters, his face dripping. "Time for a rest."
He settles under a tree and wonders, "Why does
playing in the sun always make me so hot?"

Energy from the Sun

You feel hot when you play in the sun because
energy from the sun—sunlight—makes the atoms in
your body move faster and faster. Sunlight also
supplies most of the energy used on the earth.

But what is energy? To a scientist, **energy** is the
ability to do work or to change matter. Sunlight does
work in many ways. For example, it heats air that,
in turn, causes winds to blow. Sunlight also changes
matter, as was done in the Discover Activity. The
same energy that makes you hot can
turn an ice cube into a pool
of water or even melt
glaciers.

▼ *Hot! Hot! Hot! The sun's
waves beat down with
tremendous energy!*

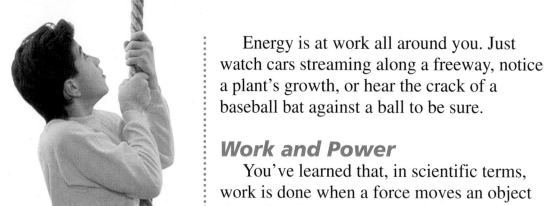

Energy is at work all around you. Just watch cars streaming along a freeway, notice a plant's growth, or hear the crack of a baseball bat against a ball to be sure.

Work and Power

You've learned that, in scientific terms, work is done when a force moves an object through a distance—in the direction of the force. You also might have figured out that work can't be done without using energy.

Look at Julio and Josh climbing ropes. Energy released from the food they've eaten is stored in their bodies. As they pull themselves up the rope, this energy changes into motion. The energy change produces the work. The "objects" are Julio and Josh and the "distance" is the length of the rope.

Energy and work are very closely related. In fact, scientists measure the change in energy by measuring the amount of work done. Scientists use the same unit of measurement for energy and work—the joule (jül). One joule is a very small amount of energy or work. You'd use about nine joules of energy to lift the average textbook one meter above your desk.

Now imagine that you're standing in the gym with Julio and Josh. Your classmates' shouts echo all around, but you ignore the noise. You have a job to do. Taking a stopwatch from your pocket you shout, "Ready, set, go!"

Your job is to measure Julio's and Josh's **power,** or the rate at which work is done. For Julio or Josh, the rate at which work is done means how long it takes to go up the rope.

▲ *Julio and Josh change energy into motion.*

Josh smiles when you tell him that he climbed the rope in twelve seconds. "OK, Julio. Ready, set, go!" you shout again. Julio scurries quickly to the top of the rope. "Six seconds!" you signal when he reaches the top.

Julio and Josh did the same amount of work, because Julio and Josh were the same weight and they climbed the same distance. But Julio did the work twice as fast, so he had twice the power.

You can see the unit of power scientists use written on light bulbs. It's the unit *watt*. This power unit was named for James Watt, one of the inventors of the steam engine. But in the late 1800s, Watt himself used another power unit—the horsepower—to compare the power of his steam engine with the power of a horse. He found that his horse could lift or pull a 550-pound weight a distance of one foot in one second. So he called this amount of power 1 horsepower. How much horsepower would it take for an engine to lift the same weight 2 feet off the ground in one second ?

▲ In the 1800s, James Watt used a horse to estimate power. This led to the unit horsepower. Today scientists measure power in watts.

The words *watt* and *horsepower* might seem confusing, but they're really not. Both describe power, and, in fact, one can be used for the other, because 1 horsepower equals 746 watts. Still, light bulbs marked ⅓ horsepower instead of 100 watts might seem rather strange!

Student Power!

How much power did Julio need to climb the rope for 30 seconds? First find out how much work he did.

Work = Force X Distance

The table shows the measurements you need. The force is his weight, which is in newtons (N).

	Julio	Josh
Force (in newtons)	300	300
Distance (in meters)	3	3
Time (in seconds)	30	60

Work = Force X Distance
= 300 N X 3 m
= 900 N-m

If 1 N-m equals 1 joule (J), then 900 N-m equals 900 J of work.

$$Power = \frac{Work}{Time} = \frac{900 J}{30 s}$$

Julio's power is 30 joules for each second—or 30 J/s.

The power produced by a 60-watt light bulb is 60 joules per second—or 60 J/s.

So, Julio's power was ½ that of a 60-watt bulb during his climb.

Julio → 30 J/s = 1
Light bulb → 60 J/s   2

What Did You Find Out?
1. *Find Josh's power (J/s) for the rope climb.*
2. *What's the power in J/s of a 100-watt bulb?*

Changing Energy

You experience every hill, turn, and loop on a roller coaster because of potential and kinetic energy.

You're sitting in the first car. It chugs slowly up the first hill. You think you'll never get to the top. But once you do, two loops loom in front of you. How will the car get safely through them and back to the beginning?

You know that energy is the ability to do work. The work you want the car to do is travel around the track. As the roller coaster's engine moves the car up this first hill, the car stores energy.

Scientists call stored energy **potential energy.** The word *potential* means "possible." If the car gains enough potential energy, it will be possible for the car to move down the hill and through that first loop!

Potential Energy

Kinetic Energy

The car sits perfectly still at the top of that first hill. It's gained all the potential energy that it can. You gasp as the car dives and you're halfway around the first loop before your stomach catches up.

The word *kinetic* means "having to do with motion." As the car plunges downward, gravity changes the potential energy to **kinetic energy,** or energy of motion. Kinetic energy carries the car to the bottom of the next hill.

The engine does the work needed to overcome the force of gravity and get the car up the hill. This work is stored in the car as potential energy. Then, the car can zoom down the hill on its own—without the help of the engine!

That's why the roller coaster is such a thrill. When you move up any part of the track, you know the car stores energy. As the stored energy changes to kinetic energy, you know you'll whoosh back down!

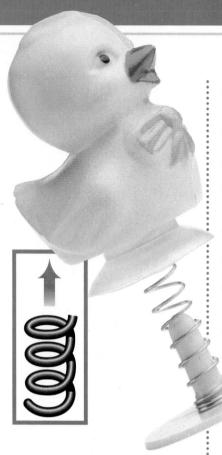

Fun With Stored Energy

Where might you expect to find potential energy? Energy can be stored in springs, against gravity, and in atoms. That sounds like serious business, doesn't it? Relax! You can actually have lots of fun storing energy.

Boing! A toy duck leaps across your desk. You're supposed to be studying, but each time the duck lands, you push it down again, and again. Soon you begin to wonder how the toy works.

Look at the spring on the toy duck. Whenever you push or pull a spring, you do work on it that's stored as potential energy. Because the work is stored, you can get it back again. It simply reappears as kinetic energy when you release the spring.

Now try to imagine the duck's jump in slow motion. First picture the duck with its spring pushed down. In this position, potential energy is stored. Next imagine the duck sailing upward. As this motion occurs, the potential energy is released. It changes into kinetic energy, or energy of motion. The kinetic energy then reappears as the potential energy decreases. But, at any given instant, the sum of the potential and kinetic energy is always the same.

You can find stored energy in many places. It's in an archer's tightly drawn bow and in a stretched rubber band. The spring in a wind-up toy stores energy when it's wound. Release the handle and watch kinetic energy reappear!

You can even store work done against the force of gravity as energy. Look at the girl in the swing on the next page. When the swing is at its highest point, work has been done against gravity. The swing stores this work as energy. At this point, the swing has all potential energy and no kinetic energy.

▼ *This spring toy demonstrates both kinetic and potential energy.*

Then as the swing sweeps down, the potential energy decreases and the kinetic energy increases. When the swing's chains hang straight down, its potential energy is smallest, and its kinetic energy is greatest. This kinetic energy carries the swing up again.

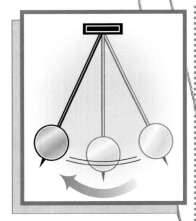

▼ As the girl swings, energy changes from potential to kinetic and back to potential.

The energy put into the swing to get it moving changes back and forth, from potential energy to kinetic energy. But you know that a swing doesn't keep going forever! Unless you keep pumping or someone pushes you, friction between you and air particles slows and then stops your swing.

You'll learn a lot about energy if you push a sled up a hill. The higher the hill, the more work you will have to do, and the more energy you will store in the sled. The sled's potential energy is greater at the top than at the bottom of the hill. You can enjoy your ride as the pull of gravity changes the potential energy to kinetic energy and carries you down.

Checkpoint

1. List 2 actions that show sunlight is energy.
2. How are work and power related?
3. How can you tell by looking at an object that it has kinetic energy?
4. What happens to the potential energy in a ball you have thrown up into the air?
5. Take Action! Use a piece of elastic to demonstrate how potential and kinetic energy change from one to another.

Activity

Using Potential Energy

Before an object can do work, it must store energy. How can you give an object potential energy? Try this activity to find out.

Picture A

Picture B

Picture C

Gather These Materials

2 pieces of string   pencil
2 blocks of wood   paper
masking tape   meter stick

Follow This Procedure

1 Make a chart like the one on the next page. Record your observations in your chart.

2 Use the strings to hang one block of wood from a table or desk. First, tape one end of each string to one of the blocks.

3 Then, tape the free ends of the 2 strings to the edge of a desk or table so the block of wood hangs down just above the floor, but does not touch it. (Picture A)

4 Tape a sheet of paper to the floor under the block of wood. Draw a line with your pencil across the paper and under the center of the wood. (Picture B)

5 Place the second block of wood so its edge is along the line you drew on the paper. Pull the hanging block aside to be sure you get the second block in the right place. (Picture C)

6 Pretend the hanging block is a swing. Pull the hanging block toward you and up so that its bottom is 10 cm above the floor.

Predict: *What will happen when you let go of the hanging block?*

7 Let go of the hanging block of wood. Measure how far the block on the floor was pushed along the floor. Record your measurement in the chart.

8 Repeat step 6 four more times. On the first trial, pull the hanging block of wood up to 20 cm above the floor before you let it go. On the next 3 trials, pull the hanging block up to 30, 40, and then 50 cm above the floor. Record the result each time.

Record Your Results

Hanging block let go at	Distance other block moved
10 cm	
20 cm	
30 cm	
40 cm	
50 cm	

State Your Conclusions

1. How did you demonstrate potential and kinetic energy with your model?
2. At what point did the hanging block of wood have the greatest potential energy? Explain your answer.

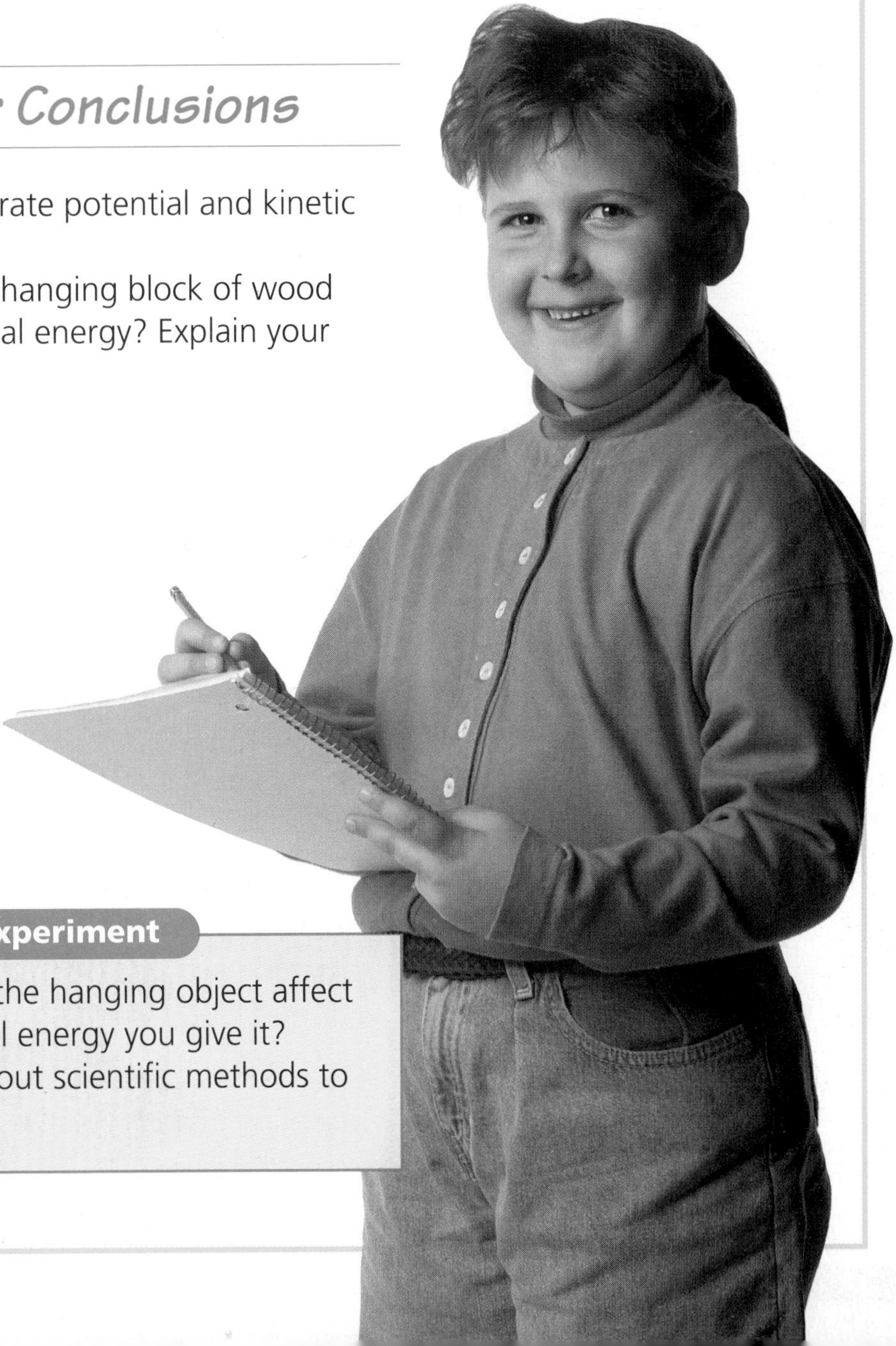

Let's Experiment

How does the mass of the hanging object affect the amount of potential energy you give it? Use what you know about scientific methods to find out.

1.2 *Energy Changes Form*

▶ **How are energy changes important to you?**

John, still hot from playing in the sun, goes into the house to cool off. As he turns on the radio, he realizes that he uses many forms of energy. The radio produces sound energy, and the lamps give light in every room. Both the radio and lamps use electrical energy. How many kinds of energy exist?

Stored Sunlight

You can find one form of energy, chemical energy, in petroleum. People burn petroleum to run cars, heat homes, and make electricity. Gasoline comes from petroleum through a refining process that also produces oil, tar, and other substances.

To find out where petroleum comes from, take yourself back in time to look at an ancient shallow sea. Algae float in the shallow water. As sunlight beats down, the algae capture the sun's energy and store it as sugars in their cells.

▼ *Energy from the sun can be stored as chemical energy for millions of years.*

For millions of years, animals of all sizes dart through the water, grazing on algae as they go. As the animals eat, they get "second-hand" sunlight from algae. When these animals die, their remains settle on the sea floor.

Suddenly, a mud slide from a nearby mountain covers the sea floor. Within seconds, all the living things—both large and small—are buried in deep mud! Mud slides occur many times over the years.

After many, many millions of years, the buried stored food in these living things changes into a pool of oil. This oil stores the sun's energy, first taken in by the algae millions of years before.

How was this energy stored all that time? It was held in the chemical bonds of the organisms. Like an atomic handcuff, a **chemical bond** is the strong attraction that holds two atoms together in a substance. For instance, chemical bonds hold hydrogen and oxygen atoms together in a water molecule. A **molecule** is the smallest bit of water that has the properties of the water. Chemical bonds hold water molecules together too.

The energy stored in chemical bonds is called chemical energy. Like the energy stored in swings and springs, the chemical energy stored in bonds is potential energy.

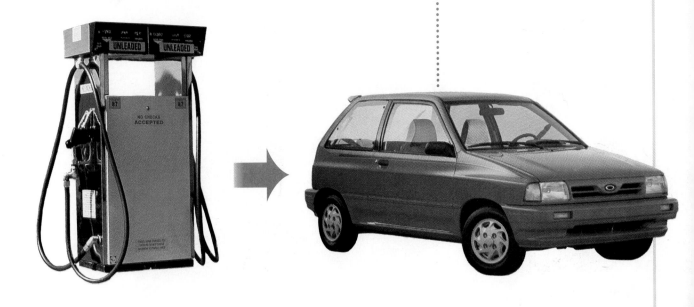

By now you may have guessed how this story ends. Imagine that you're pumping gasoline into a car. The gasoline came from that pool of petroleum holding the sun's energy. Next you hear the engine start. When this happens, the gasoline begins to burn. The potential energy in the gas changes into kinetic energy, and the car moves down the road.

Burning Charcoal

You've learned that a chemical reaction is a change that produces new substances. For this change to happen, the chemical bonds that hold together atoms and molecules must break before new chemical bonds can join other atoms and molecules.

You can't see chemical bonds break, but you can see the changes that result. Think of what happens when you toss a piece of paper into a fire. After the paper burns, nothing is left but ashes.

Many chemical reactions give off energy that can be harnessed to do useful work. Burning is probably the most familiar example of a chemical reaction that gives off energy.

➤ *Chemical reactions happen all around you.*

Burning occurs when a substance reacts with oxygen. When gasoline burns, it gives off energy. When the charcoal in the picture burns, it gives off energy as light and heat. You can feel the heat and see the light from the glowing coals.

Look at the piece of charcoal at the top. The charcoal contains atoms of carbon. Now look at the middle picture, which shows the charcoal burning. As the charcoal burns, a chemical reaction takes place between the charcoal's carbon atoms and oxygen atoms in the air. Chemists use the chemical equation below to describe this reaction.

▲ Charcoal contains carbon atoms.

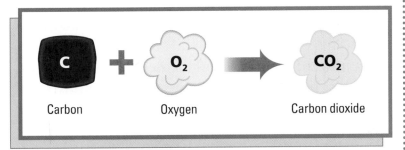

| Carbon | Oxygen | Carbon dioxide |

The chemical equation says: Carbon reacts with oxygen to make carbon dioxide gas. You can't see carbon dioxide gas when the charcoal in the grill burns, but the chemical equation tells you it is a product of the reaction.

The beginning substances in the chemical equation—carbon and oxygen—are written to the left of the arrow. The plus sign means that the carbon and oxygen are reacting. The arrow stands for the change that takes place during the reaction. Then the new substance formed by the chemical reaction is written to the right of the arrow. In this case, the arrow could point in the opposite direction too. If it did, the reaction would read: Carbon dioxide breaks down to form oxygen and carbon.

▲ The carbon atoms combine with oxygen.

If you look at the bottom picture, you can see the ash that's left. The ash is mostly minerals such as phosphorus that were mixed in the charcoal. You can no longer see the carbon because it combined with oxygen to form carbon dioxide gas.

▲ The ash contains minerals, but no carbon.

Almost everything combines with oxygen, but whether or not you notice the reaction depends on how fast it happens.

Nearly all substances on earth can combine with oxygen, yet you don't see them burning. Because many of these reactions take place very slowly, you don't notice that they release heat. This is what happens when iron combines with oxygen. If you leave nails like these outdoors, atoms of iron in the nails join with atoms of oxygen from the air. This slow chemical reaction forms rust and releases heat. Leaving the nails in a damp place causes the nails to rust faster, because water speeds up the reaction.

While some reactions take a long time, others happen more quickly. When candles like these burn, you can actually watch the chemical reaction taking place. The flame burns brightly, wax drips down the side of the candle, and a small stream of smoke curls upward. You can feel the heat and see light.

KABOOM! Explosions occur when a substance combines with oxygen in an instant. As you might expect, explosions release light and heat very quickly.

Conservation of Mass and Energy

If the rusty nail crumbles in your hand, you might think that the iron in the nail is gone. You might also think that the energy released during the reaction has disappeared. But the atoms of iron have simply combined with other atoms, making a new substance, and the energy has changed into heat that radiated away. Mass and energy are neither created nor destroyed during chemical reactions. They just change forms.

➤ You can watch this chemical reaction as it happens!

Looking at a single system will make this idea clear. A system is a collection or set of things that are related. Your bug collection, an atom, a fish tank, your state, and a desert are all systems.

A forest is a system consisting of many parts including animals, plants, air, rocks, soil, and water. Energy from sunlight supports the whole system. So this "forest system" contains a certain amount of energy and a certain amount of mass.

Imagine that lightning strikes this system and a chemical reaction, a raging forest fire, results. When the fire dies out, only charred tree stumps and smoke remain. The forest seems to have vanished! But neither mass nor energy was created or destroyed in the fire. They just changed form.

The burning trees released energy in the form of heat and light. The trees' mass became gases and particles that escaped as smoke. In other words, the energy and mass of the forest changed form and moved to other systems or off into space.

▲ *Explosions are the very rapid combining of oxygen and another substance.*

From Batteries to Music

When energy changes form, it makes things happen. Notice in the picture how this changing energy makes objects useful. When you turn on a lamp, electrical energy changes to light and heat. The light helps you see in the dark, but the heat simply causes the air around the lamp to become hotter. The toaster uses electrical energy, too. What changes do you think happen there?

Electrical energy changes into mechanical energy in the ceiling fan. Friction between the fan's blades and molecules in the air produce heat. But again, the heat is wasted because it drifts away and is no longer of any use to you.

Batteries provide energy for the pencil sharpener and the radio. How can a battery give energy? Inside the battery, a chemical reaction releases chemical energy, which produces electrical energy. The electrical energy then changes to sound energy in the radio and to mechanical energy in the pencil sharpener.

Each time energy changes form, some useful work is done. Some not so useful work is done, too—"waste" heat is produced. But the total amount of energy stays the same. It just changes from one form to another.

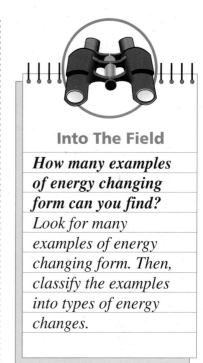

Into The Field

How many examples of energy changing form can you find?
Look for many examples of energy changing form. Then, classify the examples into types of energy changes.

▲ *Batteries are just one of the objects that you can find in your home in which energy changes form.*

Checkpoint

1. Why do you think petroleum is called a fossil fuel?
2. With what element must substances combine in order to burn?
3. What happens to the mass in the leaves of a tree when the tree burns?
4. What happens when energy changes form?
5. **Take Action!** Survey your home for objects that change energy from one form to another.

Activity

Energy Changes Form

You observe energy changing form all around you. How can you change chemical energy to heat? Try this activity to find out.

Picture A

Picture B

Picture C

Gather These Materials

cover goggles
tall, thin jar
graduated cylinder
water

thermometer
spoonful of calcium
  chloride
stirrer

Follow This Procedure

1 Make a chart like the one on the next page. Record your observations in your chart.

2 Put on your cover goggles.

3 Use the graduated cylinder to measure 25 mL of water. Then pour the water into the tall jar. (Picture A)

4 Now measure and record the temperature of the water in the jar. (Picture B) *CAUTION: Handle the thermometer carefully.*

Predict: What effect will the calcium chloride have on the water?

5 Carefully put a spoonful of calcium chloride into the water. (Picture C) Use the stirrer to gently mix the calcium chloride in the water. Immediately note the temperature of the water. Record the temperature on your chart.

6 Measure and record the temperature of the water every 30 seconds for 2 more minutes.

State Your Conclusions

1. What happened when you added calcium chloride to the water?

2. What do you think might have caused the water temperature to change? Explain.

Let's Experiment

How would changing the amount of calcium chloride added to the water affect the water's temperature change? Use what you know about scientific methods to find out.

Record Your Results

	Temperature
Water without chemical	
Water with chemical	
Water after 30 seconds	
Water after 60 seconds	
Water after 90 seconds	
Water after 120 seconds	

Identifying Relevant Facts

The information you use to draw a conclusion may not be relevant or have anything to do with your problem. You need relevant facts to draw conclusions.

Thinking It Through

A perpetual motion machine would keep running forever without needing more energy. Is this possible? Read these facts.

Fact 1: Machines lose energy due to friction. Outside energy sources replace lost energy.

Fact 2: A perpetual motion machine could be used to power many vehicles.

Conclusion: A perpetual motion machine probably is not possible.

Now ask yourself these questions.

Does Fact 1 affect the conclusion? Yes. A machine that loses energy will need more energy to keep it going, and cannot be a perpetual motion machine.

For Fact 2, ask the same question. Fact 2 does not affect the conclusion. Therefore, Fact 2 is not relevant.

When identifying a relevant fact, do not judge whether or not the fact is true or false. A false statement can be relevant if the false statement affects the conclusion.

Your Turn

Explain which facts are relevant.

Fact 1: Oil helps cut down on friction between moving parts.

Fact 2: Potential energy changes to kinetic when an object falls.

Fact 3: A moving object stops because of friction.

Fact 4: Lifting an object gives it potential energy.

Conclusion: Kinetic energy increases as a car rolls down a hill.

Chapter Review

Thinking Back

1. Explain why sunlight is **energy**.
2. Name two units of **power** and tell what they describe.
3. What is the difference between **kinetic energy** and **potential energy**?
4. Tell how potential energy and kinetic energy change back and forth in a moving swing.
5. Explain how **chemical bonds** and potential energy are related.
6. Explain what happens to **molecules** during a chemical reaction.
7. Describe the chemical reaction that occurs as a candle burns.
8. Explain why mass and energy are not destroyed during a chemical reaction in a system.
9. How does energy change form when you turn on a battery-operated tape recorder?

Connecting Ideas

1. Copy the concept map. Use the terms at the right to complete the map about energy.

kinetic　　　**matter**
potential　　**work**

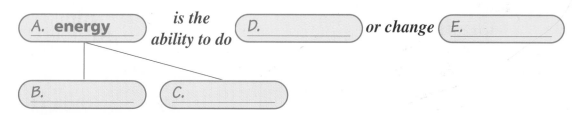

A. **energy** _is the ability to do_ D. _or change_ E.

B.　　　　C.

2. Write a sentence or two about the ideas shown in the concept map.

Gathering Evidence

1. In the Activity on page 12, what led you to conclude that increasing the height of the hanging block of wood would increase the amount of potential energy?
2. In the Activity on page 22, how did you know a chemical reaction occurred?

Doing Science!

1. **Design an activity** to show that sunlight is energy.
2. **Invent a device** that could be used to keep a bicycle that is stored outdoors free from rust.

Solar Energy

No kidding! You can really cook a potato with sunlight?

Can you build a solar cooker?

Design and construct a solar cooker to cook a small potato. Use any materials that you can think of. Place your potato in the cooker. How long did it take to cook your potato?

For Discussion

1. How well does your solar potato cooker work?
2. How could you change your cooker design to make the potato cook even faster?

2.1 Using the Sun's Energy

▶ *Is sunlight hot enough to cook food?*

"I can't believe the sun cooked the whole meal!"
"This pizza is fantastic!"
"Everything tastes just like it does at home!"

For the last two years, students in El Paso, Texas, have enjoyed a unique experience with their teacher, Louise Bergdahl. Comments such as those above describe a dinner they prepared last year. The dinner was the result of a science project called *Here Comes the Sun.*

The 60 creative sixth graders heard a speaker from the Department of Energy. They saw slides showing special ovens used in Guatemala, a Central American country where fuel is scarce. These ovens help the people there cook food cheaply. The ovens, called solar ovens, use the sun's energy to cook food. *Sol* is the word for sun in the Latin language. Each student worked with partners to make a real solar oven like you did in the Discover Activity. Students built their ovens in about four hours of class time. Then they cooked a meal in them. But the project involved more than building ovens. Ms. Bergdahl's class has also achieved local fame. They have been featured in newspaper articles and have appeared on local TV.

▼ *Kira Kawakami checks the finishing touches on a solar oven she helped build.*

Solar Bake Off

Join Kira, and her partners Erica and Michael, as they make a solar oven. They begin by discussing how solar ovens work. Flaps covered with aluminum foil bounce sunlight into a box. The flaps can be adjusted to follow the sun as it moves. The sunlight streams through a clear glass or plastic lid into the box. Because the inside of the box is black, the box absorbs the sun's energy and gets hot. The lid holds the heat in. The oven grows hot, then hotter. Finally it becomes hot enough to cook food.

Next Kira, Erica, and Michael begin to work. Erica paints the inside of a small box with a special black paint made for use on barbeque grills. Michael places rocks in the bottom of a larger box to anchor it. When the paint dries, they fit the small box inside the larger one. They fill the space between the two boxes with crumpled newspaper. Then Erica notices that other students are using different materials between the two boxes.

▼ *The solar oven bounces the sun's energy inside the box, absorbs it, and traps the built-up heat.*

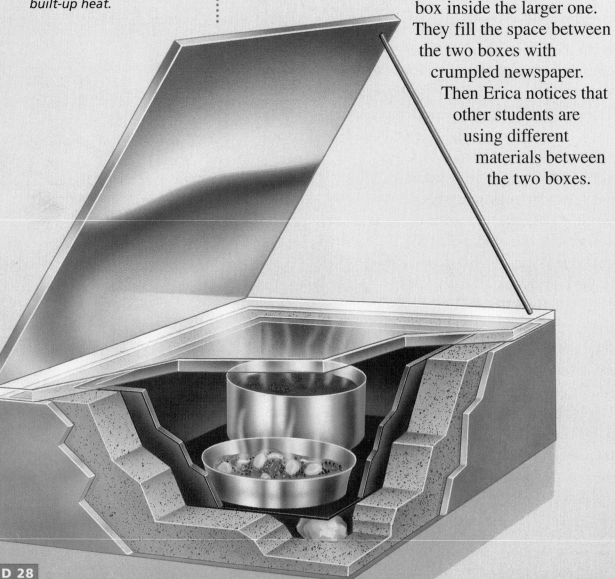

One team is especially inventive. They're filling soda cans with sand to place in the empty space. Ms. Bergdahl explains that sand surrounding the heated box will prevent heat from escaping through the oven into the ground.

Next Erica and Kira glue aluminum foil onto a large square of cardboard to make the flap. After they attach the flap, they support it with a stick so it won't blow closed. Then Michael begins the last step: taping a piece of glass onto the box.

As each team puts the finishing touches on their ovens, excitement fills the air. Looking around, the group sees that none of the ovens look the same. Most ovens are bigger than theirs. Some are black, and others are covered in foil.

Finally the day of the bake-off arrives, along with cloudy skies. On the playground, students put chicken, potatoes, pizza, and other foods into their ovens. And they watch the clouds.

But the ovens begin to heat as soon as the sun appears. Many quickly rise past 75° Celsius. Temperatures above 75° Celsius are needed to kill bacteria, so the food will be safe to eat. Although solar ovens can reach 150° Celsius, most food takes about three times longer to cook than at home. At noon, the food is ready. Kira, Erica, and Michael proudly serve a meal cooked by the sun.

▲ Ms. Cole helps Erica Whitehead, Kira, and Michael Chuilli assemble their oven.

▼ The solar oven's inventor, Sherry Cole, puts the pizza into the oven while Kira and Erica anxiously wait for lunch!

Catching Rays

Throughout the ages, people have used what they know about sunlight to help keep homes and buildings warm or cool.

Try to imagine how much energy all the world's people use in one year. That's how much energy the sun sends to the earth every 40 minutes! How can you make use of some of this energy? You do it every time you sit in the sunshine to warm yourself—just as people have done throughout history.

During prehistoric times, early peoples in Europe and Asia used caves as shelters. Instead of living deep inside the caves, they lived near the mouths. This choice probably was made to take advantage of the light and warmth of the sun. From then on, people have been directing the energy of the sun.

900 North America The Anasazi Indians built their homes in the sides of south-facing cliffs so all levels received full sun. The buildings were made of adobe, stone, and mud, which absorbed the sun's heat by day and released it at night.

200 Europe The ancient Romans first used transparent glass to cover windows, letting in light and heat and keeping out rain and cold.

500 Asia Chinese cities were planned so the gates and main rooms of buildings faced south. Translucent rice paper or silk covered windows, acting much like glass.

| 100 | 500 | 1000 |

Ancient Times

1933 Chicago Architect George Keck "rediscovered" the heating effects of the sun when he used mostly glass to cover the House of Tomorrow for the World's Fair. Later, a local newspaper coined the term *solar home.*

1990 United States Glass has become an inexpensive building material, and many architects like the way it looks. The mirrored surface reverses the effects of the summer sun. Much light is reflected, allowing the building to stay cooler.

1962 England Emslie Morgan built a school with a glass south wall. Studies show over 50% of the building's heat comes from the sun and the rest comes from electric lights and the students!

1820 England Greenhouses provided lavish indoor gardens and radiated heat to the rest of the house.

| 1800 | 1900 | 2000 |

Modern Times

Skylab orbited the earth for six years, running on solar energy.

Electricity from the Sun

Solar energy can do more than cook food and keep buildings warm. This plentiful, free energy source can also power equipment such as space vehicles, cars, calculators, and watches.

If you could harness *all* the sun's energy, in less than one hour you would have enough energy to take care of the world's energy needs for a full year. Scientists hope to make widespread use of this vast source of energy. This action would make people less dependent on fossil fuels.

Solar cells are one method of using solar energy. Solar cells change solar energy directly into electrical energy. Solar cells are made of silicon, one of the elements in sand. The solar cells of *Skylab* are on the four windmill-like panels and the two large wing-like panels attached at the upper end. First launched in 1973, *Skylab* orbited the earth until 1979. During that time, three separate teams of astronauts and scientists lived aboard the spacecraft.

Solar cells can also power vehicles on the ground. Look at the sleek race car shown here. This car has reached speeds of about 115 kilometers per hour for short periods of time!

Solar powered cars might be in everyone's driveway in the future.

In 1990, 32 solar powered cars raced from Michigan to Florida. Each car was designed so that the solar panels could catch the sun at all angles. The cars covered over 2600 kilometers of highways in 11 days. To others on the roads, the cars probably looked as if they had come from another planet!

Unlike gasoline, the sun's energy was free to the drivers in the race. But the cars themselves were quite expensive. One cost $800,000. The solar panel alone for another one cost $6 million!

Cost is only one problem experts face as they study solar power. Two others are that solar cells generate very small amounts of electricity and they take a lot of energy to make. The cells convert only about one-tenth of the solar energy they receive into electrical energy. Scientists hope that future solar cells will convert one-third of the energy they receive into electricity.

However, because solar cells produce small amounts of electricity, they can easily power small objects like the calculator you see on this page. The calculator needs only sunlight—or even lamplight—to keep running!

▲ Small items like this calculator are much less expensive to run on solar energy than batteries.

Checkpoint

1. What purpose does the flap on a solar oven serve?
2. Name one way buildings can take advantage of the sun's energy for heating.
3. Why are small items such as calculators suitable for solar cells?
4. **Take Action!** Track the path of the sunlight on your school during the day. Develop a plan for how your school might take advantage of solar energy for some of its heating needs.

Activity

Storing Solar Energy

How do objects differ in their ability to store solar energy? Try this activity to find out.

Picture A

Gather These Materials

cover goggles
cardboard box with a lid
black paint
paint brush
4 soup cans
sand
pebbles

water
torn paper or newspaper
masking tape
4 thermometers
clock or timer
oven mitts

Follow This Procedure

1 Make a chart like the one on the next page. Record your observations in your chart.

2 Put on your cover goggles.

3 Paint the outside of the box black. Be careful not to get any paint on your clothes or skin. Let the box dry completely. (Picture A)

4 Fill one can with sand, one with pebbles, one with water, and one with torn paper. (Picture B)

5 Use the masking tape to label each can and carefully put a thermometer in it.
CAUTION: Be extremely careful not to break the thermometers you put into the sand and pebbles.

6 After 2 minutes, read the temperature of each substance. Record the temperature in your chart.

7 Put the cans inside the black box. (Picture C) Take out the thermometers.

Picture B

Picture C

Temperature	Sand	Pebbles	Water	Paper
Before placed in sun				
After 1 hour in sun				
Out of sun for 10 min.				
Out of sun for 20 min.				
Out of sun for 30 min.				

Predict: *Will all 4 temperatures go up and down by the same amounts?*

8 Put the lid on the box and leave it in the sun for one hour.

9 Put on oven mitts and then move the box to the shade. *CAUTION: Handle the box carefully. It will be hot.*

10 Carefully put a thermometer in each can. After one minute, read the temperature in each can and record it on your chart. Read and record the temperature again after 10 minutes, 20 minutes, and 30 minutes.

State Your Conclusions

1. How did the temperatures compare after sitting in the sun? in the shade?
2. Which substance stored heat longest?

Let's Experiment

What other kinds of materials store solar energy well? Use what you know about scientific methods to find out.

2.2 *Waves of Light*

What is light?

Your favorite baseball player strides to the plate to bat. He slams the first pitch high into the air. You leap up to watch the ball. Even though you've got on your best sunglasses, you're suddenly blinded by a flash of sunlight and miss the play. For an instant, you wish you could turn the sun on and off.

Electromagnetic Radiation

Imagine that you really could turn the sun on and off by simply flipping a switch. The sky is pitch black, so you flip the switch to "on." In an instant, the sun begins to give off energy. It travels in all directions—some speeding toward Earth.

Eight minutes later, the solar energy reaches Earth. The waves bounce off everything around you and you suddenly see all these objects. Other waves—or rays—arrive at the same time. Radio waves, microwaves, infrared waves, ultraviolet waves, X rays, and gamma rays also travel to Earth. Some of these waves don't reach the ground. Others do, but you don't sense their presence.

Of course you can't turn the sun off and on. But the sun's energy really does travel in waves. Energy moving in waves through space is called electromagnetic radiation. All electromagnetic waves travel at 300,000,000 meters per second, which is called the "speed of light."

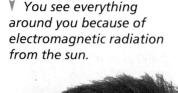

▼ *You see everything around you because of electromagnetic radiation from the sun.*

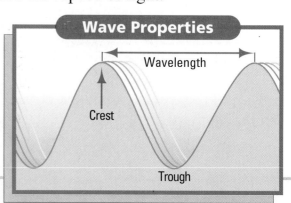

Wave Properties

Wavelength

Crest

Trough

◄ *Waves traveling in all directions can produce glare that blocks your view of the items behind the glass of the window.*

Some properties of electromagnetic waves resemble the properties of waves that ripple outward from a rock thrown in a pond. Look at the diagram on page 36 that shows these properties. One wavelength is the distance from one point on a wave to the same point on the next wave. The top of each wave is the crest and the bottom of each is the trough. So the distance from crest to crest or from trough to trough is the wavelength. Scientists use these points to study the motion of electromagnetic waves.

Sun Shades

All the things you can see either give off light waves or reflect light waves. You can see yourself in a mirror because light waves bounce, or reflect, from its shiny surface.

So how do sunglasses with polarizing lenses help you see on a bright day? Light waves vibrate in all directions. Your eyes see this jumble of waves as a glare. Polarizing lenses block out much of the jumble. They admit waves vibrating in only one direction—up and down. Thus they block much of the glare. You can see the difference in how the light passes through polarizing lenses and what a difference this makes in the photographs on this page.

▼ *Polarizing lenses block some of the jumble of light waves and thus reduce glare. Now you can see the shirts in the window.*

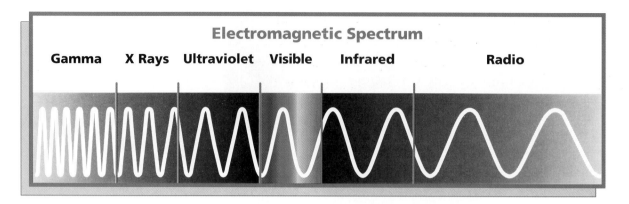

Electromagnetic Spectrum

| Gamma | X Rays | Ultraviolet | Visible | Infrared | Radio |

▲ *The waves of the electromagnetic spectrum show a pattern of increasing wavelengths and decreasing energy.*

Long to Short Waves

If you could see all electromagnetic radiation, two characteristics would stand out. First you would notice that the different types have different wavelengths. For example, X rays have shorter wavelengths than those of infrared. Next you would notice that shorter wavelengths have more energy. Gamma rays have the most energy and radio waves have the least.

If you then made a graph comparing the different wavelengths, you would discover a scale, or spectrum. The electromagnetic spectrum is the arrangement of electromagnetic radiation by wavelength. Your graph might look like the diagram above. In it, the shortest wavelengths are at one end and the longest at the other.

Visible

Electromagnetic energy is at work all around you. For instance, radio waves carry signals from radio stations to radios, microwaves heat food, and gamma rays help doctors kill bacteria on needles. However, you're most familiar with light—the only wavelengths of electromagnetic radiation you can see. These wavelengths are called visible light—or just light. Most of the visible light on the earth comes from the sun. But other light sources, such as those shown, also exist. Some, like the fire, give a bright light, while others, like the flashlight fish, give only a little light.

You see visible light as "white" light, but it really contains bands of different colors. When you stare at a rainbow arching across the sky, you can see the different wavelengths of white light—red, orange, yellow, green, blue, indigo, and violet.

Checkpoint

1. How fast do radio waves travel?
2. How do polarizing lenses reduce glare?
3. Compare the amount of energy in gamma waves with that in infrared waves.
4. **Take Action!** Make a poster of the electromagnetic spectrum. Use diagrams of the waves and pictures of people using the waves.

▼ *While the visible spectrum contains the only wavelengths you can see, it's really a very tiny part of the electromagnetic spectrum.*

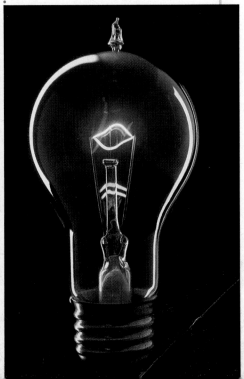

2.3 *Sun and Air*

▶ *Is sunlight good for your skin?*

Ouch! If you've ever stayed out in the sun too long, you know how painful a bad sunburn can be. After all, a sunburn means that the sun has burned your skin. However, you can prevent sunburns. Simply limit the time you spend in the sun, even on cloudy days, and use sunblock on your skin.

The Atmosphere

The ultraviolet light in electromagnetic radiation can be harmful to humans. Luckily, however, the earth's atmosphere keeps most of these harmful wavelengths away from the earth.

Have you ever wrapped yourself up in a blanket or two to keep warm? The earth's atmosphere is a layered mixture of gases that holds in the solar warmth and protects the earth like a blanket. These gases are mostly nitrogen and oxygen—with tiny amounts of many other gases.

Gravity pulls gas particles in the air toward the earth, so air is more dense near the ground. It is less dense, or thinner, higher in the atmosphere. The upper atmosphere extends far into space and gradually fades out to nothing.

People live in the lowest layer of gases, or the troposphere, which extends from sea level upward about 11 kilometers. There the sun's energy creates winds and weather. It causes water to evaporate from seas, lakes, rivers, and from growing plants. This water vapor forms clouds and then falls again as rain or snow.

▼ *You should protect yourself from harmful UV radiation.*

As the sun's electromagnetic radiation moves through the atmosphere, different things happen to it.

The earth's atmosphere acts like a screen for the sun's electromagnetic waves. It allows the longer wavelengths such as radio waves to pass through, but it blocks many of the shorter wavelengths.

Most of the wavelengths that pass through the atmosphere are visible light, or sunlight. As you can see on the diagram, several things happen to this sunlight. Air and clouds absorb some of it. They also reflect some of it back into space. The rest of the sunlight reaches the earth's surface. Notice that at the surface, sunlight is either absorbed by the land and water, or reflected.

Some ultraviolet wavelengths—or UV waves— also make it through the atmosphere. But look out! UV wavelengths spell danger. They cause your skin to become sunburned, and they can even cause skin cancer. However, most of the harmful UV wavelengths never reach the ground because they are absorbed by ozone, a gas in the atmosphere.

Sunblock!

How does the girl's blue sunblock, which contains zinc oxide, protect her from harmful radiation? Let's investigate.

What To Do
A. Dim the room lights.
B. Staple a sheet of clear plastic to the yellow side of light-sensitive paper.
C. Use sunblock with zinc oxide to write the letter *S* on the plastic as shown below.

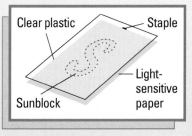

D. Expose the paper to sunlight for 5 minutes.
E. Quickly soak and rinse the paper in water for one minute. Let the paper dry.
F. Observe the paper after it dries. Blue areas show where few light waves, including harmful ultraviolet waves, reached the light-sensitive paper.

Record Your Results

	Color of Paper
With Sunblock	
Without Sunblock	

What Did You Find Out?
1. *How did the thickness of the sunblock affect the amount of light that reached the paper?*
2. *How does sunblock keep your skin safe from the sun?*

D 41

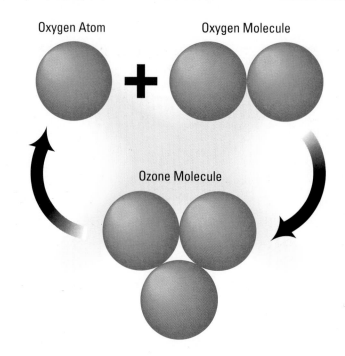

Oxygen Atom

Oxygen Molecule

Ozone Molecule

➤ Ozone both forms and breaks down in the atmosphere.

Ozone—Earth's Sunblock

You would never breathe a poisonous gas on purpose. But you breathe one in smog, the pollution caused by burning gasoline. Smog contains a large amount of ozone, which is a form of oxygen that's poisonous. You might think ozone is odd because it protects people when it's high in the atmosphere. Yet ozone harms people when it's near the ground.

Large cities often have problems with smog. If winds don't spread the smog to other areas, it becomes concentrated over a city. Then, city officials might declare an *ozone alert*. During these alerts, doctors suggest that people stay indoors as much as possible and avoid heavy exercise.

Each molecule of ozone contains three atoms of oxygen. The diagram above shows ozone breaking down and forming. Notice that O is one atom of oxygen, O_2 is an oxygen molecule, and O_3 is an ozone molecule. The arrows show that the reaction runs either forward or backward.

How do these reactions work? In one reaction, O combines with O_2 to form O_3. In the reverse reaction, O_3 breaks down into O and O_2. Both reactions take place in the atmosphere. So ozone both forms and breaks down in the atmosphere.

Scientists worry that gases from human activities are invading the "good" ozone. The invaders are gases that contain chlorine, fluorine, and carbon. These gases are called CFCs for short. CFCs are found in air conditioners, refrigerators, and some spray cans. If you have ever used spray paint, you might have released CFCs into the atmosphere.

Molecules of ozone are no match for the CFCs. CFCs rise in the atmosphere without changing into simpler substances. As they rise, they cause reactions that break ozone down into O and O_2. Each CFC molecule can destroy as many as 10,000 ozone molecules!

The map shows a hole scientists have found in the ozone layer above the South Pole. They don't know whether this hole is permanent, but it appears to be getting bigger. Scientists think worldwide use of CFCs caused the hole to appear. The hole lets ultraviolet radiation pass through the atmosphere to the ground where it is dangerous to all living things. Today, scientists and government leaders all over the world are working to ban CFCs.

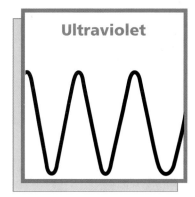

Ultraviolet

▼ *CFCs from spray cans and other sources might have caused the hole in the ozone layer, shown here by the pink to purple colors.*

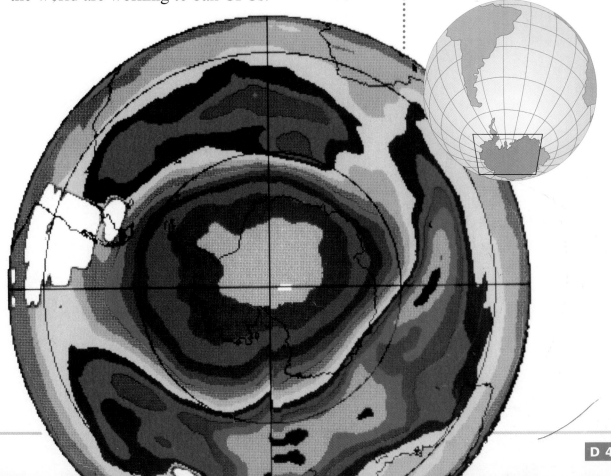

Everyone's Greenhouse

Have you heard of the "greenhouse effect?" To understand this effect, think about what can happen to a closed car out in the sun. The car's windows let the sunlight in, but block the heat from moving back out again. So the inside of the car gets very hot. A glass greenhouse works the same way.

Carbon dioxide, water vapor, and certain other gases in the air are called "greenhouse gases," because they act like the glass in cars and in greenhouses. These gases let sunlight pass through to the ground, but they don't let heat from the ground pass directly back through the air and escape into space. Like the seats and steering wheel in the hot, closed car, the earth becomes warmer because of the greenhouse gases. Overall the greenhouse effect is good because it keeps the world warm enough for plants and animals to live. But too much of the greenhouse effect is not good.

▼ *The greenhouse effect is very important to life on the earth, but making the effect stronger might cause harm.*

Look at the picture to see how the earth could become too warm. The ground gets hotter as it absorbs sunlight. This causes the ground to give off, or radiate, its heat as infrared wavelengths. Most of these infrared wavelengths are absorbed by the greenhouse gases in the air—especially carbon dioxide and water vapor. In return, these gases give off infrared wavelengths that travel back to the ground, and another cycle begins.

Luckily, air always contains greenhouse gases, otherwise you probably wouldn't be here to read about the greenhouse effect! However, the worldwide increase in the burning of coal, oil, and wood is creating more greenhouse gases, especially carbon dioxide. Scientists think this increase will strengthen the greenhouse effect and change climates around the world. Some hypothesize that glaciers will melt, causing oceans to rise. Others think that the earth might become colder. In the meantime, people throughout the world are trying to limit production of greenhouse gases.

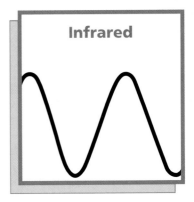

Infrared

Checkpoint

1. Why don't most harmful UV rays reach the earth's surface?
2. How can ozone be both helpful and harmful?
3. What might have caused the hole in the ozone layer?
4. What are the greenhouse gases?
5. **Take Action!** Survey the spray cans in the grocery store. Make a list of products that do not use CFCs in their spray cans.

Into The Field

Is the temperature inside a greenhouse different from the temperature outside? Use a thermometer and a clear plastic jar with a lid to make a model of a greenhouse. Record what you find out.

Carbon Dioxide and the Greenhouse Effect

What effect does the amount of carbon dioxide in the atmosphere have on the greenhouse effect? Try this activity to find out.

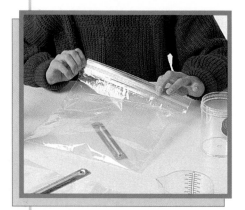

Picture A

Picture B

Picture C

Gather These Materials

cover goggles
2 self-sealing plastic
  bags
2 thermometers
large spoon

baking soda
2 plastic jars
vinegar

Follow This Procedure

1 Make a chart like the one on the next page. Record your observations in your chart.

2 Put on your cover goggles.

3 Carefully place a thermometer in one of the plastic bags.

4 Close the bag leaving just a small part of the seal open. Blow as much air as possible inside. Close the bag tightly so no air escapes. (Picture A)

5 Carefully place the other thermometer in the second plastic bag. Put 2 large spoonfuls of baking soda in 1 plastic jar. Place the jar in the bag. Hold the bag so very little air is inside.

6 Fill the other jar about one-fourth full. Carefully pour the vinegar into the jar in the bag. (Picture B)

7 Quickly close the bag so that the forming gas does not escape. (Picture C)

Predict: *What effect will the sun have on the 2 bags of gas?*

8 Record the temperature of the gas in each bag on your chart.

9 Place both bags in the sun for 5 minutes. Record the temperatures of both bags every minute.

State Your Conclusions

1. How did the temperatures of the gases in the 2 bags compare before they were placed in the sun? after they had been in the sun for 5 minutes?

2. When vinegar and baking soda mix, a chemical reaction occurs that releases carbon dioxide. How does the activity show that carbon dioxide is a greenhouse gas?

3. Based on what you know about the products of burning fossil fuels, why do you think people should try to limit this action?

Record Your Results

Temperature	Air	Carbon dioxide
Before placed in sun		
1 min. in sun		
2 min. in sun		
3 min. in sun		
4 min. in sun		
5 min. in sun		

Let's Experiment

What would happen if you doubled the amount of carbon dioxide in the second bag? Use what you know about scientific methods to find out.

Identifying Bias

To make up your mind about an issue, you might seek information from others. But even an expert on a subject can be biased, or present only the facts that support his or her view. You can make better decisions if you can identify biased information.

Thinking It Through

Suppose people in your area are voting on whether to raise money to build a new railroad line. Two experts discuss the issue on TV.

Ms. Padua I think enough public money has already been spent on mass transportation. Railroads cost a lot to run. The train's schedule may not be convenient for passengers wanting to take public transportation. Besides, many people drive cars. Trucks are more convenient, and cheaper than trains to transport goods.

Mr. Reed I think the increase in the greenhouse effect is being caused by so many people driving. Trucks and cars cause much more pollution than trains. The railroad system would be more convenient if money were spent to extend it to more towns. The railroad system can do studies to decide when passengers would find it convenient for the train to stop in their town.

One way to find out if people are biased is to learn about what affects their viewpoints. Ms. Padua is from the trucking union. She may be giving only the facts favorable to trucks. Mr. Reed heads an environmental organization. He may not care about the cost. Both have good points, but their biases may keep them from presenting all the facts fairly.

Your Turn

Find two people who drive to work. Ask them if they would take a train or bus to work if it were available. Have them explain why or why not. Do you think either person is presenting biased information?

Chapter Review

Thinking Back

1. Why did the students paint the inside of the solar oven black?
2. List ways people throughout history have used the sun's energy to heat buildings.
3. What kind of energy change occurs in a solar cell?
4. How does **electromagnetic radiation** reach Earth?
5. What is the electromagnetic spectrum?
6. How does ozone help humans?
7. Compare the structure of an oxygen molecule with that of an ozone molecule.
8. Why are scientists and government leaders working to ban CFCs?
9. Why are carbon dioxide and water vapor called "greenhouse gases"?

Connecting Ideas

1. Copy the concept map. Use the terms at the right to complete the map about electromagnetic radiation.

electromagnetic radiation
gamma rays   **light waves**
radio waves

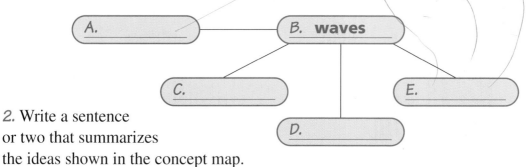

2. Write a sentence or two that summarizes the ideas shown in the concept map.

Gathering Evidence

1. In the Activity on page 34, how did you determine which material stored heat from the sun the longest?
2. In the Activity on page 46, what led you to conclude that increasing the amount of carbon dioxide in the bag would increase the temperature in the bag?

Doing Science!

1. *Create a poster* that explains why it is important to wear a sunblock when out in the sun.
2. *Write a skit* that would compare the different wavelengths and amounts of energy in the various kinds of waves in the electromagnetic spectrum.

Using Sunshine

In the summer, I water my plants almost every day.

Discover Activity

Does sunlight affect how quickly plants lose water?

Use your pencil to punch a hole in a file card. Put the card on top of a cup half filled with water. Then, put the stem of a freshly cut leaf through the hole. Make sure the leaf stem is in the water. Cover the leaf with another cup. Make another setup just like this one. Place one setup in the shade and one in the sunlight. Observe after two hours.

For Discussion

1. *Compare the amount of water in each setup.*
2. *Compare your setups with others. Do all plants give off water at the same rate?*

3.1 *Trapped Sunlight*

How do plants get energy?

If you've ever taken care of plants, you know what happens to plants when they're left in dark rooms for very long. Keiko found out the hard way! When she got home after being gone three weeks, leaves on her plants were pale and whitish instead of green. She had forgotten to raise her window shade before she left, so her bedroom was very dark. If she'd been gone much longer, her plants would have died!

Photosynthesis

Plants need light. They trap the light energy and use it to make sugars through the process of **photosynthesis** (fō′ tō sin′ thə sis). This process includes many chemical reactions that take place only in sunlight or lamplight. Greenhouses like the one here provide enough light for plants to carry out photosynthesis.

▼ *Greenhouses provide the right conditions for plants to carry out photosynthesis.*

Sunlight and Green Leaves

Have you ever discovered green stains on your jeans after playing outside? Those stains came from chlorophyll, a substance that gives plants their green color. Chlorophyll plays an important role in photosynthesis!

The diagram shows you that plants use water and carbon dioxide in the process of photosynthesis. Carbon dioxide and water take different paths to get inside a leaf. Water from the soil enters the leaf through the roots of the plant and carbon dioxide enters the leaf from the air.

Once inside the leaf, the water and carbon dioxide come together in cells that have chloroplasts. Photosynthesis takes place in the chloroplasts. Chlorophyll, the green stain on your jeans, is found in these chloroplasts.

Photosynthesis occurs in two stages. During the first stage, chlorophyll absorbs sunlight. Light energy is changed into chemical energy, and water breaks down into hydrogen and oxygen.

Recall that chemical energy is potential energy, because it's stored in the chemical bonds of molecules. When this chemical energy is released, it powers the reactions in the next stage.

During the second stage of photosynthesis, chloroplasts use hydrogen and carbon dioxide to make sugars for the plant. Now, some of the sun's energy is stored in the chemical bonds of the sugar molecules. These sugars are the plant's food.

Photosynthesis also produces oxygen. The plant uses some of this oxygen to release the chemical energy stored in the sugars it makes. But the plant makes more oxygen than it uses. The extra oxygen escapes from the leaves and goes into the air.

This process might sound complicated, but you can summarize all the changes that happen during photosynthesis in one sentence! *In sunlight, green leaves use carbon dioxide and water to make sugars, and oxygen is released*. The diagram says the same thing, but it uses pictures as well as words.

▼ Photosynthesis occurs in the cells of green plants, algae, and other organisms that contain chlorophyll.

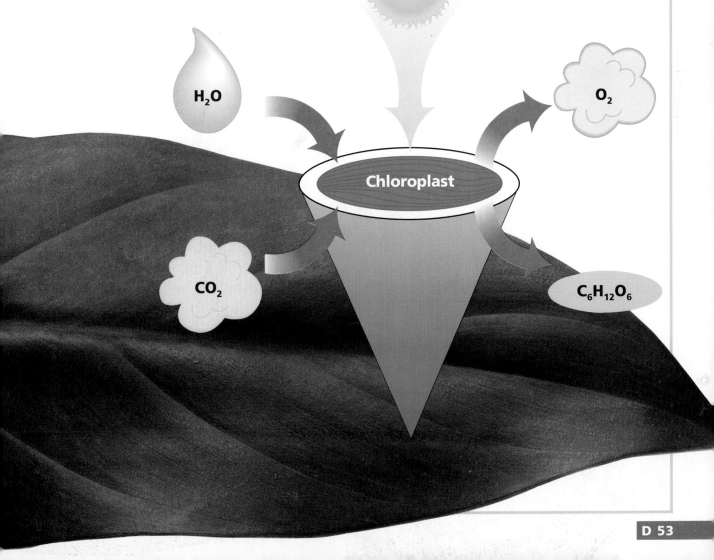

Sunlight

H_2O

O_2

Chloroplast

CO_2

$C_6H_{12}O_6$

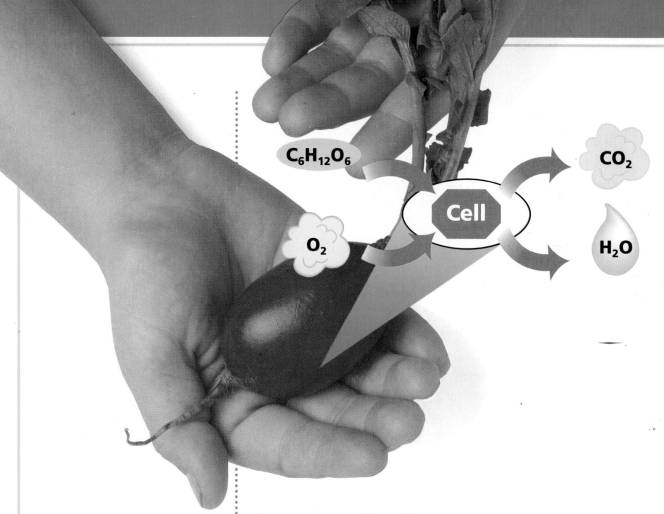

$C_6H_{12}O_6$

O_2

Cell

CO_2

H_2O

▲ *Respiration occurs in the cells of all living things.*

Sugars and Cells

Plant cells need energy to carry out the jobs they do. Those cells with chloroplasts absorb the energy of sunlight and store it in sugars that the other cells use. But cells of other plant parts that don't have chloroplasts, such as roots, need energy too. How does the stored energy get to these cells?

Tubes in the plant carry the sugars from the leaves to other parts of the plant. Once there, some sugars are stored for later use. For instance, the radish root contains sugars that were made in its leaves. When you eat a radish, you're eating those sugars stored in the radish root.

How does a plant release the energy stored in the sugar? **Respiration** is the process in which sugar's energy is released for use in the plant. During respiration, sugar reacts with oxygen to make carbon dioxide and water. As these sugar molecules break down, energy is released. Plant cells use this energy to grow, make new cells, and just stay alive.

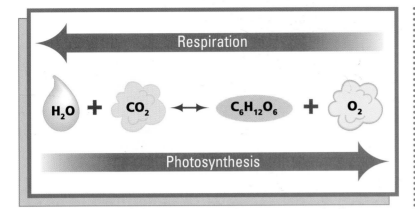

◄ This reaction happens both forward and backward.

Photosynthesis and Respiration

Read the chemical equation above. It says: Water reacts with carbon dioxide to make sugar and oxygen. You might have noticed that you just read the description of photosynthesis.

Now read the same equation backward. It says: Oxygen reacts with sugar to make carbon dioxide and water. This sentence describes respiration.

That's right. Respiration is the reverse of photosynthesis! As you study the table, you'll see that the reactions are "opposites" in other ways too.

Now you know how the sun's energy changes to chemical energy. Like calculators and watches, plants run on solar energy, too!

▼ Photosynthesis and respiration are "opposite" reactions.

Photosynthesis	Respiration
Stores energy	Releases energy
Occurs in cells with chlorophyll	Occurs in all cells
Takes place mostly in daylight	Takes place day or night
Produces oxygen, uses carbon dioxide	Produces carbon dioxide, uses oxygen

Checkpoint

1. What is the result of photosynthesis?
2. Where does photosynthesis take place?
3. How do plants use their stored energy?
4. Explain how photosynthesis and respiration are reverse reactions.
5. **Take Action!** Observe plants in an area. Sketch their positions—which have higher or lower branches and so on. How does the plant's position help it get sunlight?

Activity

Plants and Sunlight

What happens to green plants that do not get sunlight? Try this activity to find out.

Picture A

Picture B

Picture C

Gather These Materials

scissors
2 identical house plants
   such as coleus or
   philodendron

aluminum foil
masking tape
metric ruler

Follow This Procedure

1 Make a chart like the one on the next page. Record your observations in your chart.

2 Cut out 5 pieces of aluminum foil, each about 12 cm square. Use the scissors carefully. (Picture A)

3 Gently wrap a piece of the aluminum foil around one of the leaves on one of the plants. Use the masking tape to hold the foil in place. Be sure the leaf is covered completely. (Picture B)

4 Cover 4 more leaves on the same plant with foil. (Picture C)

5 Place both plants on a sunny windowsill for 7 days.

Predict: What will happen to the leaves that have been covered?

6 Uncover the leaves. Record your observations.

State Your Conclusions

1. What happened to the leaves that were covered with aluminum foil?

2. What happened to the leaves and the plant that were not covered with the foil?

3. Based on what you have learned and observed, what explanation can you give for the change of color in the leaves that were covered with foil? What if all the leaves on the plant had been covered with foil?

Record Your Results

Observations	
Leaves foil-covered	
Leaves not covered	

Let's Experiment

How do you think plants might grow to take advantage of the most sunlight? Use what you know about scientific methods to set up an experiment using plants and light from different directions.

3.2 *Food for Energy*

▶ **What happens to the food you eat?**

It's a great day for the school picnic. You race to the table with big juicy slices of watermelon and grab one. It's so delicious you go back again and again and again! A few hours later, you begin to feel sick. You say, "I never want to eat watermelon again!" But you know you'll feel better later.

Digestion Begins in the Mouth

The breaking down of food into forms your body can use is called **digestion.** When you eat, food travels in tubes through your digestive system—from your mouth through your intestines. Your body digests food as it moves along on this long journey. The first stop along the way is your mouth.

Crunch! When you pop a cracker into your mouth, you don't swallow it whole. Instead, you begin to chew it. Crunch, crunch, crunch! Your body can digest small pieces of food more easily than large pieces. So chewing plays an important role in digestion. Your teeth grind, mash, bite, and tear food into small pieces.

Your tongue helps soften the food by mixing it with saliva, the watery substance in your mouth. Enzymes in saliva help break down food even further. An **enzyme** is a substance that controls how quickly a chemical reaction occurs in your body.

▼ *This girl is storing energy!*

Enzymes are like traffic controllers guiding traffic along kilometers of roadways. They speed up or slow down thousands of chemical reactions as the food moves along. Each chemical reaction breaks larger food molecules down into smaller molecules. Each enzyme does one job in one certain type of chemical reaction. Then when the food molecules are finally small enough, they pass through the walls of the digestive system into your body.

However, the cracker being crushed by your teeth is hours away from that step. As you chew the cracker, an enzyme in your saliva helps break down the cracker. Then your tongue pushes the softened cracker to the back of your mouth to begin the next stage of its journey.

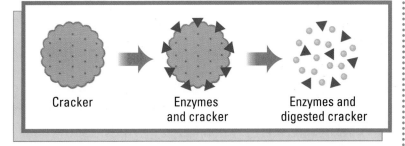

| Cracker | Enzymes and cracker | Enzymes and digested cracker |

▲ *Chewing and mixing food with saliva is the first step in digestion.*

Gulp! The cracker passes from your mouth into your esophagus. This tube connects your mouth and your stomach. It's about as long as the distance from your wrist to your elbow. Ringlike muscles surround the esophagus. These muscles push the cracker through the esophagus just like you might push a marble through a rubber tube. This action controls how much and how fast food moves along.

Tracking Your Food

The cracker soon reaches your stomach, although it no longer looks much like a cracker. The softened mass breaks down even more in the stomach. But enzymes don't begin to work on meat and other foods containing proteins until after they reach the stomach.

The inside of the stomach looks like a chamber lined with wrinkles and folds. This stomach lining makes two types of chemicals: enzymes and liquids called gastric juices.

Imagine that you're sinking your teeth into a big lemon. Its sour, biting juice squirts into your mouth. Your lips pucker and your face twists. Like the sour lemon juice, gastric juices contain an acid. But the acid in your stomach is much stronger than lemon juice! Gastric juices pour into the stomach as the food enters it. There the juices mix with the food.

These strong acids physically break down food. Besides that action, they kill many of the bacteria in the food and cause enzymes to start chemical reactions. The enzymes begin to break down foods such as the proteins of meat and cheese.

Next the stomach begins moving! Like a mixer whipping eggs, flour, and milk, the stomach begins churning. It mixes enzymes, gastric juices, and food pieces together. During this process, the cracker you ate becomes part of that acid liquid.

Gastric juices churning in an empty stomach make your stomach "growl." If you ate only one cracker, your stomach might be telling you it wants more!

➤ Food takes about a 9-meter journey through your digestive system.

Esophagus

Liver

Stomach

Pancreas

Small intestine

Large intestine

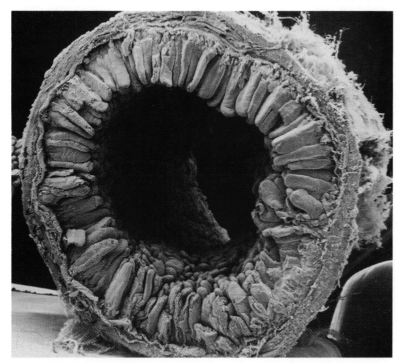

Tissues and Organs: *A Text-Atlas of Scanning Electron Microscopy* by R.G. Kessel and Randy H. Kardon. © 1979 W.H. Freeman and Company.

◄ The small intestine is lined with villi, fingerlike extensions that make more room for nutrients to be absorbed.

Notice how the small intestine turns and twists in the lower part of the trunk. On the next part of its journey, the food travels through this tube, which is 7 meters long in an adult!

Most digestion occurs in the small intestine. More enzymes and chemicals pass into the small intestine from other organs. For example, enzymes made in the pancreas pass through tubes into the upper part of the small intestine. Bile, a substance that breaks down fats, comes from the liver. These substances, along with enzymes in the small intestine, attack the liquid from the stomach.

The picture above shows tiny, fingerlike structures called villi that line the small intestine. The digested molecules of food leave the small intestine through these structures. They pass through the villi into blood vessels as nutrients. Your body uses nutrients to build new cells, to repair cells, or for energy to run, jump, and play. The blood circulates through the body carrying the nutrients. They pass from the blood into other cells of your body.

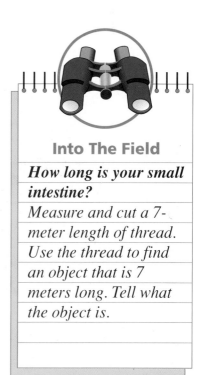

Into The Field

How long is your small intestine?

Measure and cut a 7-meter length of thread. Use the thread to find an object that is 7 meters long. Tell what the object is.

Food Changes to Energy

▼ You can be active because your cells carry out respiration.

The cracker you ate hours ago is now digested. It has broken down into sugars. These sugar molecules are now zipping along in your bloodstream carrying stored chemical energy. Imagine that these sugar molecules have just arrived at the cell. Now follow them through respiration to see how the stored energy in food is released for use.

First, the sugar molecules pass through the lining of the blood vessel into the cell. Between the blood vessel and the cell is a fluid that bathes the cells. The sugar enters this fluid, and then passes through the cell membrane. Once inside the cell, the sugar molecules combine with oxygen.

You take in oxygen when you breathe. It passes from your nose into your lungs. Then it moves into the bloodstream and is carried to the cells of the body.

Just like respiration in plants, sugar and oxygen combine to make carbon dioxide and water in your cells too. The carbon dioxide dissolves in blood and it goes to the lungs. It leaves your body as a gas, and you breathe it out through your nose or mouth.

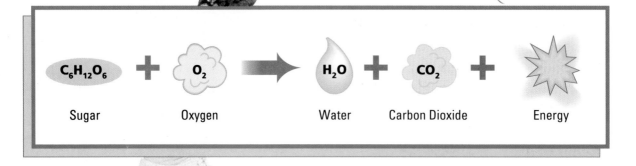

$C_6H_{12}O_6$	+	O_2	→	H_2O	+	CO_2	+	
Sugar		Oxygen		Water		Carbon Dioxide		Energy

Like the electricity needed to run a factory, the energy released during respiration runs your body. Your body stores some of the energy and uses the rest of it.

You store energy as fat. When you get cold, your body releases its stored energy and warms you. So a certain amount of fat on your body is healthful. Besides insulating your body, fat provides energy for work and play.

Energy is also stored in your muscle tissues. However, muscle tissue breaks down and releases this energy only when the body is actually starving and no other source of energy is left.

Your body quickly uses most of the energy you take in. Your body uses energy for all your body functions. Some released energy is used to grow and maintain your cells. Released energy is also used to do special jobs, such as seeing and hearing. You use energy when you talk on the phone, do your homework, watch TV, and when you sleep. And of course, the energy powers your muscles.

Imagine that you're on a long hike and that you've walked several kilometers. You have used your muscles so much that they cannot release enough energy. So your muscles feel tired. You sit on a rock to rest. While you rest, your muscle cells keep working. They receive more and more oxygen and sugars from your blood. And they get rid of waste products. After a while, the cells are ready to release more energy, and you feel rested enough to finish the hike.

Checkpoint

1. What role do enzymes play in digestion?
2. Where does most of the digestion occur?
3. What does respiration do for you?
4. **Take Action!** Stir lemon juice into a glass of milk. Watch for a few minutes. Compare this to what happens in the stomach during digestion.

HEALTH

Counting Calories

You've probably heard the word *Calorie* many times. Calories measure the energy in food, as well as the energy your body uses.

Many factors determine the number of Calories you use while doing an activity. Factors include body mass, level of fitness, the amount of fat and muscle, and air humidity and temperature.

The graph shows about how many Calories a 45-kilogram person burns per minute.

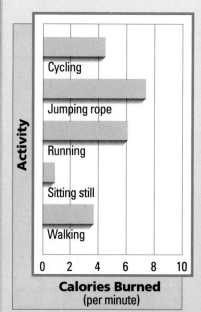

Calories Burned
(per minute)

What Did You Find Out?
1. *Which activity burns the most Calories?*
2. *How many Calories do you burn watching TV for one-half hour?*
3. *Calculate how many Calories you burn during the school day just by sitting still, walking, and running.*

Activity

Getting Through the Small Intestine

What kinds of substances can move into the bloodstream from the small intestine? Try this activity to find out.

Picture A

Gather These Materials

cover goggles	jar
metric measuring cup	funnel
water	5 coffee filters
large spoon	sugar test paper
sugar	weak iodine solution
cornstarch	dropper

Follow This Procedure

1 Make a chart like the one on the next page. Record your observations in your chart.

2 Put on your cover goggles.

3 Combine 250 mL of water, 1 spoonful of sugar, and 1 spoonful of cornstarch in the measuring cup. Stir the mixture.

4 Place the 5 coffee filters into the funnel, one filter inside the other. Fit the funnel on the top of the jar.

5 Pour the water mixture into the funnel. Be careful not to let any of the liquid spill over the top edge of the funnel. (Picture A)

Predict: *What passed through the filter paper into the jar?*

Picture B

Picture C

6 Take the funnel out of the jar. Then, test the water in the jar to see if sugar is still present. Dip a sugar test paper into the jar. Record what happens to the test paper. If sugar is present, the paper will change color. (Picture B)

7 Now test for starch. Use the dropper carefully to put 4 or 5 drops of weak iodine solution into the jar. *CAUTION: Do not get any iodine solution on your skin or clothing.* If starch is present, the reddish-brown iodine will turn the water bluish-black. (Picture C) Record your observations.

Sugar/starch mixture in jar	Color change?	
	yes	no
Sugar paper test		
Starch test with iodine		

State Your Conclusions

1. What happened to the sugar test paper when you tested the mixture in the jar for sugar? What can you conclude from this?

2. What happened to the mixture in the jar when you dropped the reddish-brown iodine solution into it? What does this tell you about the presence of starch?

3. Based on the results of your sugar and starch tests, explain the presence or absence of starch in the jar after the mixture had passed through the filter.

4. How are the coffee filters similar to the lining of the small intestine?

Let's Experiment

Both sugar and cornstarch were mixed in the water, yet only the sugar passed through the filters. Do you think salt could pass through the filters? Use what you know about scientific methods to find out.

3.3 *Nature's Balance*

> ## Why is what animals eat important?

The next time you sit under a tree, notice the rest of the plant life around you. You know from the Discover Activity that plants cycle water. But look at all the other living things. Be sure to include yourself in your picture. What other materials do they cycle? What energy sources do they use?

Energy Flow

Scientists describe organisms according to the kind of food that provides them with their energy. Organisms that make their own food using the sun's energy are called **producers**, which includes plants, algae, and other organisms with chlorophyll.

Most animals get their energy from the stored chemical energy in the food they eat. These animals are called **consumers.** Both a fox and a rabbit are consumers. The fox gets the chemical energy stored in the rabbit's cells. The rabbit got its chemical energy from energy stored in plant cells. So energy flows from producers to consumers—from the plant to the rabbit to the fox.

Scientists place consumers into three categories: herbivores, carnivores, and omnivores. The rabbit is an herbivore—an animal that eats only plants. The fox is a carnivore—an animal that eats only other animals. People and bears are omnivores because they eat both plants and animals.

▼ *Energy moves from the sun to the producers to the consumers in ecosystems.*

Food From the Sun

Energy from the sun flows through all living things in an ecosystem.

You know that in an ecosystem, producers trap the energy from the sun. The consumers then take in part of this energy.

Another level in the food chain also exists—**decomposers.** These living things, such as bacteria and fungi, break down the dead organisms. This action releases chemicals needed by other living things.

A single food chain shows only one pathway through which energy flows. A system of food chains in an ecosystem is called a **food web.** This ocean food web shows that the sun's energy flows through different pathways in the ecosystem. Follow the arrows to trace the flow of the sun's energy through this food web.

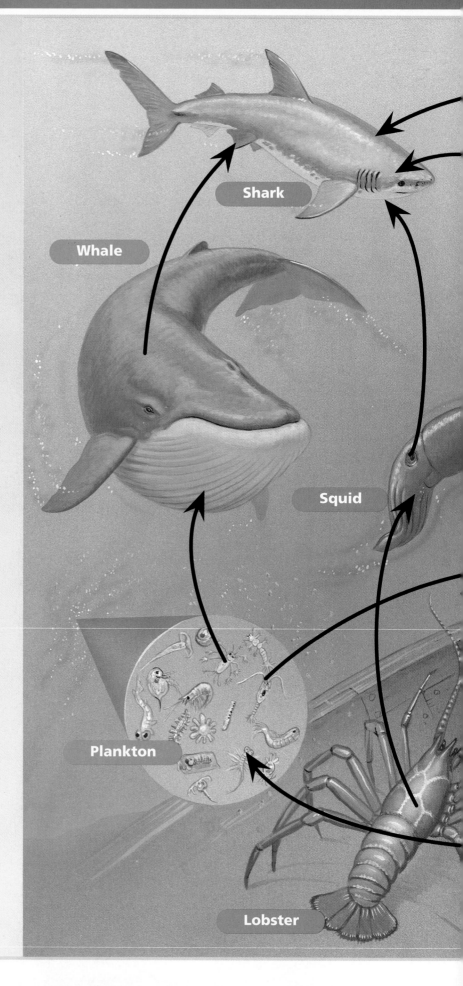

Shark

Whale

Squid

Plankton

Lobster

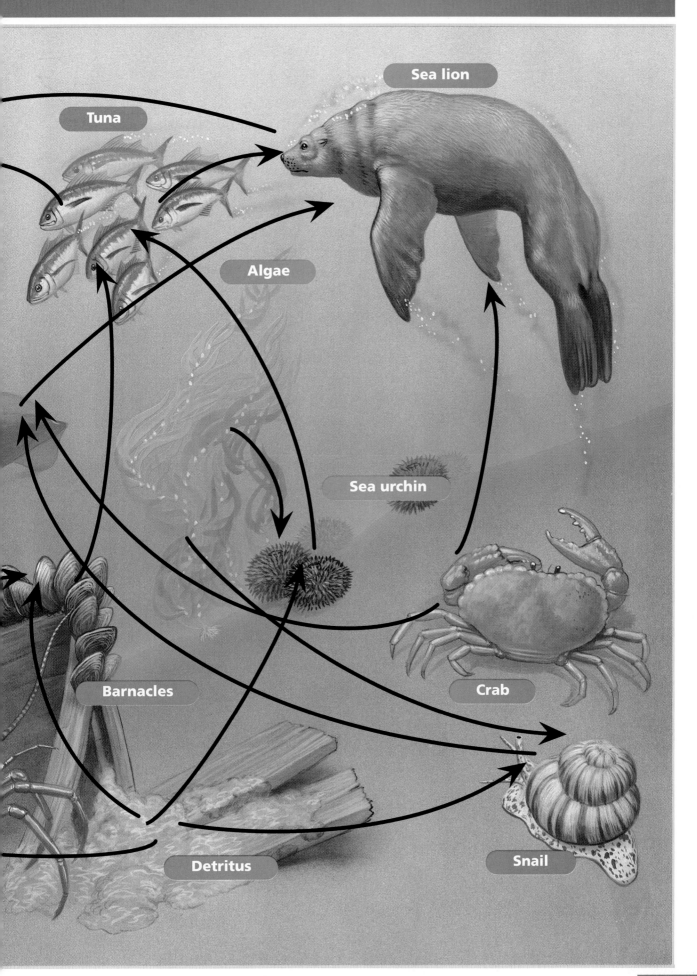

Sea lion

Tuna

Algae

Sea urchin

Crab

Barnacles

Detritus

Snail

➤ *Even you are running on sunlight!*

Back to the Sun

The picture below shows how producers and consumers recycle oxygen and carbon dioxide. During photosynthesis, producers on land and in the oceans take in carbon dioxide to make sugars. They also give off oxygen. During respiration, these producers also take in oxygen and release carbon dioxide as waste.

As if exchanging gifts, consumers and decomposers take in the oxygen released by the producers. Then during respiration, the consumers and decomposers release carbon dioxide as waste. Producers use this carbon dioxide to make sugars, and the cycle goes on.

During the carbon dioxide-oxygen cycle, producers capture the sun's energy. And as you know, most energy used on the earth can be traced back to the sun's electromagnetic radiation. This energy continuously changes form—to light energy, electrical energy, chemical energy, and others.

▼ *Because photosynthesis and respiration are opposite reactions, carbon dioxide and oxygen cycle through the atmosphere.*

Oxygen

Carbon dioxide

Much of the chemical energy stored by producers is "lost" as it flows through living organisms. Each organism uses some energy, but some also goes off into the air as heat. For example, when you eat an apple, some of the apple's chemical energy changes to heat to keep your body warm. If you ride a bike, you'll get even warmer. Some of this heat will be released into the air as you cool down again. In the air, this energy drifts away and is no longer useful.

As a result, less and less energy is passed along in each link of a food chain. Producers capture only part of the energy that reaches them. A consumer that eats only producers gets an even smaller amount of the energy. And a consumer that eats other animals gets even less of this energy. Because energy is lost at each step, food chains cannot have an unlimited number of links. Without the continuous input of energy from the sun, organisms could no longer live. Seems like everything runs on sunlight!

Checkpoint

1. Describe three types of consumers.
2. What are decomposers?
3. How is energy "lost" from a food chain?
4. Take Action! Draw a food chain using a cat, caterpillar, tree leaves, and bird. Label each as a consumer or a producer.

Having a Debate

In a debate, two groups argue an issue. Debating groups prepare by gathering information. Each group judges the information to see which facts support their arguments. Recognizing relevant and biased information will help you decide whether or not information supports your argument.

Thinking It Through

Suppose you were asked to plan a debate about eating a meatless diet. Judge these facts and conclusions.

Facts:

1. Some minerals such as iron are hard to get from a meatless diet.

2. Human stomachs can digest meat.

3. Chicken and fish are lower in fat than cheese and nuts.

Conclusion: Eating meat is necessary and healthful.

Facts:

1. Farmers must feed cattle about 7 kilograms of grain and soy to get 1 kilogram of beef. But people could eat 1 kilogram of grain and soy directly, without feeding it to cattle first.

2. Many nonmeat foods contain protein that can be eaten together to replace meat protein.

3. A high-fat diet has been linked to heart disease and some cancers.

Conclusion: A meatless diet is complete and healthful.

Judging the Facts: You could decide which facts are relevant to the conclusions. Does each fact support the conclusion? You should also think about whether the facts are being presented in a biased way. If you think they are, how would the bias affect the conclusion?

> **Your Turn**
>
> *Debate.* One team should argue in favor of eating meat. The other should argue against it. Later, discuss and judge the arguments of both sides.

Chapter Review

Thinking Back

1. How does energy change form during the first stage of **photosynthesis?**
2. Describe what happens during the second stage of photosynthesis.
3. Compare the products of photosynthesis and **respiration.**
4. How does a plant release the energy stored in sugar?
5. Describe the relationship between **enzymes** and chemical reactions.

6. How do gastric juices aid **digestion?**
7. Compare how **producers, consumers,** and **decomposers** get their energy.
8. How does energy flow through the **food web** of an ecosystem?
9. Explain how producers recycle oxygen and carbon dioxide.
10. Describe what happens to energy as it moves from producers to consumers in a food chain.

Connecting Ideas

1. Copy the concept map. Use the terms at the right to complete the map about photosynthesis and respiration.

oxygen   **carbon dioxide**
sugar   **water**

2. Write a sentence or two that summarizes the ideas shown in the concept map.

Gathering Evidence

1. In the Activity on page 56, what information did you use to predict the outcome of all the leaves of the plant being covered with foil?
2. In the Activity on page 64, what led you to conclude that coffee filters act like the lining of the small intestine?

Doing Science!

1. **Design a model** to show how food is digested in the stomach.
2. **Design a skit** to show the relationships among producers and consumers in a food web.

Watching the Ozone Hole

For the last 400 million years, ozone in the earth's atmosphere has blocked most of the dangerous ultraviolet rays from the sun. Besides causing skin cancer in humans, ultraviolet radiation can affect growth and reproduction of land and water plants.

Today, scientists conclude that the ozone layer is being destroyed, mainly by a gas called freon. You know freon as a chlorofluorocarbon, or CFC. Freon is used in refrigerators, some spray cans, air conditioners, and some plastic foam cups and packing material. When these products contain CFCs, each spray from a can, each leak from a refrigerator or air conditioner, or each burning of a foam cup spreads the CFCs into the air.

What can you and your family do about ozone depletion?

Then, the freon rises into the atmosphere and breaks apart molecules in the ozone.

Needs and Goals
What can you and your family do about ozone depletion? Think about the different sources of freon that your family uses.

- Which items do you most need to use?
- Which items could your family eliminate with the least difficulty?
- Which items could you use less?

Gathering Information
Make a table of the items containing CFCs that your family uses. Think about how often you use each of them. Then decide how you could reduce or eliminate their use.

Possible Alternatives
Air conditioners pose problems when too many are in use or they are not in good repair. Sometimes, a fan might work just as well. Also, you can check consumer magazines to find out which brands last the longest before your family buys a new one.

Plastic foam cups are especially good for hot drinks and foods. But often they can be replaced by paper, plastic, or glass cups when heat is not a factor. Also, at home or school a reusable plastic or glass cup might be just as handy.

Many products that come in spray cans also come in tubes or other kinds of containers. Also, some products in spray cans no longer contain CFCs.

Evaluating Alternatives

Copy the chart. Fill in your ideas for how your family could reduce their use of items that might release freon.

Sources of CFCs		
Item	Solution	Will I probably do it?
Air conditioner	Use less	
Spray cans	Use pump sprays instead	
Refrigerator	Check for leaks	
Hamburger boxes	Eat at places that use paper wrapping	

Making the Best Choice

Now decide which of your ideas are the best for your family. Remember that the answer may be different for every family.

Now You Do It

1. Which items that hurt the ozone layer are easiest to replace? Why?

2. Which items that hurt the ozone layer are hardest to replace? Why?

3. *On Your Own* If your school uses plastic foam cups, you and your friends could campaign or write a letter to have the cups replaced with paper ones.

4. *Critical Thinking* Many scientists think that the United States, Japan, and the countries of Western Europe are more responsible for the hole in the ozone layer than other countries are. How would you decide whether you agree or disagree?

The House of Tomorrow

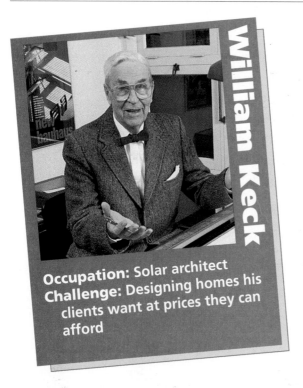

William Keck

Occupation: Solar architect
Challenge: Designing homes his clients want at prices they can afford

Since William Keck was a boy, he has looked for good values. So if you ask him why solar heating is important, he'll tell you that it saves money and it saves energy.

Mr. Keck designs solar-heated homes. He and his brother, George Keck, designed the House of Tomorrow for the 1933 World's Fair in Chicago. "On the south side of the building it had windows 12 feet high. And on a sunny winter day it would be toasty warm inside, without using a heater or a furnace."

Was your House of Tomorrow the first home with solar heat?

"As far as solar heating is concerned, there's nothing new under the sun. They were using the sun to help warm houses in northern China 5,000 years ago. And 2,000 years ago, the Greek philosopher Socrates wrote that a building with large southern exposures could be warm in winter and cool in summer."

What was the first house you built?

"When we were growing up, George and I built a clubhouse. It was an old house that we made into a warming hut for ice skating. But one of the first houses we designed was built in Arizona. First we designed it, then we went out there and built it ourselves. You learn a lot by doing."

In what other special ways can you heat buildings?

Fifty years ago Mr. Keck designed an airport hangar with pipes under the concrete floor. Hot air flowed through the pipes, keeping warm both the floor and the people working in the hangar. Besides being cheaper, it kept the workers warm when the large hangar doors were opened.

Solar Cells: Light for Power

A solar cell converts the energy of sunlight to electricity.

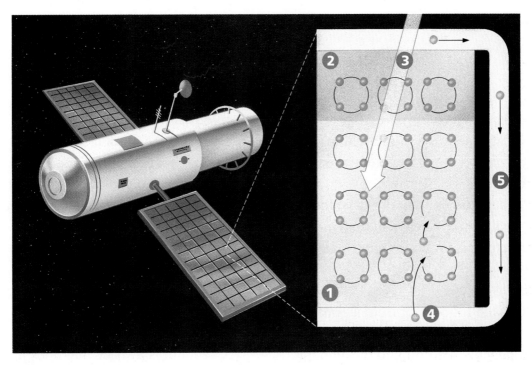

1 Some of the atoms in the bottom layer of a solar cell have fewer electrons than normal.

2 Some atoms in the top layer have extra electrons.

3 When sunlight strikes a solar cell, it knocks electrons from its atoms leaving "holes."

4 The extra electrons from the top layer move to fill in "holes" in the bottom layer.

5 The movement of the electrons creates an electric current that can power objects like satellites.

Find Out On Your Own

Find out how much light is needed to make a solar-powered calculator work. Use your findings to write directions for using the calculator.

Module Review

Making Connections

Energy

1. Explain why the total amount of energy in a system stays the same.
2. How does energy change form during photosynthesis?
3. How are potential and kinetic energy related?
4. Name the earth's main energy source.

Systems and Interactions

5. Describe how members of an ecosystem recycle oxygen and carbon dioxide through their environment.
6. How do interactions between the atmosphere and sunlight affect the amount of solar energy that reaches the earth's surface?

Using What I Learned

Categorizing

1. State whether each of the following has a greater amount of potential energy or kinetic energy.
(a) a chemical bond joining two atoms
(b) a rock rolling down a mountain
(c) a football sailing through the air
(d) a parked car

Ordering

2. Study the food chain from a grassland food web shown in the diagram. Order the organisms according to the amount of the sun's energy each receives as it feeds in the pattern shown.

Comparing

3. Compare the products of respiration and photosynthesis.
4. How are a molecule of oxygen and a molecule of ozone alike and different?

Relating

5. What job does the circulatory system play in respiration?
6. How are work, power, and energy related?

Applying

7. A vacuum is a space that does not contain any air. Could a match burn in a vacuum? Explain.

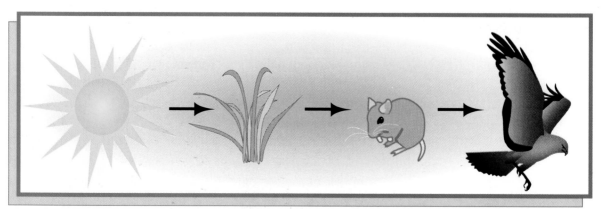

Applying What I Learned

Performance Task

Construct a covering for an ice cube that keeps solar energy from melting the ice cube. Use foil, cloth, newspaper, plastic wrap, and plastic foam. Decide where to put your covered ice cubes.

Action Project

Help educate members of your local community about the effect CFCs have on the ozone layer. Write a newsletter to your neighbors that describes this relationship and what can be done to protect the atmosphere.

Drawing

Make a drawing of a food chain that exists in your ecosystem.

Science Theater

Prepare a skit for a news broadcast describing the greenhouse effect. Explain how the earth might change if its temperature rises or cools.

Exhibitions

Make a poster or bulletin board showing the different wavelengths of the electromagnetic spectrum.

What If

What if the voters in your town had to decide whether a forested area should be cut down to make room for a large shopping mall? Supporters of the plan say that the mall will help the town by providing many new jobs for local workers. Others argue that cutting down the trees will damage the environment. What questions might you ask when forming an opinion on the issue? How would you vote on this issue?

Electricity

Electricity

What do you have in common with a bolt of lightning? Electricity! This powerful force not only creates lightning but also helps your nerves carry signals to and from your brain. In this module, you'll find out how electrical impulses travel through wires, help you see and hear, and bring the world into your living room.

CHAPTER

1 Electric Signals

What's so positive about being negative? Differences in positive and negative charges produce electricity. One type flows along circuits.

CHAPTER

2 Nerve Signals

I can't believe my eyes and ears! These amazing organs allow you to see and hear, thanks in part to electrical impulses.

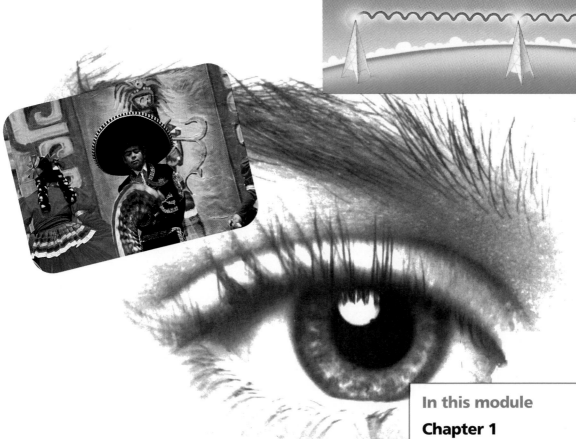

3 Signals in the Air

Is it live or is it television?

Television stations use radio waves to transmit the sights and sounds of the world into your home.

In this module

Chapter 1
Electric Signals   E 4
Chapter 2
Nerve Signals   E 30
Chapter 3
Signals in the Air   E 54

Kids Did It   E 74
Exploring Careers   E 76
How Things Work   E 77
Module Review   E 78

At the end of the book

Using Metric   1
Using Scientific Methods   2
Safety in Science   4
Experiment Skills   6
Glossary   30
Index   38
Acknowledgments   47

Electric Signals

C'mon, c'mon, you're almost there!

How can you use electric charges to win a race?

Line the inside of a box with aluminum foil. Place a few pieces of dry cereal inside. Then cover the box with clear plastic wrap. Rub the lid vigorously with a piece of nylon. Touch the lid above the cereal with your finger. What happens? In this way, try to get one piece of cereal to the other end of the box before your partner does.

For Discussion

1. *What happened when you touched the lid?*
2. *Do wool and fur have the same effect as nylon?*

1·1 *Electrical Energy*

▶ ### *How does electricity behave?*

You're just in time to watch a TV special about dinosaurs. Just as you switch on the set and settle down on the couch, rain begins to fall. Suddenly, a bright flash of lightning streaks across the sky and a crash of thunder booms. The lights go out and the TV screen goes black. What's going on?

▲ *An electric storm can affect the TV picture.*

Electric Charge

Both lightning and the energy that runs your television and lights are electricity. Although you may have read about electrical energy, you probably don't know how electricity works. To find out, you need to look inside an atom.

Protons crowd together in the nucleus of an atom. Electrons spin around the protons because the electrons are attracted to the protons. It's this force of attraction that holds the electrons in the atom.

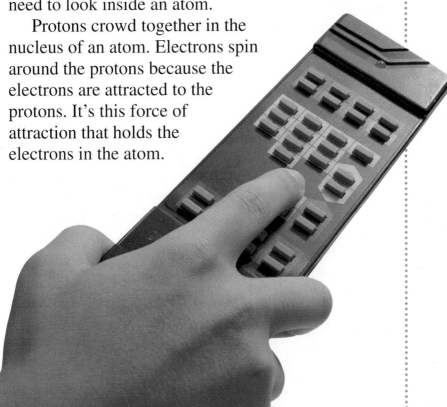

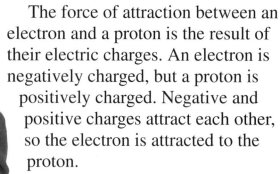

The force of attraction between an electron and a proton is the result of their electric charges. An electron is negatively charged, but a proton is positively charged. Negative and positive charges attract each other, so the electron is attracted to the proton.

Electron charges can also repel, or push away, each other. Negative charges repel negative charges. Positive charges repel positive charges.

A balanced atom has the same number of protons and electrons. The positive charges balance the negative charges, so the atom has no charge.

Jumping Electrons

Believe it or not, you deal with electric charges on a daily basis. Sometimes your hair flies away when you try to comb it. When you take a knitted hat off, your hair can stand on end. You can explain both of these events by thinking about the forces of attraction and repulsion. The hair and the comb repel each other, but the hair and the hat attract each other.

If you rub two things together, some of the electrons from the atoms in one object can jump to the atoms in the other object. Before this picture was taken, the boy rubbed each of the balloons against his hair. Friction caused some electrons in the atoms of his hair to move to the atoms of the balloons. The balloons now have more negative than positive charges, so they're negatively charged.

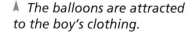
▲ The balloons are attracted to the boy's clothing.

When the boy touches the balloons to his clothes, the balloons stick to him! Why? Where the balloons touch his clothing, some electrons in his clothing are repelled by the negatively charged balloons. As a result, his clothes become positively charged. The negatively charged balloon is attracted to the positively charged clothes, so the balloon sticks to the clothes.

Jumping electrons also cause "static cling." When clothes rub together in the hot, dry air of a clothes dryer, electrons jump from one piece of clothing to another. Some clothes become negatively charged and others become positively charged. Clothes with opposite charges stick together—and to you! Using a fabric softener helps get rid of the problem of static cling.

The toy uses friction to make sparks.

Why do you see a spark when you walk across a rug and then touch a metal doorknob? As you walk across the rug, friction causes electrons to move from the rug to your shoes and into your body. You become negatively charged! Then when you touch the doorknob, the electrons jump from your hand to the doorknob. The difference in electric charge between you and the doorknob is great, so you see the jumping charges as a spark.

Friction also caused the colored sparks you see on the toy in the picture. When you pump the handle on the bottom of the toy, metal parts inside the toy rub together.

Giant Sparks

Lightning is moving electric charges.

Before a storm, negative charges build up in the bottom of clouds. These negative charges repel negative charges on the ground under the cloud.

Then, for a short time, the ground becomes positively charged. This causes current to flow between the negative cloud and the positive ground. You see this current as a giant spark—lightning!

Lightning rod

Safety during storms

An electric storm—one that produces lightning—is called a thunderstorm. Although thunder might make you jump, it really isn't dangerous. Thunder is the sound that air molecules make when they're rapidly heated by a lightning bolt.

But lightning is dangerous. It always strikes the highest object on the ground below. One way to protect a tall building or house from lightning is to put up a lightning rod. The lightning rod conducts electricity away from the building and down into the ground where it can do little harm.

You, too, risk being struck by lightning if you're the highest object in an open field. You shouldn't sit under trees either. While the tree might take the shock of the lightning bolt, you could get hit by falling branches. So whenever possible—go inside! The safest place to wait out an electric storm is inside a house or building.

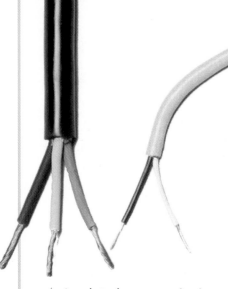

▲ Insulated copper wire is covered with plastic or rubber.

Electric Current

While a lightning bolt jumps from place to place, the electricity that runs your television behaves in a different way. Your television, lights, doorbell, and all sorts of other appliances are run by an electric current. **Electric current** is the flow of electric charge. Let's see how it works.

Suppose you have a piece of wire. The wire is made up of many atoms, all having the same number of electrons. A free, unattached electron might jump to an atom at one end of your wire, as in the diagram. A current then flows from that end of the wire to the other.

Here's what happens. The free electron can make room for itself if it pushes another electron out of the first atom. The pushed electron jumps to the next atom. But now the second atom has one extra electron, so an electron flows out of that atom and it jumps to the third atom. This flow of electrons down the wire is an electric current.

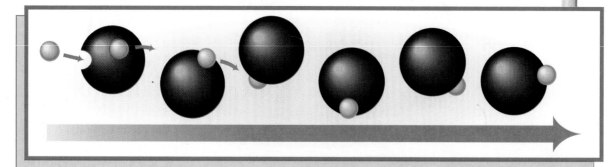

▲ In the diagram, electricity is flowing from left to right.

A **conductor** is a substance that lets electric charge pass through it. Metals are good conductors because their electrons flow more freely than the electrons in most other solids. Silver is the best conductor of the metals, but silver is too costly to use for wires. Most homes and buildings have copper wires.

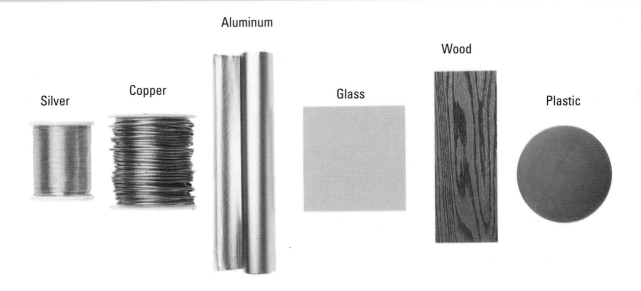

Silver Copper Aluminum Glass Wood Plastic

Best Conduction .... **Best Insulation**

Anything that slows down the flow of electric charge in a material is called resistance. Resistance changes electrical energy to heat and light. When electric current passes through wires in a light bulb, the current changes into light and heat. When current passes through a toaster, it changes to heat and light.

An **insulator** is a substance that conducts very little electricity. The things in the picture above are arranged from good conductors on the left to good insulators on the right. Materials such as plastic, wood, rubber, and glass are good insulators because their electrons do not move easily.

◣ *The best insulator among the things in the picture is plastic. The best conductor is silver.*

Checkpoint

1. What is the difference between forces of attraction and forces of repulsion?
2. What causes a spark?
3. What is the purpose of a lightning rod?
4. Why is a good conductor a poor insulator?
5. Take Action! Describe the coverings on electric wires at your home in terms of insulators or conductors.

Activity

Conductor or Insulator?

How can you find out if a material conducts electricity? Try this activity and see.

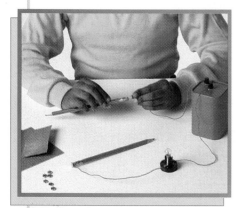

Picture A

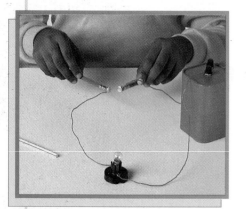

Picture B

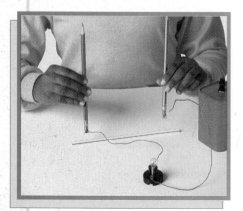

Picture C

Gather These Materials

cover goggles
3 pieces of insulated
  wire, about 18 cm long
sandpaper
2 pencils with erasers
2 thumbtacks

6-volt battery
flashlight bulb
bulb holder
coins
plastic ruler
aluminum foil

Follow This Procedure

1 Make charts like the ones on the next page. Record your observations in your charts.

2 Put on your cover goggles.

3 Use sandpaper to strip about 4 cm of insulation from each end of the insulated wires. Tightly wind one end of one wire around the point of a thumbtack. Wrap the wire about 6 times. Carefully stick the thumbtack into the eraser of one of the pencils. Make sure that the wires are secure under the thumbtack. This is one test probe. (Picture A)

4 Make a second test probe by repeating Step 3.

5 Wire the circuit. Connect the wire attached to one test probe to the battery. Connect the wire attached to the other test probe to one terminal of the bulb holder.

6 Connect one end of the third wire to the free terminal of the battery. Connect the other end to the free terminal of the bulb holder.

7 Test your circuit by touching the ends of the test probes to each other. If your circuit is connected properly, the lightbulb should light up. (Picture B)

Predict: *Which materials will conduct electricity and make the bulb light up?*

8 Test each material on the list by touching the 2 test probes to the material. (Picture C) Don't let the probes touch each other. Record your observations. Decide if the material is an insulator or a conductor.

Record Your Results

Materials	Does the bulb light?

Conductors	Insulators

State Your Conclusions

1. Which of the materials are conductors? insulators? How do you know?
2. What do all the conductors have in common?

Let's Experiment

Is salt dissolved in water a better conductor than sugar dissolved in water? Use what you know about scientific methods to find out.

1.2 *Using Electricity*

▶ **What does the power button do?**

What's the very first thing you do when you sit down to watch television? Or when you use a flashlight or a calculator? You press, flip, or turn an *off* switch to *on*. A picture appears on the TV screen, the flashlight goes on, and numbers glow on the calculator display. When you move the switch again, everything goes dark. What's happening?

Electric Circuits

When you turn on a machine that uses electricity, the current flows on a closed path called a **circuit**. The path is closed because current flows around and around the path. A circuit can have any shape and any size—as long as it's closed.

Circuits have to include a source of energy, such as a battery. Batteries give the energy needed to get the current flowing. The flashlight in the picture has two batteries and a bulb.

▼ Current moves around the circuit and lights the bulb of the flashlight.

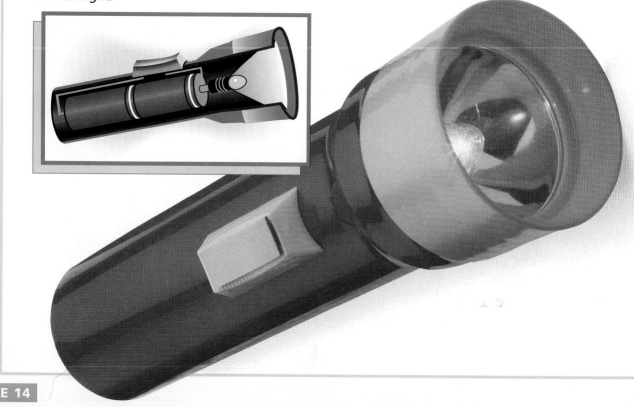

Circuits usually contain at least one device, such as the flashlight bulb, that uses the electricity. The diagram shows that when the flashlight bulb is lit, current moves from the batteries to the light bulb and back to the batteries.

What happens when you turn the flashlight on and off? When you turn the switch on, the circuit closes and current flows. When you turn the switch off, the circuit is broken and current stops flowing. Out goes the light!

Two Kinds of Circuits

If one of these pretty lights burns out, all the lights go dark. Have you ever changed each bulb on a string of lights, trying to find the one that's gone bad? If the string had fifty lights, it probably took you awhile to find the bad bulb.

This "all or nothing" situation can be traced to the circuit. When lights—or other devices—are placed one after another in one closed path, they form a series circuit.

The current in a series circuit can move along only one path. The charges have to move through every light on the circuit. If one light in a series circuit burns out, the circuit breaks and the other lights in the circuit won't light. The colored lights shown here are in a series circuit.

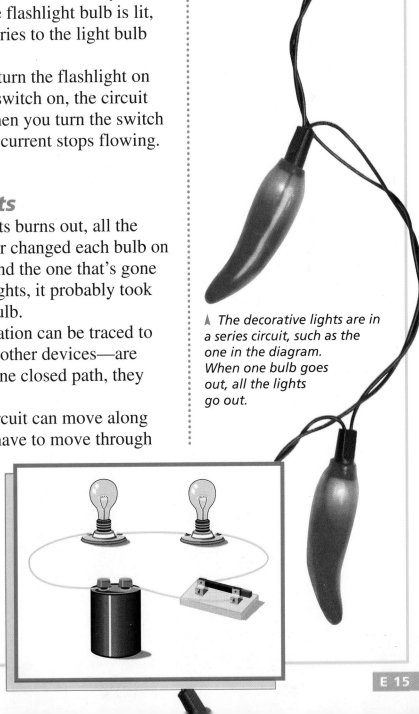

▲ The decorative lights are in a series circuit, such as the one in the diagram. When one bulb goes out, all the lights go out.

What if all the lights in your home went dark each time one bulb burned out? Or, what if you had to turn on all the electric appliances every time you turned a light on? That's what you would have to do if you had a series circuit in your home.

Luckily, the circuits in your home are parallel circuits, so you can turn on one appliance at a time. A parallel circuit allows the current to flow along more than one path. Notice in the diagram that each light has its own path—or "little circuit"—for electricity. If one of the lights in a parallel circuit burns out, the current moves right past the burned-out light and on around the circuit. Meanwhile, the other lights stay lit!

Danger: Electrical Fire

Pretend you're running the television, the toaster, an electric fan, and an iron—all at the same time. Then you turn on the microwave oven. All of a sudden, the power goes out. Your microwave oven overloaded the circuit. When wires carry too much electricity, they get hot and could cause a fire. Either fuses or circuit breakers are used in buildings and houses to help prevent electrical fires.

▼ *Electric appliances in your home are on parallel circuits such as the one in the diagram.*

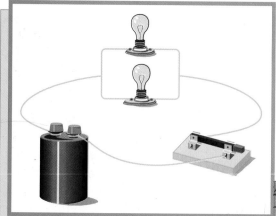

Into The Field

Where are the fuses or circuit breakers in your home?

Ask an adult to help you find them. Draw the location in your home. CAUTION: Do not touch them. Locate them only with the help of an adult.

⅄ *If the metal strip in a fuse melts, the circuit is broken.*

How does a fuse work? Look at the thin strip of metal on the top of the fuse. All the current that flows through the circuit must first flow through the metal strip. If too much current passes through the metal strip, the metal gets very hot and it melts. When the metal strip melts, the circuit is broken. Current can't flow through the wire, so the power goes out. To close the circuit again, you have to replace the old fuse with a new one. All hardware stores sell fuses.

Newer houses and buildings usually have circuit breakers instead of fuse boxes. Inside the circuit breaker is a metal strip fixed to an on-off switch that opens and closes the circuit. When too much current passes through the metal strip, it gets hot and "trips" the switch to open the circuit. As a result, the current stops flowing. To start the current flowing again, you just flip the switch to close the circuit. You don't need to replace circuit breakers like you do fuses when the power goes out.

⅄ *A circuit breaker switch*

Checkpoint

1. What parts does a circuit contain?
2. Compare series and parallel circuits.
3. What do fuses and circuit breakers do?
4. **Take Action!** Make a map of your home showing the electrical appliances you use and the location of all electrical outlets.

Activity

Making a Motor

You can make your own electric motor from simple materials you can find in your classroom. Do this activity to learn how.

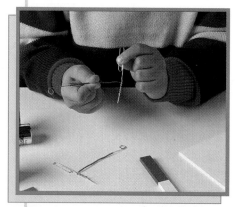

Picture A

Gather These Materials

cover goggles
2 pieces of insulated
  wire, each 20 cm long
1 piece of insulated
  wire, 200 cm long
sandpaper

2 metal paper clips
plastic foam board
2 D-cell batteries
electrician's tape
bar magnet

Follow This Procedure

1. Make a chart like the one on the next page. Record your observations in your chart.

2. Put on your cover goggles.

3. Use the sandpaper to strip 6 cm of insulation off of each end of the 3 wires.

4. Straighten the outer loop of each paper clip. Tightly wrap one end of each short wire around the straight leg of each paper clip. (Picture A) Then secure the wires with electrician's tape.

5. Make a coil from the long wire by wrapping it around one battery 20 times. Remove the coil from the battery and wrap each free end around the loops twice to hold them together. Leave the free ends sticking straight out from the coil.

6. Stick the paper clips into the board. Hang the coil between the paper clips, using the free ends of the wire to attach the coil to the clips. (Picture B)

Picture B

Picture C

7 Tape the batteries together with electrician's tape so that the positive end of one battery touches the negative end of the other battery.

8 Make a loop in the free end of each of the wires that is attached to a paper clip. Tape one of the loops so that it touches one of the free ends of one of the taped batteries.

Predict: *What happens if you hold a magnet near the coil as you complete the circuit?*

9 Ask your partner to hold the free loop of wire to the free end of the taped batteries. Hold the magnet near the coil, moving the magnet until the coil starts moving. You may need to gently nudge the coil with your finger. (Picture C)

10 Use your chart to make a drawing of your motor. Label the coil, the magnet, the energy source, and switch.

Drawing of electric motor

State Your Conclusions

1. What happened when you moved the magnet near the coil?

2. What happens to the moving coil when the current stops?

Let's Experiment

What would happen if you used a stronger magnet? Use what you know about scientific methods to find out.

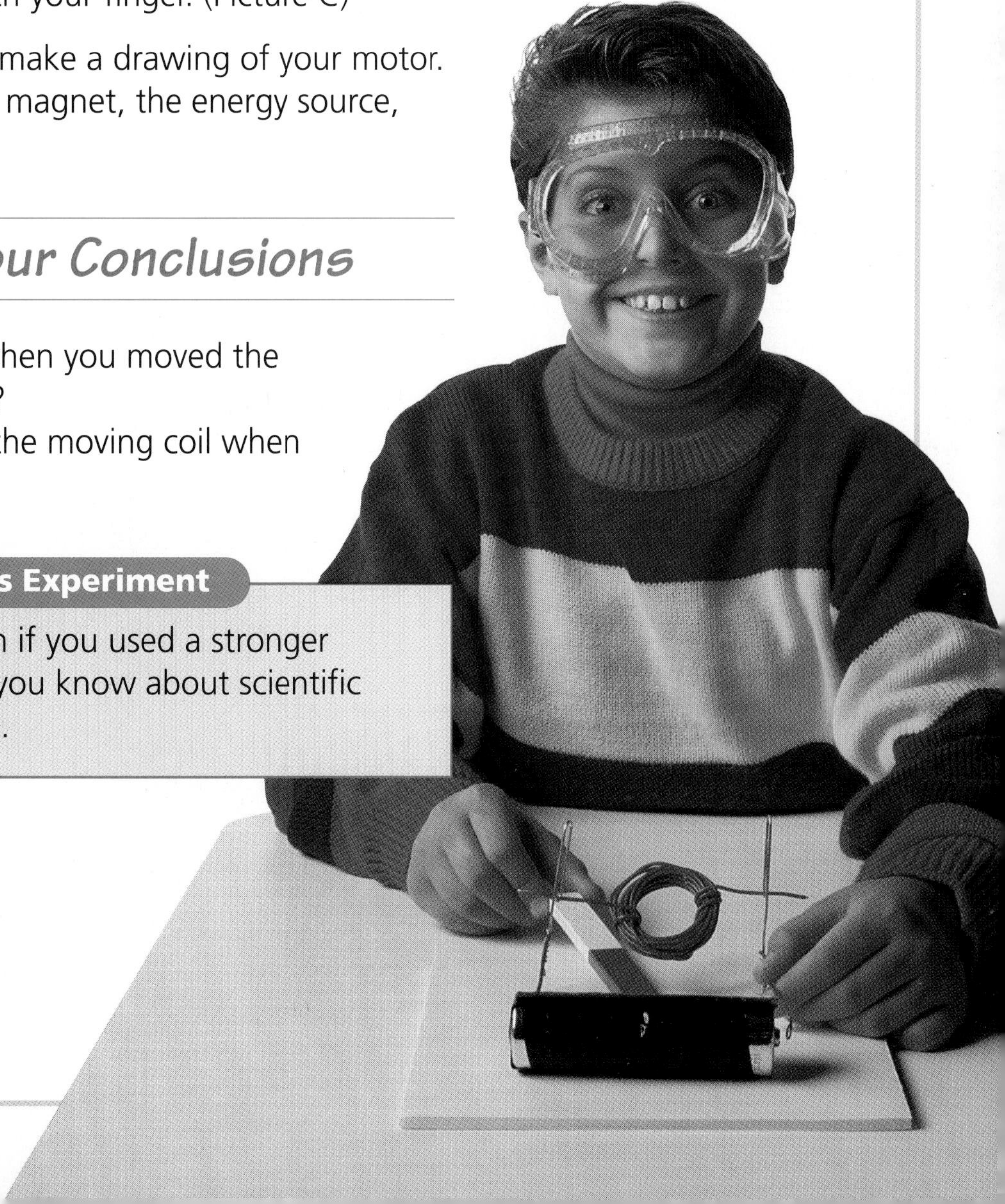

LESSON

1.3 *Magnetism*

▶ *What is magnetism?*

You've probably used magnets to stick cartoons or pictures to your refrigerator. But did you know you also use magnets when you turn on a television, a hair dryer, or your stereo? Believe it or not, you use magnets all the time!

Magnetic Fields

You've probably been playing with magnets long enough to know they attract paper clips and nails. The force of attraction that comes from a magnet is called magnetism. The **magnetic field** of a magnet is the space around the magnet where its force of attraction, or pull, is felt.

▼ *The curved lines in the picture below show the shape of the magnetic field around a bar magnet.*

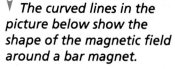

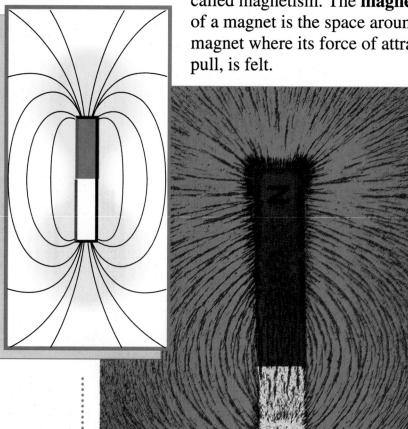

➤ *Iron filings line up in a pattern that reveals the shape of the magnetic field around a bar magnet.*

Even though you can't see a magnetic field, you can see evidence of it. The picture shows what happens when you lay a piece of clear plastic over a magnet and sprinkle iron filings on it. The filings line up in a pattern made of curved lines. If you use a bar magnet, the pattern will look like the one in the picture. But if you use a round magnet, the pattern will be different. The shape of the field depends on the shape of the magnet itself!

Notice how the iron filings seem to move out from the ends of the magnet. The lines are almost straight at the ends of the magnet, but they curve around the middle of the magnetic field. The filings form this pattern because the magnetic field is strongest near the ends of the magnet. These ends are called the magnetic poles. All magnets have two poles—a north pole and a south pole.

The magnetic poles of two magnets either pull or push each other. Does this action sound familiar? Just as electric charges attract or repel, magnetic poles attract or repel. A north pole and a south pole attract each other. But two north poles or two south poles repel each other.

Are all metals attracted to a magnet? No, if you use a copper penny or a silver ring near a magnet, nothing happens. But if you put objects made of iron near a magnet, the magnet attracts them! Magnets attract paper clips because they're made of steel, which is mostly iron. Magnets also attract cobalt and nickel.

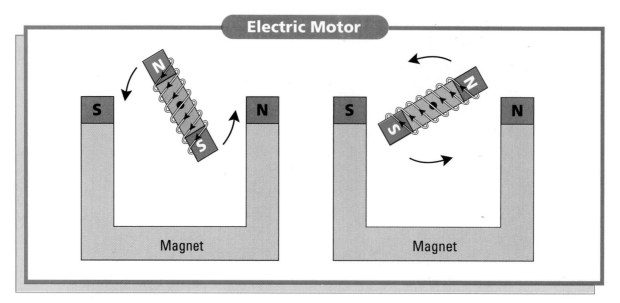

Electric Motor

Magnet

Magnet

Electric Motors

The discovery that magnetism and electricity are related led to the invention of the electric motor. You can find motors in hundreds of machines—from blenders to washers.

How are magnetism and electricity related? For one thing, electricity can be used to produce magnetism. A wire doesn't look like a magnet, but it can act like one. When an electric current runs through a wire, the current creates a magnetic field around the wire. A coil of wire produces an even stronger magnetic field than a straight wire does.

The magnetic field around a coiled wire has a north pole and a south pole just like a regular magnet has. But the coil's poles can be switched by reversing the current's direction. Then the north pole becomes the south pole and the south pole becomes the north pole. When the current is turned off, the coil of wire loses its magnetism.

The diagram shows how a motor works. A coil that can spin is placed between the poles of a U-shaped magnet. When you switch on a motor, current flows through the coil. The north pole of the coil is attracted to the south pole of the magnet. Likewise, the coil's south pole is attracted to the magnet's north pole.

Thanks to the attraction of the poles, the coil spins halfway around. Then the electric motor reverses the direction of the current in the coil.

When the current reverses, the poles of the coil also reverse. For a split second, the north pole of the coil is at the north pole of the magnet. Two like poles repel, so the coil spins halfway around again. Every time the poles of the coil reach the poles of the magnet, the current reverses. So the coil spins around and around for as long as the motor runs.

How does the spinning coil run a hair dryer fan? A fan in the dryer is tied directly to the coil. The spinning coil turns the fan blades, and air rushes from the dryer.

The mechanical energy produced by electric motors can do many different jobs. Some motors turn gears to run machines such as trains. Others turn pulleys to run appliances such as sewing machines and washing machines. All these machines depend on motors that use electricity to produce magnetism in a coil.

▼ *Inside a hair dryer is a motor. The motor is used to run a fan.*

➤ *The lines describe the earth's magnetic field.*

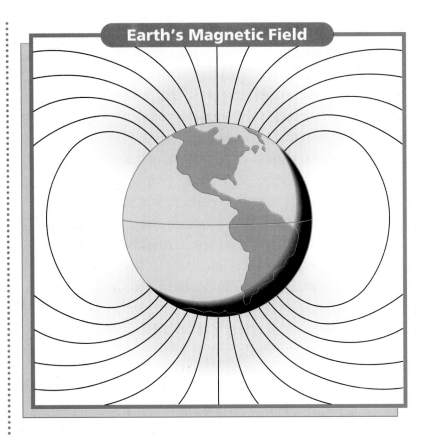

Earth's Magnetic Field

➤ *The directional compass on the next page was used during the 1600s.*

Earth: A Huge Magnet

Magnetic fields surround many planets in the solar system, including Earth. Scientists think that the movement of electrons inside Earth's core make the planet behave like a gigantic bar magnet.

Earth's magnetic field looks like the one around a bar magnet. The magnetic field is strongest at the magnetic north and south poles, just as it is for the bar magnet.

Be careful not to confuse magnetic poles with geographic poles. The geographic poles have a fixed location at each end of the earth's axis. But the magnetic poles do not line up with the geographic poles. For example, the magnetic and geographic north poles are about 1800 kilometers apart.

Besides not lining up, the magnetic poles flip-flop, or reverse, sometimes as often as every half-million years. The north magnetic pole becomes the south magnetic pole and the south magnetic pole becomes the north magnetic pole.

About 1500 years ago, the people in China invented the first directional compass. They discovered that if they tied a piece of string around a thin magnet and held on to the end of the string, the magnet would turn until its north pole faced in one particular direction. No matter where the magnet was located, its north pole always pointed in the same direction. With string and a magnet, the Chinese invented the first directional compass!

The earth's strong magnetic field makes the magnetic needle of a compass turn until its poles point north and south. The needle's "north-seeking" pole points to the magnetic north pole of the earth. Its "south-seeking" pole points to the magnetic south pole.

Hikers and explorers can use a directional compass to find directions and keep from getting lost. If a hiker faces north, east is to the right and west is to the left.

Just Passing Through

Can magnetic force pass through all materials? Let's investigate.

What To Do
A. Copy the chart below and record your observations in this chart.

	Observations
Needle	
Paper	
Paper-10	
Plastic	
Plastic-5	
Foil	
Cloth	

B. Place a sewing needle next to a magnet. What happens?
C. Repeat step B, only this time, place one piece of paper between the magnet and the needle. Record what happens.
D. Repeat step B five more times using each of the things listed below.
a) 10 sheets of paper
b) 1 sheet of plastic
c) 5 sheets of plastic
d) aluminum foil
e) cloth

What Did You Find Out?
1. *Which materials keep the magnetic force from passing through?*
2. *How does increasing the thickness of paper or plastic affect a magnet's force?*

Sunspots

A magnetic field does a lot more than run motors and spin compass needles. For instance, the sun's huge magnetic field causes radio static and brilliant displays of light in the night sky.

Because the sun is made up of very hot gases, its magnetic field is harder to describe than the earth's. Great magnetic activity produces powerful magnetic storms that move across the sun's surface. These magnetic storms show up as dark patches, called sunspots, on the sun's surface. The picture shows what sunspots look like. Never try to find sunspots. You can damage your eyes by looking directly at the sun.

Sunspots grow and shrink as they churn across the sun's surface. The number of sunspots changes from one year to the next. But every 11 years, a very large number of sunspots are visible.

Sometimes sunspots shoot huge plumes of gas into space. These gassy sprays contain electrons and other particles that have electric charges. The charged particles stream away from the sun in all directions. Some pass near the earth. The magnetic field of the earth captures some of the charged particles and pulls them toward the magnetic north and south poles.

When large numbers of charged particles enter the air near the earth's magnetic poles, they make the air glow with bright flashes and patterns of colored light like the ones in the photograph. These flashes of light are known as the northern lights in the Northern Hemisphere and the southern lights in the Southern Hemisphere.

▲ *The dark areas on the sun are known as sunspots.*

The nearer to the poles you live, the better you can see the northern or southern lights. In the Northern Hemisphere, for example, people in Alaska and northern Canada have a great view of these colorful sky shows.

Charged particles from the sun also interfere with the electricity going into businesses and homes. They can cause a sharp, brief increase in the amount of current in a wire. This increase is known as a power surge. Power surges spell trouble for machines—especially computers.

Static is most likely to interrupt television and radio shows during times of great sunspot activity. Charged particles in the air disturb the electric signals carrying the broadcast. The sun's magnetic activity reaches even into your home!

Checkpoint

1. Which elements are attracted to magnets?
2. What does electric current do to a wire?
3. How is the earth like a giant bar magnet?
4. What causes the northern lights?
5. Take Action! Sprinkle iron filings on magnets with different shapes to find their magnetic fields. Draw what you see.

▼ *The northern lights as seen from Alaska*

Making Diagrams

A diagram is a picture that helps you to see what something looks like or how it works. The diagram doesn't have to look exactly like what it is picturing. It just needs to show the main parts and how they fit together.

Thinking It Through

Look at the series circuit diagram. The wire in the circuit is shown by a curved line. The circuit is a loop with one or two batteries on it. The break in the loop is the switch. The switch is shown as a slanted line over a space in the wire. The light bulb is a device that uses the current in the circuit.

The second diagram shows a parallel circuit. This circuit powers a light bulb and a toaster, but you don't see either of them! Instead, each is shown by a zigzag line between dots. A zigzag line stands for resistance. You can use the zigzag symbol for anything that uses electricity.

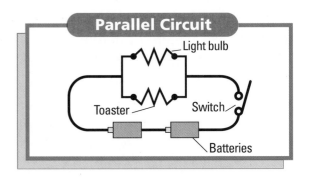

Parallel Circuit

Recall that resistance is something that opposes the flow of current. Both the wires inside the light bulb and inside the toaster act as "roadblocks" to the current. As a result, these wires get hot enough to give off heat and light.

The heat and light caused by resistance allows you to see light from the bulb and browns the bread in the toaster! Notice that if the toaster breaks, the current still can run through the light bulb. If the light bulb breaks, the current still can run through the toaster.

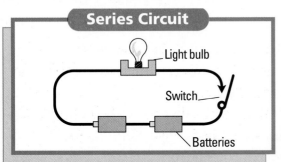

Series Circuit

Your Turn

Use the symbols to make a diagram of a series circuit that is powering a light bulb and a tape recorder. Remember that in a series circuit, all the objects using electricity are connected one following the other, along one closed path.

Chapter Review

Thinking Back

1. Compare the electric charges of protons and electrons.
2. What is thunder? A thunderstorm?
3. What is an **electric current**?
4. Give one example each for a good **conductor** and a good **insulator**.
5. Describe the parts of a **circuit**.
6. What is a parallel circuit?
7. How can a fuse help prevent a fire?
8. What is a **magnetic field**?
9. What discovery led to the invention of the electric motor?
10. How does a hiker's compass work?
11. What are sunspots?

Connecting Ideas

1. Copy the concept map. Use the terms at the right to complete the map about electrical energy.

electric current   electrons
series circuit   protons
parallel circuit

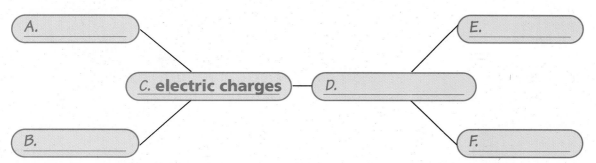

2. Write a sentence or two that summarizes the ideas shown in the concept map.

Gathering Evidence

1. In the Activity on page 12, what information did you use to predict which materials were the best conductors?
2. In the Activity on page 18, what caused the coil to behave the way it did?

Doing Science!

1. **Design an activity** to show first graders the difference between series and parallel circuits.
2. **Write a skit** that shows how different life would be if the electric motor had not been invented.

Nerve Signals

Discover Activity

What is your reaction time?

Reaction time is the length of time it takes to detect
a signal and respond to it. Have your class stand in
a circle and hold hands. Ask someone to time how
long it takes a hand squeeze to pass around the
circle. What's the reaction time for the group?

Beginning

End

For Discussion

1. How will reaction times change with practice?
2. How would you find your average reaction time?

2.1 Nervous System

> **How does your body receive, interpret, and send messages?**

Watching TV while you eat a snack seems pretty simple, but, it's not as easy as you think! While you're watching and eating, your body's working hard to keep track of the things going on around you. You're aware of the light and sounds from the TV, the taste and smell of the food, and the movements of your hands, mouth, and eyes. How does your body do all this at one time?

Signals in the Body

When something happens around you, your body gets a signal. It reacts to the signal by sending messages throughout your body. The messages travel through your nerve cells.

Your body has billions of nerve cells. These cells link your eyes, nose, ears, mouth, skin, and other body parts to your brain and spinal cord. Your brain, nerve cells, and spinal cord make up your nervous system.

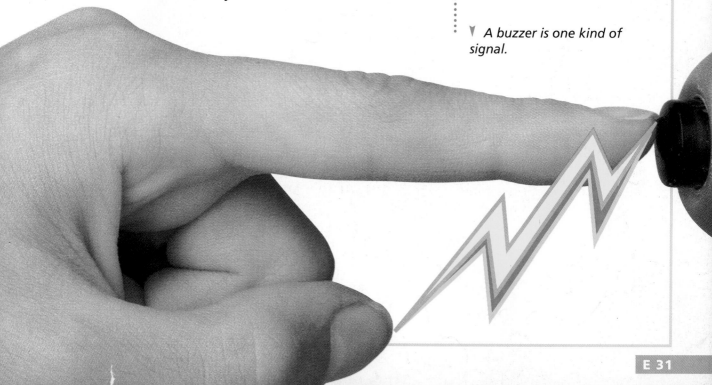

▼ *A buzzer is one kind of signal.*

▶ *Patting a dog stimulates nerve cells in your hand.*

The nervous system is similar to an electric circuit, because it sends electric signals back and forth through your body. When you get a message from the outside world—like the odor of warm bread—nerve cells in your nose "record" the message and turn it into an electric signal. The signal then travels through the nerve to the brain cells. The brain acts as a control center, where incoming signals are received and interpreted.

When your brain receives the odor signal from your nose, your brain quickly interprets the signal. Then your brain sends its own signals to other parts of your body. For example, your brain might tell your mouth to take a bite of that nice, warm bread.

The Nerve Network

You might be wondering how all this electricity gets inside your body. Substances in your nerve cells produce electric charges, just as a battery produces the charges that run in circuits.

Nerve cells vary in shape and size. Most are very tiny, but nerve cells in a human's leg can be 75 centimeters long!

The picture shows the parts of a nerve cell. Short, spreading branches called dendrites connect to the cell body. One long branch called an axon stretches away from the cell body.

Messages travel along a nerve cell from the dendrites to the axon. When a nerve cell is stimulated, as it was when you smelled the warm bread, for example, chemical reactions take place inside the dendrites. The nerve cell fires off an electric signal that races through the cell body to the axon. When the signal gets to the end of the axon, it triggers a reaction in the next set of dendrites, and the process starts again.

You might expect nerve cells to be hooked together so that messages can flow through nerves like electricity flows through a wire. But this is not the case. Actually, a small gap separates the axon of one cell from the dendrites of the next. This gap, called a synapse, is filled with liquid.

When an electric signal reaches the end of an axon, the axon quickly releases a chemical. Bits of this chemical race across the liquid that fills the synapse. When the chemical reaches the dendrite of the next cell, it sets off chemical reactions that start the electric signal in the next cell.

All this action takes place in a split second, so each nerve cell is immediately ready to send another signal down the line. In fact, a single nerve can send up to 1000 signals a second! The number of signals sent each second tells the brain how strong an odor is, how loud a sound is, how far you move your finger, or how broadly you smile.

Checkpoint

1. What does your nervous system do?
2. Describe three parts of a nerve cell.
3. **Take Action!** Use yarn to make a model of two nerve cells. Tape your model onto paper and label three parts.

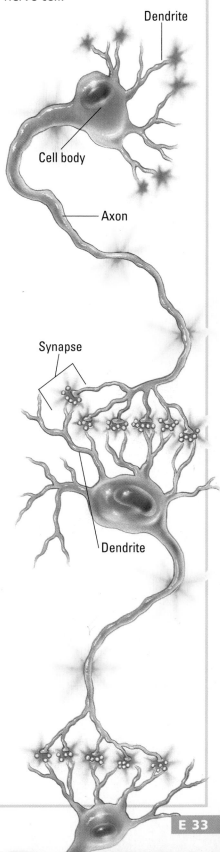

▼ A message moves from the dendrite through the cell body and the axon, across the synapse, and into the dendrite of the next nerve cell.

Dendrite

Cell body

Axon

Synapse

Dendrite

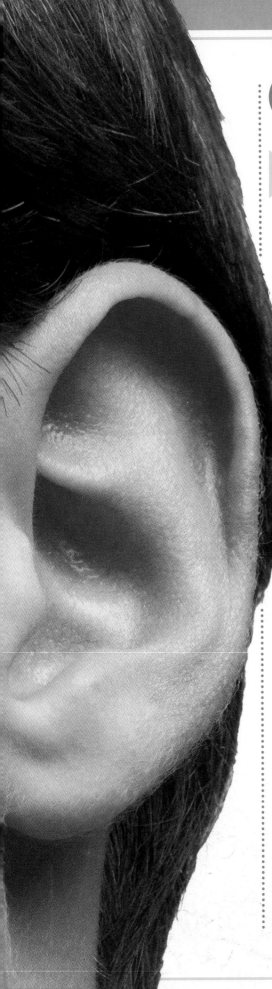

2.2 *Hear the Sound!*

▶ *How do your ears work?*

Next time you watch television, close your eyes and listen. What do you hear? Besides the sounds from the television, you might hear people talking in the kitchen and cars outside on the street. But what exactly are these sounds? And how do you hear them?

Sound Waves

You can find out what sound is by carefully stretching a rubber band tightly and plucking it with your finger. The plucking causes the rubber band to move back and forth, or vibrate, very quickly. At the same time, the rubber band makes a humming sound. If you touch the rubber band to keep it from vibrating, the hum stops, too.

Vibrations produce sounds. You hear the sound of a drum when you hit a drum head and make it vibrate. You hear sounds from a TV or radio when parts inside the speakers vibrate. People hear your voice when the vocal chords in your throat vibrate.

Some things vibrate, or move back and forth, very slowly. Slow vibrations make low sounds, like the boom of a bass drum or a fog horn. Rapid vibrations make high sounds, like the sound of a guitar string or a high note in music.

Sound is a form of energy that moves in waves. For example, you give the strings of a guitar energy when you pluck them. This energy makes the strings move back and forth. Then, gas molecules in the air next to the strings begin to vibrate too. They bump against other molecules, and make them vibrate. In this way, sound waves move through the air.

Many of the sounds you hear travel through the air. But sound waves also travel through liquids and solids. When you go swimming, you can hear sounds underwater because sound waves move through water. You can even hear yourself crunch foods such as celery because sound waves move through the bones in your head!

The sounds you hear in one ear are a little different from the sounds you hear in the other ear. Because you have two ears, you can tell that sounds are coming from different places.

Sound engineers, who make compact discs and tapes, record music and other sounds in stereo. The engineers use at least two differently placed microphones to record the music. When you play the music through two stereo speakers, sounds for the left ear come through one speaker, and sounds for the right ear come through the other speaker.

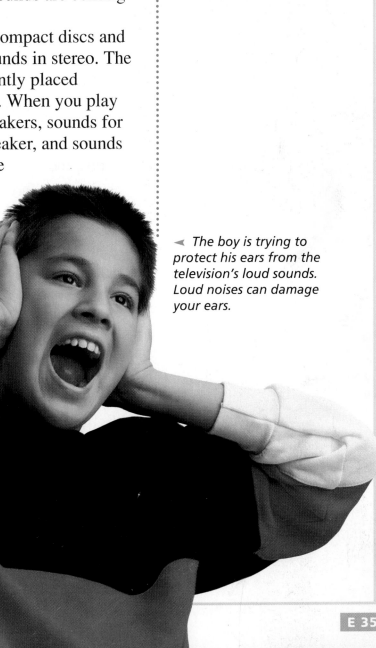

◄ *The boy is trying to protect his ears from the television's loud sounds. Loud noises can damage your ears.*

Ears for Hearing and Balance

Your ears are much more than flaps on the sides of your head. The most important parts of your ears are inside your head. Find the ear parts in the picture, as you read about how the ear works.

A shrieking siren sends sound waves through the air. The flaps on the sides of your head—your outer ears—catch the sound waves as they pass by. Each outer ear funnels the sound waves into a tubelike passage inside your head that leads to the eardrum.

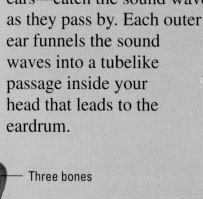

Nerve to brain

Three bones

Cochlea

Eardrum

Your eardrum stretches across the tube like a skin stretched over a drum. When sound waves hit the eardrum, the eardrum vibrates. These vibrations travel through three connected bones that are smaller than a matchhead.

The bones create a new set of waves that enter the cochlea. You can see that the cochlea is shaped like a snail shell. It's filled with a liquid and lined with tiny, hairlike cells. As the waves pass through the liquid, the hairlike cells begin to wiggle.

Notice that the sound of the siren has traveled through air, solid, and liquid. That's quite a trip, and it's a fast one too! In the cochlea, the journey's almost over because the wiggling cells excite tiny nerve cells.

In the nerve cells, the sound waves change to electric signals that race along nerve cells to the brain. It's up to your brain to interpret the signals and tell you that you hear a siren!

Your ears also help you keep your balance. You need your sense of balance to keep from falling. The parts of the inner ear that look like loops help you stay upright—whether you're sitting, standing, walking, running, or spinning like the dancer in the picture.

▲ *Parts inside the ears help people maintain their balance.*

As you move, your inner ears pick up changes in the position of your body and of your head. If you tilt or turn your head, these parts of your ear send signals to your brain. Then your brain sends out signals that tell your muscles what to do to keep you from falling.

Important information for balance also comes from other parts of your body. Your eyes send signals to your brain to tell it where you are in relation to the ground. Nerve cells in the soles of your feet and the joints of your legs send signals to tell your brain how your weight is distributed. Together, these signals and the signals from your ears help you keep your balance.

Sound and Temperatures

Have you ever noticed that a sound carries farther at some times than it does at others? For example, you might be able to hear a train whistle or traffic on the street much better at night than you can during the day. Night sounds are sharper partly because your home is quiet at night.

However, the temperature of the air also affects how sound travels. Sound waves move faster in warm air than in cold air. Also, sound waves tend to bend when they travel through air where the temperature is uneven.

The dog in the picture doesn't hear the boy calling during the day, but does hear him calling at night. When air near the ground is warm, sound waves tend to bend upward toward the cooler air. Sound waves don't hit the dog's ears, so the dog doesn't wake up.

When air near the ground is cold and the air above is warmer, sound waves tend to bend downward. Then, the dog hears the boy.

▼ *The dog sleeps soundly during the day, but at night he hears the boy call him.*

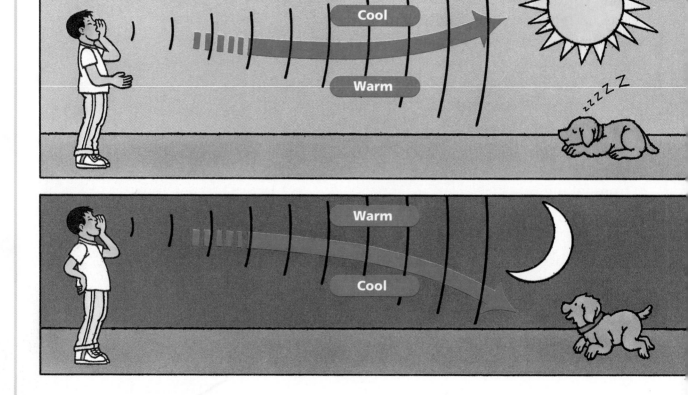

▲ *Listening rooms are designed to make full use of echoes.*

Controlling Sound Waves

Shout into a large, empty hall. Do you hear the echo? When you hear echoes in a room, you're hearing sound waves bouncing off—or reflecting from—surfaces, such as walls, ceilings, and floors.

The way sound travels in a room depends on the room's shape and what's in the room. Sound waves bounce best from hard, smooth surfaces. Soft, bumpy surfaces tend to absorb sound and cut down on echoes.

People can make rooms quieter by putting up ceiling tiles with small holes in them. Drapes, carpeting, and furniture help absorb sound, too.

In concert halls and theaters, however, echoes can improve sound. Echoes can make the music sound better and help everyone in the audience hear. Grooves in the ceilings, walls, and floors are used to control how the sound bounces.

Checkpoint

1. How does sound move?
2. What energy change enables you to hear?
3. Explain why carpets cut down on noise.
4. How does air temperature affect sound?
5. **Take Action!** Hum to yourself. Describe what you feel, where you feel it, and tell what's happening.

Speed of Sound

Usually, sound travels faster through liquids and solids than it does through air. For example, sound travels more than four times faster through water than it does through air. As a result, two whales can communicate more quickly underwater! Other factors, such as

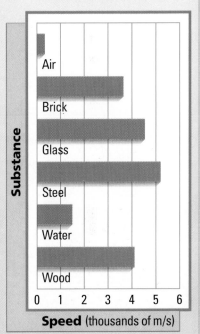

temperature, also affect the speed of sound. Sound travels faster in warm air than in cold air.

What Did You Find Out?
1. *What is the speed of sound through glass?*
2. *Does sound travel faster through brick or through wood? brick or steel?*
3. *How long does it take for sound to travel 4500 meters through water?*

Activity

Sounding Out

What kinds of materials can you use to deaden sound? Try this activity to find out.

Picture A

Picture B

Picture C

Gather These Materials

wooden desk or table or a piece of wood

tuning fork

assorted materials to test

Follow This Procedure

1 Make a chart like the one on the next page. Record your observations in your chart.

2 Strike the side of a tuning fork against your hand and place its handle on your desk, on a wooden table, or on a piece of wood. Listen to the sound the tuning fork makes. (Picture A)

3 List all the materials you will test as sound insulators in your chart.

4 Place one of the materials to test on top of your desk, table, or piece of wood. (Picture B) Strike the tuning fork and place its handle on the material. Record on your chart your observations about the loudness of the sound.

Predict: **Which materials do you think will deaden the sound of the tuning fork?**

5 Repeat Step 4 for all the other materials you listed in your chart. (Picture C)

Record Your Results

Material	Observation of sound	Rating as insulator

6 When you have finished testing all the materials, use your observations to help you rate them for their ability to deaden sound. Use a numbering system to rate the sound produced, where lower numbers indicate a softer sound and higher numbers indicate a louder sound.

State Your Conclusions

1. Which materials were best for deadening the sound of the tuning fork?
2. Do your results agree with what you learned in the chapter about controlling sound waves? Explain.
3. Using what you have learned in the chapter, tell how the sound insulators you tested deaden sound.

Let's Experiment

Which types of materials do you think will make sounds seem louder? Use what you know about scientific methods to find out.

2.3 *See the Picture!*

▶ *How do your eyes work?*

When you watch a movie in a theater, you know that the movie actors aren't really in the theater. Instead, they're just pictures on a screen. But what about your own eyes? Do the things you see live inside your head, or are they just pictures on a screen? Read on and find out.

Eyes For Seeing

Your eyes not only help you see motion when you watch movies, they also observe the objects around you. They quickly adjust to different amounts of light, and see all the colors of the rainbow. Your eyes are like a camera.

Find the eye parts in the picture as you read how your eyes help you find a snack. You're hungry, so you start looking for something to eat. Your eyes scan the kitchen table and stop at the banana. Light rays bounce off the banana and travel to your eyes. But the rays must enter your eyes before you can see the banana.

The eyeball is covered with a tough, white layer, known as the white of the eye. However, on the seeing part of the eye, this layer is clear and it is called the cornea. The cornea bends the banana's light rays as they enter the eye. Then the rays pass through the pupil—an opening in the eye that can expand and contract. The pupil looks like a tiny black dot, but it's really a hole.

The lens of your eye lies behind the pupil. Like the cornea, the lens bends the banana's light rays. After passing through the lens, the light rays form an upside-down image of the banana on the retina—the back part of the eye. The image is also reversed from left to right.

Thousands of tiny cells called rods and cones cover the retina. A bundle of nerves called the optic nerve connects the rods and cones to the brain. When light rays from the banana hit the retina, the rods and cones detect the rays and convert them into signals that the optic nerve carries to your brain. The signals carry information about the color, size, and shape of the image you're looking at.

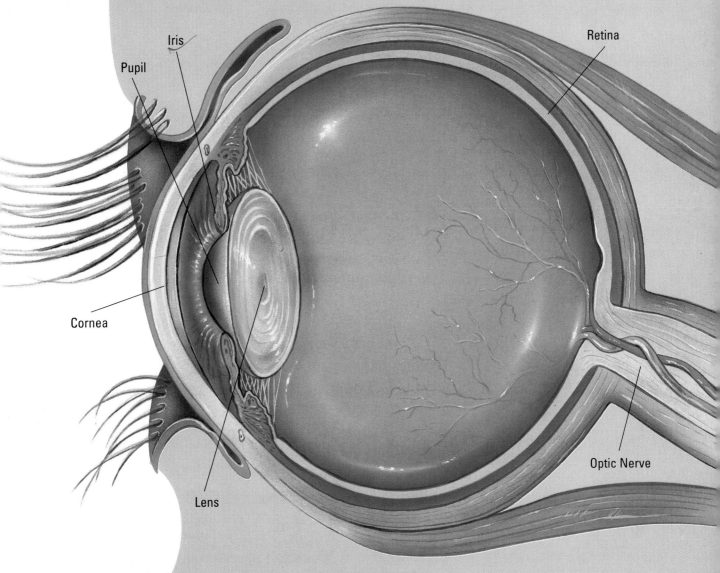

Iris

Pupil

Retina

Cornea

Optic Nerve

Lens

Your brain interprets these signals and tells you that you're looking at a banana. It also lets you know that the banana isn't upside down and reversed from left to right. Your brain helps you see the banana as it really is.

▲ *More light can come into the pupil of this eye than the pupil of the eye to the right.*

Now that you can see the banana, you remember why you were looking for it in the first place. You reach out, take a banana off the table, and peel it. Thanks to your eyes, you've found something to eat.

Seeing Clearly

Light enters a camera through a small, round opening. On many cameras, you can control the amount of light entering the camera by making the opening larger or smaller. The colored part of your eye—the iris—is a doughnut-shaped muscle that does the same thing.

In bright light, your irises contract, and your pupils get smaller. So less light gets into your eyes. This is a good thing, because too much light can damage the retina. In dim light, your irises expand. The pupils get bigger and more light enters the eyes.

Other things besides light can change the size of the pupils. Strong emotions, such as fear or excitement, can make the pupils larger. Taking certain medicines can also change the size of the pupils, causing them to get larger or smaller.

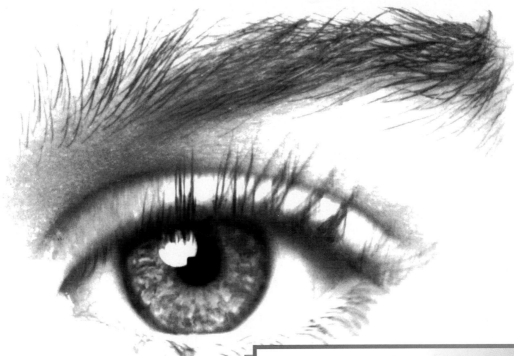

Once light waves get in, the lenses help bring the light waves together, or focus them. Muscles make the lens thinner, to see distant objects, or thicker, to see nearby objects. Because the lenses can change shape, clear images form on your retinas, as shown in the top diagram.

In spite of this, some people still see fuzzy images. If you're nearsighted, images form in front of your retina. You can see things up close, but watching a flyball in the distance is a problem!

If you're farsighted, images form beyond your retina, as shown in the diagram. You have no problem tracking flyballs, it's threading a needle that bothers you!

Wearing eyeglasses or contact lenses usually corrects both sight problems. Putting a glass or plastic lens close to the eye makes the image focus on the retina, where it's supposed to be.

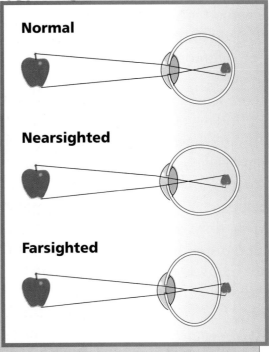

Normal

Nearsighted

Farsighted

⋏ *For normal vision, the image forms on the retina at the back of the eye. If a person is nearsighted or farsighted, the image doesn't form on the retina.*

Now You See It, Now You Don't

Some pictures trick your eyes into seeing something that isn't there!

Let's take a look at some "tricky" pictures. Read in this column about each pattern and take a good look! Then, skip ahead to page 47 to find out more about the picture.

A. Stare at this picture. What do you see where the yellow lines cross among the squares? Are the spots really there? Check page 47!

B. What do you notice about the spiraling lines? Can you tell where the spirals begin and end?

C. As you stare at this pattern, turn the book clockwise halfway around and back again quickly. How does the pattern change?

D. Look at the pairs of up and down lines. Are the pairs of lines crooked or straight?

(A)

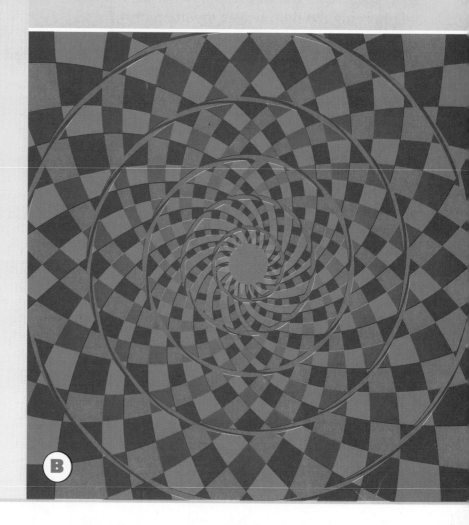

(B)

C

D

A. Are the gray spots really there? No, they aren't. When you blink your eyes the spots go away!

B. If you can't tell where the spirals begin and end, there's a reason. The spirals aren't spirals—they're circles! The design around each circle makes you think you're looking at spirals. Trace one spiral with your finger, and you'll see!

C. The design seems to get bigger and smaller as you turn the book. You know the design doesn't change size, but your eyes tell you it does!

D. If you put a ruler on the lines in each set, you'll see that all the lines are parallel. The short slanted lines drawn on each up and down line make the lines look crooked.

You rely on your eyes to give you accurate information about the world. But colors, patterns, and motion can affect what your brain perceives. You can't always believe what you see!

Into The Field

How do distant objects look compared to objects that are nearby?

While you're outside, look at a distant object. Then look at something nearby. Compare your vision for near and far objects.

Sight Tricks

Your eyes and brain trick you into seeing things move on a movie or TV screen. When you see an animal run, you are seeing a series of "still" pictures flash in front of you, one right after the other! You think it's moving because your brain stores each picture for about one-tenth of a second after the picture is gone. If more than ten still pictures pass in front of your eyes each second, the pictures seem to be joined together and the animal moves.

Your brain also makes your eyes work as a team. When you look at something, your left eye forms one image and your right eye forms a slightly different image! Try covering your left eye and looking at a picture or poster on the wall. Then cover your right eye and look at it again. What you'll see are two different views of the same thing. Look once more with both eyes open, and you'll see only one view!

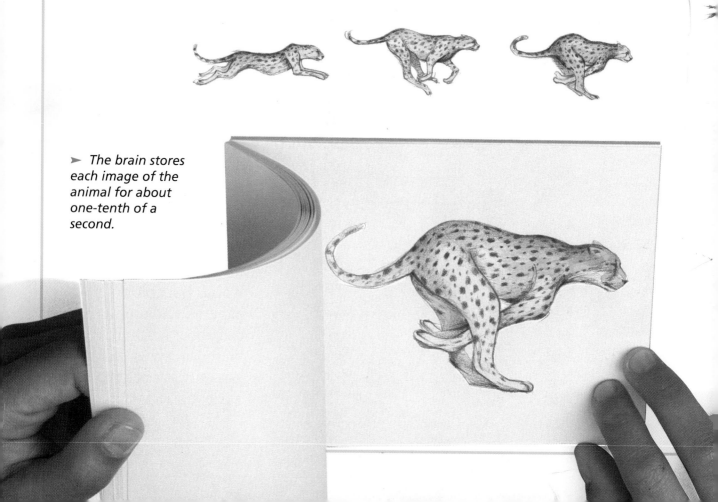

➤ The brain stores each image of the animal for about one-tenth of a second.

▲ *The puddle of water on the road is a mirage.*

When you look with both eyes, your brain gets signals from two images and puts one on top of the other to form one image that has depth to it. Your brain helps you see that a ball is round instead of flat. It also helps you decide how far away a car is before you cross the street!

Light itself—not your brain—is responsible for this sight trick. Suppose you're riding in a car on a hot day. You see a pool of water, like the one in the picture, on the road ahead. As you move toward the water, it moves farther away. What you're seeing is a mirage. The mirage appears because a layer of hot air near the ground bends the light waves. What your brain "thinks" is water is actually a reflection of the sky in the air near the ground.

Checkpoint

1. Where is the retina located?
2. What eye part focuses light waves?
3. How can you tell if lines are parallel?
4. How is it you can judge a car's distance?
5. **Take Action!** Look at a brightly colored object near a bright lamp. Compare this view to how the object looks without light and in a dim light.

Activity

Moving Pictures

You can make moving pictures yourself with only a pencil and a few pieces of paper. Try this activity to find out how.

Picture A

Picture B

Picture C

Gather These Materials

cover goggles

circular object for tracing

scissors

colored pencils or
  crayons

clear tape

small gummed-edge
  notepad sheets

2 index cards

Follow This Procedure

1. Make a chart like the one on the next page. Record your observations in your chart.

2. Put on your cover goggles.

3. Trace 2 identical circles on the index cards. Cut out the circles.

4. Draw a picture on the unlined side of each circle. Your 2 drawings should be related. For example, you might draw a fish on one circle and a pond on the other circle.

5. Tape the circles together picture sides out and with a pencil stuck between them. (Picture A)

Predict: *How will the pictures look when you twirl the pencil?*

6. Twirl the pencil and watch what happens to your pictures. Record your observations in your chart.

7 Next, think up a series of 8 or more related drawings you can make to show a simple action. The drawings in Picture B will give you an idea.

8 Draw your pictures on the sheets of a gummed-edge notepad. Make your first drawing on the back page of the notepad. Change the second picture slightly to show the first step in the action. Continue making changes as you draw the series of pictures. (Picture C)

9 Flip through your notepad from back to front. Record your observations in your chart.

Record Your Results

Action	Observations
Twirling pencil with 2 pictures taped to it	
Flipping through flip-book with series of drawings	

State Your Conclusions

1. What happens when you twirl the pencil and when you flip through the flip-book?

2. How are the movies you made similar to motion pictures?

Let's Experiment

Could you use pictures on a flap pin-wheel to make moving pictures? Use what you have learned about scientific methods to find out.

Observations at a Campsite

People's sightings, umpire's calls—both depend on careful observations. Yet when several people watch an event, they often don't see the same things, or describe what they see in the same way.

Scientists describe their observations very carefully. In addition, they make many, many observations during experiments before they accept their data as reliable or correct.

Thinking It Through

Imagine you are a park ranger. Two witnesses tell you about an animal that has been stealing food from campsites.

Witness 1: The animal was large and had dark fur. It had striped markings on its face. I don't think it had a tail.

Witness 2: When it stood on its hind legs it was about up to my waist, and I'm about 175 centimeters tall. It was limping. The animal had black and white markings on its face and tail. Its fur was darker than the picnic table.

Before you can determine what the animal really looks like, you might think through a number of questions like these.

Which description is more detailed?
How might the height of the witness affect his or her description of the animal's size?
How do their descriptions agree?
How do they disagree?

You tend to pay more attention to Witness 2, because he or she provides more detail and gives support for each observation.

You decide that the points where the witnesses agree are most likely to be true. So, you conclude that the animal had dark fur and striped markings on its face. You believe the food snatcher must be a raccoon!

Your Turn

Work with a partner. Both of you look at your teacher's desk for a few seconds. Then turn away from the desk. Write a description of your observations of the desk.

Now compare your descriptions. Did you both describe the same things? Are your observations clear and accurate? If not, don't give up! You can improve your observing skills by being alert and watching what's going on around you!

Chapter Review

Thinking Back

1. Compare your nervous system to an electric circuit. Explain how the two systems are alike and different.
2. What causes a sound?
3. Describe the path sound waves take as they move through your ears.
4. What is an echo?
5. What can uneven air temperature do to sound waves?
6. How are the lenses in your eyes useful for good vision?
7. Compare the location of images in the eyes for normal, nearsighted, and farsighted vision.
8. Give one example that shows why you can't believe everything you see.
9. What can cause a mirage such as water on the road?

Connecting Ideas

1. Copy the concept map. Use the terms at the right to complete the map describing the movement of signals along a nerve cell.

axon   **dendrite**

synapse

A. **nerve cell body** → B. _____ → C. _____ → D. _____

2. Write a sentence or two that summarizes the ideas shown in the concept map.

Gathering Evidence

1. In the Activity on page 40, how could you have predicted which materials make the sounds louder?
2. In the Activity on page 50, what did you have to do in order to see movement when you spun the pencil?

Doing Science!

1. *Design an activity* to prove that soft, bumpy surfaces absorb sound waves.
2. *Make a poster* showing people using senses of seeing, hearing, touching, smelling, or tasting, and relate the picture to the nervous system.

Signals in the Air

Let's try a party line with three people!

How can you make a string telephone work?

Punch a hole in the bottoms of two paper cups. Push one end of a long piece of string through the hole in each cup. Hold the string in place by tying it to a paperclip. Pull the string tight and don't let it touch anything. Try out your telephone. How well does it work?

For Discussion

1. *How can you make your telephone work better?*

2. *What's the longest possible string for the phone?*

3.1 *Radio Waves*

How does television work?

The word *television* means "pictures from far away." And that's just what you see when you watch this Cinco de Mayo parade that's in honor of Mexico's Independence Day. Seeing the floats decorated with flowers on TV is the next best thing to being there yourself.

Types of Radio Waves

In order for you to see the dancers and hear the bands, light and sound have to be changed to a form of energy that's movable and fast. TV cameras and microphones capture the sights and sounds as electric signals. These signals are changed to radio waves that travel through space to your TV.

Radio waves are one form of energy used to carry signals for television. Radio waves also carry the music and talk shows you hear on your radio. Microwave ovens, radar devices, and computer networks use radio waves too!

You might recall that radio waves are energy that travels in straight lines through empty space. But not all radio waves are the same length. The shortest radio waves are less than one centimeter long and the longest stretch more than one kilometer.

▲ *The Cinco de Mayo parade in San Francisco*

When you listen to a radio, you're making use of medium to long radio waves. You can see in the top diagram that long waves follow the curve of the earth. In this way, they can travel thousands of kilometers. You might be able to hear music from radio stations thousands of kilometers away.

➤ Long radio waves

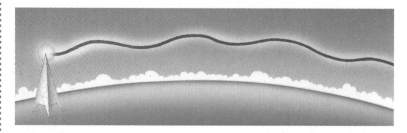

Medium-length radio waves bounce back and forth between layers high in the atmosphere and the ground, as shown. Like long waves, medium-length radio waves can travel great distances.

➤ Medium-length radio waves

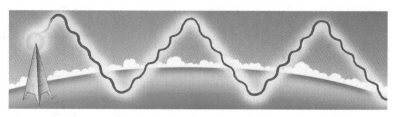

Short radio waves can be used to carry TV signals and FM radio broadcasts. It's easier to send large amounts of information quickly with short wavelengths than with long ones. Short waves don't travel far because they don't bounce between the ground and the upper atmosphere. To go far, they need "boosts." The diagram shows that short waves must pass from one antenna to another.

➤ Short radio waves

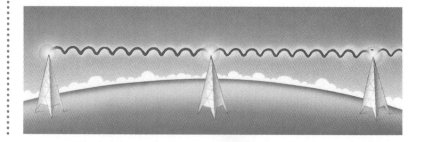

Communication Satellites

Have you ever seen a live TV program from a country halfway around the world? For this type of program, TV signals can travel as electric signals through copper cables along the ocean floor. Or, signals can travel as very short radio waves, known as microwaves, to and from satellites.

Satellites that receive and send radio waves for communications are called communication satellites. Satellites carry all kinds of signals—TV, radio, computer data, fax messages, and stereo radio.

In 1960, the first communication satellite went into orbit. Radio waves were sent to the satellite and reflected to earth. Today, hundreds of satellites are orbiting the earth. This makes it possible for people to receive TV signals from anywhere in the world.

These satellites are about 35,800 kilometers above the earth. At this height, a satellite can keep pace with the spinning earth below so the satellite stays over the same point on the ground.

You might say that satellites have "shrunk" the globe. A single one can beam signals down to an entire continent. Because radio waves travel at the speed of light, three satellites can send a signal all the way around the world in less than a second!

▲ *Communication satellite*

Checkpoint

1. Which type of radio waves carry TV signals?
2. How can signals be sent across oceans?
3. Take Action! Draw a picture of a weather satellite and of a communication satellite.

Activity

Sending Messages

The telegraph was an early method of sending long-distance messages. How does it work? Try this activity to find out.

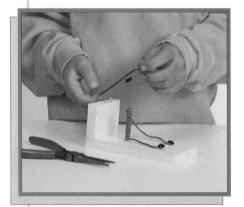

Picture A

Gather These Materials

cover goggles

4 pieces of insulated wire: 1 long, 3 short

2 plastic-foam boards, 25 cm x 6 cm x 1 cm

1 plastic-foam board, 6 cm x 6 cm x 1 cm

large nail

glue

strip of cardboard, 8 cm x 4 cm

7 thumbtacks

small hammer

metal paper clip

6-volt battery

wire cutter

Picture B

Follow This Procedure

1. Make a chart like the one on the next page. Record your observations in your chart.

2. Put on your cover goggles.

3. Make the sounder for your telegraph by gluing the small plastic-foam board to one of the larger plastic-foam boards. (Picture A)

4. Wrap the long piece of wire tightly around a nail and insert it into the bottom board. Secure the free ends of the wire with thumbtacks. Then stick a thumbtack into one end of the strip of cardboard. Carefully, hammer it down.

5. Secure the cardboard strip to the smaller plastic-foam board with another thumbtack. Make sure that the head of the thumbtack from step 4 is directly above the nail. (Picture A)

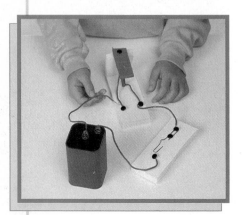

Picture C

6 Make a key for your telegraph. Unbend the paper clip part way. Use 2 thumbtacks to fasten the paper clip to the third plastic-foam board. Place a thumbtack under the free end of the paper clip so that the clip can hit the head of the thumbtack. (Picture B)

7 Connect one wire from the sounder to a terminal of the battery. Connect the other wire to the key. Wrap it tightly around the thumbtack holding down the end of the paper clip.

8 Connect the key to the battery. Run a wire from the free terminal of the battery to the thumbtack on the key that's under the free end of the paper clip. (Picture C)

> **Predict: *What happens when you press the free end of the clip on the thumbtack?***

9 Push the free end of the paper clip down on the head of the thumbtack. Observe how the sounder moves. Write your observations on your chart. Describe what happens when you tap the key. Tell what happens when you hold the key down for about one second.

State Your Conclusions

1. How does the telegraph help send signals?
2. How could you change the signals to make up a code for sending messages?

Let's Experiment

How could you change the telegraph so you could use a lightbulb as a signaling device? Use what you know about scientific methods to find out.

Record Your Results

Action with the key	Movement of the sounder
Tap the key down	
Press the key down for a second	

3.2 *TV Signals*

▶ *How does a TV program get to my set?*

Juan wants to watch the Cinco de Mayo parade. But wind and rain are whipping his rooftop antenna around, so the TV picture isn't very good. His brother puts a little rabbit-ear antenna on the set. The improved picture makes Juan wonder why antennas are so important.

Sending Signals

A TV camera changes light reflected from a parade float into electric signals. At the same time, microphones change sound waves from marching bands and voices into electric signals. At a TV station, these electric signals are combined and strengthened. Then the signals are sent out from a nearby antenna, called a transmitter. This antenna is named well because *transmit* means *to send*.

The transmitter might not be much more than a wire, but it's mounted on a tall metal tower. Radio waves travel away from the transmitter in all directions, like the ripples from a pebble dropped in a pond.

Radio waves get weaker and weaker as they move away from the transmitter. So, another antenna at a relay station picks them up and gives them a boost. Radio signals are strengthened at each station in a relay series.

Satellites are relay stations for radio waves that go across continents or oceans. These radio waves are sent to a big bowl-shaped antenna on the ground, called a satellite dish. You can see one in the picture below. The radio signals are broadcast from the dish to a communication satellite. Then the satellite reflects the set of signals back to another satellite dish on the ground.

Copper cables in the ground also are used to send electric TV signals. The cables may be present along all or part of the trip from the TV station to your set at home. Copper cables carry many other kinds of communications signals across oceans.

▼ *Tracking a television program—from the parade, to the control room in a TV station, to antennas*

What happens to the picture signal?

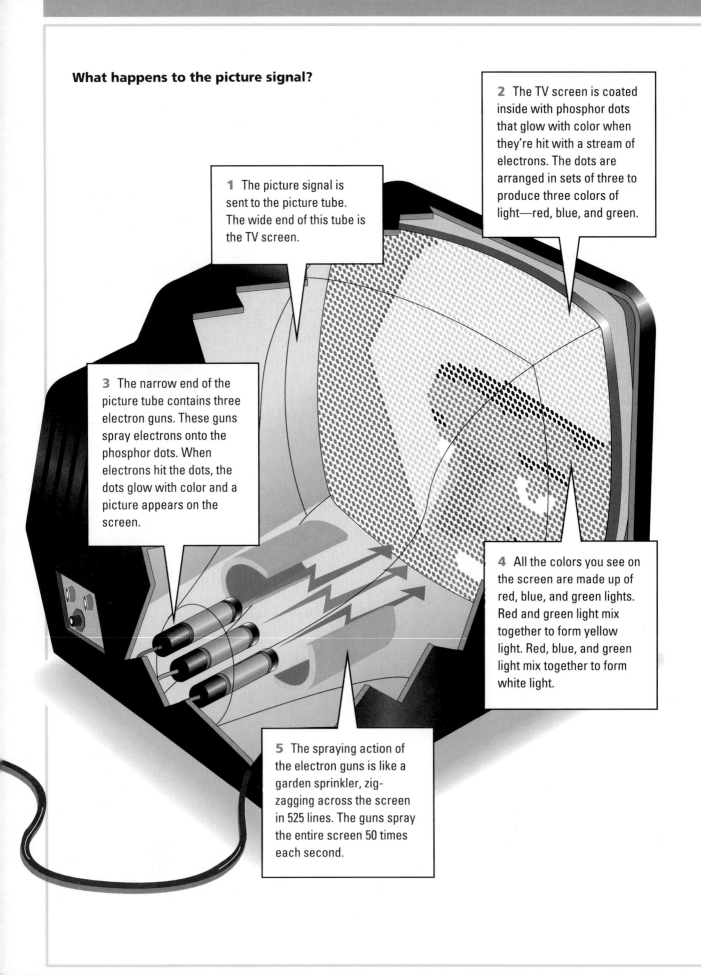

1 The picture signal is sent to the picture tube. The wide end of this tube is the TV screen.

2 The TV screen is coated inside with phosphor dots that glow with color when they're hit with a stream of electrons. The dots are arranged in sets of three to produce three colors of light—red, blue, and green.

3 The narrow end of the picture tube contains three electron guns. These guns spray electrons onto the phosphor dots. When electrons hit the dots, the dots glow with color and a picture appears on the screen.

4 All the colors you see on the screen are made up of red, blue, and green lights. Red and green light mix together to form yellow light. Red, blue, and green light mix together to form white light.

5 The spraying action of the electron guns is like a garden sprinkler, zig-zagging across the screen in 525 lines. The guns spray the entire screen 50 times each second.

Receiving TV Signals

Did you know your television set works like a TV camera in reverse? Your TV turns radio waves back into the sights and sounds of the parade.

When you turn on a television, radio waves picked up by your antenna go into the TV as electric signals. Or, if you have cable television, electric signals come into your set from copper cables.

These signals change as they pass through the tuner, the loudspeakers, and the picture tube—three important parts of a television. The tuner is the part of the television controlled by the knobs or buttons on the front of the set.

The tuner breaks the electric signals into picture signals and sound signals. Then it sends sound to the loudspeaker and pictures to the picture tube.

Inside the loudspeaker, the sound signals make a cardboard cone vibrate. The vibrating cone produces sound waves. At the same time, picture signals go into the picture tube. Read through the page to the left to see how moving pictures form on a television screen. Because the speakers and the picture tube work together, you can see the band members in the Cinco de Mayo parade march while you're listening to their music.

Checkpoint

1. What is a relay station?
2. What are three main parts of a TV set?
3. Take Action! Draw a picture using only small dots of color. How is this like the picture on a television screen?

Optical Fibers

Optical fibers are rapidly replacing copper wires for sending TV and telephone signals. Optical fibers are thin rods of transparent material—usually glass or plastic—that are covered by another material. Light rays enter one end of an optical fiber and are reflected along the length of the optical fiber.

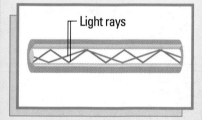

Light rays

For sending signals, optical fibers have many advantages over copper cables. For example, a pair of copper telephone wires can carry only about 50 telephone conversations at one time. A pair of optical fibers, however, can carry more than 80,000 calls at once!

What Did You Find Out?
1. *How many pairs of copper wires are needed to carry 80,000 calls at once?*
2. *How do signals move through optical fibers?*
3. *Compare the kind of signals sent through copper cables and through optical fibers.*

Activity

Tuning in the Radio

Are radio signals really in the air everywhere? Try this activity to find out more about radio waves.

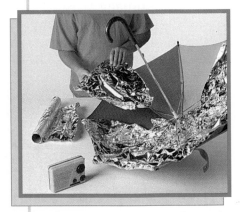

Picture A

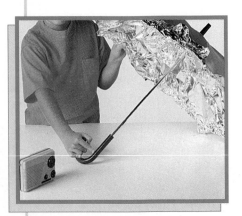

Picture B

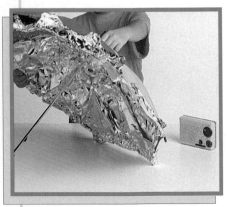

Picture C

Gather These Materials

cover goggles
heavy-duty aluminum foil
  to line umbrella

small portable radio
umbrella

Follow This Procedure

1 Make a chart like the one on the next page. Record your observations in your chart.

2 Put on your cover goggles.

3 Open the umbrella and line the inside of it with aluminum foil. In this activity, the umbrella will act as an antenna for your radio. (Picture A) Keep the umbrella away from the radio until you're ready to use it in Step 6.

4 Turn the radio dial all the way to the left and then turn the radio on. Slowly turn the dial to the right and find five weak stations. Write the numbers of each station in your chart.

5 Turn the radio station to the first weak radio station listed in your chart. Move the radio around until you get the best possible sound from this station.

Predict: **In which direction will the antenna work best?**

6 Now put the umbrella behind the radio so the aluminum foil faces toward the radio. Slowly move the umbrella closer to or farther away from the radio until you find the spot where the sound is best for that station. (Picture B)

7 Next, put the umbrella in front of the radio so that the foil faces away from the radio. Slowly move the umbrella closer to or farther away from the radio until you find the spot where the sound is best for that station. (Picture C)

8 Decide whether the station's sound is better with the foil facing toward or away from the radio. Record your answer in your chart.

9 Repeat Steps 5 through 8 for the other stations in your chart.

Record Your Results

Station number	Umbrella position for best reception

State Your Conclusions

1. Which way did the umbrella improve radio reception, with the foil facing toward or away from the radio?

2. What do you think happens when radio waves in the air meet with the foil?

Let's Experiment

Would your results change if you lined the umbrella with wax paper? Use what you know about scientific methods to find out.

3.3 *The Electronic Revolution*

▶ What kind of film does a TV camera use?

Three mice in Rosa's science fair exhibit are missing! You just videotaped her exhibit, so you pop the tape into a videocassette recorder. The tape shows one of the mice clawing at a crack in the box. Thanks to electronic devices, you've solved the mystery of how the mice escaped!

Today's Video Equipment

Today, many people use videocassette recorders, known as VCRs, and some people even have video cameras. A video camera changes light and sound to electric signals that are captured on videotape. The tape is made of plastic, and is coated with tiny crystals of iron oxide.

Video cameras send electric signals to a small device called a recording head, located in the video recorder. The recording head uses the camera's electric signals to produce a magnetic field. As the videotape moves by the recording head, the magnetic field

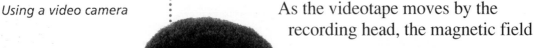

➤ *Using a video camera*

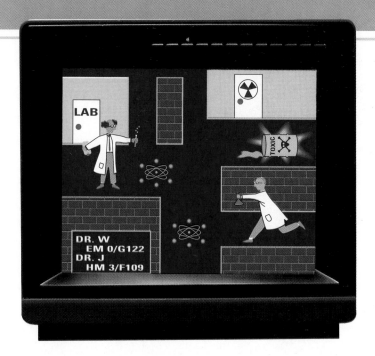

rearranges the iron oxide crystals into different patterns. The picture pattern runs down the middle of the tape and the sound pattern runs along each side.

Videotape is stored in a small, plastic box called a videocassette. The tape winds around spools inside the videocassette.

When you play a cassette on a VCR, the VCR translates the pattern on the tape into electric signals that your TV turns into sights and sounds.

If you want to record television programs yourself, you can buy a videocassette with blank magnetic tape. When you record a program, a new magnetic pattern forms on the tape. When you rewind the tape and record a new program, you rearrange the iron oxide on the tape.

Recording on magnetic tape has many advantages. Unlike film for cameras, you don't have to take magnetic tape to the store to be "developed." Instead, you can play it back instantly using a VCR and television. Camera film can be used only once, but magnetic tapes can be used over and over!

▼ *Having fun with an electronic game*

A Long View of Television

Inventors put the discoveries of science to work and created television.

In the late 1800s, scientific discoveries led to the invention of television. Scientists learned how to change sound and light into electric signals, how to send these signals out, and how to turn them back into sound and light in your TV set. One by one, devices that paved the way for TV popped on the scene.

The first TV pictures were black and white. They included so many jiggling white dots that the pictures looked "snowy!" Over the years, TV technology improved rapidly. Pictures got sharper, color was added, and signals could be received from all over the world. Today, with home video equipment, you can even make your own TV shows!

Early TV Broadcasts Here's what television looked like in the late 1920s. The picture shows a cartoon character, Felix the Cat. TV signals were sent from New York City to Kansas.

Crookes Tube During the 1870s, Sir William Crookes, a British scientist, built a special glass tube from which most of the air had been removed, called a vacuum tube.

Braun's Tube In 1897, Karl Braun of Germany changed the Crookes tube so that the electric current hit a screen, producing a pattern of light. This was the forerunner of the TV picture tube!

1900	1925

Vacuum tube From the 1920s to the 1950s, large vacuum tubes were used in radios, televisions, and computers. They controlled the electronic signals that operated these devices.

TV for the Home By the 1950s, television sets were part of the furniture in millions of American homes. The first color television broadcast was made in 1950.

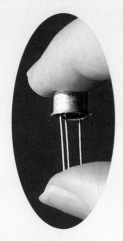

Transistors In the 1950s and 1960s, transistors replaced large vacuum tubes in radios, televisions, and other electronic devices. A transistor is a small electronic device.

Video from Space In 1969, people all over the world watched as American astronauts became the first humans to walk on the moon. Today you can see video images from other planets in the solar system!

| 1950 | 1975 | 2000 |

The electronic future

Looking Ahead

What does the future hold for television? Look ahead to the year 2005. Instead of watching a space program on a small TV screen as you do now, you watch it on a large, flat screen that fills a wall!

As you watch, you zoom in and freeze part of the action. You click your remote control, and instantly get an up-close view of the spacecraft. Click again and the action freezes. Later, you decide to watch part of the news. You press another switch, and the news station appears in one corner of the television screen, while the space program still covers the rest of the screen.

The "zoom," "freeze," and "split-screen" features are available on television today. These features are made possible by adding computers to televisions. However, televisions with features like these are still too expensive for most people.

Another improvement you might see on TV is High Definition Television, or HDTV. *High Definition* means that the picture is very sharp and clear. HDTV uses a picture tube that puts 1025 lines of dots on the screen instead of the 525 lines on today's models. The added lines mean more dots and sharper, clearer pictures.

In the years ahead, you probably will use computers to tell your TV what you want it to do for you. In fact, it's safe to predict that computers will be doing much more for you at home. For example, you might be using one computer to run your TV, video recorder, stereo, phone, furnace, lights, and washing machine.

How might a computer change your life? Well, you might be able to see someone on the TV screen while you talk to him or her on the phone. You might not have to go to the store very often, because you might use your computer and TV to do your shopping from your living room.

You might even be able to work on your computer at home instead of going out to work at an office every day. Sounds like science fiction, doesn't it? Wait for future developments!

Into The Field

Find the infrared sensors on the remote control of a TV. Ask an adult to help you find out where and how the infrared rays are given off by the remote control. Then try different ways to turn off the TV using the remote control.

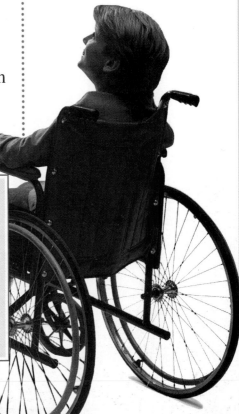

Checkpoint

1. What are two advantages of magnetic tape over regular film?
2. Which device led to the picture tube?
3. How does HDTV get such a clear picture?
4. **Take Action!** Draw and label a picture showing the path of TV signals from a TV station to your home.

Gathering Information

Suppose your family is looking for ways to cut down on the amount of electricity they use. You've had a family meeting and your job is to gather information about the costs of running appliances.

Thinking It Through

To carry out your task, you'll want to consider questions such as these.

How much does it cost to run an appliance for one hour?

Check to see which of the appliances listed in the table you have at home.

How can I estimate how much it costs to run one of the appliances listed in the table for one month?

Keep a record of how many hours each appliance runs during one month. For example, you might keep a record of how many hours the TV is on during one month. Suppose your record shows that the TV was on for 100 hours during the

month. The table shows that the TV costs about 1.6 cents per hour to run. So, the estimated cost per month is $1.60.

What kind of recommendations could I make?

Look at your records. List the appliances in order of how costly each is and how important you think the usage is.

Operating Costs of Appliances

Appliance	Approximate cost to use
Air conditioner	9.0 cents per hour
Dishwasher	9.0 cents per hour
Microwave oven	10.0 cents per hour
Range oven	25.0 cents per hour
Television	1.6 cents per hour
Light bulb	0.8 cents per hour

Your Turn

Electric energy is measured in units called kilowatt-hours. Look at your family's last electric bill to see: how many kilowatt-hours you used; the cost per kilowatt-hour; and the total cost for the month. Divide the total cost by the number of days in the month to find the average cost of electricity for each day.

Chapter Review

Thinking Back

1. List four things that use radio waves to carry signals.
2. Why must short radio waves travel from one antenna to another?
3. What are communication satellites and how are they used?
4. Why are a microphone and a TV camera needed for televising shows?
5. A TV set works like a TV camera in reverse. Explain this statement.
6. Why is the tape in a video cassette called a magnetic tape?
7. Describe a Crookes tube and tell what part of a TV set is similar to this tube.
8. What is the benefit of adding computers to television sets?

Connecting Ideas

1. Copy the concept map. Use the terms to the right to complete the map about the sending of radio waves.

**rooftop antenna   radio waves
transmitter**

A. **electric signals** — B. _____ — C. _____ — D. _____

2. Write a sentence or two that summarizes the main idea in the concept map.

Gathering Evidence

1. In the Activity on page 58, explain how the paperclip and tack relate to the switch in a circuit.
2. In the Activity on page 64, what information did you use to predict how the position of the umbrella can change the loudness of the radio program?

Doing Science!

1. *Write a skit* telling a story about how a TV program is broadcast and sent into people's homes.
2. *Build a model* that shows the main parts of a TV set. Use the picture showing the inside of a television as your guide.

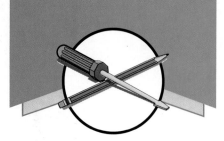

Helping Others to "See"

Think about how you find your way around your school. How much do you depend on your sight to get from your classroom to the cafeteria? How much do you depend on your sight to do such things as measure an exact amount of sugar into a measuring cup? People who can't see have to find different ways to do such tasks. Some young inventors are helping to come up with solutions to these challenges.

How much do you depend on your sight to get from your classroom to the cafeteria?

Eden Fricke is a fifteen-year-old student at Linton High School in Schenectady, New York. Her idea seems simple, but it made a big difference to blind students. She created a floor plan of her school in Braille!

Braille is a type of writing in which letters are made out of combinations of raised dots. People read Braille by feeling the dots with their fingers. Braille is used for books, music, and even for numbers on elevator buttons.

Now, thanks to Eden and her new friend Chris Walters, a map of Linton High School has been produced in Braille. To make the map accurate, Eden had to talk to the school's architects and the Northeastern Association for the Blind. Chris, who has been blind since birth, helped Eden put the Braille map on a sheet of thin metal.

Blind students can now get directions to any spot in the school just by running their fingers over the map. Eden is already planning more projects such as Braille room numbers on classroom doors and a Braille menu in the cafeteria.

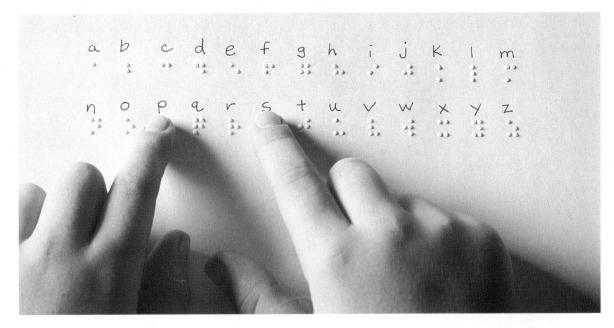

For her idea, Eden won a prize in the 1990 General Electric Company's Ingenuity Challenge 300. But for Chris, the rewards are even greater. "There are people who don't even realize there are blind people in the school," says Chris. "I'm glad to see somebody's paying attention."

Braille is an important part of another invention by a student. Fourteen-year-old, Tova Leigh, of Pepperell, Massachusetts, has invented what she calls the "Braille Pail" for the Invent America Contest at her school. Tova had the idea of putting Braille markings inside a measuring cup. Now anyone can pour and measure exact amounts by feel.

The Invention of Braille

An interesting sidelight to all these stories is the history of Braille itself. This alphabet was invented in 1824 by Louis Braille of France, who was himself blind.

Braille uses different dot patterns, containing from one to six dots. This pattern has 63 possible arrangements— enough for the alphabet, numbers, and punctuation marks. Louis Braille was only 15 when he came up with his easy-to-read dot system.

On Your Own

1. How do the other senses help a blind person? Get a bag. Put some things in it, such as a pencil, some coins, a paper clip, a peanut, and other things. Trade bags with a friend. Close your eyes. Pull an object out of the bag. Without looking, figure out what the object is. What senses help you decide?

2. Do you know anyone who is blind? Talk with that person and find out what would be helpful to her or him. For example, what is the best way to help a blind person whom you meet on the street?

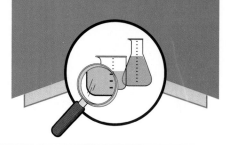

Ask a Television Engineer

Occupation: Television engineer
Hobbies: Photography, playing guitar, skiing, traveling
Goal: To one day be an independent producer

Ask Tony about TV magic and you may not like his answers. He'll tell you how it's done, and that there's no magic to it, just lots of switches, buttons, and TV monitors. And lots of work. Tony Torres is a television engineer. He's one of the people making the TV "magic" happen.

What does a TV engineer do?

"There are many different jobs. One job is being the switcher. That's the person who sits next to the director during a 'live' television broadcast, such as the local news. In front of the switcher is a big board with blinking lights and buttons to push. Beyond that is a wall filled with 20 television screens. Some of the screens show what's happening on the live television show. Others show what will be coming up in a few seconds or in a few minutes."

What do you do with all the buttons and switches?

"Some are used to cut, or change, to the next piece of videotape. Some are used for special effects."

How do you make special effects?

"Do you ever watch the local weather forecast? Usually you see the forecaster standing in front of a big map, pointing out different areas on the map. But in fact, the map is very small and the forecaster is not standing anywhere near it. The forecaster and the map are put together by the switcher. First, the weather map is called up on a computer. Then, a television camera shoots the forecaster standing in front of a green background. The switcher can block out the green color, making the background completely disappear. Then, the image of the forecaster is keyed over, or put on top of, the weather map. And what you see is the weather news."

Battery: A Power Source

How does the battery in a flashlight work? It works like the one below, which is called a dry cell.

1 A zinc can inside the battery contains a moist paste of two compounds. In the center of the can is a carbon rod. The can is covered by cardboard or metal to keep air out of the battery.

2 The compounds in the zinc can react very slowly. This reaction produces new compounds and releases electrons. When you turn on the flashlight, you close the circuit and these electrons begin to flow out of the battery and through the circuit.

4 In time, the chemical reaction inside the battery stops. Then, current no longer flows when the flashlight is turned on and the bulb no longer lights up. You need a new battery!

3 The electrons flow from the battery to the light bulb and back to the battery. They provide the electrical energy needed to light the bulb.

Find Out On Your Own

Use an encyclopedia to find the story about the invention of the battery. Pretend you are a reporter and your job is to write a short newspaper article about your findings.

Module Review

Making Connections

Energy

1. Describe an energy change that occurs at a transmitting station.
2. What energy change takes place in the cochlea of the ear?
3. How are electricity and magnetism related?

Systems and Interactions

4. A string of decorative lights has one burned out light, but the other lights are still on. What does this indicate about how the bulbs are wired together in a circuit?
5. Explain how vision depends on the fact that the brain and the eyes work together.

Using What I Learned

Comparing

1. How are lightning and a spark alike?
2. How are the screen of a television picture tube and the retina of an eye alike?

Ordering

3. Order each of the following parts of the eye to show the path light takes when it enters the eye: lens, optic nerve, cornea, retina, pupil.

Applying

4. Why is the fact that a circuit breaker opens when it reaches a certain temperature an important safety feature?
5. How do the brain and eye work together so you can see movies?

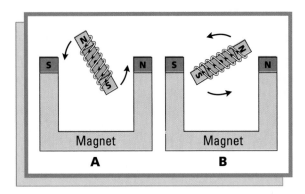

Relating

6. In what way is the relationship between electrons and protons like that of the one between a magnet and a paper clip?
7. Tell how the amount of light entering your eyes is related to the size of the pupils in your eyes.

Communicating

8. Draw a diagram that illustrates the magnetic field of a bar magnet.

Categorizing

9. Categorize each of the following substances as either a conductor or an insulator of electricity: wood, silver, glass, wool, and copper.

Observing

10. What happens to the coil shown in diagram A to the left
a) if the direction of the current reverses?
b) if the direction of the current stays the same and doesn't reverse?
c) if the current stops?
Which of the above (a, b, or c) is shown in diagram B?

Applying What I Learned

Performance Task

Use a piece of wool cloth and an inflated balloon to show that friction can cause an imbalance of electrical charge in a substance. Be sure to wear cover goggles.

Drawing

Make a poster showing sound waves sent from a ship down into the ocean. The sound waves are reflected from the ocean bottom back up to the ship. On the poster, explain how the depth of the ocean can be determined in this way.

Science Theater

Write a skit about an early explorer such as Cortez trying to explain to Native Americans in Central America how a directional compass works.

Exhibitions

Make a picture for the bulletin board showing what happens when you use a VCR to tape a television program.

What If

What if you were asked to design a new auditorium for your school? The auditorium is to be used for plays and musical concerts. How would you structure the room? What kinds of building materials would you use in the room? Make a sketch to show your design.

Living Off the Land

Living Off the Land

Land ho! Land covers less than one third of the earth's surface. Good farm land covers even less—and it comes with lots of bugs. In this module, you'll find out how farmers and scientists are working together to grow more food from the land, while fighting off an ever-growing army of insects.

CHAPTER

1 Planet of Plants

Can you smell danger in the air?
Some plants may use chemical odors to warn their comrades of approaching danger.

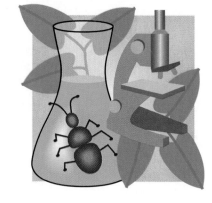

CHAPTER

2 Growing Plants

How is a flower like a factory?
Both manufacture products. For flowers, the products are life-giving seeds.

CHAPTER

3 Gardening Plants

Green thumbs are as close as your fingers. Know-how and hard work can produce gardens that are bursting with life and food.

In this module

Planet of Plants

I can't smell anything yet!

Discover Activity

What do odors tell you?

Your classmates should stand in different parts of the classroom. You or your teacher will open a bottle containing a liquid. As soon as your classmates smell the substance, they should raise their hands. Wait until all hands are raised. Repeat with a new substance.

For Discussion

1. *How did the odors travel throughout the room?*
2. *What was your reaction to each odor?*

1·1 *Stalk Talk*

▶ *Do plants communicate with each other?*

Something's happened. You've shrunk to the size of a peanut. You have wings and long, floppy antennae. You are teetering on a potato leaf in a vegetable jungle. Corn, squash, and potato plants tower over you. As you can see, it's lunchtime. And the potato plant just happens to be your favorite snack. You're a Colorado potato beetle! Farmers and gardeners don't like you very much.

The garden is hopping—like a school cafeteria. You hear the crunch of insects chewing, and the hum of "conversation"—buzzing, chirping, and chattering. A mingling of smells is in the air—the scents of tasty foods, a whiff of sweet perfume.

You move on to the next potato plant. But its leaves taste *bad*. "Bleech!" you say and spit it out. Sounds weird, but sometimes you feel like the plants get the word that you're hanging around. They seem to make themselves taste awful before you have a chance to chow down. You squat on a leaf and scratch your head.

◄ *What kinds of communication do you see in this cartoon?*

Plant Talk Hypothesis

Scientists are scratching their heads, too. They're asking themselves: Do plants really "talk" back and forth? Do they communicate and warn each other, as this cartoon suggests? Does one plant "say" to its neighbor, "Hey, the bug that likes potato leaves is heading your way"?

Scientists have found that certain plants have a way of protecting themselves from attacking insects. These plants have "buzzers" that go off when insects take nips out of them. When the chomping begins, an alarm signal travels through the plant. This signal causes the plant to make chemicals that are bad news for the munching insects. The anti-insect chemicals poison the insects or stunt their growth.

Now scientists are testing a related idea about alarm signals—the "plant talk" hypothesis. Some scientists think that a plant can do more than just protect itself. They think a plant can also send out an alarm signal that warns its neighbors of danger.

▼ *Describe what you think is happening in this cartoon.*

The hypothesis goes like this: After an insect chews a leaf, the injured plant releases a chemical that floats through the air. Remember that in the Discover Activity you learned how chemicals travel through air. You also found out that different smells cause you to respond in different ways. For example, some of the odors might have caused you to turn away or hold your nose.

According to the hypothesis, the chemical signal given off by the injured plant may cause a response in other plants. The chemical may act as a warning that shouts "Pests at lunch!" With early warning, nearby plants can start to make anti-insect chemicals *before* they get nipped by the pests.

In the laboratory, scientists found evidence to support the plant talk hypothesis. Sagebrush plants contain a chemical that some scientists think is a powerful alarm signal. The scientists tested their idea by doing the experiment pictured here. They put sagebrush plants and tomato plants together in air-tight jars. Guess what happened? Tests showed that the tomato plants began to make anti-insect chemicals. The scientists concluded that the alarm signals given off by sagebrush traveled through the air and caused this response in the tomato plants. To further test their hypothesis, the scientists put tomato plants in the air-tight jars *without* sagebrush plants. These tomato plants did not produce the anti-insect chemicals.

Do scientists need more evidence for the plant talk hypothesis? Of course they do! Remember, they did their tests in the laboratory. Plants don't normally grow in jars. Now scientists are doing new experiments that are testing the hypothesis out-of-doors in the plants' own territory.

▲ A chemical in the sagebrush plant on the right spreads through the air in this jar. The chemical may act as a signal to the tomato plant nearby.

Hormones control the growth of an apple seedling.

Developing shoot

Developing roots

Seedcase

Plant Signals

Scientists don't know for certain whether chemical signals travel from plant to plant. But they are quite sure about one thing. Chemical signals do travel *inside* a plant—from one part of a plant to another part.

When you plant an apple seed, what causes the seed to crack open? What causes a tiny root to come out of the seedcase first, and push downward into the soil? What causes a young shoot to poke through the ground and grow upward?

Chemicals called hormones control all of these activities. A **hormone** is a chemical messenger with a precise list of instructions.

A single plant contains a crew of hormones, each with its own assignment. One hormone is in charge of making roots grow downward. Another directs a stem to grow toward sunlight. When the time is right, other hormones make an apple ripen and turn red, or a maple leaf change color.

Hormones control all the activities connected with the growth and development of plants, such as this apple tree. In turn, the long days of summer, the cold nights of winter, and other signs from nature control hormones. Environmental signals—which you call the changing seasons—help control how hormones are made and released within plants.

Most hormones are produced in one part of a plant, but they have their effect in another part of the plant. So, how do they get the job done? Hormones move through tubes that carry food throughout a plant. And hormones are constantly on the march inside a plant. For example, one hormone is in charge of making a plant bend toward light. This hormone is produced in the very tip of the stem, but it travels down into the stem with its instructions.

As chemical messengers, hormones don't waste words. A tiny amount of a hormone can bring about a big change in a plant. For example, an extremely small quantity of a kind of growth hormone causes the shoot and root of an apple seedling to grow longer.

Besides controlling activities in different parts of the plant, hormones sometimes control each other. When it's time for a plant to reproduce, the hormone in charge of fruit-ripening has control over the hormone that keeps the fruit green.

Hormones control the ripening of the apples on this tree.

Checkpoint

1. Why must scientists design experiments that will test the plant talk hypothesis out-of-doors?
2. List four activities of plants that are controlled by hormones.
3. **Take Action!** Put a very ripe banana and a green tomato in a covered shoe box. Wait a few days and open the box. Observe how a hormone given off by the banana has ripened the tomato.

Activity

Putting Down Roots

People can use plant hormones to help plants grow. Try this activity to see how rooting hormones work.

Picture A

Gather These Materials

cover goggles
2 clear plastic cups
vermiculite
pencil
mature plant (coleus)

rooting hormone
2 clear plastic bags
masking tape
water

Follow This Procedure

1 Make a chart like the one on the next page. Record your observations in the chart.

2 Put on your cover goggles.

3 Fill your 2 cups with moist vermiculite.

4 Use a pencil to poke 2 holes in the vermiculite in each cup. The holes should be up against the inside wall of each cup. (Picture A)

5 Take 2 small cuttings from the coleus plant. Insert a cutting in each of the holes in one cup. You should be able to view the tips of the cuttings through the side of the cup. (Picture B)

6 Pack some more vermiculite around the cuttings to hold them in place.

7 Take 2 more cuttings from the coleus plant. Have your teacher dip the ends of the cuttings in the rooting hormone.

Picture B

Picture C

8 Plant these cuttings in the second cup. Follow the same procedure you used for the first cuttings.

9 Place a clear plastic bag over each cup. Loosely tape the bag in place. (Picture C)

Predict: **Which cuttings will have greater root growth?**

10 Keep your cuttings in a warm place with plenty of light. Remove the plastic bags to water the plant cuttings as needed.

11 Check your cuttings every day. Look for root growth. Record your observations.

Record Your Results

Observations		
Date	Cuttings with root hormone	Cuttings without root hormone

State Your Conclusions

1. How did the root growth differ in your 2 cups?
2. Do you think that the root hormone helped the plant grow roots? Explain.
3. How would using rooting hormones be helpful to farmers or gardeners?

Let's Experiment

Do you think that some types of plants grow roots faster than others? Use what you know about scientific methods to find out.

1.2 *The Talking Planet*

▶ *What's the flower telling the butterfly?*

While scientists continue to explore the idea of plants "talking" to other plants, they know that plants do "talk" to insects. Plants produce chemical signals that contain important messages.

A smell is a message. Flowers attract insects with fragrances that say, "Here's food for you." Butterflies are attracted to flowers that smell sweet. Beetles are attracted to flowers with spicy scents.

A bad taste is another message. Some flowers contain a poison called pyrethrum (pī rē′thrəm). Its message is blunt: "Bug off!" An insect gets the message after its first taste.

Signals in the Soil

Insects aren't the only organisms that get messages from plants. Tiny bacteria in the soil receive messages from plants called legumes (leg′yüms). And the bacteria actually "talk" back!

▼ *Take a look under the ground at the roots of this alfalfa plant. Find the nodules where bacteria live.*

Legumes are plants such as soybeans, peas, and alfalfa. These plants can change nitrogen gas in the air to forms of nitrogen that plants need for growth. Well, the legumes don't exactly do this on their own. The plants provide homes and food for bacteria called *Rhizobium* (rī zō′bi um). But the bacteria do the work.

As the pictures show, the legumes construct little bumps called nodules on their roots. The nodules become a home and factory for the bacteria. The bacteria live inside the nodules and feed on sugars made by the plant. In return, the bacteria make the nitrogen compounds that the plants need for growth. So, as you can see, both the plants and the bacteria benefit from this partnership.

How do legumes and *Rhizobium* get together? Molecular biologist Sharon Long discovered that alfalfa plants and *Rhizobium* "talk" to one another. Alfalfa starts the "conversation" by sending out a chemical called a flavonoid. The chemical puts out a call to all *Rhizobium* in the soil: "Come to work in exchange for room and board."

When the *Rhizobium* receive the message, they send their own chemical reply. They release a chemical into the soil that carries this message to the alfalfa plant: "We'll be there soon. Start making our nodule homes." Long and her co-workers think the conversation continues. They are doing experiments to find out what the alfalfa says next.

▲ Scientists are using microscopes and other tools to study these Rhizobium bacteria, which are found inside alfalfa nodules.

▲ Each antenna of the male silkworm moth may have 70 branches. Each branch has thousands of hairs that detect tiny amounts of female sex pheromones.

Talking Long Distance

As you learned, a hormone works *within* a living thing, where it carries messages to certain parts of the organism. A **pheromone** is a chemical that communicates information between two or more members of the same species. You might say that pheromones are long-distance hormones.

Pheromones are especially important in insect communication. Some insects, like butterflies, live by themselves. Others—like ants, aphids, and honeybees—live in large, crowded communities.

Without pheromones two tiny insects might *never* find each other in the thick grass. In many species, a female releases a sex pheromone that causes a male of her species to stop in his tracks. He picks up the signal with long, feathery antennae like those in the picture. The antennae can detect very tiny amounts of the female pheromone. When a male detects the scent, he will follow the fragrant pheromone path directly to the female. The male might then release his own pheromone to let the female know that she is about to be "courted."

Why are sex pheromones important? Well, the answer isn't exactly romance, as the cartoon suggests. Sex pheromones are necessary for the survival of a species. They help males and females of the same species find each other so that they can reproduce.

Pheromones work just as well for insects that live in large groups. Pheromones broadcast information quickly, which can be very important when danger threatens. When a honeybee stings an enemy, the bee releases a pheromone that smells like bananas. The pheromone travels quickly through the air, sending an alarm message to other honeybees. When the other bees smell this alarm pheromone, they're attracted to it. They quickly gather and get ready to help defend the hive.

Checkpoint

1. Give an example of a chemical signal that a plant sends to another organism.
2. What are sex pheromones and why are they important in insect communication?
3. **Take Action!** By releasing a pheromone onto the ground, an ant can lay a scent trail that guides other ants to a food source. Use peppermint extract to make a scent trail. Then have your classmates try to follow the trail to the "food."

▲ *Sex pheromones are an important kind of chemical communication between males and females of the same species.*

1.3 *Getting The Bugs Out*

▶ **How can chemical signals help farmers?**

It's night—your favorite time—and you're flying through a field of tomatoes. You're a fuzzy, brown cabbage looper moth, a male of your species. Suddenly your antennae pick up an *irresistible* fragrance. The message shrieks like a siren: *Female! Female! Female!* You make a beeline—oops, a mothline— toward the smell. Finally, you land in this strange-looking cardboard box. Hmmm. Other males are in here, but, hey, where's the female? You have been trapped by two tomato farmers with a keen interest in cabbage loopers, beet army worms, and other tomato pests.

Science and Farming

The tomato farmers are a husband-and-wife team who are working with scientists to find ways to reduce the amount of chemicals people put on crops. They catch male cabbage loopers by attracting them into traps that are baited with sex pheromones of female cabbage loopers.

The farmers count the male moths in the pheromone traps. The count helps farmers determine how many female moths are in the field laying eggs on the tomatoes. The eggs will hatch into larvae that will worm their way into the farmers' tomatoes.

▲ *This pheromone trap is used to attract and trap many kinds of insect pests, including these cabbage looper moths.*

If the numbers of trapped males are high, the farmers will apply insecticide to control the cabbage looper larvae. If the numbers are low, no insecticide is necessary.

Scientific knowledge about plant chemical signals can also be put to work in fields and gardens. For years, farmers and gardeners have used sprays containing pyrethrums as insecticides. The "Don't eat me!" message of pyrethrums keeps plant-eating insects away from crops.

With more research, scientists and farmers may find that the alarm chemical made by sagebrush plants can be useful. By spraying the chemical on fields, crops might begin to make the chemicals that protect them from plant-eating insects.

Today, more than ever before, scientists and farmers are working together to use what they know about plants and insects. Their work is helping find better ways to grow crops, such as the enormous wheat crop shown below. Thanks to their work, you can leave a grocery store with a shopping cart filled to the brim with tasty, nutritious foods!

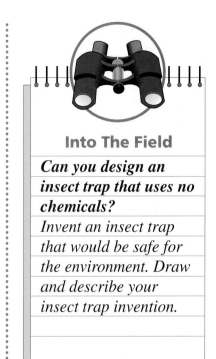

Into The Field

Can you design an insect trap that uses no chemicals?

Invent an insect trap that would be safe for the environment. Draw and describe your insect trap invention.

▼ Farm machines called combines harvest a wheat crop.

The Age of DDT

Ever since farming began 8000 years ago, people have been trying to get rid of insects and other crop pests. Early methods of pest control were hard work. People tried trapping insects, swatting them, and scaring them away. In some parts of the world entire villages still tramp through the fields beating drums to scare off grasshoppers.

A history of pest control methods is shown in the timeline on the next few pages. Follow the dates and pictures as you read. In the 1800s, people began to use chemicals to kill insect pests. A chemical that kills pests that damage crops is a **pesticide** (pes′tə sīd). Back in the 1800s, most pesticides contained metals, such as arsenic, copper, and mercury. Some of these pesticides can be very poisonous. They often killed the plants as well as the insects!

In 1939, an accidental discovery made people in this century very dependent on pesticides. In that year, Swiss chemist Paul Müller discovered that a chemical called DDT killed moths that ate wool clothes. So he began to investigate DDT. Müller found that DDT was a powerful insecticide that killed many other kinds of insects.

Ancient times

Chrysanthemum petals are crushed to make the insecticide pyrethrum.

Late 200s

The Chinese begin to use yellow citrus killer-ants to control insect pests in their mandarin orange groves.

Mid 1800s

Vineyards in France are treated with carbon bisulfide to kill aphids that destroy grape vines.

1939

Dr. Paul Müller discovers that dichloro-diphenyl-trichloro-ethane, or DDT, can kill insects.

1942–1945
World War II soldiers use shaker-top cans to dust powdered DDT on their clothing.

1946
Airplanes are used to apply DDT over large areas of farmlands. Many airplanes were those used during World War II.

1948
Dr. Paul Müller wins a Nobel Prize for discovering that DDT could be used as a pesticide.

During World War II, DDT was used to kill disease-carrying insects such as head lice and mosquitoes. DDT saved thousands of soldiers who would have died of diseases, such as typhus and malaria, that these insects carry. Shortly after the war, Paul Müller won a Nobel Prize for his life-saving discovery.

In the 1950s, people turned their attention to a peacetime problem—how to produce food for the world's growing population. Farmers began to use DDT in their fields. At first, people were very excited about the new "wonder" chemical. Farmers discovered that DDT killed a wide variety of crop pests. But that's not all. DDT was also cheap and easy to use.

It wasn't long before farmers were using DDT on everything. Harvests were gigantic! It looked as if the problem of feeding the world was solved. But slowly people began to realize that DDT affected more than just insect pests. By the 1960s, people began to see that DDT was poisoning *everything*—the soil, rivers, lakes, wildlife, and people!

A New Day in Pest Control

The timeline on this page continues to 1972—an important date in the history of pest control. In 1972, a law was passed that made the use of DDT illegal in the United States. People's views about pesticides were changing. By that time a great deal of evidence showed that DDT was harming the environment. And the poisonous effects of DDT lasted a long time.

Studies also showed that DDT wasn't working anymore. Malaria was on the rise again. Why? Mosquitoes that carried malaria had developed resistance to DDT—the pesticide no longer had any effect on them.

Crop pests were also becoming resistant to DDT. The more the farmers applied DDT, the less it worked. Heavy use of DDT was causing more and more insects to become resistant to the chemical.

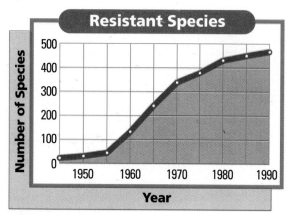

Resistant Species

Number of Species vs. Year

1955

The numbers of insects resistant to pesticides begin to increase sharply.

1960s

As the harmful effects of DDT become known, people begin to protest against the use of DDT.

1972

The United States government bans most uses of DDT, including its use in farming.

Farmers were also discouraged to find that their fields had greater numbers of pests than ever before. What was going on? For one thing, DDT was also killing the natural enemies of insect pests. With their enemies wiped out, the populations of the pests could increase rapidly.

But what has happened since 1972? Many chemical pesticides quickly replaced DDT, but they have the same problems. Many of these pesticides harm the environment. In fact, some of these chemicals are even more poisonous than DDT. And, as you can see in the graph, many kinds of insects have developed resistance to pesticides. Of these resistant species, many are disease-carrying insects and serious crop pests.

For more than 50 years, people have been waging all-out chemical warfare against insects. At one time, people believed that chemical pesticides would solve the problem of producing food for the world's growing population. But sometimes crop losses are just as high as they were before so many chemicals were used. By now, you probably wonder, "Who's winning this war?"

Solving the problems of pest control is an exciting challenge for scientists and farmers. How can they develop new chemicals and methods that do the job safely and inexpensively—and still grow enough food for people everywhere?

Many farmers are using smaller amounts of chemicals. Farmers are also applying chemicals to their fields less often. And some farmers, called organic farmers, don't use any chemicals at all. Farmers are also using biological pest control. A **biological control** is a method that uses natural enemies to control insects. As you read on, you will see that biological control is one way farmers can work *with*, not against, nature.

1976
Farmers begin to experiment with a new pest control method—integrated pest management.

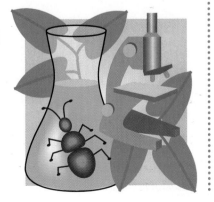

1980s
Organically grown fruits and vegetables become available in many grocery stores and farm stands.

1990s
Researchers continue to develop new chemicals and methods to control crop pests.

Battle of the Bugs

Some insects can help solve pest problems on farms and in gardens.

You're a farmer with a big problem. Your farm has been invaded by pests. Grasshoppers are chewing your corn plants. Aphids are sucking sap from your pea plants. Weevils are gnawing holes in your pepper blossoms. Stalk borers are burrowing into the stems of your squash plants.

How are you going to solve your problem? Well, you just might want to bring in *more* insects! In nature, many kinds of insects kill other insects. In this way, the populations of certain kinds of insects are kept under control.

Today, many farmers and gardeners control pests the natural way. They are learning how to use helpful insects to control the number of harmful insects that attack their crops.

Praying mantis
Eats most kinds of insect pests, including weevils, grasshoppers, aphids, and stalk borers.

Ladybug
Eats mainly aphids, but also eats stalk borers, weevils, whiteflies, and Colorado potato beetles.

Braconid wasp
Lays eggs inside the larvae of cabbage looper moths, grain weevils, cabbage butterflies, and tomato hornworms.

Take a look at the insects shown here. They should be very welcome in gardens and on farms. Why? These helpful insects kill many kinds of crop-damaging pests. Here's how they do it.

Ladybugs and praying mantises are the lions and tigers of the insect world. These hungry hunters have chewing mouthparts, which they use to devour many kinds of garden and crop pests.

Assassin bugs are hunters, too. But these bugs have sucking mouthparts. An assassin bug holds its victim, or prey, with powerful front legs. Then the assassin bug uses its long, curved beak to pierce its prey and suck out its body fluids.

Some kinds of female wasps kill pests in another way. These wasps lay one or more eggs inside the body of an insect pest. When the egg hatches, the larva—or young— feeds on the insect's internal organs, killing it from the inside out.

Assassin bug
Attacks many kinds of leafhoppers, caterpillars, and aphids, as well as Colorado potato beetles.

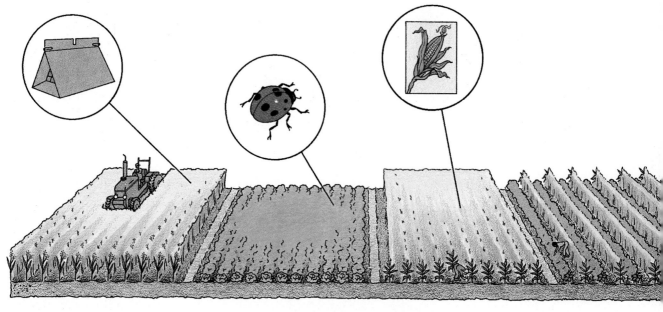

Traps provide farmers with information about the kinds and numbers of pests in fields.

Natural enemies are used as biological controls of crop-damaging insects.

Pest-resistant varieties of crops are grown.

▲ What are some advantages of using IPM?

Integrated Pest Management

As you learned, many farmers are beginning to think that they can't solve pest problems with chemicals alone. Pesticides are getting expensive and they don't always work.

Some farmers are trying a different strategy—Integrated Pest Management, or IPM for short. It works like this. Farmers use a combination of ways to control insects. That's what the word *integrated* means. Some of the methods that are parts of IPM are shown in the diagram.

IPM is not easy. Farmers who use IPM must have a great deal of knowledge about both plants and pests. Farmers must also make careful, often difficult, choices. For example, when farmers find insect damage in their fields, they must decide what to do. Will biological control work or should a pesticide be used? Whenever possible, farmers avoid using chemicals to kill crop-damaging insects. They also try to avoid using weed killers, or herbicides (hėr′bə sīds). Instead, farmers control weeds by pulling them out.

Crops are planted in narrow rows to create shade that prevents weed growth.

Chemical pesticides are used only when other pest control methods fail.

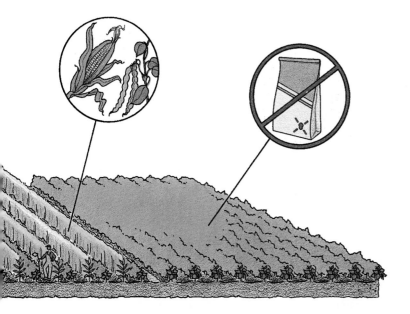

In Indonesia, the government gave rice farmers a crash course in IPM. Farmers were spraying pesticides on their rice paddies up to eight times a season to kill pests called planthoppers. The more they sprayed, the more planthoppers there were. The pesticides were killing spiders that eat planthoppers!

So, the government banned many kinds of pesticides and taught the farmers ways to bring back the spiders. In three years, farmers were using 90 percent less pesticides. What about the spiders? They were back at work, eating planthoppers.

Checkpoint

1. How can farmers use insect pheromones?
2. List the benefits and dangers of DDT.
3. What is organic farming?
4. Give an example of biological control.
5. What is IPM?
6. **Take Action!** Read the warnings on flea powders to find out about the dangers of using these pesticides on pets.

Evaluating IPM

In Indonesia, integrated pest management, or IPM, is being used to control planthoppers. Farmers have stopped spraying their rice fields with pesticides. Instead, farmers are using spiders, which are natural enemies of planthoppers, as biological controls. This chart shows the results of Indonesia's IPM program.

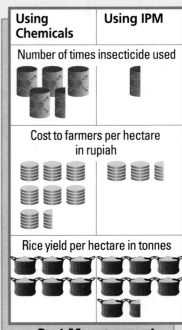

Using Chemicals	Using IPM
Number of times insecticide used	
Cost to farmers per hectare in rupiah	
Rice yield per hectare in tonnes	

Pest Management

What Did You Find Out?
1. *How does the cost of IPM compare to the cost of using chemicals?*
2. *How do the two crop yields compare?*
3. *Which method of pest control got better results—IPM or spraying with pesticides?*

Activity

A Safe Way to Spray

There are many ways to control pests. In this activity you can make an insect spray that is safe for you to use.

Picture A

Picture C

Gather These Materials

cover goggles
1 garlic bulb
1 small onion
plastic knife
cutting board
2 mixing bowls
large measuring spoon
cayenne pepper
liter measure

water
mixing spoon
liquid soap
cheesecloth
2 spray bottles
large jar with lid
2 mature plants, same
   type and size

Follow This Procedure

1. Make a chart like the one on the next page. Record your observations in the chart.

2. Put on your cover goggles.

3. Carefully chop the garlic bulb and onion into tiny pieces. Then place them in a mixing bowl. (Picture A) Add one spoonful of cayenne pepper to the bowl.

4. Add 1 liter of water and stir. Let the mixture sit for one hour. Then stir in one spoonful of liquid soap. (Picture B)

5. Pour the mixture through a few layers of cheesecloth into another mixing bowl. Then pour some of the liquid into a spray bottle. Pour the rest into a jar. Close the jar tightly, and put it in the refrigerator. It will keep for up to one week.

Picture B

6 Fill the other spray bottle with water.

7 Put both plants outside. Once each day, lightly spray one plant with your insect spray. Spray the other plant lightly with water. (Picture C)

> **Predict: How do you think the insect spray will affect the plant?**

8 Observe the plants over the next few days. Water the plants as needed. Watch for insects. Record any differences between the plants in the chart.

Record Your Results

Observations		
Date	Sprayed with insect spray	Sprayed with water

State Your Conclusions

1. What are some of the advantages to using this kind of insect spray?

2. Did you notice any differences between the plant treated with the insect spray and the plant that was not treated?

Let's Experiment

Do you think your spray would keep animals away from vegetable plants in a garden? Use what you know about scientific methods to find out.

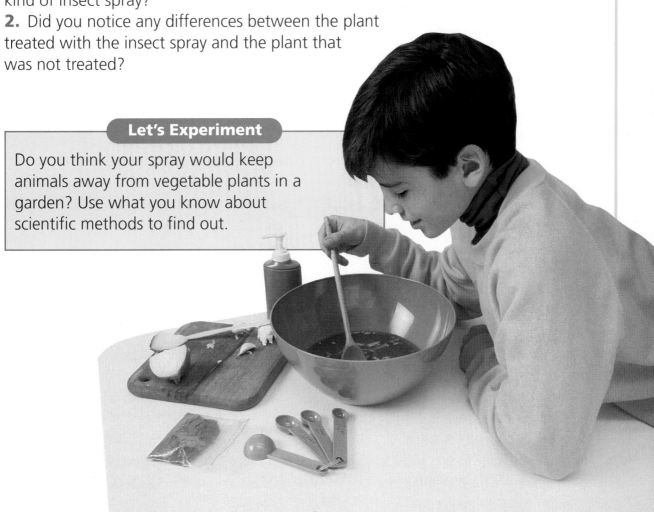

Analyzing Cause and Effect

When making a complex decision, such as whether or not to use pesticides, causes and effects are important to consider. A cause is an event that makes another event happen. The result is called the effect. Often an effect becomes the cause of another event.

Thinking It Through

Suppose you own a farm in California. Your crops have been invaded by swarms of tiny insects called poinsettia whiteflies. These insects destroy fruit and vegetable crops by sucking the sap from the plants' leaves. Here's how you might consider cause and effect as you decide how best to control these pests.

What crop damage will the whiteflies cause?

The whiteflies destroy plant leaves. The plants do not flower or bear fruit properly. If the whiteflies take over, part of my harvest might be lost.

What would be the effects of losing a part of my harvest?

If part of my harvest is destroyed, I'll have fewer crops to sell. Maybe I won't earn enough money to cover my costs. I might even have to go out of business. Looks like it's time to spray!

How would pesticides affect me and my family?

Pesticides might cause skin rashes or other illness. The extra pesticides will make their way down into the soil. Our drinking water might become unsafe. Maybe I'd better look for a natural way to control these pests.

What about wasps? What effect would they have on the whiteflies?

I could bring in wasps to eat the whiteflies. But I'd have to have huge numbers of wasps before they'd have any effect on the whitefly population. I wonder what other effects huge numbers of wasps might cause on my farm.

As you see, farmers and agricultural scientists must often make difficult choices. They must choose methods that have the largest number of good effects and smallest number of bad effects.

Your Turn

Whiteflies suck the sap out of leaves. The leaves turn brown and fall off. Tell how losing leaves would harm a fruit or vegetable. Explain the process in terms of cause and effect.

Chapter Review

Thinking Back

1. What is the "plant talk" hypothesis?
2. Explain what scientists observed when sagebrush and tomato plants were placed together in air-tight containers.
3. What effect do environmental signals have on the growth and development of a plant?
4. How are legumes and *Rhizobium* bacteria helpful to each other?
5. Compare a **hormone** and a **pheromone**.

6. How are sex pheromones important for the survival of a species?
7. Identify a positive and a negative effect of the **pesticide** DDT.
8. What is **biological control**?
9. Name two kinds of insects that are natural enemies of crop pests.
10. List three pest control methods used in integrated pest management.

Connecting Ideas

1. Copy the concept map. Use the terms at the right to complete the map about chemical signals.

pheromones   **hormones**
growth   **reproduction**

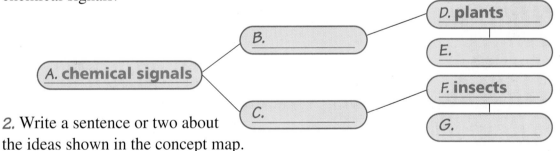

2. Write a sentence or two about the ideas shown in the concept map.

Gathering Evidence

1. In the Activity on page 10, what observations showed you that the hormone helps roots grow?
2. In the Activity on page 26, how did you know that you were making a safe insect spray?

Doing Science!

1. *Design an activity* that compares the effects of a root hormone on root growth in a coleus plant and a cactus.
2. *Develop a skit* in which you and a classmate role play a farmer and a scientist describing the benefits and problems of using pesticides.

Growing Plants

Discover Activity

What's the best way to grow peas?

Select a packet of pea seeds. Think about what conditions might affect the growth of peas. Design an experiment to find out which conditions are best for growing pea plants. Observe your plants every day for three weeks. Record your observations.

For Discussion

1. *What conditions did you test and why?*
2. *What conditions are best for growing pea plants?*

2.1 *Breaking New Ground*

▶ *What makes plants grow?*

Maybe you'd like to ask this young gardener, "What's your secret?" Well, here's what he'd tell you, "Secrets? Forget it! Growing sweet peppers isn't a big mystery. Pepper plants need six things. Supply them with these needs and you'll harvest a basketful of sweet, red peppers!"

Checklist for Growing

As you observed in the Discover Activity, plants grow and develop. Think about your pea plants. They grew from seeds into plants with slender stems, and leaves with curly threads called tendrils. If the pea plants were growing in a garden, they would have formed pods containing seeds. What does a pea plant need to grow? It must have those six things that the pepper grower talked about. To grow, plants need light, water, nutrients, the right temperature, gases in the air, and space to grow.

▼ *To produce these tasty peppers, the pepper plants need warm temperatures and plenty of space. They also need to be watered and fertilized often.*

Hydroponics: All A Plant Needs

On hydroponic farms, crops grow indoors in a nutrient-rich liquid.

Plants that grow on farms get most of the things they need from nature. But sometimes nature is undependable. Bad weather may prevent crop plants from getting the sunlight, water, or warmth they need to grow well.

Now scientists and farmers are experimenting with hydroponics, a new kind of agriculture. **Hydroponics** is the science of growing plants in a nutrient-rich liquid instead of in soil. On hydroponic farms, crops such as lettuce and spinach, are raised indoors in factory-like buildings. The plants are supplied with the things they need to grow well—air, light, nutrients, water, and proper temperature.

Light

Special grow lights are often used to help plants grow faster. Sometimes lights are turned on for 17 hours a day.

Nutrients

Nutrients—nitrogen, phosphorus, potassium, calcium, magnesium, and sulfur—are added to the water. Hormones are also added to help plants grow.

Temperature

Air temperature is carefully controlled so that plants get the warm temperatures they need. Electricity and fuels are used to heat the building.

Water

A system of pipes and sprinklers supplies plants with water. The roots of the crops hang down into a solution of water and nutrients.

Nutrients from Soil

Unlike plants in hydroponic farms, most plants grow in soil. Soil is made mostly of tiny bits of crushed rocks. As plants and animals die and decay, their remains mix with the soil, too. The plant-and-animal part of soil is called humus (hyü′məs). This wonderful mix of rock and humus contains nutrients—chemicals plants need to grow. Soil is like a bank. Plants draw nutrient "riches" from the "soil bank" just as people take money from a bank.

Some of the nutrients in soil are minerals such as phosphorus, potassium, sulfur, calcium, and magnesium. Another soil nutrient is nitrogen, the hardest nutrient for plants to get! Three-fourths of the air is nitrogen gas. But plants can't use this nitrogen. They must take in nitrogen from the soil. Some soil bacteria change nitrogen gas into nitrogen compounds that plants can use. Nitrogen compounds are also formed when dead plants decay. Plants take in and use these compounds.

The diagram shows how plants use nutrients over and over again in a cycle. In nature, plants take nutrients from the soil. When plants die and decay, the nutrients are returned to soil as humus.

▼ With your finger, trace the path of the nutrient cycle. Explain how humus is part of this cycle.

Now look at the diagram on this page. It shows that some nutrients on farmland aren't cycled, as they are in nature. When farmers harvest their crops, they take away parts of the plants that would die and become humus. It's a lot like taking money out of the bank but not putting money back. Then you have to borrow money.

When farmers take riches from the soil bank, they must borrow nutrients from fertilizers. A **fertilizer** is a substance, either chemical or natural, that adds nutrients to soil. Fertilizers are like deposits that replace money taken out of a bank. They allow farmers to keep growing crops on the land after nutrients have been removed.

Chemical fertilizers come in different forms, such as the particles you see here. Natural fertilizers include manure from cattle and other livestock. Legumes, which work with *Rhizobium* bacteria to make nitrogen, are another natural fertilizer. Sometimes farmers plant alfalfa and then plow the crop into the soil. Crops that add nitrogen to the soil in this way are called green manure.

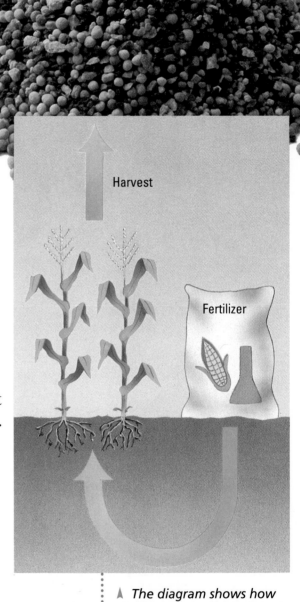

▲ The diagram shows how the nutrient cycle can be broken on farmland. How do chemical fertilizers help complete the cycle?

Checkpoint

1. What things do peppers need to grow?
2. List the benefits of hydroponic farms.
3. How does farming break nutrient cycling?
4. **Take Action!** Examine a soil sample. Separate the humus from the rocks.

Activity

Doing Away With Dirt

Can plants really grow without soil? Try this activity to see how plants grow in a hydroponic solution.

Picture A

Picture B

Picture C

Gather These Materials

cover goggles
toothpicks
2 scallions
2 narrow jars
water

marker
hydroponic solution
scissors
black construction paper
tape

Follow This Procedure

1. Make a chart like the one on the next page. Record your observations in the chart.

2. Put on your cover goggles.

3. Poke 2-3 toothpicks through the leaves of a scallion, about halfway down from the top. Then, place the scallion in a jar so the toothpicks rest on the jar's rim. The bottom of the scallion should not touch the bottom of the jar. (Picture A)

4. Pour water into the jar until it reaches just above the scallion's roots. Mark the level of the water on the jar with a marker. (Picture B)

5. Prepare another scallion as in step 3. Place it in a jar, but add hydroponic solution instead of water.

6. Wrap a piece of black construction paper around each jar, and fasten the paper with tape. The paper will keep out light, preventing algae growth in the jars. (Picture C) Place the jars in a warm, sunny place.

Record Your Results

Growth rate observations		
Date	Scallion in water	Scallion in solution

Predict: **Will the 2 scallions grow at the same rate?**

7 Check the jars every day, and add water to keep the liquid level in each jar constant. Do not add hydroponic solution to either jar.

8 Observe any changes in the scallions. Watch for root growth and leaf sprouting. Record your observations in the chart.

State Your Conclusions

1. Compare the growth of the scallions in the 2 jars.
2. What other plants do you think could be grown this way?

Let's Experiment

Do you think you could root cuttings in a hydroponic solution? Use what you know about scientific methods to find out.

2.2 *Bigger and Better*

Heads of wheat form at the top of each wheat stem. Each head is made up of clusters of flowers.

How do plants form seeds?

If you break open a sweet pepper, you'll see dozens of tiny seeds that can grow into new pepper plants. Many plants reproduce by forming seeds. When planted, a seed develops into a new plant of the same kind. How do seeds form? The seeds of fruits and vegetables develop in flowers.

How Seeds Form

How would you describe a flower? Would you use words like *beautiful, colorful, fragrant, delicate*? You probably wouldn't say *factory*, but that's a good word to describe a flower. Flowers are like factories that manufacture seeds.

Take a close look at this wheat flower as you read about the mass production of seeds. Most flowers have both the male and female machinery needed to produce seeds. The male parts are long, skinny stalks called stamens. The tips of the stamens contain millions of tiny pollen grains. Pollen contains the male sex cells, or sperm.

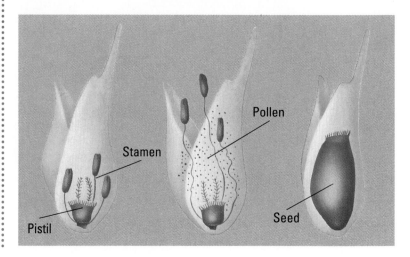

How a wheat seed forms

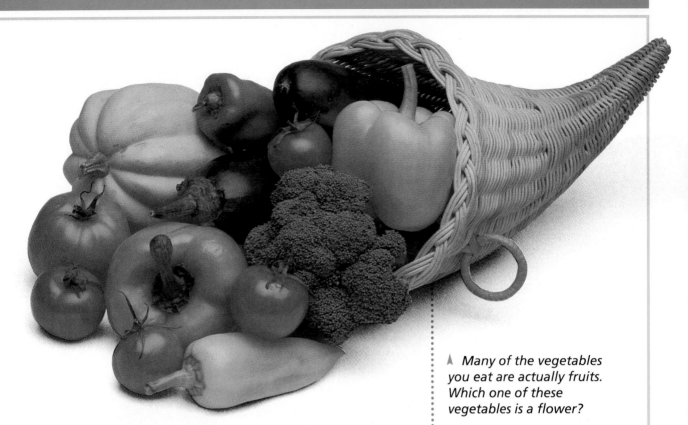

Many of the vegetables you eat are actually fruits. Which one of these vegetables is a flower?

The stamens surround the pistil, or female part of the flower. The top part of the pistil is usually sticky. The bottom part, or ovary, contains one or more ovules. Each ovule holds a female sex cell, or egg. When an egg and a sperm unite, a seed is formed.

But before a seed is formed, pollen must get to the pistil. The moving of pollen from a stamen to the sticky part of the pistil is called **pollination** (pol′ə nā′shən). This wheat flower pollinates itself. But sometimes pollen from one flower is carried by wind to another flower. Insects help pollinate other kinds of flowers. How? Pollen gets stuck to an insect's body when it lands on a flower. When the insect visits another flower, the pollen can rub off onto the sticky part of the pistil.

After pollination, a tube grows down from a pollen grain stuck to the pistil. A sperm cell from the pollen grain travels down the tube and joins with an egg inside an ovule. Then the egg cell develops into a seed—a grain of wheat! In other kinds of flowers, the ovary becomes a thick fruit that covers and protects the seed or seeds. Most of the vegetables in the picture are fruits.

Hybrids of Corn

People can control pollination to produce new varieties of plants.

What pollinated the plant that produced this tasty ear of corn—wind, an insect? It may have been a scientist!

The varieties of corn shown have different characteristics, or traits. Scientists can produce certain traits in corn and other plants by growing hybrids. A **hybrid** is an offspring of parents with different traits. To produce hybrids, scientists cross, or mate, two varieties of plants by controlling pollination. The hybrid produced by a cross has desirable traits from both parents.

Making hybrids
Scientists collect pollen from the tassel of one plant and transfer the pollen to the silk of the second plant. The second plant produces seeds, which grow into hybrid plants.

Tassel
(male part)

Silk
(female part)

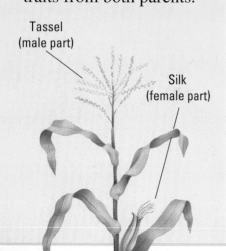

Hybrids of corn
Scientists have produced many new varieties of corn, especially hybrids of white and yellow sweet corn. Hybrids of popping corn make wholesome snacks. Hybrids of decorative corn—with red, orange, yellow, and blue kernels— make festive decorations.

Hybrid seeds
Many kinds of hybrid seeds are available, and new hybrids are developed every year.

These peas were picked from a hybrid plant that is resistant to downy mildew. The diagram shows the effects of this disease.

Sick plant

Hybrid

New Foods From Hybrids

Did you ever wonder why scientists spend so much time developing new varieties of plants? Growing hybrids solves a lot of problems for gardeners and farmers. Thanks to hybrids, farmers can grow bigger, healthier crops. That's very important in the world today, because the growing population needs a plentiful supply of nutritious foods. Growing hybrids can also help protect the environment. How? Some hybrids don't get certain diseases. Other hybrids are not as likely to be eaten by certain crop pests. When farmers plant these hybrids, they don't need to use as many chemical pesticides on their crops.

➤ *The diagram shows why this hybrid carrot is a more nourishing snack than a regular carrot.*

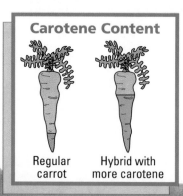

Carotene Content

Regular carrot

Hybrid with more carotene

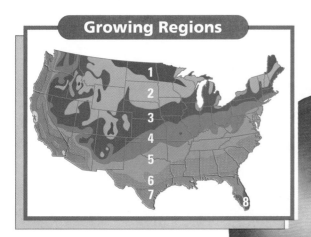

Growing Regions

The vegetables on these pages are grown from hybrid plants. The peas come from pea plants that are resistant to a disease—called downy mildew—caused by a fungus. By growing this hybrid, a farmer doesn't have to use a fungicide (fun′jə sīd), or chemical that kills the fungus. These carrots not only look good—they're good for you! They're a hybrid that contains more carotene, a source of vitamin A. Farmers will tell you that tomato plants are *slow* growers. They need long summers to bear fruit. But this tomato was picked from a hybrid plant that produces tomatoes in a shorter period of time. It's grown by farmers and gardeners who live in the northern parts of North America, where summers are short. On the map, these northern regions are shown in blue.

▲ *The map shows different growing regions. The numbers stand for average temperatures in these regions. The smaller the number, the colder the region and the shorter the growing season.*

Into The Field

How many plant hybrids have you eaten?

Look for plant hybrids in seed catalogs or on seed packages. Record all the different plant hybrids you have eaten.

Checkpoint

1. What is pollination?
2. How do scientists produce hybrid plants?
3. Describe a way in which a hybrid can improve a food crop.
4. **Take Action!** Think of new hybrids that would improve your favorite vegetables. Make a poster of your new foods.

Activity

Prize Tomatoes

When it's time to plant, gardeners can choose from a wide variety of tomato hybrids. Try this activity to see how the hybrids compare.

Picture A

Picture B

Picture C

Gather These Materials

several packages of
   different kinds of
   tomato seeds
large flower pots
soil

fertilizer
water
garden stakes
string or cloth strips

Follow This Procedure

1. Make a chart like the one on the next page. Record your observations in the chart.

2. Work as a member of a team for this activity.

3. Fill a pot with loosely packed soil. (Picture A) Choose a package of hybrid tomato seeds. Plant 4 seeds in the pot. Follow the growing instructions on the seed package. (Picture B)

4. Place the pot in a warm, sunny place. Add fertilizer and water as needed. (Picture C) Make sure that the growing conditions are the same for each team's pot of tomato plants.

> Predict: **How will the tomato plants of each team differ?**

5. Check your plant every day. When the seeds have sprouted, remove all but the largest sprout. When the plant is about 15 cm tall, use cloth strips to tie a stake to the plant to help it stand up.

Record Your Results

Observations			
Date	Growth rate	Flowering	Fruit production

6 Care for your tomato plant over a period of several months. Observe how quickly your plant grows, when it flowers, and when it produces fruit. Note how many tomatoes your plant produces. Record this information. Compare your data with those of other teams.

7 Compare the package description of your hybrid to your actual results. Then, compare your tomato plant to the plants of other teams.

State Your Conclusions

1. How did the growth of the various plants compare to their descriptions on the packages of seeds?

2. How did the various tomato plants and tomatoes compare?

3. Which hybrid would you choose for your garden? Why?

Let's Experiment

How do you think you could improve the growing conditions to make the best-growing tomatoes grow even better? Use what you know about scientific methods to find out.

2.3 *A New Crop of Crops*

How can a plant be part firefly?

Here's a riddle for you to solve. What has green leaves and glows like a firefly? Did you guess a firefly plant? Well, firefly plants don't exist. Or do they? In a famous experiment shown here, scientists made a kind of "hybrid" using a firefly and a plant. A new technology makes it possible to cross two very different kinds of living things. What is this new technology? Before you learn about it, you need to learn about genes.

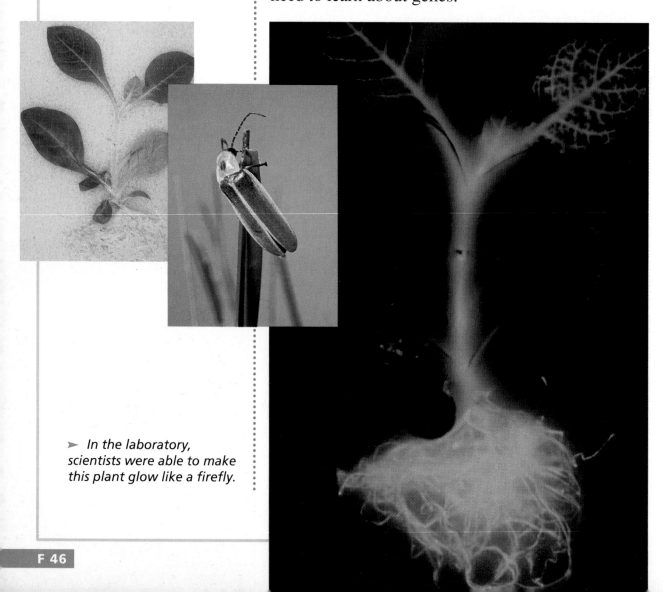

➤ In the laboratory, scientists were able to make this plant glow like a firefly.

Working With Genes

Take another look at the firefly. It's easy to see that this organism has a set of characteristics, or traits—six legs, hard outer wings, yellow stripes, saw-shaped antennae. The organ that produces a firefly's glow is another trait. Each kind of organism has its own traits.

The cells of organisms contain information that controls traits. For example, a firefly's cells contain the information about the organ that makes a firefly glow. A wheat plant's cells contain information about the color and shape of wheat flowers. Where is this information? The nucleus of each cell contains threadlike strands called chromosomes (krō′mə sōms). Each chromosome is divided into sections called genes. A **gene** is a unit of information that controls a trait.

Each kind of living thing has a set of genes that controls its traits. Genes that control a firefly's traits are different from genes that control a plant's traits. And the genes of different organisms do not mix. Why? In nature fireflies mate with fireflies, cats mate with cats, wheat plants pollinate wheat plants. You won't find a firefly plant in nature. So how did scientists make one in a laboratory?

As scientists learned about genes, they wondered whether a gene from one organism could be put into another organism. They developed a technology to do just that. **Genetic engineering** is a way to change the traits of an organism by changing its genes. Using genetic engineering, scientists removed a gene from a firefly and added it to a plant. The plant glowed like a firefly!

Scientists are using genetic engineering to produce new varieties of crop plants. These new plants can help farmers in the same ways hybrids do. For example, scientists might be able to give crop plants new genes that would protect the plants from insect pests. Then farmers wouldn't have to use as many pesticides on their crops.

Locating Your Genes

Like all humans, you have 23 pairs of chromosomes. Each chromosome is made up of thousands of sections called genes. Scientists are learning to locate specific genes on each human chromosome. For example, scientists have found the locations of genes for certain inherited diseases.

This chart shows the approximate number of genes in a human. The chart also shows the number of human genes whose exact location is known.

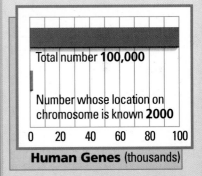

Total number **100,000**

Number whose location on chromosome is known **2000**

0   20   40   60   80   100

Human Genes (thousands)

What Did You Find Out?
1. *About how many genes do you have?*
2. *About how many of these genes have been located? How many must still be located?*
3. *What would be the advantage of locating the gene for a specific disease?*

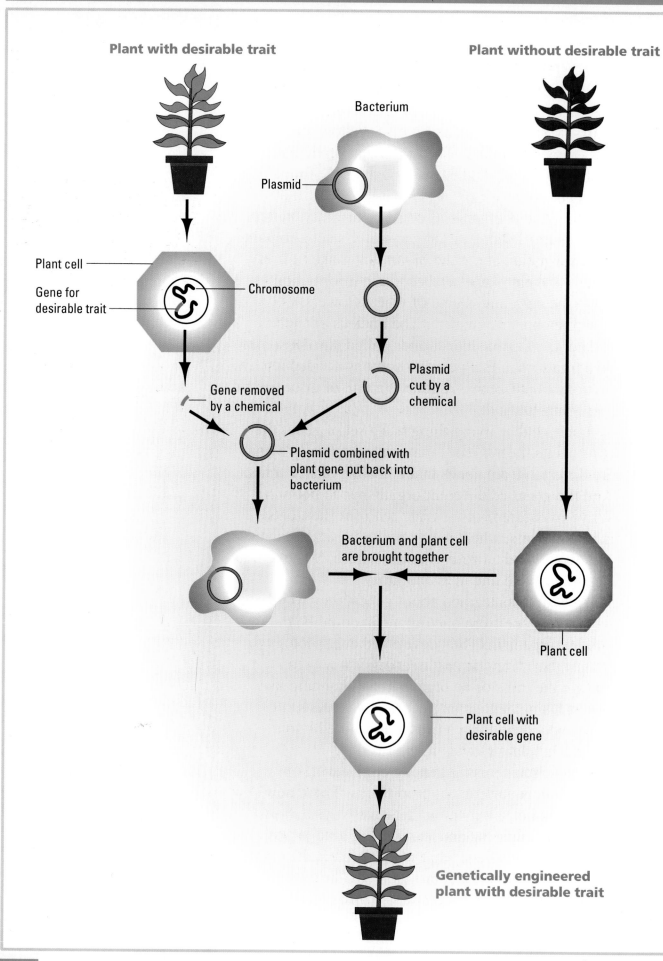

Plant with desirable trait

Plant without desirable trait

Bacterium

Plasmid

Plant cell

Gene for desirable trait

Chromosome

Plasmid cut by a chemical

Gene removed by a chemical

Plasmid combined with plant gene put back into bacterium

Bacterium and plant cell are brought together

Plant cell

Plant cell with desirable gene

Genetically engineered plant with desirable trait

Genetic Engineering

How does genetic engineering work? Scientists use several different methods. One way is to use a carrier—an organism that carries the gene from one organism to another. This method is shown in the diagram. Touch each step as you follow the procedure of transferring a gene from one kind of plant to another kind of plant.

First, scientists choose two plants. One of the plants has a desirable trait, such as resistance to a particular disease. The second plant does not have this desirable trait. Next, scientists take a cell from the plant with the desirable trait, and remove the gene that controls the trait. How do they do it? Scientists use a special chemical to cut the gene out of the chromosome.

Then the gene is put inside a carrier organism—a bacterium. Remember, bacteria are simple, one-celled organisms. Many kinds of bacteria have a ringlike structure called a plasmid. Scientists remove the plasmid from the bacterium and cut it so that it has two "sticky" ends. Then scientists "glue" the plant gene to the sticky ends of the plasmid. Finally, the plasmid is put back into the bacterium. Now the bacterium is ready to carry the new gene to the second plant.

In the last steps, scientists take a cell from the plant that doesn't have the trait. They put this cell into contact with the bacterium. The bacterium infects the plant cell with a disease. During the infection, the new gene becomes part of the chromosome in the plant cell.

But one more step remains. The plant cell—with its new gene—must grow into a new plant, with roots, stems, and leaves. Scientists place the cell in a liquid that contains nutrients and plant hormones. The plant cell grows and develops into a young plant. All the cells in the new plant have the gene that controls the new trait. So, the genetically engineered plant has resistance to disease!

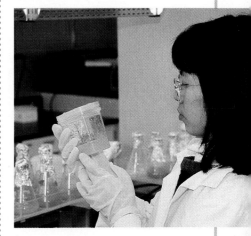

▲ *This scientist is growing new plants from plant cells.*

▲ *These farmers sell their vegetables at an open air market in India.*

Designer Foods

How might plants with new genes help farmers, like those in this picture, grow food? Well, think about what plants need to grow. Remember that plants need nutrients. Ask farmers to name the secret to growing large crops, and they'll say, "Nitrogen!" Ask farmers to name a nutrient that is often missing in soil, and they'll say, "Nitrogen!" To make up for this shortage, many farmers use chemical fertilizers that contain nitrogen.

But chemical fertilizers are getting more expensive. Also, they can be harmful to the environment. When rain falls, fertilizers wash from the soil into rivers and lakes. The nutrients in fertilizers cause water pollution. To solve these problems, scientists are trying to develop new kinds of plants that don't need to be fertilized. Instead, the plants would make their own natural fertilizers—nitrogen compounds. Remember that legumes make nitrogen compounds, with the help of *Rhizobium* bacteria. Now scientists are planning different ways to get other crop plants—corn, wheat, and rice—to make nitrogen compounds, too.

One kind of experiment is shown in the diagram. You might call it the "fix it yourself" experiment. Why? It's working with the group of genes that control *Rhizobium's* ability to "fix" nitrogen, or change nitrogen gas into nitrogen compounds. Using the methods you just learned about, scientists plan to remove the genes from *Rhizobium* bacteria.

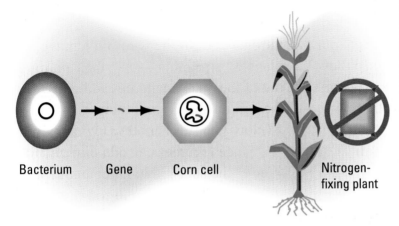

◄ *A nitrogen-fixing corn plant might be produced by genetic engineering. As you can see, this plant would not need chemical fertilizer.*

Bacterium   Gene   Corn cell   Nitrogen-fixing plant

Next, the scientists would try to put the genes into cells of corn, wheat, or rice plants. The scientists hope that the genetically engineered plants would be able to do what *Rhizobium* does—make nitrogen compounds. If these genetic engineering experiments work, just think about what it would mean. All the corn fields and wheat fields in the world might not need to be fertilized for nitrogen!

Checkpoint

1. What does genetic engineering allow scientists to do?
2. How do scientists use bacteria in genetic engineering experiments?
3. How are scientists using genetic engineering to develop new crop plants?
4. **Take Action!** Make a diagram that shows how a gene from a soybean plant might be put inside a corn plant to produce a corn plant with nodules.

Forming a Hypothesis

Scientists often make observations about nature that they can't explain. Once they notice a problem, or something they can't explain, scientists make a hypothesis—a likely explanation for a problem. Then scientists test their hypotheses with experiments.

Thinking It Through

About 100 years ago, scientists like Dr. George Washington Carver began to experiment with ways to help farmers improve their soil. Here are steps he took and you might follow to make and test a hypothesis.

1. You observe two fields, one planted with cotton and one planted with peanuts. The fields began with identical soil. The first year, both fields yield good crops. But each year thereafter, the soil in the cotton field gets poorer in quality, and the cotton crop gets worse. You see no difference in the peanut crop.

2. You form a hypothesis—cotton wears out the soil and peanuts enrich it.

3. You test your hypothesis in the laboratory by trying to find how peanut and cotton plants differ. You discover that cotton takes an important nutrient,

nitrogen, out of the soil. But legumes— plants like peanuts —take their nitrogen out of the air. So legumes add nitrogen to the soil instead of removing it.

4. Now you form another hypothesis: Since legumes can add nitrogen to the soil, planting legumes should add nitrogen to soil that does not have enough nitrogen.

5. You test this hypothesis in the field. In your test you find a field in which cotton is no longer growing well. You test the soil and find that it is very low in nitrogen. Then you plant a legume such as peanuts instead of cotton. After a few growing seasons, you test the soil again. It is now rich in nitrogen. You conclude that your hypothesis is valid because your data supports the hypothesis.

Your Turn

Use what you learned in this chapter to form a hypothesis about some aspect of farming. State your hypothesis. List the facts on which your idea is based. Tell how you would test the hypothesis.

Chapter Review

Thinking Back

1. Identify six things all plants need to grow and develop.
2. What is **hydroponics**?
3. Explain how bacteria in the soil can help plants grow.
4. Why do farmers add **fertilizer** to the soil in which crops have grown?
5. Identify the male and female parts of a flower.
6. Describe the role insects play in **pollination**.
7. What is a hybrid?
8. Explain how growing **hybrids** can help protect the environment.
9. Describe the relationship between **genes**, chromosomes, and traits.
10. What is the role of bacteria in **genetic engineering**?

Connecting Ideas

1. Copy the concept map. Use the terms at the right to complete the map about how pollination occurs.

pistil   pollination
stamen   ovule

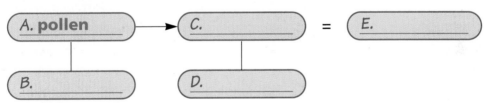

2. Write a sentence or two about the ideas shown in the concept map.

Gathering Evidence

1. In the Activity on page 36, what information did you use to predict whether the two scallions would grow at the same rate?
2. In the Activity on page 44, how did you know that the tomatoes produced from the various plants would have different traits?

Doing Science!

1. *Invent and name* a new hybrid vegetable that you would produce by crossing two varieties of plants. Make a poster showing the traits of the hybrid and its parents.
2. *Design a demonstration* to show how the male and female parts of flowers can vary from one kind of plant to another.

3

Gardening Plants

> I wonder if any worms are in here!

How can you grow an indoor mini-garden?

Think about what you learned about growing plants. Use this information to plan an indoor mini-garden. Choose the seeds you want to plant and the growing conditions for them. Observe your garden for about three weeks.

For Discussion

1. *How well did your garden grow?*
2. *What choices did you make in planning and caring for your garden?*

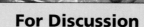

3.1 Growing A Garden

▶ *How would you grow a vegetable garden?*

You've learned a lot about plants and what they need to grow. When you did the Discover Activity, you used what you know to grow an indoor garden.

Now think about how you would plant a garden outdoors. Where would you begin? A good place to start would be to collect the items you see here. You'll also need a garden book. Why? It will tell you what your plants need to grow. For example, each kind of plant needs a certain kind of soil, a certain amount of sunlight, and a certain kind of fertilizer. If you don't know what your plants need, you won't be harvesting many vegetables!

Pretend you are going to plant and care for a garden. Then play the garden game on the following pages. Pick the crop that you'd most like to grow. As you read, use the boxes to make decisions about how to grow your crop. Each box has four choices. Pick the choice you think is best for *your* crop. When you're finished, see whether your choices helped your crop grow.

▼ *Garden gloves and a trowel make planting seeds easier. A trowel is a tool with a pointed scoop for digging holes and loosening soil.*

Planting a Crop

The box on this page gives planting instructions for four kinds of crops. Read about each crop. Then decide which crop you'd like to grow.

Tomatoes were brought to Europe from South America in the 1500s, where they were grown in gardens for their pretty fruits. But before the 1800s, many people didn't eat tomatoes. Back then, people thought tomatoes were poisonous.

Corn is actually the grain crop maize, which was first grown in North America over 6000 years ago. After European settlers arrived, they took maize to Europe, where it is an important grain crop too.

Carrots are roots of a plant that was first grown in Europe around the Mediterranean Sea. Carrots were among the first plants brought to North America by explorers.

Strawberries that grow in gardens are probably a hybrid of many kinds of strawberry plants that once grew wild in North and South America.

▲ *Seeds of fruits and vegetables are many sizes, shapes, and colors. Which of these seeds can you identify?*

Pick a Crop

Tomatoes Start seeds in pots 6 weeks before you'll plant. Set seedlings 46 centimeters apart and slightly deeper than they were growing in the pots.

Corn Plant corn seeds in holes 3 centimeters deep and 5 centimeters apart. Put 4 to 6 seeds in each hole. Thin plants for final spacing of 30 centimeters.

Carrots Plant seeds about 0.6 centimeters deep and in rows that have the soil loosened to the depth of about 20 centimeters.

Strawberries Plant seedlings in holes about 20 centimeters deep. Spread out the roots. Space the plants at least 60 centimeters apart.

Where you plant your crop is an important decision. To choose the best plot for your crop, think about three things. How much sunlight does my crop need? How much space does my crop need? What kind of soil does my crop need?

You should also keep in mind that some plants are hardy—they can grow in places where they might not get all the things they need. Other plants are delicate and won't grow well in places where they don't get enough sunlight or space to grow in.

Before you plant, you should do one more thing—test your soil. A soil test tells how acid or alkaline (al′kə līn) your soil is. Some plants grow best in acid soil while others grow best in alkaline soil. Numbers called pH numbers measure how acid or alkaline the soil is. A pH number below 7 is acid. A pH number above 7 is alkaline. Most plants grow best in soil that is slightly acid—pH 6.5. And few plants can grow at all in soil that is more acid than pH 4 or more alkaline than pH 8.

▲ The dark color of this garden soil is a sign that it is rich in humus.

Pick a Plot

This spot is a sunny, open field, about 12 meters by 8 meters. It's the best plot on your land.

This spot is a patch of sandy soil that is in the shade for part of the day. The sunniest section is about 3 meters by 4 meters.

This plot is a small, gently sloping section, about 3 meters by 1 meter. It gets full sun for most of the day.

This corner section of land gets full sun and has rich soil. Too bad it's only 2 meters by 2 meters.

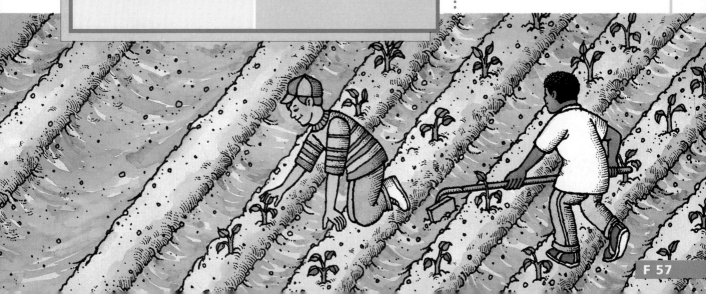

Caring For a Crop

You've planted your crop. Now you're ready to take care of it! Part of this job is making sure your soil has enough nutrients for growing plants. How? You need to add fertilizer to the soil. Remember that fertilizers contain nutrients that plants need.

Deciding what fertilizer to use isn't easy. Fertilizers have different ingredients and some fertilizers cost more than others do. You can buy chemical fertilizers that are special mixtures for certain types of plants. The packages have labels that list three numbers. The numbers tell the percentages of nitrogen, phosphorus, and potassium they contain. A 5-10-5 label would have 5% nitrogen, 10% phosphorus, and 5% potassium.

You must also decide when to fertilize. Some plants grow better if you add fertilizer before you plant. Other plants need to be fertilized while they are growing. When you add fertilizer, remember this rule: the more nitrogen, the less you should use.

▲ *Lettuce needs nitrogen-rich soil to produce dark green leaves.*

Pick a Fertilizer

This fertilizer is a 5-10-10 mixture of nutrients. Use it on a crop that needs twice as much phosphorus as nitrogen.

This fertilizer is a 10-20-20 mixture. Use it *before* you plant this delicate crop. Once planted, this crop should not be fertilized.

This 5-10-5 fertilizer is used on a crop that needs lots of nitrogen. Fertilize once a month. Follow the directions to make sure you add enough fertilizer.

This fertilizer is a 10-10-10 mixture. Use it on a crop that needs high amounts of soil nutrients. Fertilize after the crop sprouts and again in a few weeks.

Taking care of your crop also involves protecting it from insect pests. But before you decide how to get rid of your pests, you better make sure they really are "pests"! The praying mantis on this page may not look like something you'd want hanging around your garden. But as you learned, a praying mantis eats many kinds of insect pests. And ladybugs have an enormous appetite for harmful aphids. So keep in mind that you can use other insects to control your garden pests.

You can also use other plants! Some plants make chemicals with odors or tastes that keep insect pests away. Growing these plants next to your crop can help control pests.

Chances are you won't have to use chemical pesticides. A few insects can't eat up all the plants! But pesticides may be needed for large numbers of pests. Then, two rules should be remembered. Follow the label instructions carefully. And it's better to use too little than too much.

▲ *A praying mantis is a predator—a hunter that captures and eats its victim.*

Pick a Pest Control Method

Pull out any plants that look sickly to prevent diseases from spreading. Cover the soil with ground-up corn cobs to stop weeds from growing.

Plant the herbs rosemary and sage nearby to help keep pests away. You don't need to use chemical pesticides on this hardy crop.

This crop attracts many pests, so you might need to use a pesticide. Plant onions or potatoes with this crop to help control pests.

Plant asparagus around this crop to keep pests away. Get some ladybugs, which eat harmful aphids. Pick off the hornworm caterpillars.

Harvesting a Crop

If all your choices had the same color box, then your garden grew quite well! Now read about what each crop needs to grow. Once you know more about these crops, play the game again. See if you make better choices this time.

Corn is the crop that needs the most space. It also needs lots of sunlight and nutrient-rich soil. Corn plants must be close together so that wind can pollinate the corn flowers. If wind can't blow pollen from one plant to another, you'll get no ears!

Like corn, tomatoes need a sunny place to grow. But they don't need as much space. Tomatoes grow best in soil that has high amounts of nitrogen and phosphorus.

Carrots are hardy—they grow without special care. Carrots can grow in partial sun and they aren't harmed by many pests. Sandy soil and low amounts of fertilizer are best for carrots. Too much nitrogen can cause carrots to become forked.

Strawberry plants need lots of sunlight, but not a lot of space. In fact, you can even grow strawberry plants in barrels or large flower boxes. Strawberry plants aren't hardy—they often get diseases. Fertilizers should be used *before* planting to prevent damage to the fruit.

➤ *Many gardeners make compost in a wire bin, or composter, like the one shown here.*

▲ *What garden wastes do you see in this compost?*

Once fall comes, you may think your job is done. But fall is the time to get your garden ready for next year. A good way to do this is by making **compost**—a kind of natural fertilizer. As you can see, compost is made of the same things humus is made of—dead plant materials. So, like humus, compost is rich in nutrients that plants need.

How do you make compost? At the end of the growing season, pile the dead plants in a big heap. You can also add grass clippings, weeds, leaves, and kitchen scraps, such as apple peelings. Shovel a layer of soil onto the compost heap. Keep adding layers of plant materials and soil whenever you have any garden wastes. As the plant materials decay, compost forms.

When spring arrives, the nutrient-rich compost will be ready to shovel into your garden soil. By adding compost to the soil, you are helping to complete the nutrient cycle you learned about!

Checkpoint

1. How does a soil test help gardeners?
2. Why do gardeners add fertilizer to soil?
3. How does compost improve garden soil?
4. Take Action! Look in a garden book or on seed packages for the planting and care instructions for four vegetables. Use the information to design a new garden game.

Struggling Seeds

Will pH affect a seed's growth? Let's investigate.

What to Do
A. Label three cups 1, 2, and 3.
B. Add ten radish seeds to each cup. Then add water to cup 1; vinegar to cup 2; and a seltzer tablet dissolved in water to cup 3.
C. Let all the seeds soak overnight.
D. Remove the seeds from each cup and wrap them in a moist paper towel. Slide each towel into a labeled plastic bag. Seal the bag.
E. Look at the seeds every day for four days. Check for seed growth. The seed is growing when you can see small roots or a shoot. Record the number of seeds that show growth each day.

Record Your Results

Day	Number Growing		
	Cup 1	Cup 2	Cup 3
1			
2			
3			
4			

What Did You Find Out?
1. *Do radish seeds grow in vinegar, which is acid? Do they grow in the solution of the tablet dissolved in water, which is alkaline?*
2. *Why were some of the seeds soaked in water?*

Passing the Test

Whether you are growing tomatoes or petunias, you need to know if your soil is right for your plants. Try this activity to test your soil's acidity.

Picture A

Picture B

Picture C

Gather These Materials

soil sample   spoon
clean container   blue litmus paper
distilled water   stopwatch

Follow This Procedure

1 Make a chart like the one on the next page. Record your observations in the chart.

2 Collect a soil sample from your yard or school yard. Put the sample in a clean container.

3 Use the spoon to mix the soil sample with enough distilled water for the soil to become muddy, about as thick as applesauce. (Picture A) You will be using litmus paper to test the soil sample. This paper changes color when it is dipped in acid.

4 Insert 3 pieces of blue litmus paper halfway into the muddy soil. The top half of each paper should not get wet. Wait 10 seconds. Then, remove one piece of the litmus paper. Rinse it off with distilled water. (Picture B)

5 Note the color of the litmus paper you removed. If the litmus paper is pink or red, your soil is acid. If the paper is still blue, wait another 5 minutes, and then remove the second piece of litmus paper.

6 If the second piece of litmus paper is pink, this shows that your soil is moderately acid. Record your results. If this second piece is blue, wait another 10 minutes. Then remove the last piece of litmus paper.

7 If the last piece is pink, your soil is slightly acid. If it is still blue, your soil is not acid at all. (Picture C) Record your results.

Record Your Results

	Color of litmus paper
First piece of litmus paper	
Second piece of litmus paper	
Third piece of litmus paper	
Result: Soil sample is _____	

State Your Conclusions

1. What were the results of your soil test?

2. How do you think gardeners could use this type of information when they get ready to grow their plants?

Let's Experiment

What do you think would happen to the acidity of the soil if you add lime to it? Use what you know about scientific methods to find out.

3.2 *The World's Garden*

▶ **What's it like to be a farmer?**

Gardening is like farming without a lot of worries. Gardeners don't have to make money on their crop. They don't have to pay taxes or borrow money from the bank. Gardening is fun; farming is business. But gardeners and farmers make the same kinds of decisions. So learning how to take care of a garden can help you understand what it's like to take care of a farm.

Farming Today

Suddenly you're in a farmer's boots and blue jeans. You're riding a tractor in an enormous field. Yikes! Your small garden is now a huge farm! What are you going to do now? How much fertilizer will your soil need? What pesticides should you use?

You don't have time or money to test every part of your land for soil pH. So, you'll do what farmers have done for thousands of years. You'll estimate, or use what you know to make a good guess.

▼ *What problems does this new fertilizer truck help farmers solve?*

You're also going to estimate how much fertilizer your soil needs. And you'll follow this rule—more is better than less. By adding more fertilizer than you think you need, you make sure that even your worst soil has enough nutrients.

Then you remember reading about a new kind of truck that can help you take the guesswork out of soil testing and fertilizing. You make a phone call to the company. Someone from the company brings a truck to your farm and takes you for a ride.

Wow! This truck is amazing. It has a computer on board. Data about your soil is put into the computer. The data come from soil tests, pictures of your land taken by satellites, and soil maps made by the government. The computer hums as it analyzes the data. Then it chooses the exact amounts of nutrients that are best for your soil. The truck mixes the nutrients together to make a special fertilizer—just for *your* land! A few seconds later, the fertilizer comes pouring out.

In no time at all, this super new machine fertilizes all your fields and your ride is over. You can't believe what it can do! It makes decisions for you. It can help you save money on fertilizer. You'd never use too much fertilizer again. And that would be good news for the environment. You remember how fertilizers polluted a nearby stream. Then you close your eyes and imagine your fields at harvest time. Because your soil has just the right kinds of nutrients, your crops should be larger than ever! Finally, you shake your head and wonder, "Farming sure is changing. What will it be like in the future?"

▲ Computerized soil maps, like this one, are analyzed by a computer in the cab of the truck. The different colors represent different kinds of soil.

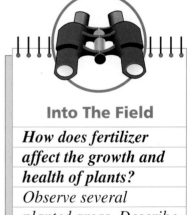

Into The Field

How does fertilizer affect the growth and health of plants?

Observe several planted areas. Describe the appearance of the plants. Find out whether each planted area is fertilized.

Bypassing the Farm

Someday food may be produced without growing crops.

Imagine growing food without planting crops! A new method may be used to do that.

Tissue culture is a method of growing living tissues outside an organism. To make a tissue culture, scientists remove tissue from an organism and place the tissue in a growing medium. A medium is a liquid that contains growth hormones, water, and nutrients.

Scientists are using tissue cultures to grow cells of crop plants. For example, one scientist made a tissue culture of the juice sacs inside an orange. The juice sacs multiplied on their own and produced orange juice—without any orange trees! In the future, tissue-culture factories, like the ones shown here, may produce foods.

1 **Planting trees**
Fast-growing trees supply the sugars for growing mediums.

5 **Distributing food**
The foods are taken to market. Tissue-culture factories can be located anywhere and can operate all year.

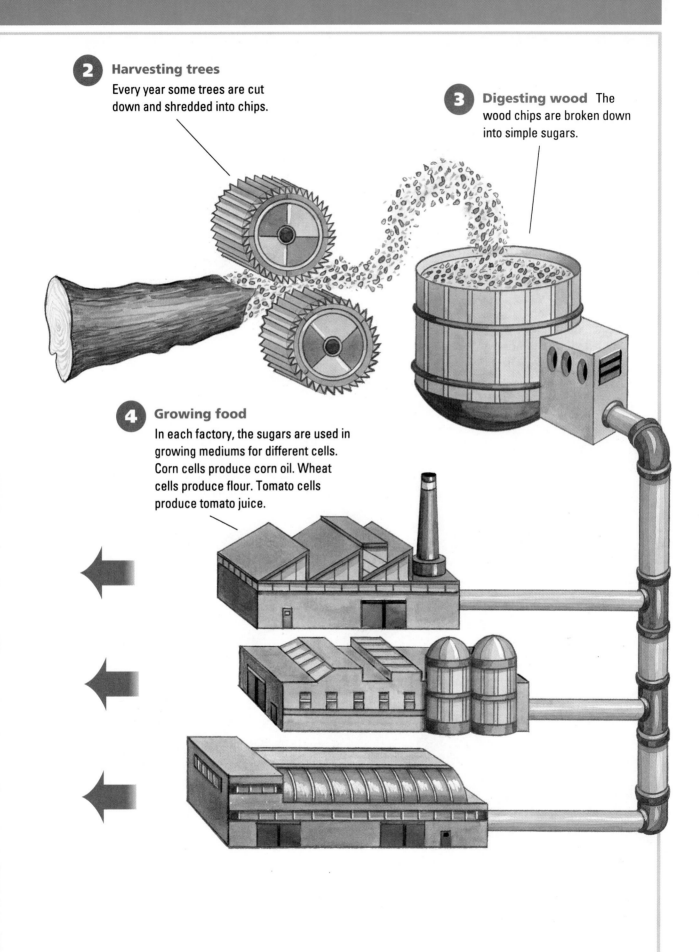

2 **Harvesting trees**
Every year some trees are cut down and shredded into chips.

3 **Digesting wood** The wood chips are broken down into simple sugars.

4 **Growing food**
In each factory, the sugars are used in growing mediums for different cells. Corn cells produce corn oil. Wheat cells produce flour. Tomato cells produce tomato juice.

Farming in Space

The year is 2060. You just came from your job in the crop chamber. You and 10,000 other people live and work in a giant wheel spinning in space. As you begin a letter to your grandparents back on Earth, you remember visiting their farm when you were a kid. Things sure were different then!

"Dear Granddad and Grandmother," you write, "You should see how fast plants grow in space! Out here, crops grow all year long. And they get 24 hours of sunlight every day. No wonder we space farmers produce lots of food in our space station! Besides, our crops aren't harmed by any insects. Everything that comes on board our space station is checked to make sure no pests are brought inside. So, we can farm without pesticides.

"And the work is fun! Most of us space farmers are also doing experiments in genetic engineering. I'm developing a new kind of 'super corn.' It grows in hot and cold temperatures. Pretty soon we'll ship some super corn back to Earth. You'll be able to grow corn in winter and in summer."

You close your letter, but add a P.S. "Sometimes I look out at our beautiful planet Earth, and it reminds me of why I'm here. We space farmers don't want to do your job. We can't produce all the food for people on Earth. We just want to find new and better ways for Earth farmers to farm. We're trying to help you grow more food in ways that will protect Earth's soil and water!"

◄ A space station might have different levels of fields, where corn, soybeans, and other crops would grow.

Checkpoint

1. What problems happen when farmers guess how much fertilizer to use?
2. How might tissue culture be used to grow foods in the future?
3. List some benefits of space farming.
4. **Take Action!** Write an advertisement describing a new kind of farm machine.

Activity

Lights On

How well will a plant grow if it is kept in the light for 24 hours a day? Try this activity and see.

Picture A

Picture B

Picture C

Gather These Materials

2 young potted plants, same type and size
masking tape
marker
metric ruler

water
grow-light or fluorescent lamp
2 large identical cardboard boxes

Follow This Procedure

1 Make a chart like the one on the next page. Record your observations in the chart.

2 Use masking tape to label one of your plants A and the other plant B. Measure the height of your 2 plants.

3 Starting in the morning, place both plants in a box. Set up the lamp so that it shines on the plants. (Picture A)

4 Allow the light to shine on the plants for 8 hours.

5 After 8 hours, remove plant A from the box, and put it into an identical box nearby. Cover the box. No light should be shining on plant A when it is in the second box. (Picture B)

6 Allow the light to shine on plant B overnight, giving it a full 24 hours of light.

7 After 24 hours, measure the height of both plants and record the measurements in the chart.

8 Put plant A back into the lighted box. Again, allow the light to shine on plant A for 8 hours and plant B for 24 hours.

> *Predict:* **Will the number of hours of light affect the growth rate of the plants?**

9 Repeat the procedure every day for 1 to 2 weeks. Water your plants, keeping the soil of each plant equally moist. Measure the height of each plant at the end of each day. (Picture C) Record this information in your chart.

Record Your Results

	Height - Plant A	Height - Plant B
Start		
Day 1		
Day 2		
Day 3		
Day 4		
Day 5		
Day 6		
Day 7		

State Your Conclusions

1. Describe any differences you saw in the growth of the 2 plants.
2. Where could you set up a farm where the plants could get light 24 hours a day?
3. If you had a farm here on Earth, what would be the advantages of giving plants 24 hours of light each day? What would be the disadvantages?

Let's Experiment

Now that you have seen how the amount of light can affect plant growth, do you think the type of light could make a difference? Use what you know about scientific methods to find out.

Organizing Information

You don't always find the information you need by reading sentences and paragraphs. Information also appears in other forms, such as tables, charts, graphs, and diagrams. In a table, a list of subjects is organized into two or more columns.

Thinking it Through

Let's say you're planning a garden. You've decided that you don't want to use pesticides on your plants. You look for facts on how to grow plants without pesticides, and you find this table.

Keeping Away Pests

Plant...	near...	to keep away...
herbs (sage, thyme)	lettuce, cabbage	slugs, cabbage butterflies
garlic	strawberry plants, fruit trees	fungus
marigolds	tomato plants, cabbage	most harmful insects
onions	carrots	carrot flies

1. Notice that the vertical columns on the table are three lists. The list on the left is of plants that keep away pests. The list on the right names pests that harm plants. The list in the center column is of plants that are threatened by the pests.

2. Notice that you can make a sentence by reading one line from left to right across the columns. For example, "Plant herbs near lettuce and cabbage to keep away slugs and cabbage butterflies." Say a sentence out loud as you read each line across.

Your Turn

Use the table to plan a naturally pest-free garden. Organize the information about your plan by drawing a map or diagram.

Chapter Review

Thinking Back

1. What planting information do you need to know when you plant seeds?
2. What does a soil test tell you?
3. When testing the soil of a plot of land, you find it has a pH number of 3. Is this land suitable for farming? Explain.
4. Identify three elements found in chemical fertilizers.

5. Explain how certain plants can be used to control pests.
6. How is **compost** like humus?
7. How can a computer be used to help farmers fertilize their soil?
8. What is **tissue culture**?
9. Would a space farm need pesticides? Explain why or why not.

Connecting Ideas

1. Copy the concept map. Use the terms at the right to complete the map about soil testing.

acid soil   **alkaline soil**   **pH number**

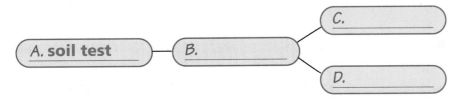

A. soil test — B. _____ — C. _____ / D. _____

2. Write a sentence or two that summarizes the ideas shown in the concept map.

Gathering Evidence

1. In the Activity on page 62, why was it important that you only touched the top, dry part of the paper?
2. In the Activity on page 70, what information did you use to predict whether the number of hours of light would affect the plants' growth rate?

Doing Science!

1. *Design an activity* to show that most plants grow best in soil with a pH of about 6.5.
2. *Develop a skit* to show what life in a space farm might be like.

The Green Teams

City gardens and parks provide open space where people can relax and feel less crowded. The plants and trees help to freshen the city's air. Green leaves and colorful flowers brighten the dull surroundings.

In cities across the United States, people are teaming up to create more green spaces. Students just like you are important members of the teams. Students help improve their communities' environments in many ways. They clear bricks and debris from abandoned lots. They haul dirt and plant flowers. They build playgrounds. They pick up litter and water the grass.

Families from the neighborhood can grow their own flowers and vegetables.

There's a community park in Chicago that's so lovely people call it *El Paraíso,* which means "the paradise" in Spanish. El Paraíso was once an empty lot filled with garbage and rubble. The community stepped in. They didn't want the land to go to waste. So they got permission from the city to turn the site into a park that the whole neighborhood could enjoy. Students and other people in the community worked together. Local businesses donated plants and building materials. Volunteers cleared and fenced the land and planned the layout of the park. They set aside one part for people to sit in and enjoy the surroundings. Another part of the park was set aside as a community garden, where families from the neighborhood can grow their own flowers and vegetables.

In New York City, about 600 older students take part in the Community Volunteer Corps (CVC). These students work on many projects, including ones that help the environment. One CVC project called Lots for Tots has changed several vacant lots into safe playgrounds for small children. CVC volunteers also work in Operation Greenthumb, creating and taking care of public parks. While these students are creating green spaces, they are also training for future jobs.

One CVC project was to reopen a children's garden. First the workers cleared out mounds of rocks, weeds, and trash. Then they built four plant beds and began a garden. In the spring of 1991, the garden produced its first harvest in

30 years! Now students from a local school help keep the garden growing.

Is there a place in your community that could use a spot of green? Maybe a "green team" in your area could use your help. Or perhaps you could start a green team of your own!

On Your Own

To learn what other kids are doing to beautify their communities, write to Renew America. This organization keeps a record of environmental projects going on around the country.

Sweet Potatoes in Space

Dr. Audrey Trotman

Occupation: Agricultural microbiologist
Words to remember: "Science is fun. It's something anyone can do."

Have you ever tried a sweet potato cookie? Have you ever eaten bread made from sweet potato flour? Researchers at Tuskegee University in Alabama are trying to come up with a variety of uses for sweet potatoes and their leaves. Other researchers are trying to find ways to recycle the parts of the plant that cannot be eaten. Still others are studying the best ways to grow sweet potatoes in a hydroponic medium, or nutrient solution. Dr. Audrey Trotman is one of these researchers. She is an agricultural microbiologist—a scientist who studies microorganisms that affect crops.

Why is there so much interest in sweet potatoes?

"Sweet potatoes are just one of the food crops that NASA would like to raise in space. Others include foods such as rice, wheat, white potatoes, soybeans, peanuts, and lettuce. At Tuskegee we're finding out as much as possible about sweet potatoes."

Why do they need to grow plants?

"Some flights, such as the year-long planned flight to Mars, will be too long to carry prepared foods. The answer is to grow the food where it's needed. But in space there will be limits."

What kinds of limits?

"First of all, soil will not be used. We're working with a hydroponic medium that would supply all the nutrients the sweet potato plant needs. One of the main needs of any plant is a source of nitrogen. Some types of bacteria, called nitrogen-fixing bacteria, form compounds that contain nitrogen. I'm working to find how many of these bacteria to add to the hydroponic medium. We're also studying the best way to grow the bacteria in space."

Biosphere II: Farming Under Glass

Biosphere II is a large glass building that is sealed off from the rest of the world. Inside are several miniature environments that resemble places on the earth. Air, water, and wastes are recycled.

1 The rainforest produces oxygen.

2 The ocean supplies water.

3 The wetlands include a beach, a saltwater marsh, and a freshwater marsh.

4 The desert is separated from other areas by dense, thorny shrubs. The savanna is a grassland area.

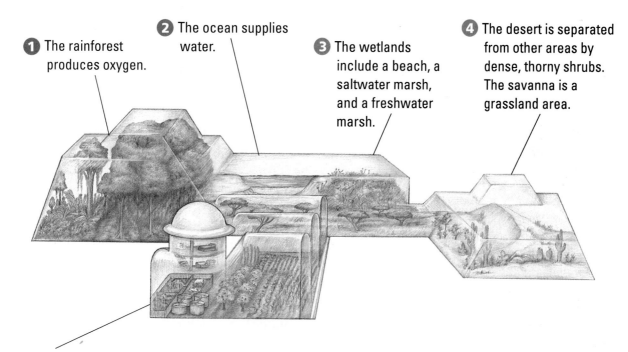

5 The agricultural section contains living quarters for eight people as well as a farm. Biosphere II residents raise fish in large tanks. Nitrogen-rich water from the fish tanks is used to fertilize crops, which are grown by hydroponics. Ladybugs and wasps are used instead of chemicals to control crop pests.

Find Out On Your Own

Check current science magazines for reports on the progress of the Biosphere II experiment. Find magazine articles in the library by using the *Readers' Guide to Periodical Literature*.

Module Review

Making Connections

Patterns of Change

1. Explain the effect that harvesting crops has on the cycling of nutrients.
2. Describe how hormones cause the changes that occur when an apple seed develops into a tree.
3. Methods of dealing with crop pests have changed over time. List several reasons why people's ideas changed.

Modeling

4. How does the use of chemical fertilizer model the effect humus has on soil?
5. How does growing crops in a greenhouse model space farming?
6. How did the choices you made in the garden game model those you would make when you grow houseplants?

Using What I Learned

Observing

1. Identify the parts of the plant shown in the diagram.
2. How do the wheat flowers shown below differ from corn flowers?

Categorizing

3. Categorize plant parts shown in the diagram as either "male" or "female."

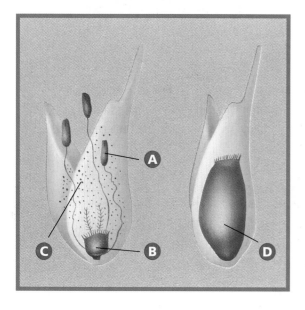

Comparing

4. Compare a pH reading of 4 with a reading of 8.
5. How do the traits of a hybrid compare with those of the parent plants?
6. Compare the different methods of pest control used since the early days of farming.

Relating

7. Suppose a disease greatly reduced the population of *Rhizobium* bacteria. What effect might this have on plant populations?

Communicating

8. Draw a diagram to show how pollination occurs between two different plants.

Applying

9. How would the development of genetically engineered plants that could make nitrogen compounds benefit the environment?

Applying What I Learned

Performance Task

Use seedlings of two different kinds of plants, a fluorescent lamp, water, soil with a pH of 5, and a 10-20-20 fertilizer to show that each kind of plant has its own special needs.

Drawing

Design a poster that illustrates the steps that might produce a genetically engineered corn plant that can change nitrogen gas into nitrogen compounds.

Exhibitions

Make a poster or bulletin board that identifies organisms produced by either hybridizing or genetic engineering. Next to each organism, identify the desirable traits it shows.

What If

What if your community is considering passing a law that prohibits the use of pesticides in the community? What things would you consider in deciding your opinion on the issue? List reasons both for and against the new law. Then decide how you would vote.

Using Metric

About 1 centimeter

About 1 millimeter

About 1 meter

Water boils (100°C)

Normal body temperature (37°C)

Water freezes (0°C)

1 cm
1 cm
1 square centimeter

1 cm
1 cm
1 cm
1 cubic centimeter

About 1 kilogram

Degrees Celsius

11 football fields end to end is about 1 kilometer

1 liter of milk

Using Scientific Methods

Scientists ask many questions. The answers cannot always be found in books. In fact, no one may know the answers. Then scientists use scientific methods to find answers. Scientific methods include steps like those described on the next page. Sometimes the order of the steps changes. The experiments in this section give you a chance to use scientific methods to explore the world around you.

Identify Problem The problem is usually in the form of a question such as, "How does wind speed affect erosion?"

Make Observations Recorded observations become data and might include the size, color, or shape of something.

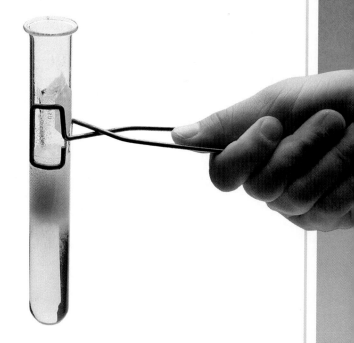

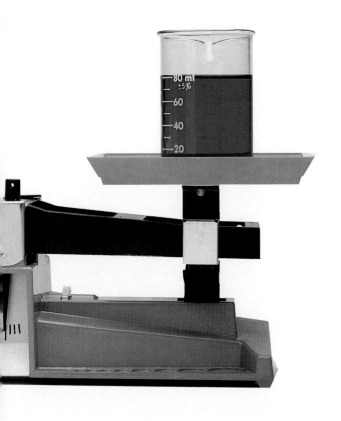

State Hypothesis A hypothesis is a likely explanation of the problem. It may turn out to be incorrect; it must be tested.

Test Hypothesis If possible, experiments are done to test the hypothesis. Experiments should be repeated to double check the results.

Collect Data The information you gather from the experiment is your data.

Study Data The data collected during an experiment is better understood if it is organized into charts and graphs. Then you can easily see what it all means.

Make Conclusions The conclusion relates to the hypothesis. You might conclude your hypothesis is correct, or that it is incorrect.

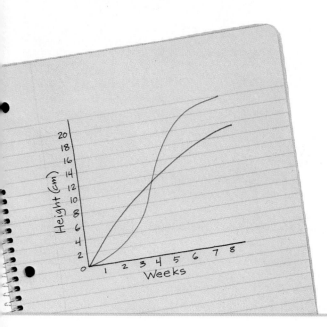

Safety in Science

Scientists know they must work safely when doing experiments. You need to be careful when doing experiments too. Here are some safety tips to remember.

Safety Tips

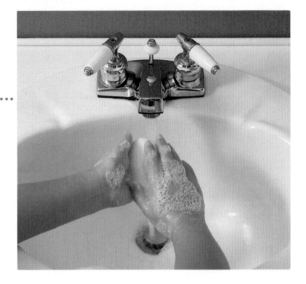

- Read each experiment carefully.

- Wear cover goggles when needed.

- Clean up spills right away.

- Never taste or smell substances unless directed to do so by your teacher.

- Handle sharp items carefully.

- Tape sharp edges of materials.

- Handle thermometers carefully.

- Put materials away when you finish an experiment.

- Wash your hands after each experiment.

Making Conclusions

Experimenting with Dyes for Cell Parts

Maria observed an onion cell through a microscope during her science class. She learned that cells had a nucleus and a cell wall. Maria wondered if cell parts would show up more clearly when stained with dye.

With her teacher's permission, Maria set up an experiment using black ink and green food coloring as dyes. She put a thin piece of onion skin on each of three microscope slides. She added a drop of black ink to one slide, a drop of food coloring to another, and a drop of water to the third. Then she put a coverslip on each slide.

Maria observed the slides under a microscope. She saw the nuclei of the cells on the slide with black ink very clearly. Nuclei did not show up as well on the slide with green food coloring. Nuclei of cells from the slide with water looked the same color as the rest of the cell. Maria studied her results to decide what they meant. She concluded that cell parts show up more clearly when stained with black ink.

Thinking About the Experiment

Maria used her observations to make a conclusion. Every experiment must be set up so that a conclusion can be drawn after the observations are made or data are collected. The conclusion must be supported by the data.

1. What was Maria's conclusion?

2. Which observations led Maria to her conclusion?

Anything in the experiment that could be changed is a variable. A control is the part of the experiment that does not have the variable being tested. The slide with only water was a control.

3. In Maria's experiment, what was the variable that changed from one setup to the other?

4. How did the control help Maria reach her conclusion?

Try It!

Try Maria's experiment and see if you come to the same conclusion.

Problem

What substance makes cell parts more visible under a microscope?

Hypothesis

Dye will make cell parts show up more clearly.

Materials

black ink
green food
    coloring
water
medicine
    dropper

microscope
3 microscope slides
    with coverslips
3 thin pieces of onion
    skin
tweezers

Procedure

1. Use the tweezers to pull 3 thin pieces of onion skin from a fresh onion bulb.

2. Place a piece of onion skin on each of the microscope slides.

3. With the medicine dropper, place a drop of water on one slide, a drop of green food coloring on another, and a drop of black ink on the third.

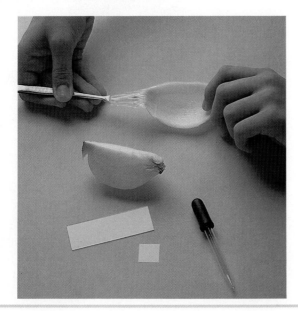

4. Cover each slide with a coverslip.

5. Examine the 3 slides under a microscope.

6. Record your observations on a table like the one below.

Data and Observations

Substance added	Visible cell parts

Conclusion

Write your conclusion based on your data and observations.

Practice

Making Conclusions

Scientists use a purple dye called Gram stain to classify bacteria into two major groups. Suppose you added Gram stain to two kinds of bacteria. One kind turned purple. The other kind did not turn purple.

1. What conclusion can you draw about how cells of different bacteria absorb this stain?

2. What conclusion can you draw about how the bacteria can be classified?

Collecting Data

Experimenting with Balloon Rockets

Jim and his father were looking at a rocket engine in a space museum. Jim noticed the opening where gases leave the engine. He wondered if the size of the opening had anything to do with the engine's power.

Jim remembered a time when he was washing his family's car. There was a spray nozzle on the end of the hose. As he changed the size of the opening of the nozzle, Jim had to hold the hose tightly to keep it from twisting in his hand because the force of the water became stronger. If he turned the nozzle so that its opening changed size again, the water did not have as much force.

Jim thought that a rocket engine with a bigger opening might push the rocket farther than an engine with a small opening. He decided to do an experiment to test his hypothesis.

Thinking About the Experiment

Jim wanted to collect data that would help him test his hypothesis. In the procedure on the next page, Jim had to change only one variable.

1. What was the variable that Jim tested?
2. What did Jim's data describe?

In collecting data, Jim recorded that the balloon moved about 2.5 meters in the first test. In the second test, it moved about 3.5 meters. In the third test, it moved about 5 meters.

3. Which nozzle size caused the balloon to move the greatest distance?

Based on the data he collected, Jim made a conclusion about his hypothesis.

4. What was Jim's hypothesis?
5. Based on the data in questions 3 and 4, what do you think Jim concluded about his hypothesis?

Try It!

Try Jim's experiment and see if you come to the same conclusion.

Problem

How does the size of the balloon opening affect how far a balloon rocket travels?

Hypothesis

A balloon rocket with a large opening will travel farther than a balloon rocket with a small opening.

Materials

cover goggles	cardboard, at least
8 meters of nylon	6 cm x 6 cm
fishing line	pencil
balloon	masking tape
paper clip	meter stick
scissors	straw

Procedure

1 Cut a 5 cm circle from cardboard.

2 Using the pencil point, make a very small hole in the center of the cardboard.

3 Thread the open end of a balloon through the hole and blow up the balloon. Measure the length of the balloon.

4 Use a paper clip to close the opening of the balloon.

5 Tape a straw to the top of the balloon so that one end of the straw is pointed in the same direction as the opening.

6 Thread the fishing line through the straw. Have a partner hold one end. You hold the other. Stretch it out.

7 Remove the paper clip from the opening. Measure and record how far the balloon moves along the string.

8 Make the hole in the cardboard circle larger. Inflate the balloon to the same size as in step 3. Repeat steps 4–7.

9 Remove the cardboard circle. Inflate the balloon again to the same size. The opening will be at its biggest this time. Repeat steps 4–7.

Data and Observations

Opening size	Distance balloon moves
Small	
Bigger	
Biggest	

Conclusion

Write your conclusion based on your data and observations.

Practice

Collecting Data

Suppose you wanted to collect data about how balloon size affects the distance traveled.

1. What data would you collect about the size of the balloon?

2. What might your hypothesis be?

3. How would you change this experiment so that you could collect data to test your hypothesis?

Testing a Hypothesis

Experimenting with Solids

Sally watched her parents move into their new house. Her father could not fit a bookcase through a door. He took the bookcase apart. It then fit easily through the door.

Sally thought of a hypothesis to explain what she saw. Her hypothesis was that the parts of any object take up less space than the object itself does. She decided she would do an experiment to test her hypothesis.

Sally wanted to use a solid in the experiment because the bookcase is a solid. At school, she had used water to measure volume. Volume tells how much space something takes up. Sally used clay for the solid and water to measure volume.

First she measured the volume of a ball of clay. Then she measured the volume of the clay pieces.

Thinking About the Experiment

Sally poured a volume of 250 milliliters of water into the cup. The difference in the water level when a solid is added to the water is the volume of the solid. The water level went up to 300 milliliters with the clay ball and up to 300 milliliters with the clay pieces.

1. What was the volume of water Sally used?

2. What did the volume rise to with the clay ball? the clay pieces?

3. What was the volume of the clay ball? the clay pieces? (Hint: The volume of the clay is the amount the water level changed.)

Sally's experiment showed that her hypothesis was not true for clay.

4. Explain why Sally's data did not support her hypothesis.

5. Write a new hypothesis that supports Sally's data.

Try It!
Try Sally's experiment and see if you come to the same conclusion.

Problem
How does the space taken up by a solid compare to the space taken up by its pieces?

Hypothesis
Recall that Sally's hypothesis was incorrect. Write your own hypothesis for this experiment.

Materials
500 mL measuring cup   water
metric ruler   clay

Procedure
1 Fill the measuring cup exactly to the 250 mL mark.

2 Use a ruler to make a ball of modeling clay that is about 5 cm in diameter.

3 Put the clay into the water. Record the water level.

4 Take the clay out and break it into small pieces.

5 Make certain that the water level is still at 250 mL.

6 Put all of the pieces into the water. Record the water level.

Data and Observations

	Volume in mL
Water	
Clay ball and water	
Clay pieces and water	

Conclusion
Write your conclusion based on your data and observations.

Practice

Testing a Hypothesis
Sally plans to try the same test on a variety of other solids. She wants to start with a block of wood and its pieces.
1. How can she change the experiment so it will work for wood?
2. Suggest some other solids she might use in the experiment.

Using Models

Experimenting with Bones

Sheila visited a skeleton display at a science museum. She noticed that the upper body and lower body seemed to meet at a bone shaped something like a triangle. A sign told Sheila that this bone was called the sacrum. Sheila thought that the sacrum must be very strong because it could hold up the other parts of the body. She wondered if other shapes, a square for example, could support as much weight as a triangle does. When she got home Sheila made a model to find out.

She decided to use flexible plastic straws for her model because she could bend them into shapes. She made a triangle and a square from the straws. To see which was stronger, she taped each shape to the end of a ruler. Then she placed books on the ruler one at a time. Sheila found that the triangle could hold up more books than the square before losing its shape.

Thinking About the Experiment

1. What problem did Sheila want to solve?

2. Write a hypothesis for the problem.

3. Sheila used a model to test her hypothesis instead of using real bones. Why?

4. Why did Sheila use flexible straws for her model?

5. How was her model like the real bone?

6. How was the model different?

7. When is it useful to use a model?

8. What conclusion did Sheila make using her model?

Sheila wanted to find out more about bones. She wanted to know what minerals are important to grow strong bones.

9. Could she use her model to answer this question? Why or why not?

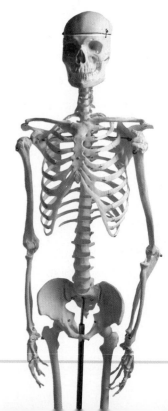

....
Try It!
Try Sheila's experiment and
see if you come to the
same conclusion.
....

Problem
Does a bone shaped like a triangle support weight better than a bone shaped like a square?

Hypothesis
Write your own hypothesis for this experiment.

Materials
several books of about the same size and weight
masking tape

7 flexible plastic straws
metric ruler
scissors

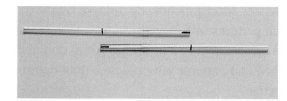

Procedure
1 Trim the long ends of the straws so that the flexible part is in the center. Stretch out the flexible part.

2 Cut 2 slits about 1 cm long at either end of each straw.

3 Use 3 of the straws to make a triangle by fitting the ends together.

4 Use the other 4 straws to make a square.

5 Tape one side of the triangle and one side of the square to the table so that they stand upright.

6 Hold the ruler so that one end is on the table and the other end is supported by the top of the triangle. Fasten the ruler to the triangle with tape.

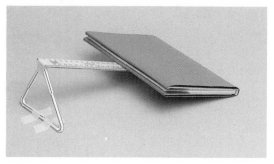

7 Place a book on the ruler. Keep adding books until the triangle begins to come apart.

8 Repeat steps 6 and 7 with the square. Compare the difference in the strength of the two shapes.

Data and Observations

Shape	Number of books supported
Triangle	
Square	

Conclusion
Write your conclusion based on your data and observations.

Practice

Using Models
Suppose you wanted to show how the bones work inside a joint, such as the shoulder or the knee. Look at a picture of a skeleton to get an idea.
1. What would the model have to do to show how the joint works?
2. Probably several different materials could be used to make a model of a joint. What materials can you think of?
3. How would your model be similar to the real body part?
4. How would it be different?

Collecting Data

Experimenting with Practice

Tina was taking piano lessons. She knew that the more she practiced a song, the faster and better she could play it. She wondered if practicing could help a person do any activity faster.

Tina asked Andy to help her find out. Tina traced Andy's right hand on a piece of paper. On the drawing, Tina numbered the fingers 1 through 5 with Andy's thumb being 1. Then Tina asked Andy to tap his fingers in the order 43512. Tina timed how long Andy took to tap this order five times. She wrote the time on a chart. Next, Tina told Andy to practice tapping 43512 for two minutes. Andy practiced. Tina timed him again.

Next, Tina traced Andy's left hand and numbered the fingers. She had Andy tap in the order 25134 five times. Tina wrote down the time. Then she had Andy practice with his left hand for two minutes. Finally, Tina timed Andy again and wrote down the time.

Thinking About the Experiment

Tina was collecting data each time she wrote down how long Andy took to do a finger pattern five times.

1. Why was it important for Tina to write down her data after each step?

2. How is using a data chart like the one on the next page helpful?

Tina's data showed that Andy did five right-hand patterns in 15 seconds before practice. After practice, he did five right-hand patterns in 5 seconds.

3. How many times faster did Andy do the right-hand patterns after practice than before practice?

Tina's data showed that, with practice, Andy cut his left-hand time from 10 seconds to 5 seconds.

4. For which hand did Andy show the most improvement?

5. Did all the data Tina collected support her hypothesis? Explain.

6. Based on his data, what conclusion do you think Tina made?

Try It!
Try Tina's experiment and
see if you come to the
same conclusion.

Problem
Does practice decrease the time needed to do an activity?

Hypothesis
Practice decreases the time needed to do an activity.

Materials
paper | watch or clock with
pen | a second hand

Procedure
1 Trace your partner's right hand on a piece of paper.

2 On the drawing, number the fingers 1 to 5 starting with the thumb.

3 Ask your partner to tap his or her fingers in the order 43512 while you time the activity.

4 Record the time your partner needed to tap 43512 five times in a chart like the one below.

5 Have your partner practice tapping the pattern for 2 minutes.

6 Repeat steps 3 and 4.

7 Repeat steps 1-6 using the left hand and having your partner tap in the order 25134.

Data and Observations

	Right hand	Left hand
Time before practice		
Time after practice		

Conclusion
Write your conclusion based on your data and observations.

Practice

Collecting Data
1. Tina wondered how Andy would do if he stopped practicing for a few hours and then tried to do the patterns again. What might Tina's hypothesis be?
2. How would you change the experiment so that you could collect data on how stopping practice affects learning?

Studying Data

Experimenting with Water and Sand

Mike lived near a large lake. Sometimes in summer he spent a day at the beach. He noticed that in the morning, the sand on the beach was cool. In the afternoon, the sand was so hot it burned his feet. Mike wondered why the water in the lake did not heat up during the day as the sand did. He thought of this hypothesis to answer his question: *Under a heat source, sand heats up faster than water.*

Mike decided to try an experiment to test his hypothesis. He carefully collected and studied his data. Then he made conclusions about whether sand heats faster than water.

Thinking About the Experiment
The purpose of an experiment is to collect data about the problem being solved. To help study the data, it can be arranged in a table.

1. What kind of data would Mike want to collect in his experiment?

2. Why would Mike want to collect his data at regular times?

3. What should Mike do with his data to help study it?

4. How would studying the data help Mike test his hypothesis?

Mike could use the information in his data table to make a graph. A graph is very useful for showing changes that occur during an experiment. A graph has two lines that cross, or intersect. Each of the two lines in a graph is used to show one kind of measurement data.

5. What information can Mike show on each of the two lines in a graph?

Try It!

Try Mike's experiment and see if you come to the same conclusion.

Problem

Why does lake water not heat up during a warm day like sand does?

Hypothesis

Sand heats up faster than water.

Materials

2 aluminum pie pans

water at room temperature

sand

2 thermometers

meter stick

clock or watch with second hand

2 200-watt lamps with reflectors and stands

Procedure

1. Fill a pie pan with water. Fill the other pan to the same level with sand.

2. Place the pans about a meter apart on a flat surface. Let the pans stand for about 2 hours to be sure they are at the same temperature.

3. Place a thermometer at the same depth in the middle of each pan. Record the temperatures in the pans in a chart like the one shown.

4. Place the lamps about 40 cm above the pans. Direct the light straight down onto the pans.

5. Measure and record the temperature of each pan every 5 minutes for the next 30 minutes.

Data and Observations

Time (minutes)	Temperature	
	Water	Sand
0		
5		
10		
15		
20		
25		
30		

Conclusion

Write your conclusion based on your data and observations.

Practice

Studying Data

Suppose you wanted to find out whether sand or water cools down faster.

1. What might be your hypothesis?
2. How would you set up an experiment to test your hypothesis?
3. What data would you want to collect and study?
4. How would you organize your data?

Making Observations

MODULE E

Experimenting with Magnetic Fields

Juanita was studying magnets in science. She was very interested in the shapes of magnetic fields. She remembered a picture in her science text that showed how iron filings lined up around a magnet. Juanita wondered if magnets of different shapes had magnetic fields of different shapes. She set up an experiment to find out.

Juanita placed some iron powder in a jar that contained cooking oil. She shook the jar and held it over a magnet. The iron powder lined up to show a three-dimensional pattern of the magnetic field. Juanita made careful observations of the magnetic field. She tried several different magnets. Juanita was able to compare the magnetic fields of magnets of different shapes by making detailed drawings.

Thinking About the Experiment

One important part of making observations is to be able to notice differences. Juanita observed that iron powder seemed to build up on the ends of one of the magnets she tested.

1. What does this observation indicate?

When making good observations it is important to notice not only changes, but also where changes do not occur. Juanita noticed that the iron powder near the top of the oil was not affected by the magnet.

2. Is this an important observation for Juanita to make? Explain.

When making observations it is important to make an accurate record of what you observe. Juanita decided to record her observations by making a drawing of what she saw.

3. How else might Juanita have recorded her observations?

Try It!

Try Juanita's experiment and see if you come to the same conclusion.

Problem

How does the shape of a magnet affect the shape of its magnetic field?

Hypothesis

Magnets of different shapes have magnetic fields of different shapes.

Materials

small plastic jar
  with lid
vegetable oil
teaspoon

iron powder
magnets of
  different shapes

Procedure

1 Fill the plastic jar to about 2.5 cm from the top with clear vegetable oil.

2 Add one teaspoon of powdered iron to the oil. Put on the lid and make sure that it is tightly closed. Shake the jar to mix the iron and oil.

3 Hold the jar steady over each type of magnet you wish to test. Notice what happens to the particles of iron in the oil.

4 Record your observations by making drawings. Draw the pattern of what you see around the magnets you are using.

Data and Observations

Magnetic field pattern

Conclusion

Write your conclusion based on your data and observations.

Collecting Data

Experimenting with an Electromagnet

After studying electromagnets in science, Nathan and Mike decided to do an experiment with electromagnets. They each used a book that told them how to build an electromagnet.

The boys tested their electromagnets by trying to pick up small iron and steel objects. Nathan's electromagnet seemed stronger than Mike's. Mike noticed that Nathan was using two batteries, while he was using only one. Mike wondered if the number of batteries made a difference in an electromagnet's strength. The boys decided to do an experiment to find out.

Thinking About the Experiment

In order to collect data that would help them reach a conclusion, Nathan and Mike had to choose one variable to test.

1. What variable did Nathan and Mike test?

2. Why would Nathan and Mike want to use only paper clips instead of several different iron and steel items?

Each time the boys added a battery to the electromagnet, they collected new data. The one-battery magnet picked up three clips. The two-battery magnet picked up seven clips. The three-battery magnet picked up ten clips.

3. Which electromagnet was weakest?

4. Which electromagnet was strongest?

Nathan and Mike concluded that an electromagnet is made stronger by adding more batteries to it.

5. Does Nathan and Mike's data support their conclusion? Explain your answer.

6. Suppose Nathan and Mike had added a fourth battery to their electromagnet and tested it. Would the electromagnet have picked up more or fewer clips than it did with three batteries? Explain your answer.

Try It!

Try Nathan and Mike's experiment and see if you come to the same conclusion.

Problem

What affects the strength of an electromagnet?

Hypothesis

Adding batteries to an electromagnet makes it stronger.

Materials

3 flashlight batteries
insulated copper wire
sandpaper

large nail
small paper clips
masking tape

Procedure

1 Use sandpaper to remove 1 cm of insulation from the wire's ends.

2 Wind the wire around the nail at least 30 times. Do not let the wire coils overlap.

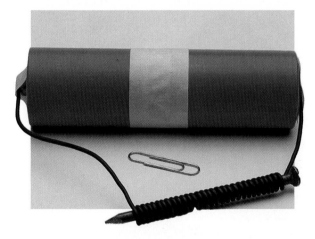

3 Tape 1 end of the wire to 1 end of a battery. Tape the other end of the wire to the other end of the battery.

4 Try to pick up paper clips with the nail. Count and record the number of clips that the magnet picks up.

5 Take the ends of the wire off the battery.

6 Connect 2 batteries by placing the positive (+) end of 1 battery to the negative (-) end of another. Tape the batteries together tightly.

7 Tape the ends of the wire to the free ends of the batteries.

8 Repeat steps 4 and 5.

9 Take the wires off the batteries and add a third battery to the series. Make sure you only connect a positive end with a negative end.

10 Repeat steps 4 and 5.

Data and Observations

Batteries	Paper clips
1	
2	
3	

Conclusion

Write your conclusion based on your data and observations.

Practice

Collecting Data

1. Suppose you wanted to test how the size of the nail affects the strength of an electromagnet. How would you change the experiment above?

2. Instead of collecting data about the number of clips picked up by different numbers of batteries, what data would you collect?

Making Conclusions

MODULE E

Experimenting with a Wet Cell

Alicia had learned that the current in a wet cell battery is caused by electrons flowing through a liquid containing an acid. She knew that some foods have juices that contain acids. She wondered if some foods contain strong enough acids to make a wet cell battery. She decided to do an experiment to find out.

Alicia's teacher told her that a compass needle will move when an electric current flows near it. Alicia wrapped wire around a compass. She taped one end of the wire to a copper strip and the other end to a zinc strip. She pushed the two metal strips into a hot dog bun. She observed the compass needle to see if it moved. It did not.

Alicia repeated this procedure three times, using a lemon, a head of lettuce, and an orange.

Thinking About the Experiment
Alicia used the data she collected to make conclusions. Alicia recorded that the needle moved when she used the orange and the lemon. It did not move when she used the hot dog bun or the lettuce.

1. With what foods did current flow?

2. What proof did Alicia have that current flowed with the foods listed in question 1?

Alicia concluded that some citrus fruits contain acids strong enough to make a wet cell battery.

3. Was Alicia's conclusion correct? Explain your answer.

Lemons and oranges are citrus fruits.

4. If Alicia had concluded that all citrus fruits work in a wet cell battery, would you agree with her conclusion? Explain your answer.

Try It!

Try Alicia's experiment and see if you come to the same conclusion.

Problem

Is the acid in some foods strong enough to be used to make a wet cell battery?

Hypothesis

Some foods contain strong enough acids to make a wet cell battery.

Materials

compass	lemon
insulated copper wire	hot dog bun
cover goggles	head of lettuce
masking tape	orange
copper strip, 2 cm wide, 10 cm long	sandpaper
	pencil
zinc strip 2 cm wide, 10 cm long	metric ruler

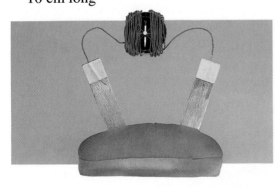

Procedure

1 Put on your cover goggles. Rub the metal strips with sandpaper until the strips are shiny.

2 Use the sandpaper to remove 3 cm of insulation from each end of the wire.

3 Wrap the wire around the compass 25 times. Make sure the wire loops all go in the same direction.

4 Tape one end of the wire to the copper strip. Tape the other end of the wire to the zinc strip.

5 Turn the compass so that the needle is in line with the wire coils.

6 Make a small pencil mark 3 cm from the bottom of each metal strip.

7 Make two small pencil marks 4 cm apart on the bun. Push the ends of the metal strips 3 cm into the bun.

8 Observe the compass needle and record your observation.

9 Press and roll the lemon on a table or desk top. Repeat steps 7-8 using the lemon.

10 Repeat steps 7-8 using the lettuce.

11 Press and roll the orange. Repeat steps 7-8 using the orange.

Data and Observations

Food used	Needle moves	Current flows
Hot dog bun		
Lemon		
Lettuce		
Orange		

Conclusion

Write your conclusion based on your data and observations.

Experiment Skills
Setting Up a Control

Experimenting with Plant Responses

Kristi wanted to have a plant for her room. She made a cutting from a large plant and placed it in a jar of water. After a few days, she saw roots growing straight downward from the plant into the water. Kristi wondered if plant roots always grow downward, with gravity. Kristi wondered what would happen if she could turn a plant upside down. Would the roots bend and start to grow in the opposite direction? She did an experiment to find out.

Kristi used corn seeds that she soaked in water. She put the seeds on paper towels placed against the inside of two jars containing some water. In a few days, the young roots grew straight downward. Kristi turned one jar upside down so the roots pointed upward. A few days later she noticed the roots bent all the way around so they were starting to grow downward. She compared them to the roots of the seedlings in the upright jar. The seeds in the upright jar had grown straight down without bending.

Thinking About the Experiment

Kristi did something to Jar A that she did not do to Jar B. The part that is different is the variable being tested.

1. What is the variable being tested?

Kristi's experiment also had a control. A control is part of the experiment that does not have the variable.

2. Which group of seedlings were the control?

3. How did having a control help Kristi see the results of the experiment?

4. Suppose Kristi did not use control plants. Could she be sure that turning the plants caused the roots to change direction? Why or why not?

5. Suppose Kristi forgot to add water to the control plants. How would this affect her results?

6. Why should the control in the experiment have all conditions the same *except* for the tested variable?

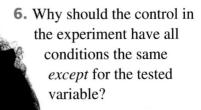

Try It!

Try Kristi's experiment and see if you come to the same conclusion.

Problem
How do plant roots respond to gravity?

Hypothesis
Plant roots always grow downward with gravity.

Materials

2 pieces of cardboard	2 jars with lids
8 corn seeds	marker
dish	paper towel
graduated cylinder	water

Procedure

1 Place the corn seeds in a dish of water. Soak them overnight.

2 Mark the two jar lids *A* and *B*.

3 Fold a paper towel so that it fits flat around the inside of each jar. Wedge a piece of cardboard up against it so that the paper towel stays up against the side of the jar.

4 In each jar, put 4 soaked corn seeds between the paper towel and the side of the jar. Place the seeds so the pointed ends are downward. The paper towel should keep the seeds in place.

5 Add 50 mL water to the bottom of each jar and cover.

6 Keep both jars in a dark place.

7 After 3 days, observe the direction of the root growth of the seedlings in each jar.

8 Place Jar *A* on its side. Make sure the lid is screwed on tightly. Leave Jar *B* upright.

9 Observe both jars after another 3 days.

10 Place Jar *A* so it is upside down. Observe again after 3 days.

Data and Observations

Observations of Root Growth		
Day	Jar A	Jar B
3		
6		
9		

Conclusion
Write your conclusion based on your data and observations.

Practice

Setting up a Control
Suppose you wanted to find out if plant stems always grow upward. You might use three potted plants. One pot could be placed on its side. Another would hang from a rope so it is upside down.
1. What should you do with the third pot?
2. What is the variable being tested in your experiment?
3. What is the control in your experiment?

Collecting Data

Experimenting with Plant Shoots

One day Erin watched her aunt snip buds off the tops of plants she had grown in pots on her windowsill. She told Erin that removing the top bud caused the plants to grow new buds and shoots. These buds and shoots grew from the sides of the main stem. If she did not snip the top buds, she explained, the plants would grow tall but would have fewer side shoots.

Erin set up an experiment to test how removing buds from plants would affect their growth. She used six plants growing in small pots. The plants ranged between twelve centimeters and fifteen centimeters in height, and each had nearly the same number of shoots growing from the sides of the main stem.

Erin snipped the top bud off three of the plants and did nothing to the other three plants. After ten days she counted the number of side shoots on each plant and measured each plant's height.

Thinking About the Experiment

Erin used only one kind of plant in her experiment. Suppose she had compared different kinds of plants.

1. Explain why this would have made the experiment more difficult for Erin to make conclusions from her data.

Erin collected data about six plants— three with the top bud removed and three without the top bud removed.

2. Why did Erin not use just one plant with a top bud and one without?

3. Explain why Erin did not remove the top bud from plants in pots 1 to 3.

4. Why did Erin choose plants that were about the same height and had about the same number of stems at the start of the experiment?

5. Why was it necessary to put all of the plants on the same sunny windowsill?

Try It!

Try Erin's experiment and see if you come to the same conclusion.

Problem

How does removing the bud from the top of some plants affect their growth?

Hypothesis

Some plants grow new shoots from the sides of the main stem after a top bud is removed.

Materials

6 potted plants,   metric ruler
   each 12 cm   masking tape
   to 15 cm tall   marker

Procedure

1 Place a piece of masking tape on the side of each pot. Use the tape to label the pots, *1, 2,* and *3.*

2 Label the other pots *4, 5,* and *6.*

3 Using your fingertips pinch off the top bud on the three plants in pots *4-6.*

4 Measure the heights of all of the plants and record these in the data table.

5 Count the number of side shoots on each plant. Record the numbers in the data table.

6 Place the plants on a sunny windowsill and let them stay there for 8 days. Do not forget to water them regularly.

7 After 8 days, measure the height of each plant and record the measurements in the data table.

8 Count the number of side shoots on each plant and record these in the data table.

Data and Observations

	Plants					
Height	1	2	3	4	5	6
Day 1						
Day 8						
Shoots						
Day 1						
Day 8						

Conclusion

Write your conclusion based on your data and observations.

Practice

Collecting Data

Suppose you wanted to see how removing the end buds from all the side stems of a plant affected its growth.

1. What kind of data might you collect?

2. What characteristics might you look for in a plant to make collecting your data easier?

3. Make a data table that you might use to record your observations.

Setting Up an Experiment

Experimenting with Plants

Chang learned that plants are adapted to different climates. He thought that water probably passes out of a forest plant faster than it does from a desert plant. He collected a green leaf from a tree in his yard and a small piece of a jade plant. A jade plant has small, thick leaves and is similar to a desert plant.

Chang set up an experiment. He put water in three clear plastic cups. He hung the tree leaf over one cup and the piece of jade plant over another cup so that each was in water. Thus, both could absorb water. The third cup contained only water. He covered each of the three cups with another cup.

Chang put the three pairs of cups in the same place. He observed the top cups for several days.

Thinking About the Experiment

Chang wanted to compare the rate at which water was released to the air from each plant.

1. What is the purpose of the upper cups?

2. What did Chang expect to see in the upper cups?

For his comparison, Chang needed a control. The control is the part of the setup that is not affected by what happens to the leaves.

3. Which part of the setup was the control in this experiment?

4. Why was the control important in Chang's experiment?

5. Why did Chang leave all three setups in the same location?

Try It!

Try Chang's experiment and see if you come to the same conclusion.

....

Problem

Does water pass out of a forest plant faster than from a desert plant?

Hypothesis

Forest plants release water more quickly than do desert plants.

Materials

green leaf
6 clear plastic
   cups
small stem with
   leaves from
   a jade plant
nail

3 squares of
   cardboard large
   enough to cover
   the cups
tape
water

Procedure

1 Fill 3 of the plastic cups two-thirds full with water.

2 Use a nail to pierce the center of each cardboard square.

3 Place the plant stems through two of the cardboard squares.

4 Put each square on top of a cup. Make sure the two plant stems are in the water.

5 Use tape to hold the cardboard onto the cups.

6 Place an empty cup over each square. Tape it securely to the cardboard.

7 Place the three setups in the same location .

8 Observe the top cups for several days.

Data and Observations

	Day 1	Day 2
Forest Leaf		
Jade plant		
No plant		

Conclusion

Write your conclusion based on your data and observations.

Practice

Setting Up an Experiment
Explain how you would change the experiment above to find out each of the following.
1. What could you do to measure the amount of water absorbed by each plant?
2. What could you do to find out how temperature affects the amount of water released by a plant?

Glossary

A

acceleration (ak sel′ə rā′shən), the rate of change of velocity.

acid (as′id), substance with a pH lower than 7; a compound that releases hydrogen ions in water.

air resistance (ar ri zis′təns), the opposition to motion caused by air particles.

alga (al′gə), one of a group of freshwater or saltwater producers classified in the protist kingdom.

alkaline (al′kə līn), refers to a base; describes a substance with a pH higher than 7.

animalcule (an′ə mal′kyül), name used by Leeuwenhoek to describe the microscopic organisms he observed.

antenna (an ten′ə), device for receiving and sending radio waves.

atmosphere (at′me sfir), layered mixture of gases surrounding the earth.

atom (at′əm), basic unit of all matter.

atomic number, the number of protons in the nucleus of the atom.

autonomic (ô′tə nom′ik) **nervous system,** controls involuntary processes such as breathing and digestion.

axon (ak′son), part of the nerve cell that carries impulses away from the cell body.

B

bacteria (bak tir′ē ə), group of microscopic nonphotosynthetic one-celled organisms classified in the moneran kingdom.

ball and socket joint, one of the five kinds of joints in the body; allows circular motion.

bile (bīl), a bitter, greenish-yellow liquid that aids digestion; released by the liver.

biological (bī′ ə loj′ ə kəl) **control,** method that uses natural enemies to control insects.

C

Calorie (kal′ ər ē), measure of the amount of energy in foods; the amount of energy needed to raise the temperature of one kilogram of water one degree Celsius.

carbon dioxide (kär′ bən dī ok′ sīd), a gas in air; each molecule consists of one atom of carbon, two atoms of oxygen.

carnivore (kär′ nə vôr), consumer that eats only other consumers.

cartilage (kär′ tl ij), tough, elastic, flexible material that covers bones in joints to prevent friction and absorb vibrations.

cell (sel), the basic living unit of an organism.

CFC, abbreviation for chlorofluorocarbon gas; a gas in the atmosphere that can break down ozone molecules.

chemical (kem′ ə kəl) **bond,** the strong attraction that holds two atoms together in a substance.

chemical energy, energy stored in the chemical bonds between atoms and molecules.

chemical equation (i kwā′ zhən), an arrangement of symbols, formulas, and numbers that are used to describe a chemical reaction.

chemical reaction, a process that produces one or more new substances.

chlorophyll (klôr′ ə fil), green substance in producers that absorbs light energy for photosynthesis.

chloroplast (klôr′ ə plast), organelle in producers that contains chlorophyll.

chromosome (krō′ mə sōm), threadlike strand that is made up of genes; found in the nucleus of a cell.

circuit (sėr′ kit), a closed path through which current flows.

circuit breaker, safety device that automatically opens an electric circuit when too much current flows through it.

circulatory (sėr′ kyə lə tôr ē) **system,** the network of arteries and veins that carries blood throughout an organism.

classify (klas′ ə fī), to sort into groups based on similarities and differences.

cleavage (klē′ vij), the way a crystal splits into pieces with flat surfaces.

cochlea (kok′ lē ə), spiral shaped structure in the inner ear filled with fluid and lined with tiny, hairlike cells.

complex machine, machine made up of many simple and compound machines that is usually powered by electricity or fuel.

compost (kom′ post), mixture of decaying leaves, manure, and other material that forms a kind of natural fertilizer.

compound (kom′ pound), substance produced when atoms of two or more elements combine.

compound machine, a machine that is a combination of two or more simple machines.

comsat (kom′ sat′), a communications satellite.

conductor (kən duk′ ter), a material that transmits heat or electricity.

consumer (kən sü′ mər), organisms that get their energy from the stored chemical energy in the food they eat.

control (kən trōl′), the part of an experiment that does not have the variable being tested.

cornea (kôr′ nē ə), the transparent part of the outer coat of the eyeball, covering the iris and pupil.

crest (krest), highest point on a wave.

crystal (kris′tl), structural unit in most solids that has an orderly, repeating arrangement.

cytoplasm (sī tə plaz′əm), clear, jellylike fluid substance between the nuclear membrane and the cell membrane; contains all the cell's organelles and aids in moving material within the cell.

D

DDT, abbreviation for dichloro-diphenyl-trichloro-ethane, a powerful insecticide.

decomposer (dē′kəm pō′zer), organism that helps to break down and decay dead organisms and the wastes of living organisms.

dendrite (den′drīt), part of a nerve cell where nerve impulses begin and then travel through to the cell body.

depressant (di pres′nt), kind of drug, such as alcohol and tranquilizers, that slows down the nervous system and reduces reaction time.

digestion (də jes′chen), the breaking down of food into forms animals can use.

drag, the disturbance of air or water caused by motion that slows the body down.

E

eardrum, the thin skin that covers the end of the ear canal.

echo (ek′ō), reflected sound waves.

egg (eg), female sex cell.

electric (i lek′trik) **current,** the flow of electric charge.

electrical (i lek′trə kəl) **energy,** kind of energy carried by moving charges.

electromagnetic (i lek′trō mag net′ik) **wave,** energy that travels through space at a speed of 300,000,000 meters per second.

electromagnetic radiation (rā′də ā′shən), energy moving in waves through space.

electromagnetic spectrum (spek′trəm), scale of electromagnetic waves from shortest to longest or longest to shortest.

electron (i lek′tron), negatively charged particle that moves around the nucleus of an atom.

electron cloud model, current model of the atom that states that the exact location of the electrons is unknown.

element (el′ə mənt), any substance made of only one kind of atom; one of 109 basic substances that cannot be broken down by chemical reactions.

energy (en′ər jē), the ability to do work or change matter; usually expressed in joules.

enzyme (en′zīm), substance that controls how quickly chemical reactions occur in the body.

epithelial (ep′ə thē′lē əl) **cell,** kind of cell that forms the skin and linings of organs such as the mouth and intestines.

esophagus (ē sof′ə gəs), the tube that carries food and fluids from the mouth to the stomach.

eukaryote (yü kar′ē ōt), organism made of cells that contain many different structures surrounded by thin coverings called membranes.

F

farsighted (fär′sī′tid), kind of sight where images form beyond the retina and are not seen clearly.

fertilizer (fėr′tl ī′zər), substance, either chemical or natural, spread over or put into the soil to supply missing nutrients.

fixed joint, one of five kinds of joints in the body; does not allow movement.

food chain, simple feeding pattern that shows the transfer of energy from one organism to another.

food web, system of food chains in an ecosystem that shows how energy flows through the ecosystem.

force (fôrs), a push or a pull.

friction (frik′shən), force between surfaces that resists the motion of one surface past another surface.

fruit (früt), thickened ovary that covers and protects the seed or seeds.

fulcrum (ful′krəm), point on which a lever is supported and turns.

fungicide (fun′jə sīd), any chemical that kills fungus.

fuse (fyüz), safety device in which a metal strip melts to open a circuit when too much current flows through it.

G

gastric (gas′ trik) **juice,** strong acid made in the stomach that aids digestion.

gear (gir), toothed wheel that developed from the wheel and the lever.

gene (jēn), a unit of information that controls a trait.

genetic engineering (jə net′ik en′jə nir′ing), a technology to change the traits of an organism by changing its genes.

geode (jē′ōd), rock usually having a cavity lined with crystals or other mineral matter.

geographic (jē′ə graf′ik) **pole,** a fixed location at either end of the earth's axis.

gliding joint, one of five kinds of joints in the body; allows bones to slide past one another.

gravity (grav′ə tē), a force that exists between any two objects.

greenhouse effect, the trapping of infrared radiation from the earth by some gases.

greenhouse gas, gas in the atmosphere that traps heat near the earth's surface instead of allowing it to pass through to space.

H

HDTV, abbreviation for High Definition Television, a technology that allows a larger, clearer picture than other forms of television.

hemoglobin (hē′mə glō′bən), red-colored protein in red blood cells that carries oxygen to cells.

herbicide (hėr′bə sīd), chemical used to kill weeds.

herbivore (hėr′bə vôr), a consumer that eats only producers.

hinge joint, one of five kinds of joints in the body; allows back-and-forth movement.

hormone (hôr′mōn), chemical substance that affects growth and development of organisms.

horsepower, customary unit that measures power.

humus (hyü′məs), part of soil formed from decayed plant-and-animal matter.

hybrid (hī′brid), an offspring of parents with different traits.

hydroponics (hī′drə pon′iks), the science of growing plants in a nutrient-rich liquid instead of soil.

hypothesis (hī poth′ə sis), a likely explanation of a problem.

I

inclined (in klīnd′) **plane,** a simple machine that is a flat surface with one end higher than the other.

inertia (in ėr′shə), the tendency of a moving object to stay in motion or a resting object to stay still.

insulator (in′sə lā′tər), a material that does not conduct heat or electricity well.

integrated pest management, use of a combination of ways to control insects and other pests.

integumentary (in teg′yə men′tər ē) **system,** the system that covers and protects the body.

involuntary (in vol′ən ter′ē) **muscle,** a muscle that works without a person thinking about it.

iris (ī′ris), colored ring-shaped muscles in the eye that change the size of the pupil.

J

joint, place where bones come together.

joule (joul), metric unit used for measuring work and energy.

K

kinetic (ki net′ik) **energy,** energy of motion.

L

larva (lär′və), immature caterpillar stage of many insects.

legume (leg′yüm), certain plants whose roots have nodules that contain nitrogen-fixing bacteria.

lens, a transparent oval body in the eye directly behind the iris, that focuses light rays upon the retina.

lever (lev′ər), a simple machine made of a bar that is held up on a point, or support, called a fulcrum.

ligament (lig′ə mənt), tough strips of tissue that hold bones together at joints.

lightning (līt′ning), giant spark of moving electric charges in the atmosphere.

lubricate (lü′brə kāt), to apply oil, grease, or other substance to reduce friction.

luster (lus′tər), property that tells how a substance reflects light.

M

macrophage (mak′rō fāj), kind of white blood cell capable of absorbing and destroying waste or harmful material.

magnetic (mag net′ik) **pole,** place on a magnet where the magnetic field is strongest.

magnetic field, the space around a magnet in which an object feels a magnetic force.

magnetism (mag′nətiz′əm), the force of attraction that comes from a magnet.

marrow (mar′ō), soft tissue inside some bones that produces red blood cells.

mass (mas), the amount of material that an object has in it.

mechanical (mə kan′ə kəl) **energy,** energy an object has because of its motion and the forces acting on it.

medium (mē′dē əm), liquid that contains growth hormones, water, and nutrients.

metal (met′l), one of a group of elements that are usually solid at room temperature, are shiny, and conduct heat and electricity well.

microorganism (mī′krō ôr′gə niz′əm), organisms too small to be seen with the unaided eye.

mineral (min′ər əl), basic, solid, nonliving matter from the earth.

mitochondrion (mī tə kon′drē ən), organelle that releases energy in the cell.

model (mod′l), a picture or structure that will help to explain how something looks or works.

molecule (mol′ə kyül), the smallest bit of a compound that has the same properties of that compound.

muscular (mus′kyə lər) **system,** the muscles attached to your skeleton.

N

NASA, abbreviation for the National Aeronautics and Space Administration.

nearsighted (nir′sī′tid), kind of sight where images form in front of the retina and cannot be seen clearly.

nerve impulses, signals that relay messages between your brain and your muscles.

nervous system, system that links all parts of the body and carries information back and forth among them.

neutron (nü′tron), particle having no electric charge and found in the nucleus of the atom.

nodule (noj′ül), a small structure on the roots of legumes that contains nitrogen-fixing bacteria.

nonmetal (non met′l), one of a group of elements that cannot be polished, is brittle, and does not conduct heat or electricity.

nuclear membrane (nü′klē ər mem′brān), covering that surrounds the nucleus.

nucleus (nü′klē əs), central part of the atom; control center of the cell.

nutrient (nü′trē ənt), a substance needed for growth and survival.

O

omnivore (äm′ni′vōər), a consumer that eats both producers and consumers.

optic (op′tik) **nerve,** bundle of nerves connecting the retina to the brain.

orbit (ôr′bit), the path of an object around another object.

organ (ôr′gən), groups of tissues that work together to do a job.

organ system, groups of organs that work together to do a job.

organelle (ôr′gə nel′), structures found in the cytoplasm that do the work of the cell.

organism (ôr′gə niz′əm), a living thing made up of one cell or more.

ovule (ō′vyül), contains the female sex cell.

ozone (ō′zōn), kind of oxygen that contains three oxygen atoms per molecule.

P

pancreas (pan′krē əs), a large gland near the stomach that gives off pancreatic juice, a digestive juice which contains various enzymes, into the small intestine.

parallel (par′ə lel) **circuit,** circuit that allows the current to flow along more than one path.

periodic (pir′ē od′ik) **table,** chart that shows the orderly arrangements of the different elements based on their atomic numbers.

pesticide (pes′tə sīd), chemical that kills pests that damage crops.

pH number, number from 0-14 that tells whether a substance is acid or alkaline.

pheromone (fer ə mōn), any chemical substance that is given off by members of a species and causes other members of the species to give particular responses.

photosynthesis (fō′tō sin′thə sis), the process by which producers make sugars from sunlight, water, and carbon dioxide.

pistil (pis′tl), female part of a flower that contains the ovules.

pivot joint, one of five kinds of joints in the body; allows bones to move over and under one another.

plasmid (plaz′mid), ringlike structure of a bacterium that contains genetic material.

polarizing (pō′lə rīz′ing) **lens,** a lens that allows electromagnetic waves vibrating in one direction only to pass through.

pollen (pol′ən), tiny grain that contains the male sex cell.

pollination (pol′ə nā′shən), the movement of pollen from a stamen to a pistil.

potential (pə ten′shəl) **energy,** stored energy an object has because of its position.

power (pou′ər), rate at which work is done.

power surge (sėrj), a sharp, brief increase in the amount of current in a wire.

producer (prə dü′sər), an organism that makes its own sugars using the sun's energy.

prokaryote (prō kar′ē ōt), organism made of cells without a membrane separating organelles from the cytoplasm.

proton (prō′ton), positively charged particle in the nucleus of an atom.

pulley (pu̇l′ē), a simple machine consisting of a rope that passes over a grooved wheel.

pupil (pyü′pəl), opening into the eye through which light passes.

pyrethrum (pī rē′thrəm), chemical poison made of the powdered flower heads of any of various chrysanthemums.

Q

quark (kwôrk), a basic building block of the nucleus of an atom.

R

reflex (rē′fleks), any movement that happens automatically.

repel (ri pel′), to push away.

resistance (ri zis′təns), anything that slows down the flow of electric charge.

respiration (res′pə rā′shən), the process by which cells change sugar and oxygen into carbon dioxide and water, thereby releasing energy.

retina (ret′n ə), a layer of nerve cells in the back of the eye that contains both the rods and cones.

rolling friction, friction that results when a round object rolls over a surface.

S

saliva (sə lī′və), watery fluid in the mouth that moistens food, aids chewing and swallowing, and begins digestion.

satellite (sat′l īt), object that revolves, or moves, around another object.

scale (skāl), the size of a plan, map, drawing, or model compared with what it represents.

scanning electron microscope, tool that forms an image by sending a beam of electrons across surfaces of objects.

screw (skrü), inclined plane in a spiral form.

seed (sēd), the result of an egg and sperm joining together.

series (sir′ēz) **circuit,** circuit in which current can move only through one pathway.

simple machine (mə shēn′), tool with only one or two parts.

skeletal (skel′ə təl) **system,** the framework of bones and other parts; supports and protects the body.

sliding friction, friction that results when two solid surfaces slide across one another.

small intestine (in tes′tən), the organ of the digestive system in which most digestion takes place.

smog (smog), pollution consisting of a combination of smoke and fog in the air.

solar (sō′lər) **cell,** device that changes solar energy directly into electrical energy.

solar energy, energy from the sun.

sound energy from vibrating matter.

species (spē′shēz), a group of organisms that have similar traits and can produce offspring that can also produce offspring.

speed, measures how quickly an object moves over a certain distance.

sperm (spėrm), male sex cell.

spongy bone, layer of bone with an open, spongelike structure that makes bones lighter and easier to move.

sprocket (sprok′it), gear on a bicycle.

stamen (stā′mən), the male part of a flower that produces pollen.

stimulant (stim′yə lənt), kind of drug, such as cocaine and amphetamines, that speed up the nervous system.

stomach (stum′ək), storage sac where most food begins the digestion process.

streamlining (strēm′lin′ing), rounding of the surfaces of objects to reduce air resistance.

sunspot (sun′spot′), dark patch on the sun where a magnetic storm is occurring.

symbol (sim′bəl), one or two letters that stand for an element's name.

synapse (si naps′), gap between the dendrites of one nerve cell and the axon of the next where a nerve impulse passes from one nerve cell to another.

T

tendon (ten′dən), ropelike structure that connects muscles to bones.

theory (thē′ər ē), one or more related hypotheses supported by data that best explains things or events.

tissue (tish′ü), groups of cells of the same kind that work together to do a job.

tissue culture (kul′chər), a method of growing living tissues outside an organism.

tolerance (tol′ər əns), a user's need to take more and more of a drug to feel an effect.

trait (trāt), a particular characteristic or property of an organism.

transmission electron microscope, forms an image by transmitting a beam of electrons through thinly-sliced objects.

transmitter (tran smit′ər), antenna that sends out radio waves.

tread (tred), the grooves and ridges on a bicycle tire.

troposphere (trop′ə sfir), lowest level of the atmosphere from sea level up to about 11 kilometers.

trough (trôf), lowest point of a wave.

V

vacuole (vak′yü ōl), organelle of storage in the cell.

variable (ver′ē ə bəl), anything in an experiment that can be changed.

velocity (və los′ə tē), value giving the speed and direction in which an object is moving.

vibration (vī brā′shən), rapid back-and-forth motion.

villus (vil′əs), tiny fingerlike projection in the small intestine that increases the area for absorption of food.

visible (viz′ə bəl) **light,** light that humans can see.

voluntary (vol′ən ter′ē) **muscle,** muscle that a person can control with thought.

W

watt (wot), metric unit that measures power.

wavelength (wāv′lengkth′), distance from one point on a wave to the same point on the next wave.

wedge (wej), a simple machine used to cut or split an object.

weight (wāt), the amount of force that gravity exerts on a mass.

weightlessness (wāt′lis nis), a condition in which the pull of gravity is balanced by other motion.

wheel and axle, simple machine that consists of a wheel and a shaft that turns with the wheel and supports its center.

work (werk), product of the force exerted on an object and the distance the force moves the object in the direction of the force; expressed in newton-meters or joules.

Index

Acknowledgments

ScottForesman

Editorial: Terry Flohr, Janet Helenthal, Judy Elgin, Mary Jayne Horgan, James McPherson, Joline McVicker, Glen Phelan, Matthew Shimkus

Art and Design: Barbara Schneider, Jacqueline Kolb, George Roth, Cathy Sterrett

Picture Research/Photo Studio: Nina Page, Lynn Mooney, Judy Ladendorf, John Moore

Photo Lab/Keyline: Marilyn Sullivan, Mark Barberis, Gwen Plogman

Production: Barbara Albright, Francine Simon

Marketing: Lesa Scott, Ed Rock

Ligature, Inc.
Pupil Edition interior design and production

Unless otherwise acknowledged, all photographs are the property of ScottForesman. Unless otherwise acknowledged, all computer graphics by Ligature, Inc. Page abbreviations are as follows: **(T) top, (C) center, (B) bottom, (L) left, (R) right, (INS) inset.**

Module A
Photographs
Front & Back Cover: Background: David Scharf/Peter Arnold, Inc.   Children's Photos: John Moore

Page A2(T) DPI/Uniphoto   **A2(B)** The Granger Collection, New York   **A6(TL)** S.Meola/Visuals Unlimited   **A6(TR)** Dr.Jeremy Burgess/SPL/Photo Researchers   **A7(T)** Dr.Jeremy Burgess/SPL/Photo Researchers   **A7(B)** David Scharf/Peter Arnold, Inc. **A12(T)** R.Weldon/Gemological Institute of America **A12(T INS)** R.Weldon/Gemological Institute of America **A12(B)** Art Resource   **A12(B INS)** E.R.Degginger/Bruce Coleman, Inc.   **A13(T)** Fred Ward/Black Star   **A13(T INS)** DPI/Uniphoto   **A13(B)** Charles Moore/Black Star   **A13(B INS)** DPI/Uniphoto   **A16-17** David Scharf/Peter Arnold, Inc. **A16(B INS)** David Scharf/Peter Arnold, Inc.   **A23** Michel Viard/Peter Arnold, Inc.   **A24(T)** Photo Courtesy of Scintag, Inc. **A24-25** Alfred Pasieka/SPL/Photo Researchers   **A26** Jerry Howard/Stock Boston   **A27(B)** Myrleen Ferguson/Photo Edit **A28** Richard Megna/Fundamental Photographs **A32(R)** Lawrence Berkeley Institute   **A36** Universities Research, Inc.   **A37** Universities Research, Inc.   **A38(L)** The Granger Collection, New York   **A38(R)** The Granger Collection, New York   **A40** Yada Claassen/Stock Boston   **A41(R)** John D. Cunningham/Visuals Unlimited   **A49** Prof.J.Bories/CNRI/SPL/Photo Researchers   **A50(T)** SIU/ Visuals Unlimited **A51-52** David M.Phillips/Visuals Unlimited   **A55(L)** Dr.Jeremy Burgess/SPL/Photo Researchers   **A55(R)** The Granger Collection, New York   **A56** Biophoto Associates/SS/ Photo Researchers   **A58(L)** M.Eichelberg/Visuals Unlimited **A58(R)** Kevin Vandiver   **A59(T)** Dr.Jeremy Burgess/SPL/Photo Researchers   **A59(B)** EM Unit, British Museum of Natural History/SPL/Photo Researchers   **A60** CNRI/SPL/Photo Researchers   **A61(TL)** Dr.Tony Brain & David Parker/SPL/Photo Researchers   **A61(CL)** Dr.Tony Brain & David Parker/SPL/Photo Researchers   **A61(CR)** Dr.Tony Brain & David Parker/SPL/Photo Researchers   **A61(R)** Dr.Tony Brain & David Parker/SPL/Photo Researchers   **A64(T)** David M.Phillips/Visuals Unlimited **A64(B)** Manfred Kage/Peter Arnold, Inc.   **A65** Moredun Animal Health LTD/SPL/Photo Researchers   **A66(T INS)** Chemical Design/SPL/Photo Researchers   **A67(T INS)** Ed Reschke/Peter Arnold, Inc.   **A67(B INS)** From CORPUSCLES by Marcel Bessis.Springer-Verlag, Berlin, Heidelberg, New York. © 1974 **A70** Dan McCoy/Rainbow   **A71(L)** Manfred Kage/Peter Arnold, Inc.   **A71(C)** Leonard Lessin/Peter Arnold, Inc.

Illustrations
Page A33-35 George Kelvin   **A46** Jak Graphics **A64** Biomedia   **A65** Biomedia   **A77** George Kelvin

Module B
Photographs
Front & Back Cover: Children's Photos: John Moore

Page B3 Prof.J.Bories/CNRI/SPL/Photo Researchers **B5** Dennis O`Clair/Tony Stone Worldwide   **B16-17** Doug Arnand/Tony Stone Worldwide   **B17** Robert Harding Picture Library Ltd., London   **B18(L)** Science Museum, London **B32** Greg Vaughn/Tom Stack & Associates   **B34(L)** Steve Elmore/The Stock Market   **B34-35** Simon Nathan/The Stock Market   **B36** American Honda Motor, Co, Inc   **B37** G. Heisler/The Image Bank   **B37(T)** Reprinted with permission from POPULAR SCIENCE Magazine, copyright, 1991, TIMES MIRROR Magazines, Reprinted by permission, Los Angeles Times Syndicate.   **B37(B)** G. Heisler/The Image Bank **B43(T)** The National Motor Museum at Beaulieu, England **B43(B)** Doug Menuez/Reportage   **B44(T)** Culver Pictures **B44(B)** Culver Pictures   **B45(C)** The National Motor Museum at Beaulieu, England   **B45(T)** Vandystadt/ALLSPORT USA **B45(B)** Steven A. Heller

Illustrations
Page B2 John Burgoyne   **B17** John Burgoyne   **B18** John Burgoyne   **B19** John Burgoyne   **B20-21** John Burgoyne **B32-33** Slug Signorino   **B35** John Burgoyne   **B56** JAK Graphics   **B58** George Kelvin   **B61** Rich Lo

Module C
Photographs
Front & Back Cover: Background: Gray Mortimore/Tony Stone Worldwide   Children's Photos: John Moore

Page C2(TL) Scott Bauer/Allen Laidman Photography **C13** Mike Powell/ALLSPORT USA   **C14(T)** L. Tobey Sanford **C16(TL)** Culver Pictures   **C16-17(T)** UPI/Bettmann **C16(B)** The Granger Collection, New York   **C17(BR)** NASA **C23** Mark Seliger   **C25(T)** The Granger Collection, New York **C25(B)** American Institute of Physics,/Niehls Bohr Library Photo Collection   **C30** Manny Millan/Sports Illustrated for Kids **C32** Scott Bauer/Allen Laidman Photography   **C40** R. Calentine/Visuals Unlimited   **C41** Bob Daemmrich/Stock Boston **C46(T)** Richard Hutchings/InfoEdit   **C46(B)** Richard Hutchings/InfoEdit   **C48** Louis Psihoyos/Matrix   **C53** Focus On

Sports **C54(L)** William Meyers/Third Coast Stock
C60(T) NASA **C60(B)** NASA **C61** NASA **C68(T)** U.S. Space Camp(R) Photo **C68(C)** U.S. Space Camp(R) Photo
C68(B) NASA **C69(C)** U.S. Space Camp(R) Photo
C69(T) NASA **C69(B)** U.S. Space Camp(R) Photo
C74 Doug Hoke **C75** Doug Hoke

Illustrations
Page C3 Vincent Perez **C26(T, B)** JAK Graphics
C30 Vincent Perez **C32** Vincent Perez **C38-39** Vincent Perez
C41 Vincent Perez **C62** Jacque Auger **C66-67** Randy Verougstraete **C70-71** Randy Verougstraete **C77** Rich Lo

Module D
Photographs
Front & Back Cover: Background: Tony Stone Worldwide
Children's Photos: John Moore

Page D2(T) Philip Jon Bailey/The Picture Cube **D3(C)** The Bettmann Archive **D8** Philip Jon Bailey/The Picture Cube
D9 Arnie Feinberg/The Picture Cube **D14(L)** F. Stuart Westmoreland/Tom Stack & Associates **D14(R)** Steve Ogden/Tom Stack & Associates **D15(L)** Courtesy American Petroleum Institute, Photographic and Film Archives
D15(R) Courtesy Ford Motor Company **D18(T)** Doug Sokell/Visuals Unlimited **D18(B)** Jim Cornfield/West Light
D24 Frank Cezus/Tony Stone Worldwide **D30** ASB Photos
D30-31 The Bettmann Archive **D31(TL)** Courtesy William Keck **D31(TR)** Wes Thompson/The Stock Market
D32(T) NASA **D32(B)** Greg Vaughn/Tom Stack & Associates
D37(T) Milt & Joan Mann/Cameramann International, Ltd.
D37(B) Milt & Joan Mann/Cameramann International, Ltd.
D38(L) Tony Stone Worldwide **D38(C)** COMSTOCK INC.
D38(R) COMSTOCK INC. **D39(L)** Mark Stephenson/Pacific Rim/West Light **D39(C)** Varin J. P. Jacana/Photo Researchers
D39(R) COMSTOCK INC. **D43** NASA **D51** Martin Rogers/Uniphoto **D70(R)** C.A. Morgan/Peter Arnold, Inc.
D71(T) David R. Frazier Photolibrary **D76** Brent Jones/Scott, Foresman

Illustrations
Page D7 Clint Hansen **D28** Steve Fuller **D37** Teri McDermott **D41** Wild Onion Studio **D44-45** Wild Onion Studio **D48** Simon Galkin **D60** Teri McDermott
D66-67 Walter Stuart **D68-69** Walter Stuart **D70** Wild Onion Studio **D77** George Kelvin

Module E
Photographs
Front & Back Cover: Background: Grant Heilman Photography
Children's Photos: John Moore

Page E3(C) David Ryan/DDB Stock Photo **E89** Kent Wood/Peter Arnold, Inc. **E9(T)** Grant Heilman Photography
E25 Michael Holford **E26** NASA **E27** Johnny Johnson/Alaska Photo/All Stock **E37** Alan Becker/The Image Bank
E39 Robert Frerck/Odyssey Productions, Chicago **E49(T)** John D. Cunningham/Visuals Unlimited **E55(T)** David Ryan/DDB Stock Photo **E55(B)** David Ryan/DDB Stock Photo **E57** Chris Alan Wilton/The Image Bank **E60(T)** Robert Fried/DDB Stock Photo **E60(BL)** Diane Johnson/Tony Stone Worldwide
E60-61(B) Lawrence Ruggeri/Third Coast Stock **E61(T)** Bill Gallery/Stock Boston **E61(BR)** Erika Craddock/Tony Stone Worldwide **E68(T)** David Sarnoff Library **E68(B)** Science Museum, London **E69(TL)** Culver Pictures **E69(TR)** Science Museum, London **E69(BL)** Dan McCoy/Rainbow

E69(BR) NASA **E74** Courtesy of Judy Leigh, Vanen Brook High School, Pepperell, MA. **E76** Mike Kelly/Scott, Foresman

Illustrations
Page E3 Dale Glasgow **E6** Mas Miyamoto **E9** Joe Rogers
E16 Carl Kock **E22** JAK Graphics **E33** Teri McDermott
E36 Teri McDermott **E38** Mas Miyamoto **E43** JAK Graphics
E43 Teri McDermott **E48** Susan Spellman **E52** JAK Graphics
E56 Dale Glasgow **E70** Sharmen Liao **E72** Carl Kock
E77 George Kelvin

Module F
Photographs
Front & Back Cover: Background: W.H.Hodge/Peter Arnold, Inc. Children's Photos: John Moore

Page F3(T) Peter Menzel/Stock Boston **F2(B)** Robert Wagoner/The Stock Market **F3L(C)** David Hanson/Tony Stone Worldwide **F7** Edward Farmer and Clarence Ryan/Washington State University, Institute of Biological Chemistry, Pullman
F8 Patrick Eggelston/Visuals Unlimited **F9** W.H. Hodge/Peter Arnold, Inc. **F12(L)** Grant Heilman Photography **F12(R)** Runk Schoenberger/Grant Heilman Photography **F13(T)** COMSTOCK INC. **F13(B)** C.P. Vance/Visuals Unlimited **F14** Hans Pfletschinger/Peter Arnold, Inc. **F17** Ray Atkeson/The Stock Market **F18(L)** Courtesy of the Trustees of the British Museum
F18 UPI/Bettmann **F19(L)** UPI/Bettmann **F19(R)** Dick Thomas/Visuals Unlimited **F20** FPG **F21(T)** Steve Smith/West Light **F22(T)** Hans Pfletschinger/Peter Arnold, Inc.
F22(B) D. Hagemann/Okapia/Photo Researchers **F23(T)** Science VU/Visuals Unlimited **F23(B)** Stephen Dalton/Photo Researchers **F31** Robert Wagoner/The Stock Market
F32-33 Bill Ross/West Light **F40** John Colwell/Grant Heilman Photography **F40-41** Swarthout/The Stock Market
F41(T) Peter Menzel/Stock Boston **F43(T)** Grant Heilman Photography **F46(L)** by copyright permission of the AAAS.
F46(C) Runk & Schoenberger/Grant Heilman Photography
F46(R) by copyright permission of the AAAS. **F49** David M Dennis/Tom Stack & Associates **F50** David Hanson/Tony Stone Worldwide **F52** AP/Wide World **F64** Roger Knutson/Soil Teq Inc **F65(T)** Linhoff/Soil Teq Inc **F65** Soil Teq Inc
F76 Audrey Trotman

Illustrations
Page F5 Carl Kock **F6** Carl Kock **F8** Ebet Dudley
F15 Carl Kock **F16** Laurie O'Keefe **F24-25** Nancy Lee Walter **F34** Wild Onion Studio **F35** Wild Onion Studio
F38 Wild Onion Studio **F40** Wild Onion Studio **F42** Wild Onion Studio **F56-57** Mas Miyamoto **F58-59** Mas Miyamoto
F59(T) Carla Simmons **F60** Mas Miyamoto **F66-67** Simon Galkin **F68** George Kelvin **F70** Laurie O'Keefe
F78 Wild Onion Studio